PRAIS

Unmasking Your Soul

"*Unmasking Your Soul* is one of those books that truly offers deep, lasting, soul-fulfilling transformation. The simple and enjoyable act of reading what Anümani has written is life-changing, because while she shares powerful personal stories, practical teaching, and inspirational wisdom, it is the energy with which she offers such that will transform every cell of your being and the very way you live in the world. So I encourage you to read every word of this book and receive the profound gifts in between the lines. There is mystery, magic, and magnificence here for YOU!"

— **Christine Kloser**
The Transformation Catalyst
Award-winning author, coach, and mentor
www.ChristineKloser.com

"*Unmasking Your Soul brings together an enriching mix of the mystical with real-life stories and practical tools to empower you to create the life you desire*—a GREATful Life of confidence, joy and success—on your terms! My dear friend and mentor, Eileen Anümani Santos, gracefully takes you on a powerful journey of self-discovery. Use the gems in this treasure of a book to transform your life (however you want) with loving wisdom and soul!"

— **Stephanie Bavaro**
GREATful StoryTeacher, Virtual Business Executive, #1 international bestselling author, and CEO of GREATful Woman®
www.GREATfulWoman.com

"Why are you here? Who are you? Are you fulfilling your life's purpose? How can you live the life and the love that you truly desire? Anümani shares many of the stories, lessons and advice in *Unmasking Your Soul* that have not only helped me personally, but can also help you find your unique answers to profound questions like these. She is a gifted author, speaker, coach, artist, musician, and healer. I am blessed to have had her on my "team" for many years, and with this book, you can too!"

— **Sofia Milan**
America's Sweetest and Spiciest Relationship Expert, and CEO of the Sofia Milan Company
www.SofiaMilanBooks.com

"Beyond your physical expression, is the core of your being—the Soul. Eileen Anümani Santos has created a blueprint to gently unmask that core essence. Through a masterful blend of real-life stories, divine teachings, guided meditations, and exercises, she helps renew your relationship with your Soul. On this sacred journey you discover your true purpose and are given the tools to heal what stands in the way of being able to live an empowered and authentic life. This book will change your life!"

— **Reverend Dr. Pedro Power**
International bestselling author,
Founder of the International Metaphysics Center,
Metaphysical Pastoral Psychologist, Minister and Practitioner,
Transformational Healer, Spiritual Guide, and Soul Coach
www.InternationalMetaphysicsCenter.com

UNMASKING YOUR SOUL

A Transformational Journey of
Truth, Light, and Healing

UNMASKING YOUR SOUL

Copyright© 2016 by Eileen Santos

Published by:
Transformation Books
211 Pauline Drive #513
York, PA 17402
www.TransformationBooks.com

ISBN # 978-1-945252-20-4
Library of Congress Control No: 2016962136

Cover Design: Kristi Santos
Editor: Marlene Oulton
Proofreader: Gwen Hoffnagle
Midwife: Carrie Jareed
Pastel Paintings: Eileen Anümani Santos
Soul Chamber Symbol Illustrations: Kristi Santos
Author photograph: Katy Timney, www.katyrosephotography.com

Printed in the United States of America

THIS BOOK IS DEDICATED TO...

My beloved God, with whom I co-created these words.
My beloved guides and all the divine beings who chose
to bring love to these pages.

My eternal Twin Soul. You are always in my heart.

Mom and Dad, gracias por tú amor eterno.
My beloved Santos family who cheered me on to the finish line.
My goddaughter, Vanessa Angelyss, who has been a bright light on my
journey and a reminder that love is what matters most in life.

And those who are here now and ready to unmask their Souls.

CONTENTS

A DIVINE MESSAGE FOR YOU, BELOVED READER

In the beginning, you emerged from a seed of **Love**. **Love** became the anchor for your Soul and all that you are. As you emerged into physical form, that **love** remained within you... in a place of oneness with the Divine. In the stillness you can call upon it in a moment's breath. Herein lies the secret to that which you've been seeking all your life.

In this seed of **love** that makes up your Soul's DNA, is the **Truth** of your existence and your unique purpose in this life. Unmask it, accept it, be grateful for it.

You were born in this time to bring your unique seed to humanity. You are on Earth now with a specific purpose that only **Your Light** can deliver. Within your Soul you hold the container for the unfolding of this purpose. Receive it, commune with it, nurture it.

The seed is ready to be harvested. Your Soul calls to you to embrace the **truth** of your existence. The fire has ignited your Soul and the power of your divinity is exposed to the masses. Embrace **truth** without fear. Show your true face to the world—the need to hide no longer serves you. Shine **your light** to the world. Feel it, know it, embrace it.

As the seedling hatches, **Healing** occurs, and you transform into the **real you**—the you that you've always been, the you that your Soul knows is the divine receptacle of God's **love**—every breath, every word, and every action instilled with the expression of your divinity. As you emerge, empowered to be the real you, life transforms with you and the Universe supports you in the unfolding of your Soul's purpose. Believe it, trust it, surrender to it.

You have returned to the purest form of your existence—**love**—and this new you knows no boundaries of limitation or desire. All it knows is that with **love** anything and everything is possible.

And so it is. The **empowered you** begins anew.

THE MAP

The Unmasking Your Soul Blueprint

From my own transformational journey of over twelve years emerged the **Unmasking Your Soul Blueprint**™. I didn't realize it at the time, but God was deliberately taking me through my own healing and transformation so I could share this teaching with you. You're going to read the word *God* a lot throughout this book. To me God represents the ultimate source of higher consciousness that lives and breathes through each of us. If the word *God* doesn't resonate with you, I encourage you to replace it with a word or words that fit your own spiritual beliefs and values. I also call God the Divine, Creator, and Source, and whenever you see these words you can think of the name that fits the higher power or higher consciousness of your own beliefs.

I had not put into words the three stages I describe in *Unmasking Your Soul* until a dream revealed these three words to me: "*Truth.Light.Healing.*" And I mean Spirit gave them to me exactly as you see them written, periods and all.

The **Unmasking Your Soul Blueprint** is built on the foundation of these three key stages: *Truth, Light, and Healing.* Each stage helps you connect more deeply with an aspect of you that has been hidden, masked, or forgotten so you can heal and transform that part of you to its original form of wholeness and completeness. As you immerse yourself in the divine teachings of this process, you emerge as the ***REAL YOU***.

These were the words given to me by the Divine to describe each stage:

- ***Truth***: To begin the healing process, accept and awaken to the *divine truth* within your Soul. Accepting the truth is a journey of self-discovery in which you UNMASK those areas of your life that are keeping you from expressing your most authentic you.
- ***Light***: As you experience this awakening and pierce the spiritual veil, you shift from a sense of separateness to one of connectedness. As you CONNECT with your authentic you—your *divine light*—you shed the hurts and ego-driven behaviors that no longer serve you.

- *Healing*: As you fully EMBODY your divine expression, you unlock your Soul's DNA and begin living a more joyful, passionate, inspired, Soul-driven life.

You can download the blueprint at: **www.UnmaskingYourSoul.com/Blueprint.**

At each stage, every truth you unmask allows you to reconnect with the truest essence of your Soul. Your Soul, or *Alma* in Spanish, serves as your compass for True North. This is the only direction that brings you true fulfillment in your life. Your goal is to align with your Soul's purpose. Only then will life become easier for you.

At the center of the blueprint is where you reconnect with your Soul and the core of who you really are. At your core you are **LOVE**, a true essence of light and magnificence. You really are powerful beyond measure. It's just that the noise of your thoughts and mind gets in the way of that pureness of love, peace, and joy. But if you commit to working on **YOU** and building your spiritual muscle, the rewards are immeasurable. I know you want to live on purpose, fearlessly, otherwise you wouldn't be reading these words.

What does **Truth, Light, and Healing** really mean? In Stage 1, **Truth**, I help you discover what needs to be unmasked. Is it your *divine purpose*? Do you need to heal something very painful that happened to you that's holding you back from embracing your power fully? Or do you want to reduce the stress and anxiety in your body so you can see your life choices more clearly? Whatever it may be, together we'll create the space for you to listen to what your Soul wants to tell you, here and now, at this moment in your life.

> *Your Soul serves as your compass for True North.*

Truth begins with a willingness to change your life. It requires both *intention* and *choice*: 1) intention to heal, transform, and receive whatever the Divine is ready to help you discover about who you really are; and 2) making the choice to take that first step in **unmasking** those areas of your life that still hold you back.

Allowing free will to flow without resistance is what enables you to make your choice with greater ease. It's like you're dancing with the flow of the Universe and your dance changes based on how the unfolding of your life needs to happen. Don't resist the flow. Instead, align with the flow, and with alignment comes ease and grace. Deepak Chopra calls this the "Law of Least Effort" in his book *The Seven Spiritual Laws of Success*. What follows is the desire—the fluid that ignites your Soul to pursue your dreams without hesitation. The Universe is ready and willing to give you all you need and deserve, but it's up to you to open the door. And the door will only open when what you seek is in alignment with what you're here to do.

In Stage 2, **Light**, you cultivate a deeper relationship with your divine expression, the **light of YOU**. The deeper you go, the more you're able to shed the ego-driven behaviors that hold you back from being the **REAL YOU**. In this stage I teach you to build your spiritual muscle. Transformation doesn't happen without some work. You must commit to *YOU* daily. This means finding your rhythm to connect with the Divine. We're all different, so trust your intuition when building your spiritual practice. There are so many ways to connect with the Divine. Meditation, prayer, and chanting are examples of techniques that can help you connect with the *divine mind*. The key is connecting with the stillness within you. It is within the stillness that you find all the answers you seek.

For years my preferred spiritual practices have been prayer and meditation. Your Soul already knows how you're meant to connect with your divine expression, so trust in that feeling. Find those activities that help you connect to that state of stillness and quiet in which all seems to melt away, completely lifted as if by magic. When you connect to your "God-vibration," you experience the magnificence of feeling embraced by the deepest love that has ever existed. You are God's beloved child, worthy of all and more. It is hard for the human mind to fathom the depths of this type of love. Once you connect with the Divine in this way, you'll always seek refuge in this loving vibration.

In my most difficult moments, it was God's loving voice that allowed me to stay centered, even amid the chaos surrounding me. I knew I would be taken care of no matter what. You, too, will always be held lovingly in God's arms. Imagine a life fully bathed and immersed in this unconditional love. This is within your reach, if you allow it to be so.

When you're living on purpose, things flow through you, not around you.

And in Stage 3, *Healing*, you embody your true essence, *the infinite-loving YOU*, and this is when the biggest transformation occurs. When you embody the highest version of you, guided by your Soul, your life shifts dramatically. You're able to live in a state of connectedness instead of separateness. You experience oneness with the Divine that allows you to manifest your Soul's purpose, and you do this with devotion, passion, and dedication.

When you're living on purpose, things flow through you, not around you. You become high on life because all you do emerges from your deepest desires, fueling the manifestation of your Soul-driven life. In the *Healing* stage you work in concert with your divine expression to bring about love and healing in you. As you heal, you heal those around you. As you embody your Soul, your Soul embodies you and you reach true mastery in your life.

The Unmasking of My Soul

Unmasking Your Soul

by Eileen Anümani Santos

Your Soul speaks to you in many ways. Listen to the quiet whisper in your ear, in your heart, and in your mind. What does this whisper say?

Your Soul says, The unfolding has begun. I am here awaiting your arrival to celebrate your divinity with you… awaken to my calling.

SOUL… **S**acred **O**penness to **U**niversal **L**ight… you are the light… you are the light… you are the light… divine and sacred… all-knowing, all-loving, all-being. We are one, not separate, but one—one with all that is. In this place of oneness, all that exists is the purity of *divine light* and love. In this place all that holds you back melts away… and you become nameless, bodiless, and pure… pure of mind… pure of spirit… pure of Soul.

Here we recognize each other's divinity. We recognize that we are spiritual beings having human experiences… and it is in this unity of one mind, one body, one Soul that we feel strength in numbers… strength in our power… the shining of our lights to the world.

Walk with me today and remove your mask—the mask that has held you back from radiating your true essence… your true gifts… the true you… a divine, sacred being of light. It is time to shine your light to the world. See me within you… see me shine the light on your wounds, transforming the darkness into the light. As you remove your mask, a euphoria of joy and love permeate the essence of your being. It is me… your divine essence. And as you look closer, you recognize me… the true you… you remember who you really are and are meant to be in this life.

As you bare your Soul to me… you feel such freedom… such light… such love. A passion has been reignited within you. It is through me that you become you. It is through me that you are empowered to embrace your light… your divinity… your infinite-loving self. In this remembrance, I ask you to surrender to me. Take off your mask and see the unfolding as I guide you in manifesting your destiny. What joy! What magnificence! What elation! Celebrate with me today as we rejoice in our divinity… and the grace of the Universe. It finally has all come together… bringing respite to me, your Soul.

PREFACE

Since you're reading these words, you know without a doubt that there's a yearning deep inside you to live a more Soul-driven life. Like me, you're ready to transform your life; to *unmask your Soul*. I lived most of my life wearing a mask—a mask that was based in fear of being me.

How is it that you came to live a life that doesn't feel completely fulfilling? In my case I spent most of my life pretending to be someone I wasn't because I was afraid of being judged, even though I yearned to be accepted and loved by others. But in 2003, at the age of thirty-eight, something happened that changed my life forever. I had a dream, but not just any dream; this one was mystical and powerful. It was the first time I heard God's voice, loud and clear. It went like this:

> *I'm in an elevator in a tall office building, a skyscraper, with three other women. As the elevator descends, suddenly the cable breaks loose. The elevator plummets so rapidly it makes a hole in the side of the building and lands on a muddy, dark river of emotional turmoil. The elevator skids on its back over the top of the river, with its doors open to the sky. As I look towards the bank of the river, I see a woman in white robes with blond hair—she's my guardian angel. She reaches down into the elevator and pulls me to safety. As I get myself together, I notice that I've lost my wedding ring. I search high and low, and even ask a security guard who appeared in the dream to help me find it, but to no avail. As I wrestle with anxiety and emotion, I hear this strong, calming voice, God's voice. "My Child," He says, "I have a mission for you. One that you won't understand right now, but be patient, for in time all will be revealed to you."*

When I woke up from this dream there was no mistaking what course of action I had to take. Until that point I had been living a life full of lies. I was wearing a mask—several in fact. There had been so many signs that something was dreadfully wrong in my life, but I had ignored them all. At the time I was employed as a marketing executive for a small student loan company, and I spent mindless days of endlessly working. I had become a workaholic to avoid the truth of what was waiting for me at home—a very unhealthy relationship.

To most people I seemed very successful and happy, but the truth is that inside I was a mess. I had lived most of my life pleasing others, doing what I thought was expected of me, and not really listening to the yearning of my Soul, which was asking for a happier, more loving, and healthier life. As I worked to meet the demands of my outer world, I had unknowingly closed myself off from my inner world, from my connection to spirit—to the Divine which had always been very strong in my adolescence.

This dream unleashed a chain of events that changed me forever. I began to remember something very painful from my childhood that I had conveniently "forgotten." I had visions of being sexually abused at the age of four by a relative whom I'd trusted. In the darkness he would whisper, "It's okay, don't be afraid." For years I was afraid of the dark and couldn't understand why until that moment.

My body was overwhelmed with all that was going on. Between the memories of the sexual abuse and the unhealthy relationship I was experiencing at home, my body went into overload. I began having fainting spells (a sign of my consciousness wanting to awaken), and yet when I went to my doctors they couldn't find a medical condition for what I was experiencing. All the chaos (reminiscent of the muddy waters in the dream) in my outer world was just a reflection of the turmoil and pain I had been carrying for so long.

The epiphany had come in the form of that vivid dream. The Universe was yelling loud and clear, "Wake up, Eileen. It's time for you to wake up from your stupor." And wake up I did. Immediately I knew this was a direct sign from God that I needed to change my life and step into my power.

Shortly thereafter I separated from my husband. While the ending of this relationship turned out to be more difficult than I imagined, I found a new spark of faith and light within me—a spiritual awakening that transformed me forever.

"Why me?" I asked God the day He told me He had a mission for me. Somehow I had forgotten that my Soul had volunteered for this task. I had conveniently forgotten that before I arrived at that point I had made a commitment to share my gifts with the world. Why? Because it was easier to forget than to courageously embrace the uncertainty of being ME. But despite my fear and feelings of being overwhelmed, I found the inner strength to embrace my divinity and witness the divinely orchestrated unmasking of each chamber of my Soul.

With each passing day I discovered Soulful gifts that had been dormant since my childhood. Art was the first to emerge. No surprise that the first pastel I was guided to paint was of my own awakening and was called *Spiritual Awakening*. I remember loving art so much as a child, but I never gave myself permission to follow this passion. I was too busy living my life for others rather than living it for *me*. Then other creative expressions emerged: songwriting and singing, poetry, and writing. I had been giving my power away to others for so long that I had trouble speaking my truth and really using my voice as God intended. It was no coincidence that I was being guided to sing so I could heal that part of me that I had shut down for so long in fear of not being loved or accepted.

Then the Universe began to send new people into my life, people who would contribute to my spiritual growth. One of these happened to be an accountant turned energy healer. I could relate to him because I had lived most of my life in the corporate world as well; first as an engineer, then as a consultant, and then as a marketing executive. It was no coincidence that I met this energy healer.

I became so fond of his work that I decided to take one of his meditation classes. And that's when a perfect stranger taking the same class came up to me and said, "Do you know you're meant to be a healer?" I didn't know what to say. This wasn't something I expected to hear.

True love sometimes shows up in our lives when we least expect it and in packages that can challenge us to our core.

As all of my hidden treasures began to emerge, I also discovered that *true love* sometimes shows up in our lives when we least expect it and in packages that can challenge us to our core. When I sought counsel from friends and family to support me through these major life changes, I unexpectedly met my Twin Soul. It was incredibly powerful, yet challenging at the same time, because she was a woman. This was against everything I had been raised to believe was acceptable.

What made this relationship so different was the instant kinship and Soul connection I felt in her presence. It was like we had known each other forever, beyond time and space. But as the closeness grew, I realized I was feeling more than gratitude and friendship; I was feeling deep, profound love. This love was deeper than any love I had experienced to that point.

I immediately resisted the feelings. How could this be? How could I be in love with a woman? That was not the way I had imagined my life. The truth is I was more concerned about what my family and others would say than about how I was really feeling. At that point I still didn't love myself enough to know that once again I was giving my power away to others. This was my decision to make, yet I was afraid to lose those I loved the most. I had grown up in a Catholic, Puerto Rican household, and all I could think about was how my mother was going to react.

Well, believe it or not, it was a movie that helped me better understand what was going on inside me. Yet again, the Universe supported me on my journey and gave me exactly what I needed to clear some of my confusion and doubt. On a Saturday afternoon I happened to be surfing channels and saw a movie called *An Unexpected Love* ready to air on the Lifetime Network. I immediately felt called to watch the movie, and it turned out to be the best medicine for my aching heart.

In this movie the main character, Kate Mayer (played by Leslie Hope), seems to have it all: a nice suburban house, two loving children, and a devoted husband. But Kate is anything but happy. Not only is she disappointed in her marriage, she is disillusioned with her entire life. In her pursuit of happiness, she files for divorce and gets a job working in a small real estate agency. Kate becomes good friends with her boss, Mac, who is a woman. When she discovers she has fallen deeply in love with Mac, everything in her life begins to change.

It's clear that this is a movie of a woman's emotional journey of self-discovery. Kate finally takes off her mask and discovers who she really is. For the first time in her life she gives herself permission to follow her deepest desires. I can certainly relate to Kate's story. You see, I, too, was on a journey of self-discovery and at a crossroads in my life. Watching this movie was certainly divinely guided. It helped me accept what I was feeling without guilt or shame.

Just as quickly as the Divine challenged what I believed to be acceptable in my life, it provided me with the experiences to gain greater clarity about my truth. The Divine helped me understand that this type of sacred love chooses you, you don't choose it. Despite the package being different from what I imagined (gender in my case, but it can come in any form—age, religion, etc.), this kind of love has its own Soul language and is an unstoppable force that is divinely orchestrated. And with that realization I was able to accept it without guilt or shame, and receive it as a sacred gift from the Universe.

Some time after leaving my marriage, I found the courage to admit my feelings to my newfound love. Let's put it this way: things didn't go as I had hoped. She told me I was confusing her kindness and friendship for something else. This really broke my heart because deep down I knew there was a profound, deep Soul connection between us as if we had been together many times before in other lifetimes.

As I reflect back on that moment, I recognize that neither one of us was ready for the sacredness of this type of relationship. I had lots to shed and heal, and the Divine was preparing me to transition into my "purpose-work"—that which reflects my *divine purpose*. I needed to be able to do that on my own without any other distractions. You attract into your life what you live within. This means that before you can create a sacred, soulmate relationship, you must create the sacred space within to receive such a powerful and deep love into your life.

No matter what has happened to you, I know you can transcend it. If I was able to break free from my old life, you can too. Listen to your Soul's yearning in this moment and see where it takes you. In the main chapters of this book, I gently guide you through a transformational journey of *Truth, Light, and Healing*. On this sacred journey you'll identify in what parts of your life you're wearing a mask. We'll work together to help you remove those masks and connect more deeply with your Soul to awaken your own power, intuition, and wisdom.

There is something unique you hold within you.

There is a deeper part of you that knows that you are here for a reason. That Soul part of you also knows that you're more than just human flesh. There is something unique you hold within you that only you have. Imagine that. That unique seed is your higher purpose. And through my own story of unmasking in the pages that follow, I want to help you discover what that is. Beneath all the masks you've been holding on to so tightly lies the *divine* part of you that is so much more expansive. I want you to read the words that follow and hold them in your heart as you begin this journey with me:

You are love and deeply loved by the Universe.

You are a luminous being of light.

You are what the world is waiting for.

That unique seed is your higher purpose.

As you prepare for this journey, there may be a part of you doubting that you'll be able to get the breakthroughs or transformation you seek. Or perhaps there's an unsettling fear in the pit of your stomach. As you step into the edge of your comfort zone, doubts and fears are likely to arise. That's actually a good thing. On the other side of those fears and doubts lies the clarity, healing, and transformation your Soul desires for you. Maybe you don't believe me in this moment, but please stick with me on this journey. You'll be glad you did!

May the unmasking of your Soul be filled with love and grace!

EILEEN ANÜMANI SANTOS, *UNMASKING YOUR SOUL* C. 2014

Unmasking Your Soul is about becoming the ***real you***. This is not just about unmasking your human-self, but your spiritual-self as well. When you commit to becoming the highest version of you, the Divine conspires to make it happen for you. When you *open your heart* and *remove your mask*, the most authentic you emerges—your divine expression embodied in the human vessel. Allow your Soul to guide you on this journey of self-discovery.

***UNMASK your SOUL* and become the REAL YOU!**

INTRODUCTION

Becoming the Divine Curator of Your Soul

At this point you might be asking yourself, "Why so much talk about the Soul, and why should I listen to what it's saying?" To answer those questions, I want to begin by sharing the conversation that occurred between my Higher-Self and me that culminated in the seeds of this book. In these pages I define the Higher-Self as the *divine* part of you that is the vehicle through which the Soul communicates with you. The conversation went like this:

Me: I seek the truth... the truth of me. What is the truth of me?

Higher-Self: Your spiritual-self... that part of you that is all-knowing, all-loving, and all-being.

Me: Why now?

Higher-Self: Why not? You're ready, right?

Me: So you say. Am I ready? My ego wants me to believe not. No longer will I stand for this giving my power away again and again to my ego. All my life I've given my power away to others and dimmed the brightness of my light, yet all along it was my ego making me believe I wasn't good enough, I wasn't capable enough, not smart enough, not beautiful enough, not worthy of the life I so desired. But no more. I am good enough. I am worthy enough. I am enough and more. I AM that I AM.

I connect with you, my infinite-loving Soul, allowing you to be my true guide. I am ready! I am ready! I am ready!

I remove this ego mask—this illusion of what my ego wants me to believe is the real me, but is not. That mask is but an illusion of the power I have continuously given away to my ego—that part of me that uses my past pain to "keep me safe" in an illusory world created by fear.

Higher-Self: I was waiting for you to say you were ready. Let me help you unmask your Soul once and for all.

If in that moment I hadn't listened to my Soul, this book would never have been written. This is why it's so important to connect deeply with your Soul and discover what it's trying to tell you. Your Soul is the receptacle of your wisdom—wisdom you have accumulated over lifetimes. Your Soul is the holder of what you've already experienced, as well as what you're meant to experience in this moment in this life. When this conversation happened with my Higher-Self, I wanted to know more, so I asked more questions. And these are the responses I got:

Me: Where does my Soul reside?

Higher-Self: It is that part of you that is all-loving, all-knowing, and all-being. You are a Soul with a body, not a body with a Soul. Your Soul is so expansive that the body is too limited to hold its expansiveness. Your Soul is within and without… the outermost layer in which all things reside… body, mind, and spirit. It is infinite and all-knowing, connected with all there is. It carries your karma and wisdom from all that you have lived and experienced as a spirit and Soul.

Me: What does this mean: "as a spirit and as a Soul"?

Higher-Self: Spirit is the *you* you are now in this life. It embodies your spiritual connection to Source. Soul encompasses all that and more. The Soul already has lived this many times—an accumulation of spiritual experiences past, present, and future, all in parallel, all happening at the same time. Your spirit is the embodiment of your *divinity* in your current life.

Why is this important to know? Because in this vast and expansive expression of yourself that sits beyond time and space exist twelve chambers. Each carries a Soul virtue that unlocks your true expression as a being of light.

In *Unmasking Your Soul* I guide you on a journey of unmasking these twelve chambers—a transformational journey of self-discovery through which you become the curator of your Soul and discover what the canvas of your Soul looks like.

I'll be your guide on this journey. Consider yourself the pilgrim on the road to discovering the deepest parts of you that reside within your Soul. This road is full of twists and turns that ultimately lead to the truth that only you can discover. On this journey you'll become the *divine curator* of your journey to self-discovery, unmasking each and every chamber of your Soul. I open the door for you, but you must be the one to walk through it.

Each chamber houses information that perhaps has remained hidden from you until now. Maybe subconsciously it has been too painful for you to face, or your ego is trying to keep you chained to a past laden with fear. But fear is not always the enemy. Fear can act as a motivator to change your life, especially as you become aware of the consequences of allowing fear to paralyze you into non-action and complacency.

Together the twelve chambers create the tapestry of your true essence and form the DNA of your Soul.

Together we'll unmask twelve Soul virtues that form the fibers of your true essence, being, and Soul. As we remove each layer of illusion and woundedness, the true you emerges and the positive aspects of each of your Soul's chambers flows in your life. Together the twelve chambers create the tapestry of your true essence and form the DNA of your Soul. They are the strands of your Soul's DNA that allow you to embody the highest version of you in your physical form.

Throughout ancient history the number twelve has played a very significant and mystical role in the eventuating of cosmic order. In simple terms, it represents wholeness and the completion of God's creation. This became clear to me when the Divine revealed the connection through one of my paintings, entitled *My Journey in Puzzle Pieces*. I created this pastel in 2010, and it was my first self-portrait. This painting represents the canvas of my Soul and captures my own transformational journey since my dream of awakening in 2003.

When I drew this, I was guided to create twelve puzzle pieces and was specifically instructed to leave puzzle piece number twelve blank. I had no idea at the time that this section was to represent the new life that would unfold for me twelve years later. I didn't understand the significance until I began writing this book. You see, my journey began in 2003 with my dream of awakening, and twelve years later I'm sharing this story with you.

Because you're reading this book, you, like me, are on a journey that may represent one of the most life-changing times of your life. Your Soul will give you the keys to unlock what has remained hidden until now, but only you can decide if you're willing to take the actions that will allow you to transform your life and become the real you— the you your Soul has been whispering for you to become.

Why Take This Journey with Me?

When you open up to Spirit, that higher power that connects us all, you experience loving grace and divine synchronicity as the weaving of a beautiful tapestry of YOU. Each thread is carefully placed at the exact moment it's needed to bring together the most amazing expression of YOU to the world. I want to reassure you that you are

> *When you open up to Spirit you experience loving grace and divine synchronicity.*

needed in the world. You carry a unique purpose that only you can bring to the world. I ask you to breathe that knowing into your heart.

Feel it and believe it in the deepest parts of your Heart and Soul. Only by believing and embracing your divinity can you truly reemerge as the precious gem that you are, immersed in God's vibration of wholeness and completeness. You matter, and you matter a lot—more than your ego-mind allows you to understand. This cannot be understood through words or thoughts. This must be experienced through your spirit and Soul.

In this oneness with your Soul, your senses become alive in a way that boggles the mind. In this journey of unmasking and truth, what matters most is the heart. This is where you must focus your attention. Your heart center is the portal to your divinity and your oneness with God. It's where you radiate your own God-vibration. When the noise in the outer world becomes overwhelming, this is your place of respite and knowing that all will be okay.

As you begin to open your Heart and Soul, you notice the signs that the Universe is sending you. You see new opportunities knocking at your door. And when those opportunities come, you need only choose whether or not to take action. Decide whether or not you want to walk through the door. The more you connect with your Soul, the deeper you go and the easier it is to make choices that align with your Soul's purpose. The same goes for our journey together. Decide whether or not you're willing to take the actions to **unmask** and **discover** the **real you.**

In the movie *The Matrix*, Keanu Reeves plays the hero (Neo) in a virtual world filled with illusion and run by machines (akin to the ego-mind). Initially Neo doesn't believe that he's "The One"—the one meant to save humanity. Morpheus, played by Laurence Fishburne, is Neo's guide to the understanding of his true purpose. One of my favorite lines in the movie is when Morpheus tells Neo, "I'm trying to free your mind, Neo. But I can only show you the door. You're the one that has to walk through it." This is the same for you. I can guide you to the doorway that leads to your Soul, but you have to decide whether or not you're willing to walk through the doorway and connect with it.

At the beginning of the movie, Neo doesn't believe in himself, yet Morpheus knows deep within his Soul that Neo is meant for greatness. You were born with this same greatness. It is inherent in your Soul and just waiting to blossom. Sometimes we cannot see what others see in us. I can't tell you how many times that has happened to me in my life. And that did not change until I learned to love myself again. Just like me, Neo had to experience great turmoil and the potential loss of loved ones to break free from the chains that were holding him back from expressing his authentic self. As Neo embraces his gifts, a miracle occurs. He becomes what he has always been and is able to serve his purpose in leading a cause for humanity against "the machines."

You, too, have a cause to fight for in this world. That cause can be big or small, but the important thing is for you to discover what it is. Why are you here? What is your purpose? Or, as said in Spanish, *Cual es tú propósito?* I want to help you become your own Neo. Embrace your *GIFTS*. Embrace your *PURPOSE* in the world. Embrace your *LIGHT*. Embrace the *LOVE* that you are. Become the signpost for spiritual understanding and evolution in the world. Bring all this into your being, into every part of your life, no matter where that is.

The more light you shine, the more the world transforms into Heaven on Earth.

The more light you shine, the more the world transforms into Heaven on Earth. I am counting on you to *BE YOU* so the world can benefit from your magnificence. Shine your light brightly and live on purpose, fearlessly. I promise to hold your hand every step of the way through the material written on each page of this book.

As your guide on this journey, my heartfelt desire is to return you to your original state of wholeness and completeness. I want to help you remove the layers of your outer existence that hold you back from being the highest version of *YOU* that you can be—as God intended it to be. That outer existence is filled with lots of "noise," memories, pain, and emotions that create a film of muck, or *porquería*, as we say in Spanish, that is a projection of all the hurt you carry inside. The more wounds you carry inside, the more your outer world reflects that. If you've ever heard the saying "As within, so without," then you understand that your outer world is a reflection of your inner world.

If I can do it, so can you. Who would've thought that an engineer turned marketing executive would transform into a minister, healer, artist, singer, and author. Not me. I never imagined that would be me. In fact, I got caught up in the whole "moving up the corporate ladder" bit for a long time. Even though I was constantly given signs from the Universe, I ignored them all. And the pain continued to accumulate, year after year; because when you don't tend to your inner sanctuary, it floods with corrosion until you burst. Usually that means that something dramatic has to happen for you to wake up and really "see" what has always been there. I also know that everything happens for a reason and in divine order. I needed to experience all those painful moments so I could be present with you here, now, to guide you on your own journey of self-discovery.

So we are partners on this road of transformation and healing. Ultimately you have the *power to heal*, to be *YOU*. I will help you tap into your senses, your spiritual gifts, your divinity, and your Higher-Self so you can emerge as the beautiful, radiant YOU that you are. No longer will you need to hide under the masks, fears, and illusions that no longer serve you. You can have it all if you commit to loving **YOU** in a way you've never experienced before. *Self-love* is the Soul virtue that creates the opening and space for the type of transformation I speak of. No surprise, it's the first chamber we'll focus on in "Chapter 1: Returning to Divine Love." It's what I had to relearn when my life changed forever in 2003.

If you say yes and commit to unmasking your Soul, you're agreeing to be the *divine curator of your Soul*. Each chapter that follows takes you on a gentle journey of self-discovery. Through poetry, art, divine teachings, guided meditations, journaling, and rituals, your Soul will speak to you every step of the way. All you have to do is be open, be gentle with yourself, and commit to this transformational journey of *Truth, Light, and Healing*.

Showing up to LOVE YOU is the key to unmasking your Soul and your destiny.

Taking the first step and showing up to **LOVE YOU** is the key to unmasking your Soul and your destiny. Take the key in your hand and unlock the door. Open the door. Walk through the doorway. If you walked through the doorway, congratulations! Take a moment now to take a deep breath and set your intentions for this journey.

With much gratitude and love, I open my heart to you. May your journey bring you the grace and glory you deserve!

The Structure of Each Chapter

Each chapter begins with a poem, then moves into the teachings of that Soul chamber. Each chapter also includes one or more guided meditations that are the foundation for eliciting healing, Soul insights, and shifts in consciousness. The journey then continues with journaling exercises and five rituals to help you embody the particular Soul virtue being discussed in that chapter.

Every chapter ends with one of my Soul paintings and a message from that painting. Each painting was divinely channeled and holds messages and energetic impressions of the Soul that bring healing to the bearer. In the "Rituals" section of each chapter, I ask you to meditate with the paintings so you can receive the healing light they hold. As you work with these paintings, pay attention to where you're being drawn in. This will give you clues about where you might need to release old wounds and pain.

How to Prepare for Your Journey

This is a very sacred journey you're about to embark on. Sacred because it is about YOU and the *unmasking of your Soul*. This is not the type of book to rush through.

Instead, imagine that this journey is a spiritual pilgrimage to your SOUL—the highest version of YOU. Therefore treat it with care, and above all, be gentle with yourself as you move through your unmasking.

Before you get started, here are a couple of things you'll need as you work through each chapter:

- *A Sacred Space.* This is a sacred journey of self-discovery; an unmasking of your Soul. That being said, I suggest that you create a sacred space in your home (if you don't already have one) where you can go to engage with the depths of your Soul and with this book as your companion. Make this space your sacred space, where you do those things that elicit that type of feeling in you. For me that means lighting a candle, some incense, and inviting God and my spiritual team into my space through a prayer of intention or an invocation. For you it might be something different. It doesn't matter what it is, only that when you do it, you feel that you're opening the doorway to commune with God—the Divine. Why am I suggesting this? Because the more you go to the same spot to work on YOU, the more energy you build in that space to support you in your transformational journey. I suggest that you perform the exercises, guided meditations, and rituals suggested throughout the book with this in mind. Here is a sample invocation you can use or modify to fit your own beliefs and divine expression:

    Heavenly Father, Dear God, Dear Spirit, as I begin this process of remembrance of the love that I AM, please bring forth protection and guidance so that all that transpires may be for my highest good. I am eternally grateful for your love and support on my journey of self-discovery. Today I commit to loving myself once again. I ask for your assistance in releasing anything holding me back from being love in this moment and fully unmasking my Soul. Help me be open to the grace of your healing. And so it is.

- *A Journal.* I'm a big believer in using journaling as a spiritual practice to bring about healing. In each chapter you'll find exercises that typically follow some type of guided meditation. I recommend you use one journal to document your entire journey and insights from each chapter. That way you can look back and see how what you're experiencing connects together.

- *A Recording Device.* Every chapter has one or more guided meditations. It can be distracting to try to read the words of a guided meditation and still connect with its healing or activating energies. If that is the case, I suggest you record the guided meditations in your own voice on a digital recorder, iPad, iPhone, or other "smart" device. You have access to the audio versions of the guided meditations at the end of each chapter (twelve in total) at **www. UnmaskingYourSoul.com/Meditations**.

- *The Canvas of Your Soul.* I provide a PDF of the **Unmasking Your Soul Blueprint** that serves as the *Canvas of Your Soul*. You can download the PDF at **www.UnmaskingYourSoul.com/Blueprint**. As you move through each chapter, pick phrases, words, or symbols that represent your experience from that chapter. You can make this canvas your own piece of artwork, representing your transformational journey of self-discovery. You can even color, paint, write, or cut images from magazines that depict the messages and insights you received in the chapter. And best of all, you don't need to be a professional artist to do this. Just have fun and let your Soul express through you as it wants to. This will become the vision board of your Soul's unmasking and a keepsake of your journey.

EILEEN ANÜMANI SANTOS, *MY JOURNEY IN PUZZLE PIECES* C. 2010

My Journey in Puzzle Pieces shows the unfolding of my transformational journey over the last twelve years. The first puzzle piece captures the dream of awakening I had in 2003 that changed my life forever. The last puzzle piece, number twelve, is the beginning of my new life, which began when the *divine seed* was planted for me to write this book.

Join me in *DISCOVERING* your Soul's journey!

STAGE ONE: TRUTH

Unmasking Your Soul's Truth

To begin the healing process, accept and awaken to the truth within your Soul. Accepting the truth is a journey of self-discovery in which you UNMASK those areas of your life that are keeping you from expressing your most authentic you.

God's Love for You

by Eileen Anümani Santos

As I look within you, I see a heart full of love, but one that bears
pain as well.

It is time for you to release that which holds you back, for within you
is a spark of fire that is waiting to be embraced.

It is time to love thyself as God loves you, unconditionally, with no shame,
no guilt, but oneness with all of life.

How could God forsake such a loving child?

He has not. He whispers His love to you, but do you hear?

Let it be so by listening to the wind and the words that Spirit whispers
in the day and the night.

They are words of how special you are and have always been.

You are loved more than you can imagine. It is time to become one with
that love so that your heart may feel respite and heal.

Remember that with God's love, anything is possible, and so, today, begin
anew and believe it to be so.

CHAPTER 1

Soul Chamber I:
Returning to Divine Love

In the beginning, you were *love*. You were born from a vibration of eternal love. But when you took physical form, you lost the remembrance of your true essence. I'm here to remind you of that truth—that within you is the seed of eternal love, *divine love*. This seed of eternal love is located in your heart center, the portal that connects you to your *divinity*, the "God" within you.

In this chapter you begin your transformational journey with *TRUTH*. There are four chambers that you will unmask in Stage One of your journey that will connect you with your *Soul's Truth*. Your heart center (in the lower chamber of the heart) is the location of **Soul Chamber I—Divine Love,** the first of the Soul virtues that will be unmasked as you embark on your journey of wholeness. The mask associated with this first chamber is the **Mask of Separation**. The mask of separation usually occurs from an emotional state of fear—the fear to love, the fear to be loved, or the feeling of being unworthy to be loved. This chamber is represented by the archetype of the *divine beloved*. In this case the "beloved" is YOU. This chamber is all about self-love and self-acceptance. It is here where you connect with your own seed of eternal love. The sacred symbol of this chamber is the holy chalice with an inscribed infinity symbol, representing that there is no beginning or end to the source of the love that exists within you. See the image shown here.

Divine Love Symbol

This seed of eternal love that lives within your heart has its own intelligence and consciousness. Research by

the HeartMath° Institute shows that the electrical component of your heart's electro-magnetic field is about sixty times bigger than that of your brain. In addition, its magnetic component is approximately 5,000 times stronger than your brain's magnetic field. This means your heart is an intuitive and sensing organ that is capable of receiving spiritual messages directly. I call those intuitive hits and spiritual messages *clairlove*. You might have heard the term "clair" before as used in the word *clairvoyance*. In French, *clair* means "clear" and clairvoyance, therefore, means "clear-seeing." In similar form, *clairlove* refers to "clear-loving." This is about using the consciousness of your heart to help you "feel" through the heart of your *divine beloved* so that all you choose and do are actions of self-love. The more you veer from acts of self-love, the more you feel separated from God and your own divinity, as happened to me at a young age.

I remember having mystical experiences as a child in which I would leave my body and fly with the angels. This seemed to happen nightly over the course of several years. But one day I told a cousin of mine what I was experiencing, and he said I was crazy. From that day forward, I felt like an outcast and misunderstood by my own family. Eventually this led me to mistrust my divinity and even feel unworthy of love. So at a young age I shut myself off from the Divine. And this lasted until my dream of awakening in October of 2003. It was like I was asleep all those years, suppressing my spiritual essence because I felt betrayed by it.

After leaving my marriage, I began my journey of recovery and discovery in which I learned that self-love is the panacea for all our pain and suffering. The poet Rumi reminds us of the power of love: "Through Love all that is bitter will be sweet; Through Love all that is copper will be gold; Through Love all dregs will become wine; Through Love all pain will turn to medicine." Yet back in 2003, when I began my spiritual journey, I was far from truly loving myself. I had to unlearn what fear had instilled in me. I had to shed all those wounds within me and bring them to wholeness again.

And just as I prayed and opened my heart for assistance, the Divine sent me the help I needed. When I spoke to a good friend about my divorce and how much pain I was in, she recommended I read Marianne Williamson's book *A Return to Love*. In this book based on *A Course in Miracles* (a book of universal spiritual teachings from the Foundation of Inner Peace, scribed by Dr. Helen Schucman), Marianne reveals how love is a potent force that leads to inner peace and a more fulfilling life.

"Love is what we are born with. Fear is what we learn. The spiritual journey is the unlearning of fear and prejudices and the acceptance of love back in our hearts."

~ Marianne Williamson

> *Love is the anchor that holds you accountable to your truth and helps you remove the masks you're wearing.*

For so long I had been wearing a mask of separation. The pain within me kept me separated from my true expression of *divine love*. As I read Marianne's book and began to unlearn fear and separation, I discovered the love within me. It had always been there, but had been forgotten and misplaced. Love, or *amor* in Spanish, is really the answer to it all.

Love is the anchor that holds you accountable to your truth and helps you remove the masks you're wearing. When you love YOU, you tend to follow the compass to True North, the path that aligns you with your Soul's purpose. When you align with your Soul's compass, life flows effortlessly, emerging from the seeds of your greatest desires and passions. This is what ignites your Soul to create, achieve, love, and live as the **real you**. You're no longer afraid to speak your truth and stand by it. This is the path you begin today just by saying yes and being here right now.

> *We cannot love others as we were designed to until we can love ourselves first.*

We cannot love others as we were designed to until we can love ourselves first. In self-acceptance of our true identity, spiritual, physical, and emotional are all interdependent within our humanness. We are spiritual beings having human experiences. Train your mind, your heart, and your spirit to embody this truth that at your core you are a divine expression of God. It is your Soul that can guide you home to that place of innocence and purity—you, the child that once loved unconditionally. As this innocent child you knew nothing else but the purity of *divine love*, an essential ingredient of happiness and fulfillment.

Learning to love myself again has been a life-long journey for me. With each layer that is healed, I'm taken to an even deeper place of eternal love within me. The deeper I go, the more I'm able to hear the voice of my Soul guiding me to a new place of wholeness. I share with you the words of my Soul in one of those precious moments of communion. I encourage you to find a quiet place where you can read these words and really allow them to sink into your Heart and Soul. Feel and breathe every word into your existence.

I ask: What do you want to tell me today, My Dearest Soul?

My Soul responds: That you are so loved by all that is. That you are love. That I am you and you are me. That we are one. I am here to bring you to the deepest parts of your I AM.

Today I want to speak to you of self-acceptance and self-love. You have battled for many years with that part of you that you have felt to be unworthy of love and unwilling to accept yourself as you are. But today I want to change that for you.

I want to challenge your mind and your thoughts—those thoughts are not who you are. I carry within me the expression of your divinity, of your God-vibration. I share something similar to your cellular structures. I carry strands of DNA that make up who you are, what you have experienced, your gifts, your wisdom, and the lessons to be learned in this life. I am here to guide you through your sacred journey of discovery and remembrance.

In this moment I want you to acknowledge me within you. Close your eyes for a moment and feel my presence within you—in your heart center. See me seated there within you. Now we are going to remove those thoughts and memories of unworthiness and replace them with thoughts of complete love, of your being held and sustained in the arms of the Divine. Let us imprint that image in your heart. **You are always held and sustained by God's presence, the divine expression within you. Breathe that in now.**

Cannot you feel how loved you are, how magnificent you truly are, how powerful and vibrant your light is? Feel it now. **See your light encircling your being, your Soul family, your community, and the entire world. Breathe this into your heart.**

As the magnificent being that you are, you are worthy of love because you are love. My Dearest One, you are love. You originated from love, and love is at the core of your power and magnificence. Feel that love within your heart. Drink from the holy chalice of love that sits in your inner temple. Sip from this cup and connect with your true essence, love. Sip, breathe. Sip, breathe. **Believe that this is who you really are. Breathe this in now.**

As you connect with this magnificent, loving being that you are... examine what you see, what you feel. It is pure... it is calmness and serenity. You are bathed in pink light. You are safe. It is as if you are in your mother's womb, relishing in this haven of love. What is there not to love about yourself? Here... you are perfect, whole, and complete. The other is an illusion. Let us remove this illusion from your mind. Let us imprint this truth in your heart. **See and feel your wholeness and completeness. Breathe this into your heart.**

In your inner temple you are safe to be you and your vibration is that of *divine love*. Let us expand this inner temple beyond your heart. See it grow and grow, bigger and bigger, encompassing all of your body and going beyond your body. It extends twelve feet out around you. **This inner temple now expands and encompasses your entire energy field. Breathe this image into your heart center.**

See your inner world now projecting into your outer world. Your outer world is realigning to this truth of who you are… love, peace, serenity, abundance, all flowing within you and without. Those who come into your world now are aligning in their core essence of love, aligning with your vibration of *divine love*. **Imagine this now. Breathe it into your heart.**

Now practice this as much as you need to until you see your inner temple and outer world becoming permanently one.

> *Self-love is the ingredient you need to contribute to the world at your highest capacity and goodness.*

Self-love is the ingredient you need to contribute to the world at your highest capacity and goodness, the highest version of YOU. When you can love yourself as you are, you find your true voice in the world, be it your physical voice or the voice of your gifts and your purpose in life. Embracing this Soul virtue is a critical step in unmasking the ***real you***. You can only embody your truest self when you love and accept yourself completely. Without *divine love* it is practically impossible to evolve and grow into to the full embodiment of your Soul's purpose.

On my own journey I discovered three key principles that are essential in returning to *divine love*: compassion, forgiveness, and surrender. Let's look at each one now.

Compassion Helps You Recognize the Divine in Others

> *Compassion and forgiveness go hand in hand: one opens the door to the other.*

As a healer myself, I've always felt a closeness to Jesus, who's been called "The Master Healer" by many. I've experienced His presence in my own healing and in the healing work I've performed with clients. One of the qualities I admire most about Jesus is His level of compassion and forgiveness. Jesus was able to forgive even the worst of perpetrators. Even Judas, who betrayed Jesus with the infamous kiss of greeting that identified Him to the soldiers of the chief temple,

29

received full pardon. That level of compassion and forgiveness requires a deeper under-standing of and connection with your own seed of eternal love. Compassion and for-giveness go hand in hand: one opens the door to the other. When you're able to have compassion, it opens the doorway for you to then forgive.

Compassion is about empathy, sacredness, non-judgment, and being love in moments of despair, anger, loss, or fear. Compassion, fueled by your seed of eternal love, is an act of kindness, one that ultimately nurtures your Soul.

> *"When we practice loving kindness and compassion we are the first ones to profit."*
>
> **~Rumi**

Compassion emerges from a deep place of Soul connection. As you're able to rec-ognize your own divinity and the divinity of others, the seed of compassion blooms into existence in your life. When I was ready to learn this lesson, the Divine again con-spired to bring me an experience that helped guide me in the right direction.

Shortly after I began my divorce proceedings in 2004, I went on a trip to attend my company's annual customer conference. I normally like to relax on airplanes by reading a book, listening to soothing music, or even taking a nice nap. But on this day the Divine had other plans for me. I was feeling a bit down, as my divorce was really taking a toll on me. I remember I was sitting in row twelve in the aisle seat. I noticed this nice fellow and a young lady sitting next to me. I don't remember exactly how the conversation got started between us, but all of a sudden I found myself telling this perfect stranger my life story and how I was currently going through a divorce.

He shared with me that he was going to a conference as well. It was a workshop about a book he had written. The young lady sitting next to him was his teenaged daughter. And the more we talked, the more at ease I felt. It was as if his presence was helping to prepare me for what happened next.

He stood up, opened his briefcase, and pulled out a book. It was the book he had authored, and he presented it to me as a gift. He suggested I read some of it while on the plane. I almost fell over when I read the title, *Love Walked among Us: Learning to Love Like Jesus*. I decided to take his advice and began to read the book. And guess what. The first chapter was all about compassion. Yes, no coincidence. The Divine was giving me exactly what I needed in that moment. In order to begin the healing process of forgiving my ex, I had to learn to have compassion for him first.

In this same chapter of his book there was one particular line that struck me very powerfully. Paul E. Miller, the author of this book, said, "Jesus has shown us how to love: Look, feel, and then help." This is what compassion is all about. It's about really looking at the other person deeply and feeling what they are feeling. When you're able to see that deep down your perceived enemies (this could be family, friends, or co-workers) are spiritual beings having human experiences as we all are, and that their true essence is love, you understand that it was never their intention to hurt you in the first place.

> **All outward expression originates from your inner expression.**

All outward expression originates from your inner expression. Any pain in your inner world is mirrored in your outer world. This is when I began to understand that my ex's behavior stemmed from his own pain. When I was able to see beyond his human expression and connect with his spiritual essence, I understood his hurt. I could feel how much he had been carrying all his life and why I'd become the recipient of the anger, pain, and turmoil that was raging in his inner world. As I learned to have compassion for him, I was able to take the steps to forgive him and forgive myself for the times I, too, had fallen prey to my own humanness and lashed out at him.

Forgiveness as the Gateway to Freedom

So what does it mean to truly forgive? Forgiveness is about relinquishing control of the pain that makes you want to lash out against those who've hurt you. It's about discovering that you aren't defined by what happens to you; you are defined by how you react to it. It took me many years to understand this and put it into practice in my own life. Forgiveness is not easy. It takes courage and strength. But the more you open your heart to *divine love*, the easier it is to forgive. Pastor and author T. D. Jakes said this very thing: "We think that forgiveness is weakness, but it's absolutely not; it takes a very strong person to forgive."

Part of the human experience is to honor your emotions and work through them. I'm not advocating you ignore the pain, but instead go beneath the surface and discover the root of the pain and why it entered your life in the first place. Everything in life happens for a reason, even the painful experiences. At first you might not understand the "why" of things, but eventually it all makes sense.

Part of our humanness is a desire to always be "in the know" of things. So when something "bad" happens in your life, it's part of your human nature to question the "why" and get immersed in the negative emotions of the pain. But there is another way of being that can be learned so that your reaction is influenced by your connection to your seed of eternal love, your inner temple of *divine love*. From this inner temple you're able to live from a deeper level of knowing that no matter what is happening in your outer world, all will be okay. This is about living from the inside out versus outside in. When you're able to master this way of being, no matter what happens in your outside world you're able to remain centered and calm despite outside circumstances.

The first step in being able to forgive is recognizing that forgiveness has nothing to do with the person who caused you the pain; it has everything to do with you as the victim or the receiver of the pain. T. D. Jakes said, "Forgiveness does not exonerate the perpetrator. Forgiveness liberates the victim. It's a gift you give yourself." And a gift it is. It is a gift of freedom, but also plays an important role in maintaining a healthy mind and body. Let me explain why:

From an energetic standpoint, "non-forgiveness" accumulates in your energetic field and eventually manifests as illness in your body, potentially affecting the organs near your heart center, like your heart, lungs, etc. Imagine, if you will, this energetic field as a complete replica of your body that is invisible to the naked eye, just like the atoms that make up the molecules of your body, which can only be seen under powerful microscopes. The bottom line is that you're made up of energy, and this energetic field is connected to your physical body.

The other aspect of this energetic phenomenon is that when you keep this energy of non-forgiveness within you, it works its way through your subconscious, replaying the story of hurt over and over again. This, in turn, affects your beliefs about your worthiness of being loved. As this happens, it's like you continue to fuel the energy that keeps you attached to the hurt and the energy of the pain associated with the perpetrator of the hurt. You literally leave part of your energy with the perpetrator. In other words, it's like giving away that part of yourself (your energy) every time this memory replays in your subconscious. So when I speak of the gift of freedom that comes from forgiveness, one aspect of that is being able to retrieve the energy you constantly give away to this situation as it replays in your subconscious.

Why is this important? Because the more energy you give away, the weaker both your inner and outer worlds become. Again, your outer world is a reflection of your inner world, and your inner world is made up of energy. If you give away pieces of your energy (your inner world), your outer world (in this case your physical body) is affected.

The other aspect of forgiveness as a gift of freedom is that it provides the gateway to embodying your seed of eternal love, *divine love*. It is only through forgiveness that you're able to pierce through the veil of illusion that makes you believe you're separate from God and others. When you experience hurt and pain, you create a shield or a wall around your heart; but through forgiveness you can break down those walls and love again. Begin by forgiving yourself, and in turn this creates the space to forgive others.

Your heart center is the gateway to your divine essence—your God-vibration, the place where you can access and experience *divine love*. And only through the act

Your heart center is the gateway to your divine essence—your God-vibration.

of forgiveness can you find this place of infinite love again. In *A Course in Miracles*, it says, "Through your forgiveness does the truth about yourself return to your memory." What is this truth? The truth that you have a divine presence within you, and through that all-loving presence you can do anything, including healing yourself.

The more you practice forgiveness and integrate it as a spiritual tool in your life, the more you're able to see that every relationship, every person, every experience is a holy and sacred experience. You begin to see others differently—as the *divine beings* we all are. You learn to understand that we are mirrors of each other and that every experience is meant to teach you something—to illuminate the places within you and within others that lurk in the shadows of wounds that require healing and shedding. Through forgiveness you're able to radiate God's light onto those wounds and bring them back to wholeness, helping you embody your true magnificence.

I can tell you that forgiveness is possible even with the worst of offenses. I can honestly say that with all the inner work I've done, I've been able to forgive the abusers in my life. A testament to that was the day at a family barbeque when I ran into the family relative who abused me. It was the first time I had seen him in the years since discovering the memories of the sexual abuse. He showed up at the barbecue somehow. My mother said she hadn't invited him. She told me afterwards that if she'd known he was my abuser, she would've confronted him, but the Divine had carefully orchestrated this whole encounter. I had already divulged that truth to her, but something, perhaps the pain, caused her to forget the abuser's identity. Regardless, it was meant to be exactly as it happened. I was to confront my own ability to forgive.

As my relative approached me, I had no idea how I was going to react. But in that moment I was able to see him at a deeper Soul level. I knew that he carried his own pain, which caused him to act the way he did. It doesn't mean I was excusing his behavior, but in that moment I learned to recognize the divinity within him, and in that recognition felt compassion for his own wounds. And through my act of compassion came the forgiveness. So you can see how compassion leads to forgiveness.

Surrendering to Love

Living from a place of self-love, *where you embody the universal flow of divine love,* requires you to go into places where you might feel vulnerable. Perhaps you're like me. I spent most of my life building a wall around my heart—a shield to protect myself (or so I thought) from being hurt. But the more you try to shield your heart, the more you feel that something is missing in your life. Your heart is not only the doorway to *divine love* with your beloved Creator, but it is also the guidepost to living on purpose. It is from *divine love* that you can finally love yourself as God loves you. From this place you're able to commit to your Soul's purpose and say yes to receiving all the gifts the Universe wants to bestow upon you. From this place you're able to tap into your *divine spark* and express your uniqueness to the world through the career, relationships, and family that truly make your heart sing.

> **Self-love requires a commitment to healing your heart.**

Self-love requires a commitment to healing your heart and tearing down the wall that keeps you from sharing and receiving love as your Soul wants and knows you deserve. Sometimes this wall can be very thick, with perhaps lifetimes of pain and loss that still cause you to shield that expansive and magnificent power that you hold within your heart center. I truly believe **love is the answer to all that is**. Love is a state of being that transmutes all energies into light, into vibrations of existence here and beyond. Love is an unstoppable force that has the power to transcend even the most difficult situations. I experienced this in my own life in April of 2013 when I had a near-death experience.

My parents arrived at my house on a Friday evening so they could visit family nearby for Easter that coming Sunday. But when Sunday came around, I was too ill to travel. In a matter of hours I was bedridden with no clue as to what was happening to my body. Several days passed and still no improvement, so my father took me to see a doctor. Twice I was misdiagnosed. One time they claimed I had a viral infection, and the second time an upper respiratory infection. The second diagnosis just made matters worse, as the medication I was given completely irritated my stomach. Now I felt like I had this big ball in my belly that was inflamed. By day six, my condition had completely deteriorated from bad to worse. Despite forcing myself to drink liquids, my body was completely dehydrated. I could barely hold my head up, and breathing was very difficult, so my mother called the paramedics. Off we went to the hospital.

As soon as I arrived, the emergency room doctor asked one of the nurses to give me intravenous fluids. I could feel the cool liquid entering my veins and beginning to bring some respite to my lightheadedness. I was grateful that the Divine had sent me a wonderful doctor to attend to my needs. After several diagnostic tests, she returned to tell me that I had contracted influenza type B. We were there all night, and the next morning I was discharged after receiving several bags of intravenous fluids and with a new medication in hand.

Yet when I arrived home, I still felt like something was dreadfully wrong. My mother took me upstairs to my room and sat me in a massaging recliner I have next to my bed. I could feel that my body was continuing to weaken, to the point where I asked her to please contact some family members and friends and have them pray for me.

I've always known how powerful prayer can be, especially when done in community and in great numbers.

As soon as the words came out of my mouth, I could tell she became very nervous. My mother had seen me ill before, had cared for me through several knee surgeries, and knew that I could tolerate high levels of pain. For me to say I needed prayers, she immediately knew that this was more serious than she'd originally thought. Despite her initial fear, something came over her in that moment. It was as if the Holy Spirit had entered her body, and she said in Spanish, "*Vamos a darte un bañito*," which means "Let's give you a bath."

My mother proceeded to walk me over to my Jacuzzi. She sat me on a small bench while she filled the Jacuzzi with water. After helping me into the tub, she then poured small buckets of water over my head and body. I've always known how strong my mother is, but in that moment she was a pure *spiritual warrior*. Not for one minute did she give in to the fear I know she was feeling as she saw me fading away. I could sense she was praying in silence as she poured each bucket of water with such grace and love. It was as if she was performing a sacred bath ritual—a baptism of my Soul.

I grew tired sitting on the bench and asked for help in sitting down in the Jacuzzi. I then laid my head against the wall and began my own silent conversation with God. "My Dearest God," I said, "I'm scared. I feel as if my essence is leaving my body, bit by bit, minute by minute. I'm dying, but no, that can't be. I still have so much to do in this world, so many to serve. I feel like I've let you down." I saw flashes of childhood memories, cherished memories with family and friends, like a movie playing in my head.

And then God said, "My child, you could never let me down. I love you eternally and I'm here to help you find your way. You have a choice in front of you now."

"What choice is that?" I asked.

And God replied, "A choice to heal or not heal."

"I want to heal. I know I haven't yet fulfilled my purpose on Earth," I replied.

And God said, "Then I need you to recommit to your purpose right here, right now. Surrender and let go. I promise I will catch you."

In that moment I remembered the vows I had taken the previous year when I was ordained as a minister. I had vowed to serve as the healer whom God created me to be. I took a deep breath and envisioned myself surrendering and free-falling backward into God's arms. As He caught me, I felt a big release and a sense of calmness enter my body and mind.

I heard God's voice one last time. He said, "And now you shall heal."

Minutes later I arose from the water with a new will to live, determined to live on purpose. I was exceedingly grateful that my mother had listened to the divine guidance she received in that moment. The voice of her Soul became the captain of her actions.

As she surrendered to the divine will of her Soul, she was able to create the space for God's *divine love* to bring me back to life. As I stood up from the tub with little assistance, she smiled, although a bit surprised, and gave me a towel. In that moment she couldn't put how she felt into words, but she knew she had just witnessed a miracle. It took me several weeks to get back to normal, but most of all I was grateful for being alive and being given a second chance.

> **Embodying divine love requires full surrender to making yourself vulnerable to the outside world.**

Embodying *divine love*, self-love, requires full surrender to making yourself vulnerable to the outside world. This means that you're willing to give up control because there's this deeper knowing that a higher power is in control of your life. When you back off the reins and allow your Soul to lead, your life is richer and more expansive, and flows with ease and grace. People you need to meet, events that need to happen, all that you need seems to fall from the sky exactly when you need it.

On that particular day, my mother was that vessel for divine grace. She became the co-creator with God in that moment, allowing her Soul to guide the way, and then the rest unfolded as it was supposed to. It wasn't my time.

I'm so grateful because I'm now able to be here with you and serve you on your own transformational journey. Remember that *loving you* is the foundation of living a more joyful and Soul-driven life. By loving you, you open the space for experiencing that same love with your beloved, family, and friends. Here is a wonderful reminder from Louise Hay that will help you understand the importance of loving you every day: "Self-love is simply appreciating the miracle of my own being. When I really love myself, I cannot hurt myself, and I cannot hurt another person." Now let's reconnect you with your seed of eternal love, your breath of existence—*divine love*.

The meditation that follows helps you awaken to the *divine love* within you. In the meditation we'll be helping you surrender to your Soul and the truth within you. Take this time now, before you begin, to ask the Divine to help you bring to your conscious mind all that is blocking you from embodying the eternal love that you are, so you can heal and transform it.

You can record the meditation so you can close your eyes while you listen to it. For an audio version, visit **www.UnmaskingYourSoul.com/Meditations**. Sit comfortably where you won't be disturbed – with your feet flat on the floor and your hands on your knees with palms facing up. If you're an experienced meditator, use whatever position is most comfortable to you. When you're ready, please move to the meditation.

Guided Meditation: The Voice of Your Soul Awakens Your Seed of Eternal Love

Don't be dismayed, for it is here… a way to be… **a way to remember the seed of your eternal love.**

You are me, I am you, and we are one. As your Soul, I breathe through you, I share your heart, and I share your mind. **Let me in.** Let me show you how easy it can be. **BREATHE me into your heart. FEEL my vibration. We are anchored in DIVINE LOVE.** {Breathe this into your heart.}

If only you would **surrender control to me.** The Divine will always serve your best interests, and **only through surrender will you find freedom** to live a loving and joyful life. Surrender to the truth of who you are. **You are not your thoughts, your name, or your body.** {Breathe this into your being.}

Surrender to the truth of your divine being, to that part of you that has already lived more than once, that knows what steps you must take, that knows the lessons you are here to learn. I am the voice of your Soul, the voice that wants to speak to you and whisper all your **truths. Connect with that presence that is the REAL YOU. Let go now.** Breathe… breathe… breathe.

See yourself becoming one with this part of you, your Soul. The door opens in your heart. You walk through and the integration of oneness occurs. **You are love once again.** {Breathe this into your heart.}

Allow, surrender, and release the hold. Slowly your Soul comes forth to take the reins. You can now sit back and trust in the guidance of the highest version of YOU, your Soul. Action, universal movement, manifestation, all ushered in together. **Your seed of eternal love has been awakened.** {Breathe this into your heart.}

I surrender to you, my dearest Soul. We are one. I am DIVINE LOVE. I am eternal love. I commit to being the REAL ME. {Affirm this into your heart and connect with your new vibration.}

This guided meditation is a powerful tool to help you access the depths of your Soul and your seed of eternal love. It helps you go beneath the layers surrounding your heart and discover those areas that need healing and love. Each time you use the meditation, you peel back another layer of the "onion," get closer to your true expression, and align more deeply with your Soul's vibration. All the guided meditations in this book are imprinted with healing energy to help you release old, stagnant energy and activate a higher version of the divine expression that you're ready to embody.

In *Unmasking Your Soul* I ask you to journal after each meditation. I've been journaling for over ten years now, and I've found it to be an integral part of my own healing journey. As you answer the questions below, try to recall any bodily sensations you experienced during the meditation. It could be a feeling, an image, or the surfacing or releasing of physical pain.

Spend about ten to fifteen minutes journaling in a quiet place where you won't be disturbed. You can put on some soothing music or light a candle or incense to support you as you write. Just write from your Heart and Soul, and the rest will follow. Take some deep breaths as you write, allowing the words to flow through you with love and grace.

Journaling Exercise

1. Were there any moments in the meditation when your breath felt shallow? If so, what was going on in those moments?

2. Were there any specific memories or thoughts that came up as you went through the meditation? If so, how might they be related to a need to unmask your Soul?

3. How did you feel when you spoke the words **truth, surrender, divine love, freedom, being the real me**? Did any of these feel uncomfortable or not truthful to you? If so, why do you think that is? Pay attention to how your body reacted.

4. Did you discover any areas of your spirit that need healing and love?

5. Write down one or more **areas that you'd like to unmask** and practice loving again as you embark on your transformational journey.

After journaling, begin working on the **Canvas of Your Soul.** (You can download the PDF at **www.UnmaskingYourSoul.com/Blueprint.**) Pick phrases, words, or symbols and put them on section 1 of the **Truth** part of your roadmap. Make this canvas your own piece of artwork, representing your transformational journey of self-discovery. Color, paint, write, or cut images from magazines that depict the messages and insights you received in this chapter on *returning to divine love*. You don't need to be a professional artist to do this. Just let your Soul express through you as it wants to. This will become the vision board of your Soul's unmasking, a precious gift to you from your *divine beloved*.

Five Rituals to Awaken Your Divine Love Muscle

One way to awaken your *divine love* muscle is to practice rituals in which you nourish your mind, body, spirit, and Soul with acts of kindness and goodness. Most people think of rituals as celebrations of religious ceremonies, but a ritual can be any type of time-honored tradition, like having pancake breakfasts on Sundays with your family. In my household, my brothers and I had a weekend ritual of making the "Santos Special," which entailed corn flakes, hot chocolate, and melted cheese. In fact, I encourage you to create your own rituals. I give you suggestions throughout the book, but make them your own. The goal is to create sacred habits that deepen your actions of self-love and Soul nourishment.

The rituals that follow are meant to help you awaken your *divine love* muscle. You can repeat any of the rituals and the guided meditation earlier in the chapter as many times as you like. With each repetition you go deeper in accessing your *divine beloved*.

Before you begin, don't forget to create your sacred space. As mentioned above in the section about your sacred space in "How to Prepare for Your Journey," you can choose from various ways to create your sacred space including prayer, invocation, lighting a candle or incense, or playing soothing music in the background. Be sure to take some deep breaths to relax your mind and body before you begin. Connect with your Soul as you enter this sacred space.

1. One ritual to help you with compassion is to practice seeing the Divine in others. In the Indian tradition, an ancient Sanskrit greeting, *Namaste*, is used to do just that. It means "I bow to the God in you." When you use the salutation *Namaste* with someone, you're acknowledging that you see the light in them as they see the light in you. This is similar to the saying "The eyes are the window to the Soul." What you're trying to see when you look into someone's eyes is the divinity of that person. This is more a feeling than an actual physical seeing. It is about connecting to the seed of eternal love within that person as they connect with your seed, your light. One way to do this is to actually practice "seeing" and "feeling" the divinity of someone close to you: your partner, a family member, a friend, etc. As you learn to recognize the divinity within those you love, you learn to recognize it in perfect strangers. To practice this ritual, be sure your journal is handy, and do the following with a partner:

    a. Each person should sit in a comfortable chair with feet on the floor facing each other. Sit knee to knee with a small distance between your knees, no more than twelve inches. Have your journal or paper and pen available nearby. Place your hands on your knees with palms facing up and take some deep breaths together. Try to match the breathing of the other person, inhaling through your nose and exhaling slowly through your mouth. Close your eyes if it helps you focus. When you feel calm and centered, move on to the next step.

b. Open your eyes and just softly stare into the eyes of your partner. Allow your gaze to soften, allowing you to connect with the love you have for this person. Imagine a cord of pink light connecting your hearts together. Send love through this cord to your partner as they do the same to you. Continue to gaze softly into your partner's eyes. See if you can really feel into their Soul. No words are exchanged; just allow the energy to flow through you both. Do this for three to five minutes. Pay attention to the smallest of details. When you both feel complete, move on to the next step.

c. Without any vocalization from either of you, journal about what you just experienced. How did your body feel? Did your mind and Soul tell you anything about this person? Did you get any other messages about your partner or about yourself? Spend about ten to fifteen minutes journaling about this experience. When complete, share with your partner what you just wrote.

2. I've found that your inner child—the expression of your "little girl" or "little boy"—holds the bulk of the pain that causes you to separate from the *divine love* that is your true expression. To help release any pain your inner child is holding, you can do the Ho'oponopono Hawaiian ritual of reconciliation and forgiveness. This is a very powerful technique. Forgiveness begins with you. You should be able to forgive yourself first before expecting to be able to forgive others. To practice this ritual, do the following:

a. Sit down in a comfortable chair with your feet on the floor. Close your eyes and place your hands on your knees with palms facing up. Take a couple of deep breaths, inhaling through your nose and exhaling slowly through your mouth. Really pull the breath down into your heart, holding it in for a short time and then exhaling through your mouth. Take at least three deep breaths. When you feel calm and centered, move on to the next step.

b. With your eyes closed, see either your little girl or little boy standing a short distance in front of you. If you cannot visualize them, just feel their presence in front of you. Then say the following four phrases:

"I'm sorry."

"Please forgive me."

"I love you."

"Thank you."

c. Keep repeating the four phrases at least seven to ten times. You can repeat this ritual over the course of several days until you start to feel the energy shifting. Sometimes emotions or tears are released. That is a normal part of the process. Or you may not experience anything initially. There is no right answer or way. Just trust what you're feeling and continue with the process until you feel complete.

d. After completing the steps above, I recommend you take a moment to journal about your experience. Write down what you noticed about your inner child. How did they look? Were they happy or sad? Did they say anything to you, or could you feel their emotions in that moment? Writing about this may help you identify what pain you're still holding that is separating you from your true expression of *divine love*.

e. Write a letter to your little girl or little boy. This doesn't all have to be done in one sitting. I recommend you allow the Ho'oponopono to take effect over the course of a seven-day period before you move on to the next ritual. In this letter, tell your inner child all the reasons you love them. Don't judge what you're writing; just allow your heart to guide your words. Write five to ten things on your list. Now visualize or feel your inner child standing in front of you. Read to them all the items on the list. Close your eyes for a moment and just send them love, seeing beautiful pink light emerging from your heart center and bathing them completely. Just sit with that vision for several minutes, allowing yourself to truly feel this love between you.

f. You can repeat this same ritual with others you feel you need to forgive. Imagine the person you want to forgive standing in front of you. If the pain is deep or you don't feel safe around this person, you can imagine them standing farther away from you. Repeat steps a, b, and c above, replacing your little girl or little boy with the person you would like to forgive.

3. Something simple you can do to nourish your Soul and practice kindness towards yourself is to schedule "self-love" dates. On your dates you can do anything that allows you to truly refuel, recharge, and feel loved. For example, getting a massage, taking a warm bath while reading an inspirational book, going to an art museum or the theater, and taking a walk in nature are great activities. The important thing is to develop a habit and consistency in expressing love towards yourself. Create your own self-love ritual and then be sure to repeat it as often as you need it.

4. Here's a self-love ritual for cloaking yourself with a loving blanket of the Divine infused with a vibration of eternal love. Repeat this ritual throughout the day, as often as you need it.

    Imagine you're walking in a beautiful garden. As you turn, you see a bench and walk towards it. Your guardian angel is waiting for you there. As you reach the bench, your guardian angel rises to greet you. They are holding a pink cloak—your own divine blanket of eternal love. Your guardian angel places it around your shoulders and immediately you feel such divine grace, as if you're held in the arms of the Divine. Spirals of green and pink light surround your body and lift any disharmony out into the Universe. With every swirl comes a sweet lightness to your being. You feel the intense flow of love in your heart, spreading to every cell in your body. Lighter and lighter you feel, and a deep sense of knowing that you are finally home. Love is all you know now... love and only love. You smile and hug your guardian angel. As you stand basking in this moment, a beautiful blue butterfly lands on your finger. It is flapping its wings. The gentle breeze of its wings whispers to you, "This is your new beginning. Love unites us in oneness." You stare at the beauty of the butterfly and soak in all the love within and without. With gentle grace, the butterfly flies away, leaving a blue spark of light in its trail. You smile and thank the Divine for this beautiful experience. Gradually feel your presence in your body. When you're ready, you may open your eyes. Remember how safe and loved you felt as you wore your cloak of eternal love. Come here often to renew your vibration of love.

5. Meditate with my painting, **Finding Love Again**, shown at the end of the chapter. Each of my paintings was divinely channeled and holds messages and energetic impressions of the Soul that bring healing to the bearer. This particular painting holds vibrations of healing for those needing to remember their true expression of *divine love*.

    a. Close your eyes and take a breath... inhaling slowly through your nose and exhaling slowly through your mouth... and with each breath you take relax your mind, body, and spirit. Continue focusing on your breath... and with each breath allow your thoughts to pass freely... thought after thought... breath after breath... relaxing more and more deeply. Continue taking several more deep breaths. {**Repeat for one or two minutes.**}

    b. Briefly open your eyes and observe the painting. Allow yourself to be taken on a journey into the painting. Look at the images and symbols, and allow your gaze to go to one focal point in the painting. Soften your gaze as you focus on this point of interest. Breathe in its energy, seeing the symbols, images, and colors in your mind's eye. Continue breathing in the energy... breath after breath, allowing you to feel and absorb the healing energy from this focal point.

c. With your next breath, listen to the voice of your Soul. What is it communicating? What messages do you hear or feel within you as you breathe in the energy of the painting? Pay attention to where the energy is going in your body. This gives you an indication of where in your body you may need to release old energy, traumas, or wounds. Continue breathing and just go into the stillness while you connect deeper within. Allow the healing energies of the painting to penetrate your mind, body, and spirit. {**Do this for two to five minutes.**} If you feel guided, you may continue repeating this step, changing to a different focal point in the painting each time. Again, allow yourself to breathe the images, symbols, colors, and healing energies into your being.

d. Don't forget to journal about anything of significance that comes up during this experience.

Eileen Anümani Santos, *Finding Love Again,* **c. 2008**

Finding Love Again is about self-love. As you heal, grow, and are reborn into wholeness, you clear the space in your heart to attract that same love into your life. When you remember and reconnect with your true expression of *divine love*, you are able to see and experience that same *divine love* in those around you. Self-love is the foundation of being able to live a more Soul-driven life.

Be *DIVINE LOVE* today and every day!

The Spiritual Warrior Emerges

by Eileen Anümani Santos

I once believed it wasn't possible ~ possible to stand in my own divinity, in my own divine power.

But, you, Dear God, have shown me how to stand and believe that nothing has the power to hold me back: not my fear, not my ego, not the pain.

As I learn to love me again, and live in oneness with you, the Spiritual Warrior within me emerges to set me free. I am not a warrior of violence or threats; I am a warrior of light, peace, and loving power.

I stand with courage, confidence, and worthiness; for you are my rock and my strength. It is in our oneness and moments of stillness that you show me how loved I truly am. You remind me that I am safe, protected, and powerful beyond measure.

As I see myself through your eyes, I experience my sacredness and magnificence. I understand that standing in my divine power is the only way to living the life I desire.

As I embrace the Spiritual Warrior within me and anchor it in your divine love, I witness the miracles and grace that the universe brings into my life every day.

Every breath is a gift.

Every person in my life is a mirror of my own truth.

Every event is divinely ordained;

All coming together to create the canvas of my soul.

And, as this canvas emerges, no longer do the words of others stop me in my tracks.

Instead, I stand firmly in my divine power. With my newfound courage, I follow the whispers of my heart and soul. Today, I emerge as the Spiritual Warrior!

CHAPTER 2

Soul Chamber II:
Embracing Your Divine Power

Within you lies a deep well of golden light that engulfs the core of your existence. This golden light, the seat of your ***divine power***, protects and shields you from the things in your life that do not serve your highest good. Perhaps at some point the experiences of your life tainted and dimmed this light, and you forgot how divinely powerful you really are. You allowed others and circumstances to choose for you because deep down you were afraid that you would lose something dear to you if you chose for yourself. I know this to be true for many. I did this for most of my life.

Your abdomen, between the bottom of your rib cage and your navel, is the location of **Soul Chamber II—Divine Power**, the second of the Soul virtues that will be unmasked as you embark on your journey of wholeness. The mask associated with this second chamber is the ***Mask of Victimhood***. The mask of victimhood is usually connected to an emotional state of low self-esteem and shame. At a subconscious level, you might feel you don't have the freedom to make the choices that you desire. This usually stems from the fear that if you stand up for what you believe, you will compromise your safety or even experience some loss in your life, such as losing someone you love. This chamber is represented by the archetype of the ***divine warrior***. In my paintings I represented this archetype as the ***spiritual warrior***. I use these names interchangeably throughout this chapter. This chamber is all about your personal power and divine

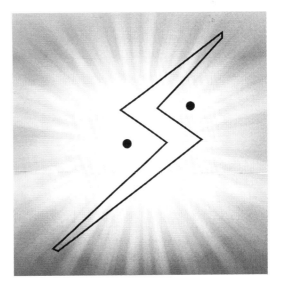

Divine Power Symbol

will—the will to take the actions that serve your highest good and align with your Soul's purpose. The sacred symbol of this chamber is the shield with the jagged *S* as shown above.

The Spiritual Warrior is the name of the painting I created in 2007. It was the first time I captured the essence of this warrior energy in my paintings. When I finished the painting, I realized it represented the archetype that I had become in order to take the actions my Soul was guiding me to take. For so long I had lived in fear: the fear of being me, the fear of standing up for what I believed, the fear of speaking my truth, the fear of standing in my power and making the choices I wanted and not the choices that others wanted for me. In her book *When Things Fall Apart*, Pema Chödrön said, "If you don't know the nature of fear, and what it feels like, then you can never be fearless. Fear is a natural reaction to moving closer to the truth." Having the courage to feel the fear, yet taking action anyway, is one of the main qualities of the *divine warrior*.

You may be asking why I paired the words *spiritual* and *warrior* together. That might seem like a contradiction. I believe there is a way to be strong, in which you embrace your *divine power*, yet do it in a loving way. Your *divine power* is fueled and anchored in *divine love instead of control or manipulation*. This means that the *spiritual warrior* is a peaceful warrior. The *spiritual warrior* is able to harness this gentle, loving power to overcome and transcend obstacles that come their way. They stand steadfast in their divinity. Their faith is unmovable and unstoppable. A *spiritual warrior* doesn't use threats or violence to get what they want. Instead, they anchor themselves in their truth, and every time they express their truth they become empowered to receive their heart's desires. Being a *spiritual warrior* means having faith in the unseen and making a commitment to embrace your purpose fearlessly, regardless of what the world around you says or does. A friend of mine told me once that "Faith is not to be grown. Faith is to be apprehended." This is about really going after it and embracing it.

> **"Faith is to believe what you do not see; the reward of that faith is to see what you believe."**
>
> **~Saint Augustine**

Jesus is the epitome of the *spiritual warrior*. He commanded His prayers into manifestation with such power, yet His touch and presence were of such gentleness. His love transmuted the darkness into the light in one instant. He had relentless courage to be who He was regardless of what others believed or said about Him. He spoke His truth no matter what. He lived on purpose and stood His ground in times of turmoil and descent. He faced His enemies with the gentle and *divine power* of the *spiritual warrior*.

You, too, can find the *spiritual warrior* within you and embrace the *divine power* you were born with. You originated from God's womb of love, and you carry the power to command your life just as Jesus did. When you stand in your power fully, life becomes non-negotiable. You no longer ask for permission; you make things happen as you tap into the divine grace of the Universe. Jesus knew that the only source of real power is within.

> *Your divine power becomes the torch that illuminates your way and melts through any challenges you face.*

Eva Bell Werber said it is so eloquently in her book *Quiet Talks with the Master*: "There is only one source of real power and that is the Holy Presence within your own soul." This Holy Presence refers to the *spiritual warrior* within you—the seat of your *divine power*. Your *divine power* becomes the torch that illuminates your way and melts through any challenges or obstacles you face. As the *spiritual warrior*, you're able to access the strength and courage you need to transcend the trials and tribulations presented to you by your Earthly experience.

Let me paint the picture of one of the most difficult days of my life when I had to call on my *divine warrior* and embrace my *divine power* more deeply than I ever had before. It was December 28th, 2003. I was sitting in a recliner chair in the living room of the condo I shared with my husband. My laptop was on my lap and I was busy working as usual. This had become my modus operandi: immerse myself in work so I wouldn't have to deal with the reality of my unhealthy marriage. In came my husband, and he said hello and sat down. Something came over me and I said, "I can't do this anymore." He looked at me with confusion in his eyes and asked, "What do you mean?" And I said, "I can't do this anymore. I can't pretend anymore that everything is okay when it's not." And he replied, "But we went out just last night and had a great time." Inside I was saying to myself, *Yes it seemed that way because I'm an expert at wearing a mask and hiding the truth.* Yet I turned to him and said, "I want out of this marriage. I refuse to do this anymore." It was the first time I had spoken my truth to him in years.

It was not as though we both hadn't tried to work things out. We had gone to counseling together. But something big changed when I heard God's voice in my dream of awakening in October of that same year. It was like this unstoppable force of *divine power* had been ignited within me and I was determined to follow through on my actions.

We both got up from where we were sitting. He went upstairs and I followed. I was so angry. He went from confusion, to doubt, to anger. He went into our master bedroom, picked up our wedding picture, and smashed it at my feet. Although very afraid for my life, in that moment I stood my ground and yelled right back at him. In hindsight, that was not the smartest thing to do, but I knew I couldn't back down. I quickly called my older brother and told him what was happening. He was my voice of reason and said, "Leave the house right now." And so I did.

I ended up in tears at my parents' house about a thirty-minute drive from ours. I was quite broken and scared, but determined to see things through. Several days later I showed up at our condo with an army of family. I was there to pick up some things so I could stay at my parents', since my husband refused to leave. He kept apologizing and pleading with me to take him back, that we could work things out. But I had heard that story many times before and had reached my limit. I refused to be the victim anymore. I knew if I wanted a happier life it was up to me to make that happen. And that is another quality of the *divine warrior*. Once the *divine warrior* makes up their mind to take action, they are relentless. I became that way too. My freedom now stood in my own hands. It was up to me to break the chains that had kept me tied to that relationship for over eleven years.

The next several months were arduous and painful. I became the target of his anger. It felt like I was being stalked by this man. He even called my place of employment, and I left that day crying of embarrassment about the shouting match that had transpired between us. In that moment I knew that no matter what, I was not going back to that old life. The minute I walked out the door of our condo, I had already made my final decision. Our relationship was over. It took another year and half to finalize our divorce, but we never saw each other again after the day I returned to the condo with my family to get some clothes. Whenever I had doubt or fear, I would think back to the day I had heard God's voice. That dream had been imprinted in the essence of my being, and I knew that I had to stay true to me, to what I was feeling.

This experience made me realize why so many people stay in unhealthy relationships, as the fear for your life can be paralyzing. Not only that, but the abuse works on your psyche. The verbal abuse I experienced made me believe at times that perhaps I deserved it. I needed to keep my mouth shut or he would get angry. Perhaps I was unworthy of the kind of love I truly desired. He always told me that the love I wanted didn't exist, but deep down I knew it did. It just wasn't possible with him.

As painful as that experience was, one of my greatest teachers was my husband. At the time I couldn't see the gift in all of this, but I certainly can now. There were times when I saw this gentle man so full of love, dreams, and aspirations. But at other times his anger outweighed the light I knew existed within him. This anger fostered a distance between us. It even kept him from being able to pursue his greatest gifts. He was an amazing poet and writer. I would tell him all the time that he needed to write a book, but he never was able to embrace that part of himself while we were together.

It took me years to heal from this experience, and as I mentioned before, it was *divine love* that helped me do it. I was finally able to forgive him and forgive myself for my contributions to the disharmony between us. Despite the pain I suffered, I came to see the divinity within him and all the moments of goodness he brought to my life and those around us. For this I am so grateful.

When you think you can't have the life you desire, know that this belief is coming from the smaller you—your ego. The bigger you knows that you really can have what warms your heart, and more. Like me, I know you, too, can embrace your *divine power* to bring goodness and joy into your life.

Look around at your life in this moment to see where you're holding yourself back from being the real you. Are you allowing yourself to be a victim? Are you giving your power away to a situation or a person? If you answered yes to either of these questions, it's time to make a different choice. Start now, in this moment. All it takes is one baby step at a time. Don't be shy in asking for help. Find someone you can trust or a support group to help you through your journey. We all need encouragement and support in life. Don't believe you need to do it alone. When you ask for help, there's always support around the corner. The Divine always hears your prayers and sends you exactly what you need in that moment. You just need to do your part.

The Consequences of Living Someone Else's Life

> *It is from the chamber of divine power that you make choices to live a life that aligns with your truth.*

It is from the chamber of *divine power* that you make choices to live a life that aligns with your truth and desires, and not the truth of others. However, when you experience powerlessness and are victimized in some way, making choices for your greater good becomes very difficult. You lose the sense of who you really are. You begin to live the life of someone else rather than your own. You become a great actor, acting out the life of someone else because subconsciously you feel you have to and that you have no other choice. An example of this might be seen in the career you chose. Did you choose it because deep down it made your heart sing? (If so, congratulations!) Or did you choose it because your parents or someone else told you that's what you needed to do? If that's the case, you might be feeling it's time to really do what fills your heart with joy.

By the time I had to choose a career, I was still wearing the mask of victimhood, although I was not consciously aware that my psyche (subconscious mind) was keeping me imprisoned in these painful memories. I had been sexually abused multiple times, by a family relative and a neighbor, at the age of four, and had repressed these memories until the age of thirty-eight because they were so painful. My dream of awakening in 2003 was the spark that uncovered these agonizing memories. I remember that the level of shame I felt was devastating. I kept going over the memories in my mind, thinking to myself, "Why didn't I scream?" I thought of myself as a strong warrior woman, yet I had been paralyzed in fear in those moments. I blamed myself for not having screamed. I was only a child, but somehow I felt I should've been able to do something.

Yet I know there was nothing I could've done to prevent or change what happened. When I told my mom about these memories, she began to blame herself, saying that perhaps there was something she could have done to prevent this from happening. I reassured her it was not her fault, nor mine for that matter. Even the most painful experiences happen for a reason. If I had not experienced that level of pain, I would not be here, now, able to tell you that despite the pain, fear, and shame of this experience, I was able to transcend it, and that I'm here to help you do the same—to help you not be the victim anymore. Because you're reading this, I know that somewhere in your life you, too, have been the victim and are now ready to heal that and let it go.

I recognize now that back in 1983 when I chose to pursue my undergraduate studies in engineering, I did so to conform to someone else's dreams and not my own. One day my older brother recommended I speak to one of his friends who was an engineer. At the time I still wasn't sure what I really wanted to do, so I thought it would be helpful to speak to someone who was already working in their chosen field. My brother's friend asked me a battery of questions about what I liked and wanted to do. Then he said, "Oh, you're great at math and science, so you should really consider being an engineer." I was grateful that he had spent the time speaking to me and encouraging me to go ahead and apply for the engineering program at a local college. At the age of eighteen I had already lost the sense of who I really was and had no clue what I wanted to do with the rest of my life.

Despite the underlying discomfort and feeling in my gut that this might not be the best choice for me, I chose to pursue an engineering degree anyway. I had always been a straight-A student in high school, but I really struggled that first year in college. Getting an A seemed beyond my reach in those days. I struggled to get a decent grade point average by the time I graduated, as the subject matter just didn't fill me. The passion was missing. But I had already said yes to obtaining that degree, and was determined not to let down those who believed in me. So I let this part of my life play out and completed my studies. I ended up taking a job in the defense industry for a large defense contractor.

Day by day the initial excitement of a new career faded. My heart was just not in it. There was no desire to do what I was doing. It became difficult to get out of bed each morning. Instead of being happy as I entered the building where I worked, my stomach would go into knots. I became a bit depressed and disappointed, as school had not prepared me for the reality of what I was facing. While I met some amazing people working for this employer, every time I went into a lab to work, my heart became very disappointed.

I had fallen in love with the image I had created of myself as this smart, strong, unstoppable, professional "woman engineer," and while deep down I believed I was all those things, the environment was proving a challenge to that image. I was always the lone female on the team among many males, and it became very clear that I was going to have to work extremely hard to get ahead in this male-dominated environment. On one of my first projects, I had been assigned, along with a group of three other associates, the task of putting together a proposal for the Navy for submarine communications. I was very excited when I first heard our company had received this project, as that meant we would get to work with some of the scientists in the Navy's research lab who were conducting some very exciting experiments with amazing results. Again, in my mind I had painted the picture of this very cool and exciting project that turned out to be totally the opposite.

My supervisor, an ex-military officer, did not provide much guidance, so I was left to paddle this boat on my own. One day I was called in to the department head's office and he began our meeting by yelling at me, asking me why the proposal sections were not complete. "Don't you realize we have a deadline?" he screamed. I sat there stupefied, with emotions welling up inside me. I had been burning the midnight oil on this project, yet there seemed to be no appreciation for my hard work. There was no opportunity to explain what was going on and the fact that I was waiting on some of the scientists to provide their portions of work for the project. I left his office, went straight to the ladies' bathroom, and locked myself in a stall to cry. "Why me?" I asked God. "How could this be happening to me?" I knew there was a lesson to be learned in all of this, so I pulled myself together and went back to work.

I soon discovered how alone I was feeling. I was incredibly homesick, as this was the first time I was away from my family. At that time they were living about three hours away from me, so I had to fend for myself and learn how to maneuver life's challenges on my own. Despite the distance, my mom and I spoke over the phone frequently and they came to visit as much as they could. My mom has always been my greatest cheerleader, even when she didn't quite understand what I was doing or wanting in my life. One day I told her how unhappy I was with things at work and she said to me in Spanish, *"No te dejes caer. Confía en Dios que todo va salir bien,"* which means "Don't let yourself fall down. Trust in God that all will be okay." In that moment that was exactly what I needed to hear.

The truth is this incident at work had opened a deeper wound than I imagined. Despite the encouragement from my mom, I became very depressed. I told a woman I had met there, who had become like my second mom, how upsetting all this was and that I felt lost. I didn't know if I could make it through this project. I'm so grateful I found this special person and allowed her into my life. I knew she had been sent by God to help me through what seemed to be a very dark night of the Soul. My Soul was calling me to greener pastures, but I had no clue what that entailed.

Because of all the experiences I had as a child when I felt like an outcast and didn't trust my own divinity, I had closed myself off from trusting my spirituality and the messages from the Divine. But the more I interacted with this woman and her family and friends, the more I was able to open myself bit by bit to the calling of my Soul. She invited me to her church one day, a Baptist church in Maryland, and I felt so loved that day. I had never met any of those people before, but they opened their hearts to me, a perfect stranger, and brought me into their house of worship. I felt so blessed to have met her. She was God's messenger to me, and slowly I began to open myself up once again to faith, trust, and a willingness to deepen my relationship with the Divine.

After this opening occurred, I paid more attention to what was happening around me and what people were saying to me, and went within more and more to seek the answers that seemed so far away from my conscious mind yet I knew were there ready to be harnessed and embraced. I just had to get out of my own way. One day at work as I completed a rotation to another department that was part of the program I had begun two years earlier, I had a conversation with the department head about my current project. We were equipping buses for the Maryland Transit Administration with a communications system that would make their service more efficient, expansive, and profitable. He was quite different from some of the other supervisors I had encountered in my workplace. He was a kind and gentle man. He told me I reminded him of his daughter. He then asked me a very important question. "Eileen, you've just completed your fourth rotation. Now you have to choose where you'd like to work in the company. Thinking about all the work you've done so far, what were the things that you really felt passionate about?"

I knew the answer was not something that would allow me to stay there, but I said it anyway: "The business and management side of things." I had gotten a glimpse of the business world through some of my projects and had started to think about getting a master's degree. Something came over him, and rather than try to convince me otherwise he encouraged me to follow my heart. He even offered to write a recommendation for my university application, which I gladly accepted. It was this conversation that led me to decide to leave that organization and apply to an MBA program. For the first time in a long time I began the process of making choices for me, choices that resonated with me despite what others said. I knew some people would challenge my desire to go back to school because of how expensive it was, but I didn't care. I was beginning to embrace the *divine warrior* within me and decided that no matter what others said, I was going to do this.

This experience taught me that sometimes you have to go through the pain (the darkness) to discover the light—to discover the gifts, the grace, and the love that the Universe has in store for you. In moments of despair, when the darkness overpowers you, know that you're never alone. God always sends a helping hand, an Earth angel to help you through it. God sent me this woman, who became my second mom away from home, as that channel for healing and awareness. Sometimes the answer is so close to you that you miss it entirely because you're not paying attention to the signs and messages being sent your way. You can stay stuck in the pain or you can choose to make a change in your life to move you forward. The same choice will give you the same result. A different choice is the only thing that will bring about a different result. So I chose differently this time around. I chose to follow my heart, and it was one of the best decisions I ever made. There were more challenges to come, but for now I had moved the needle to True North, and was beginning to follow my Soul's compass to greater fulfillment, excitement, and joy.

> *"Once you tap in, just for a moment, to the power that is you, then you allow the Universe to yield to you in the way that you intended."*
>
> ~**Abraham**

Finding Your Power in the Midst of the Stillness

Your divine power can be found in the stillness within you.

Your *divine power* can be found in the stillness within you. The more you resist the changes your Soul is prodding you to make, the more you encounter challenges and experiences that force you to choose whether you're ready or not. That has been my experience. The more you can learn to pay attention to the subtle messages that the Universe is sending you, the more you can move through the challenges with ease and grace. The subtle messages I speak of can be through human messengers or from the animal kingdom. I will discuss more about connecting with the Divine through nature in chapter 8, "Accessing Your Divine Wisdom." For now I want to tell you the story of the praying mantis that visited me one day while I was gardening:

It was a hot summer day and I had gone outside to tidy up the front yard. There were lots of dead plants due to a recent heat wave and lack of water. I started trimming one of my rose bushes. As I cleared the dried up plants, I saw a small praying mantis on the sidewalk. I looked up at the bush next to the roses, and saw a huge praying mantis (the female) sitting on one of the branches. It was completely still, not moving at all. Not too far away was the smaller one, the male, also completely still. It took me a while to see them, as they were both camouflaged. I knew by now that this was not a coincidence and there was a message in this encounter. I put down my hand tool and sat on the ground in front of the bush. I closed my eyes for a moment and just prayed for clarity and divine guidance. I took several deep breaths. As I did this, I felt this angelic presence standing behind me. I felt bathed in God's love in that moment. It was as if I were being invited to drink from God's well. It was time to enter the inner sanctum of stillness and see what message was being brought to me through these sacred creatures.

As I sat there in the hot sun, everything dissipated into the background. It was just me and the praying mantises. I watched them in their stillness and they became the object of my focus. Just as in meditation, the moment of stillness came and I heard, "It's time to make a choice, one that you've been resisting for a while now." I realized I had been deferring an important decision in my life. As I cleared out the dead plants I was reminded that there was something in my life that needed to die so that the "new" the Universe was bringing to me could have space to grow. Somehow I had planted some "weeds" in my spiritual garden, and now it was time to pull those weeds. There was something I needed to let go of because it no longer served my highest good.

Sure enough, after this sacred encounter, I was watching one of my favorite sci-fi shows, *Warehouse 13*. (I am an avid sci-fi fan so you're bound to hear more about my favorite flicks in later chapters.) One of the agents in the show who happened to study Buddhist practices said, "You can only lose what you refuse to let go of." It was clear that the praying mantises had a deeper meaning for me. When I researched the symbolic meaning, I discovered that the praying mantis is not only about practicing stillness and deliberate, focused movement, but also about redirecting energy from those things that aren't working in your life to those that are. For me that meant shedding some old beliefs that were getting in the way of my spiritual growth and evolution. It was time to make an important decision, and I knew this had to do with volunteer work I was involved in.

For a couple of years I had been splitting my free time between two spiritual centers. I was deepening spiritually, meeting others of like mind, getting the support I needed on my journey, but also teaching and sharing my spiritual gifts. But it had gotten to a point where being in both groups was becoming very unhealthy for me. I knew the choice I had to make was to leave one of the groups. For some time I had been feeling uncomfortable in one of them. Lately there had been lots of conflict between the members, and I was starting to feel like I couldn't be the real me. I felt like I had when I was in my marriage, as if I couldn't always say what I wanted to for fear of creating conflict or that I wouldn't be accepted.

Embracing your *divine power* is about allowing your body and your heart to tell you when relationships have become unhealthy, or even toxic. This was one of those moments. I was beginning to feel intoxicated with the fumes of the negative energy surrounding me in this group. It was a no-brainer to leave, right? Well, yes and no. My heart knew it was the right thing to do, but the part of me that still wanted to be accepted and loved was afraid to part ways.

It took another incident to help me understand that it really was time to leave that group. I had agreed to participate in their leadership retreat. One of the members had invited us to her place of employment, which was in a very rustic, log-cabin setting. At first I was very excited to be there, but soon the event turned into a mass of arguments and disagreements. I felt like I was being transported back in time to similar moments, like those in my marriage. I completely shut down and prayed that the time would pass quickly. I could've chosen to walk out of that mess in that moment, but I didn't have the courage, so I stayed. It didn't take long to realize that this environment was not healthy and was absolutely the opposite of what I needed in my life at the time. I was going through some big changes, and what I needed most was peace, stillness, and loving support. This last incident was the straw that broke the camel's back. I finally was able to embrace my *divine power* and not be the victim anymore. I left the group and chose to get the loving support I needed elsewhere. I had finally learned to say yes to me, to my health, and to my sanity.

Sometimes embracing your *divine power* takes some painful experiences and constant coaxing from the Divine for you to wake up and smell the coffee. But it gets easier the more you learn to pay attention to the subtle messages around you. It's like anything else: You have to practice owning your power and embracing it, just like a good athlete has to practice their sport. You have to practice going into the stillness, and once you're there, listening to the messages and the guidance that emerge from that stillness. You will have many opportunities to practice going into the stillness and listening to the Divine with the guided meditations I provide in each chapter.

> *Practice owning your power and embracing it.*

Taking Back Your Power

Have you ever been in a situation in which someone said something to you and you just went along with what they were saying, but deep down you knew it didn't fit with who you really are? Why didn't you say something? Were you afraid they would judge you? Were you afraid they would get angry with you? Were you afraid that if you said something you wouldn't be safe? If you answered yes to any of these questions, then you, like me, have experienced moments when you have given your power away.

Why might you give your power away to others? Most likely because consciously or subconsciously you believe you have to. Every time you give your power away you're acknowledging that in some way you feel beholden to being the victim. You tend to look externally for validation of who you are, what you think, how you behave, etc. And when the outside world's definition of who you should be is not in harmony with who you really are, you can deny and hide those parts of you that do not conform to how the outside world wants to define you. Lack of self-acceptance is what causes you to deny who you really are in the first place.

In the movie *X-Men First Class*, Eric (otherwise known as Magneto) said to the shapeshifting blue mutant, Raven, "If you're using half your concentration to look normal, then you're only half paying attention to whatever else you do. You want society to accept you, but you can't even accept yourself." This is how many of us function on a day-to-day basis. We're so focused on fitting in and denying who we really are that the other aspects of our beings (our Soul aspects and divinity) get pushed away and become ignored. Yet if we spent less time hiding and more time allowing our Souls and divinity to come through in our daily lives, we would set into motion clear paths for miraculous shifts to occur.

The more you live in this world, but not of it, the more your Soul can help you take guided action that fully supports your purpose on Earth. Or, said another way, the more you live from the inside out, the less the outside world can hold you back from shining your true *divine power*.

Denial of who you really are usually indicates that somewhere in your life you wore the mask of victimhood. When you wear this mask, you can find yourself blaming someone else for your circumstances. There is an underlying belief that you are powerless in this situation. I felt that way for such a long time in my marriage. I blamed my husband for the situation I was in. I felt trapped. I thought if I said what I wanted to say I would make him angry, and then that would lead to arguments, which would then lead to divorce. It was a vicious cycle. At the time there was a part of me that felt divorce was not an option since I had been raised in the Catholic faith. By now you know enough of my story to know that I overcame my underlying beliefs. It took a lot of faith, work, and support from others, and a heartfelt commitment at a Soul level, to embrace my *divine power*.

Relationships are a common area in which we give our power away. When it comes to relationships, learning to set healthy boundaries is one of the keys to mastering your personal power. Setting boundaries and recognizing when they have been overstepped has been a lifelong lesson for me. My boundaries were violated as a child, so I had to relearn what healthy boundaries are.

How do you know when others are overstepping healthy boundaries? The body is an amazing vessel. It tells you what's going on, not only within you but outside of you. I'm sure you can remember a time when your gut told you that something felt right or wrong. This is the first place you need to check in with to determine when your boundaries have been violated. Have you ever had that sick or "yucky" feeling in your stomach when you're around a particular person? Do you feel that they use fear to manipulate you? Do they act in a way that makes your stomach churn? Those are all signs of unhealthy, toxic relationships. These behaviors often come from those you love the most; and boy, how difficult it is when it's your spouse, parent, or sibling who is causing these feelings. But no one deserves that type of treatment, no matter who is causing you to feel that way. When that happens, it's time to go within and discover what choices and actions will bring you to a renewed place of love, peace, and acceptance.

Remember, *divine power* is found within the depths of your Soul. You will never find it outside of you. When you give your power away to circumstances, events, or people, you're opening the door for some level of manipulation, control, and overstepping of boundaries. The more you allow the underlying belief that you're a victim of circumstance to take hold of you, the more powerless you feel—and then you feel there's nothing you can do about it. When it comes to thoughts and energy, your underlying beliefs and thoughts create your reality. If you believe you are powerless, the Universe matches that vibration with circumstances and people who reinforce your belief of being powerless. Getting to the root of your beliefs is important so you can confront them and let them go. Remember that you're not those thoughts, nor are you those beliefs. The real you is a seed of eternal love, *divine love*.

It could be (like it was for me) that learning to embrace your *divine power* is one of your major life lessons. In any case, the first step is to recognize that you're giving your power away. You can give your power away to a multitude of things, including relationships, jobs, money, addictions, and health. Pay attention to how your body feels when you're in some of these situations. A sure sign that you're around a "toxic" person is that you feel drained and depleted by them. I call these people "energy vampires." What happens energetically is that they "suck" away your source of power, leaving you feeling depleted. Their own lack of confidence and self-acceptance causes them to leech off other unsuspecting victims to replenish their own power source.

If you answer yes to any of the following questions, there's a strong chance you're giving your power away.

- Do you feel you have to receive outside approval or acknowledgement in order to feel good about yourself?
- Do you constantly feel you're being manipulated or controlled by others; or do you find yourself trying to control others and situations?
- Do you find that others tend to overstep your boundaries? Do you find that you're surrounded by toxic friendships? Do you feel drained when you're around these people?
- Do you find yourself excessively shopping? Do you tend to buy things to make you feel good about yourself?
- Do you feel anger, resentment, and jealousy towards others?
- Have you become a workaholic? Is there a part of your life you're avoiding?
- Are your religious beliefs or your upbringing causing you to stay in situations that are not healthy for you?

Your upbringing and religious beliefs can be strong contributors to your inability to face or leave toxic situations. I remember I had a friend in high school who said her mom believed it was the woman's role to support and accept her husband's behavior, no matter what. This woman had accepted her husband's adultery for twenty years, and said in Spanish, "*Esta es mi cruz*," or "My cross to bear." In her case, she had been brought up to believe that the man takes cares of the woman, so she felt she couldn't survive on her own. But guess what. One day she finally woke up, realized she deserved better, and filed for a divorce. Her husband was shocked and angry (his bruised ego, of course). She even ended up with the house they shared. With the help of her daughters she was able to buy him out, and finally proved to herself that she could be independent and still manage on her own.

Standing up for yourself in such situations takes a lot of courage, but I know you can do it. If I could, you can, too. It's time for you to take your power back. As Marianne Williamson said, "You are powerful beyond measure." You deserve the best life you can have. That is God's desire for all His children. You deserve to be loved, nurtured, and accepted exactly as you are, because you are perfect. You are an infinite being of love and light. Your essence is love, so how can there be anything wrong? There isn't. It's time you love yourself the way God loves you. Life tends to quickly pass us by, so don't wait another moment to live the life you truly deserve, abundant in love and joy and ignited with passion for doing all that you love to do. Embrace your power today and know that you matter. You matter to the world. You have a unique purpose to fulfill. Start today, my beloved Soul. Focus on those things that replenish your power and get rid of those things that take it away, no matter what they might be. Stand in your *divine power* and take control of your life. Make your dreams and goals non-negotiable. Become that unstoppable force that is the *spiritual warrior*. Start making those choices that serve your highest good, and leave the rest; for in finding your *divine power* again, you also find your divinity.

Now let's help you activate the *spiritual warrior* within you, the seat of your *divine power*. The meditation that follows helps you awaken to the *divine power* within you. In the meditation we'll be helping you surrender to your Soul and the truth within you. Take this time now, before you begin, to ask the Divine to help you bring all that is blocking you from embodying your *divine power* to your conscious mind so you can heal and transform it.

You can record the meditation so you can close your eyes while you listen to it. For the audio version, visit **www.UnmaskingYourSoul.com/Meditations.** Sit comfortably where you won't be disturbed—with your feet flat on the floor and your hands on your knees with palms facing up. If you're an experienced meditator, use whatever position is most comfortable to you. When you're ready, please move to the meditation.

Guided Meditation: Activating the Spiritual Warrior within You

Close your eyes and start by taking three deep breaths. Breathe in deeply through your nose and out slowly through your mouth.

Now let's begin this journey of the spiritual warrior together. Let's tap into your own divine essence and the divine power within you… to awaken that which is already there.

Visualize yourself as the spiritual warrior. You're dressed with protective armor. On your head armor are the most beautiful colors of turquoise, green, fuchsia, and an orangish brown; your arm bands are also beautifully decorated in hues of turquoise, green, and fuchsia; and around your neck hangs a very special amulet—it's a sun with fifteen rays radiating from its center in hues of green and purple.

You sense you're completely protected from harm's way… but you clearly know your greatest armor is that of God's presence within you.

As you begin to walk, you see you're in an open field, very lush and green. You take a moment to admire the beauty surrounding you… the trees, the flowers, and the gentle breezes… you feel so connected to all these beautiful creations of Mother Earth. As you begin to walk again, a tiger comes to meet you. It will serve as your guide today.

You are overwhelmed by the presence of this magnificent and beautiful creature, its orange, white, and black stripes all flowing together. As you look into the tiger's eyes you immediately feel its divine connection to Source. You feel oneness with the tiger as if your bodies and Souls are joined as one… the tiger's strength and courage seem to be flowing through your veins. The tiger growls lovingly for you to follow… and so you do.

You look ahead and see the tiger is leading you into a rainforest. Although your first reaction is one of trepidation, that feeling quickly fades as you know you're being guided and protected by the Divine, and the tiger will keep you safe.

When you enter the rainforest, all your senses are immediately awakened. You see so many trees you've never seen before (bamboo, durian, and fig trees). You feel how sacred and ancient these trees are. As you look up to the branches, you see several reddish-brown orangutans. It seems as if they're smiling at you. They seem to know you're here for a special purpose and that a gift awaits you.

As you continue walking, you see a silver gibbon (a type of ape), and it's singing. You stop to listen a moment to its great call. It is a high-pitched hooting sound, and you experience vibrations in your body that bring you joy and peace. Take a moment to breathe this joy and peace into your heart center. *{Pause in silence for one minute.}*

Exotic birds fly overhead and your breath is taken away by the beauty of the orchids, flowers, and the bright-colored butterflies that fly around them—orange, yellow, and blue… just breathtaking. You feel amazingly connected to Source and Mother Earth. You stop and touch one of the ancient durian trees. You can feel its sacred energy and its connection to the rest of the rainforest.

You continue following the tiger and you see it has stopped in front of some tall vines. As you go closer, you see there is a hidden doorway behind the vines. Its brown, earthy color keeps it well camouflaged. You're guided by the tiger to open the door, and so you do. When you walk through the doorway you're transported to an ancient time. You see a beautiful stepped, golden pyramid made of bricks. It is a ziggurat of ancient Babylonian times. Its seven levels shoot up high into the sky, and at the top of the pyramid you can see there's a small shrine.

You follow the tiger and see you're approaching a very long staircase that leads up to the shrine. You begin to climb the steps. With each step you take, you feel the sacredness of the earth you walk on. You feel the presence of ancient priests and *priestesses who walked these stairs before you. You focus on your breath as you take each step, making this climb your own sacred ceremony and ritual. And as you do, you become connected to the deep, ancient energies that emanate from this magnificent structure.*

*You finally reach the top, and as you walk through the doorway of the shrine, you're amazed at the beautiful colors of the paintings and carvings on the walls. Some show religious scenes of ceremonies and rituals of these ancient times. There are brick benches against the walls with various gods and goddesses standing on them. You notice a beautiful lyre in the corner of the room. You walk over and touch it, and feel the soft angelic sounds of its Soul. Let these angelic sounds permeate your core being. {**Pause in silence for one minute.**}*

As you look to the doorway of the shrine, a high priestess enters the room. You can immediately feel the power of her presence and the ancient knowledge within her. She tells you telepathically that her name is Priestess Negara. She is dressed in a beautiful white robe decorated with colorful crystals around the neckline. She is wearing a headband that carries the most beautiful blue-colored stone that sits right over the middle of her forehead. You notice she wears an amulet similar to yours around her neck, with a sun surrounded by fifteen rays of light.

Priestess Negara comes to you and telepathically tells you to put your hands out in front of you with palms facing upward. She places her hands over your palms and immediately you feel a soothing sensation flowing through your body. She tells you she is sending you healing energy and is going to help you access the wisdom of the spiritual warrior within you.

You stand for a moment as you revel in this beautiful healing energy, and you can feel a door opening within you—it is a gateway to ancient wisdom that has lain dormant within you for many lifetimes. She is now giving you access to this wisdom.

*You see colors and images flowing through your mind and Soul. Take a minute to allow this healing energy to flow through every cell of your essence as it brings the sacred wisdom to the surface of your conscious mind. {**Pause in silence for one minute.**}*

Priestess Negara tells you to turn around and face the altar in the center of the room. You walk forward and see a beautiful blue crystal orb sitting in the center of the altar on a golden mantel. Around it sit various offerings: poppy flowers, incense, and dried fruit. She urges you to pick up the crystal orb, and you do so.

When you hold the orb in the palms of your hands, it radiates a lovely blue light. It is an Adriatic blue color—you feel the wisdom of the blue sky and ocean. When you look at Princess Negara again, you see her crystal headband and amulet radiating swirls of blue light... the swirls of light immediately enter the amulet around your neck, and you feel your heart center healing and flowing in love... feeling peace, forgiveness, and compassion for yourself and others who have hurt you in your life.

You can see your heart center expanding and radiating in the most beautiful pink light of unconditional love... divine love. You feel as if God is hugging you at this moment... a euphoria of divine love envelops your body and Soul!

*The blue light swirls all around you. As it spins, it fills the room. You feel such peace, power, and love permeating the essence of your being. As the blue light travels through every part of your body, you feel its healing power strongly. Now take a minute to allow the blue light to permeate every part of your being... every cell in your body. {**Pause in silence for one minute.**}*

When you look to see if the tiger is still there, you see a swirl of yellow light radiating from the tiger, and it enters the crystal orb in your hands. The yellow light is so bright—like the rays of the sun... warm and inviting. As it enters the orb, it transfers to your body... into your hands... your head... your arms... your torso... your feet. It enters the essence of your core being. It feels warms and vibrant and fills your abdomen with divine power. You begin to feel so confident and strong... like you can take on the world. It is as if the essence of the tiger permeated your being and you have connected fully with the spiritual warrior within you. As this is happening, the blue light of the orb continues to permeate your core and you feel its healing power. It's allowing you to fully embrace your true self... your authentic self.

*Take a moment to fully allow this divine power to integrate with your being. {**Pause in silence for two or three minutes.**}*

Priestess Negara tells you to say the following mantras with her. She tells you to practice these mantras daily, as they will help you keep the spiritual warrior activated within you. Place your hands over your stomach (your solar plexus chakra) and repeat these mantras silently three times as you hear them spoken:

- *Worthiness {**slowly repeat three times**}*
- *Goodness {**slowly repeat three times**}*
- *Confidence {**slowly repeat three times**}*

- *Loving power {**slowly repeat three times**}*
- *Strength of the spiritual warrior {**slowly repeat three times**}*

And now with the spiritual warrior fully activated within you, you know you can stand firm for what you believe in; you have returned from whence you came.

After several minutes, the orb slowly shuts down and the blue light stops radiating. You take this as your cue to put the orb back in its holder on the altar, and you thank the tiger and the Divine for this amazing gift they have given you. The tiger then guides you back to the open field from whence you began your journey today.

*As you arrive, once again you thank the tiger for being your guide today. You take a minute to savor this beautiful moment… to feel this amazing energy that is permeating within and without. You can feel the tiger's essence within you. {**Pause for ten to fifteen seconds.**} Your spiritual warrior is fully present {**pause for ten to fifteen seconds**}… and the blue light still occupies your body, bringing peace, love, and healing throughout. Take a moment more to breathe this all into your core essence. Feel the divine power in your abdomen. You have fully activated your spiritual warrior. Use this power wisely as you begin anew. Pause and slowly come back into your body.*

When you're ready, slowly come back to the present and open your eyes.

Now that you've completed the guided meditation, take some time to do some journaling. Spend about ten to fifteen minutes in a quiet place where you won't be disturbed answering the questions below. You can put on some soothing music or light a candle or incense to support you as you write. Remember, just write from your Heart and Soul, and the rest will follow. Take some deep breaths as you write, allowing the words to flow through you with love and grace.

Journaling Exercise

1. Are there any specific experiences, feelings, images, symbols, or messages you remember from the meditation? If so, write them down.

2. Are you living a life you have chosen, or are you living your life based on the needs and wants of others? Write down some examples of events, situations, or relationships in which you have given or are giving away your power.

3. How do you feel when you give your power away to the situations noted in question two? What story are you telling yourself that keeps you bound to the wants and needs of others?

4. What are the limiting beliefs that are causing you to behave this way?

5. What are some positive beliefs you can use to release and replace the old beliefs that no longer serve you? What are some steps you can take to build a more positive belief structure? Remember, you only need to take one step at a time. Even baby steps count.

6. Think of a time when you felt confident, courageous, or powerful. What about that situation allowed you to fully embrace your *divine power*?

7. What can you leverage from that experience to regain and embrace your *divine power* fully, now and in the future?

After journaling, don't forget to continue working on the **Canvas of Your Soul.** (You can download the PDF at **www.UnmaskingYourSoul.com/Blueprint.**) Pick phrases, words, or symbols and put them on section 2 of the **Truth** part of your roadmap. Make this canvas your own piece of artwork, representing your trans-formational journey of self-discovery. Color, paint, write, or cut images from magazines that depict the messages and insights you received in this chapter on *embracing your divine power*. Remember, you don't need to be a professional artist to do this. Just let your Soul express through you as it wants to. This will become the vision board of your Soul's unmasking, a precious gift to you from your *divine warrior*.

Five Rituals to Awaken Your Divine Power Muscle

The rituals below are meant to help you awaken your *divine power* muscle. You can repeat any of the rituals that follow and the exercises and guided meditations earlier in the chapter as many times as you like. With each repetition you go deeper in access-ing your *divine warrior*. As this *spiritual warrior* of light, you stand in your power, yet you're grounded in God's love. There is nothing more powerful than that.

Before you begin, don't forget to create your sacred space, and be sure to take some deep breaths to relax your mind and body. Connect with your Soul as you enter this sacred space.

1. One of the ways to practice your *divine power* is to use positive statements, or affirmations, to reinforce the thoughts and the emotional state you want to create and embrace. For this exercise I combine affirmations with some mirror work inspired by Louise Hay's teachings. Consistency is key, so try to repeat this exercise daily, even if for just a couple of minutes.

   a. Stand in front of a mirror, preferably a large, full-length mirror. Begin by looking into your eyes in the mirror and saying, "I love you, _____." (Insert your name in the blank spot.) If it were me, I would say, "I love you, Eileen." Repeat this several times looking directly into your eyes. The intention is for you to connect more deeply with your Heart and Soul. If this is difficult for you, please don't give up. This means there's a part of you that you're not loving in this moment. That's okay. Take one small step at a time. Repeat this for at least one or two minutes.

   b. Focus on your abdomen. Go back to that moment in the meditation earlier in the chapter when we activated the *spiritual warrior* within you. Remember how it felt to have the golden-yellow light from the tiger enter your abdomen? That energy is already there and awakened. Just tap into it. Feel the warmth and strength of that light, your *divine power*. Once you feel connected to that part of you, repeat the following affirmations at least three times each. In repeating the affirmations, be sure to speak the words into your eyes with emotion and feeling, and then pull the energy of the words down into your abdomen.

      "I am powerful beyond measure."

      "I embrace my *divine power* to help me create the life I deserve."

      "I am a powerful and wholesome force for goodness."

      "I am confident in my ability to make the right choices."

      "I embrace the *spiritual warrior* within me and use it wisely. "

      "I am not the victim of the world I see."

      (This last one is borrowed from the principles of the book *A Course in Miracles*. This is an important one. When you hold past trauma in your body that is unresolved, you see the world through the eyes of that wounded part of you. The more you're able to release the pain and practice embracing your *divine power*, the more you're able to see the world through the eyes of your own divinity. Use this as you would the other affirmations. It is your declaration to the world that you're releasing any attachment to the memories, traumas, and wounds that have you beholden to past events that no longer serve you.)

2. In this ritual you can try several different methods to regain or take back your power. See what resonates with your Soul and then keep practicing that particular ritual.

    a. Bring back to your conscious mind a situation in which you feel you gave your power away. Feel the energy of the situation in your body. Since this is about retrieving your power, feel it in your abdomen. As you hold the energy in your abdomen, bring golden light from above your head in through your crown and into your belly. Allow the golden light to surround the energy of this situation completely, forming a cocoon around the energy.

    b. Repeat the following two phrases: "I call all of my power back to me now. I am whole and complete." As you say the words, see the golden light in your belly completely transmuting the old energy and receiving your power back. Use this ritual as often as you need to.

    c. Another favorite ritual of mine is working with Archangel Michael to cut any negative ties that exist between me and another person so I can disconnect from someone who is draining my power and energy, and also retrieve any energy from that situation. The more we stay in toxic relationships, the more our energy is depleted. The minute you feel that something like this is going on, ask for divine intervention. I like to call on Archangel Michael and his sword of truth to assist me in these types of situations.

        i.   Start with a short invocation or prayer to request assistance from Archangel Michael: "Archangel Michael, please shine your golden light on me and help me sever any negative ties that no longer serve me in this moment. I invoke the power of your sword. May it protect and shield me from any who want to cause me harm. May your divine sword cut away the obstacles that hinder my path so I can fully embrace my *divine power*. I surrender to your will and God's grace."

        ii. Close your eyes and take at least three or four deep breaths. Visualize or feel the presence of Archangel Michael in your sacred space. Relax and allow Archangel Michael to use his sword to cut away any negative attachments and energies. Visualize or feel the movements of the sword as Archangel Michael gently and swiftly makes cuts all around you—top, bottom, and sides—every part of you severed from any obstacles. Stay in this sacred space for several minutes.

        iii. When you feel complete, slowly open your eyes. Thank the Divine and Archangel Michael for their grace and assistance.

3. This ritual requires ten tumbled yellow stones. You can purchase these very inexpensively at Amazon or a local retailer that sells rocks, stones, and crystals. I recommend either tiger's eye or citrine tumbled stones. Crystals, like humans, are made of energy, so you can use the energy of the stones to help you replenish and heal your power center. Be sure to connect with the stones before you use them. I like to hold them to my heart and ask for their divine assistance with whatever I currently need. In this case you can ask the crystals to help you heal and reenergize your *divine power* center.

   a. Prepare the place where you will lie with the crystals. You can put a blanket down on the floor or even use your bed for this ritual. You will need enough space to place the crystals in a circular fashion around your body.

   b. Take seven crystals and lay them down on the blanket or your bed. Evenly space the crystals so that they surround your entire body.

   c. Lie in the center of the crystals and place the remaining three crystals on your abdomen.

   d. Close your eyes and take several deep breaths. With your eyes closed, visualize yourself connecting with the beautiful golden light from each of the stones surrounding you and on your abdomen. With each breath you take, see yourself bringing the golden light from the stones directly into your abdomen. Breathe in the warmth, the power of these beautiful stones. Breathe in power and exhale any negative energies. Inhale goodness and golden light. Breathe out any anxiety and toxic energy. Repeat this for several minutes, then lie in the stillness for five to seven minutes.

   e. When you feel complete, slowly come back to the present and open your eyes. Thank the stones for their divine assistance.

   f. Be sure you "clear" your stones after each use with one of the following methods:

      Burn white sage or a smudge stick and pass each stone through the smoke.

      Place the stones in the moonlight overnight.

      Bury the stones in the earth overnight.

4. Now let's do a short ritual that helps you make choices that support your highest good. Use your journal or a piece of paper for this exercise. The focus is on identifying situations that are currently taking your power away, and then creating a list of choices and actions that will help you strengthen your *divine power*.

   a. Make two columns on the sheet of paper. Label the left column "Situations in which I'm Giving My Power Away." Label the right column "Choices and

Actions to Remedy These Situations." In the left column, list all the situations, events, and people that give you the sense that you're giving your power away—you feel they deplete your energy in some way. After you write the entire list, write in the right column the new choices and actions you can take to help you regain your *divine power.*

b. Once you've completed both columns to the best of your ability, pick at least one item from the list that you're ready to release and choose differently in this moment. It could be leaving a toxic friendship or relationship, changing your job or career, or releasing an old, painful memory. Once you've selected the item, write it separately on a small piece of paper in the form of a declaration. For example, "I declare that I'm choosing differently in this moment. I surrender to whatever shall be in my highest good and ask for assistance in leaving this toxic relationship. I am ready to stop giving my power away and I know I deserve a life that is filled with love, joy, and happiness."

c. Burn this piece of paper! Choose something that is fireproof in which to burn it, perhaps a glass or metal bowl, or a sacred abalone shell used for burning sage, or even in a bonfire. The act of burning this declaration serves two purposes. It helps you release the old situation to the Universe for healing, and it also shows the Universe you have chosen to serve your highest good and have set an intention at a Soul level to embrace your *divine power* in this situation. The Universe will then respond by sending you whatever you need to make this happen.

5. Meditate with my painting, ***The Spiritual Warrior***, shown at the end of the chapter. Each of my paintings was divinely channeled and holds messages and energetic impressions of the Soul that bring healing to the bearer. This particular painting holds vibrations of healing for those needing to remember their true expressions of *divine power.*

a. Close your eyes and take a breath... inhaling slowly through your nose and then exhaling slowly through your mouth... and with each breath you take relax your mind, body, and spirit. Continue focusing on your breath... and with each breath allow your thoughts to pass freely... thought after thought... breath after breath... relaxing more and more deeply. Continue taking several more deep breaths. {**Repeat for one or two minutes.**}

b. Briefly open your eyes and observe the painting. Allow yourself to be taken on a journey into the painting. Look at the images and symbols and allow your gaze to go to one focal point in the painting. Soften your gaze as you focus on this point of interest. Breathe in its energy, seeing the symbols, images, and colors in your mind's eye. Continue breathing in the energy... breath after breath, allowing you to feel and absorb the healing energy from this focal point.

c. With your next breath, listen to the voice of your Soul. What is it communicating? What messages do you hear or feel within you as you breathe in the energy of the painting? Pay attention to where the energy is going in your body. This gives you an indication of where in your body you may need to release old energy, traumas, or wounds. Continue breathing and just go into the stillness while you connect deeper within. Allow the healing energies of the painting to penetrate your mind, body, and spirit. {**Do this for two to five minutes.**} If you feel guided, you may continue repeating this step, changing to a different focal point in the painting each time. Again, allow yourself to breathe the images, symbols, colors, and healing energies into your being.

d. Don't forget to journal about anything of significance that comes up during this experience.

EILEEN ANÜMANI SANTOS, *THE SPIRITUAL WARRIOR*, C. 2008

The Spiritual Warrior is about embracing your ***divine power.*** This painting was inspired by my own journey and represents the strength and courage I had to find to align with my Soul's purpose and transform my life. When you listen with your heart and tap into the voice of your Soul, you learn to embrace the unstoppable faith of the *spiritual warrior.*

Awaken the *SPIRITUAL WARRIOR* within you and embrace your *DIVINE POWER*!

Remembering Your Divine Worthiness

by Eileen Anümani Santos

Oh, My Child, you have forgotten how magnificent and beautiful you truly are.

Fear has made you believe that you are not worthy of even being here right now in my presence. But I ask you to hold my hand and remember that infinite-loving, divine being that you are.

There is no place hidden where your love does not exist, where your presence does not exist, where your Soul does not exist.

You are here and everywhere, all at once. Beneath the fear is a dwelling where only love exists.

In this dwelling we are one: I am you and you are me, and we connect to all of consciousness in the here and beyond. I ask you to breathe in this pure vibration of eternal love and let it melt away your fear.

Beneath it all, remember that just by being born you are worthy of all the Kingdom and blessings of this Earthly plane.

You are worthy of all you desire.

You are worthy of being loved.

You are worthy of being you.

You are worthy in all that you do.

You are worthy in your words and in your actions.

You are worthy through the expression of your divinity, your Soul, the infinite-loving you that you are.

Let your worthy, magnificent you be your mindful expression in this moment and forevermore!

CHAPTER 3

Soul Chamber III:
Remembering Your Divine Worthiness

Before you were formed in the womb you were chosen by the Divine to be alive exactly in this moment. There is a reason for that. There's something you've been seeking and searching for—something, perhaps, that still seems unfulfilled in your life. But because you're reading these words, most likely there's something blocking you from discovering what that something is that is seeking its freedom from the deepest echelons of your Soul.

Worthiness is the calling card for what needs to be unmasked in your life in this moment so you can discover the truth of your existence. Right below your navel is the location of **Soul Chamber III—Divine Worthiness,** the third of the Soul virtues that will be unmasked as you continue on your journey of wholeness. The mask associated with this third chamber is the **Mask of Judgment**. The emotional state associated with it originates from feelings of unworthiness such as not feeling you're "enough" and deep feelings of guilt. This guilt is what causes you to judge yourself and fear that others will do the same. This chamber is represented by the archetype of the **divine child**. *Divine worthiness* is all about your relationship to yourself and others. The sacred symbol of this chamber is the womb of creation, the seeds of the divine feminine and divine masculine forming the seed of the *divine child* in the center. See the image shown here.

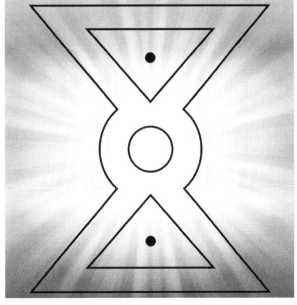

Divine Worthiness Symbol

A message from God to you:

You were chosen from one in a billion to be born as you are, a magnificent spiritual being housed in a magnificent physical vessel. I chose you to be here in this moment because there is a unique purpose you are meant to share with the world. I planted my God-seeds within you and one of those seeds contains the essence of your divinity. The seed has permeated its shell and has now grown and pushed through the fertile soil—it represents your new life. This seed contains my DNA, and so in my image you are as I AM—all-knowing, all-being, and all-loving. Your divinity is your birthright in deserving and being worthy of all that you need, and more, to support you in the fulfillment of your Soul's purpose. WORTHY, to me, means the **W**onderful, **O**mniscient, **R**espectful, **T**enacious, **H**eartfelt **Y**OU. It's time to remember that you carry this seed of worthiness within you. It has already sprouted through the fertile soil of your Heart and Soul, and now requests your undivided attention. Go within now and remember that you are worthy, that you deserve the life you dream of, and that in our oneness anything is possible, even instantaneous and magical moments of remembrance and healing.

Do you realize how special you really are? Let's see if I can convince you of this fact. The average male produces one billion sperm per month. Of those one billion sperm, one inseminated the egg from which you were born. Can you imagine being chosen from one billion sperm? That makes you damned special! I'm here to remind you (again) of how loved and special you are. When you're able to see how special you are and love yourself as much as the Divine loves you, your life flows effortlessly. You see your dreams coming to life and all that you deserve coming to you because you are open to receiving it.

> *"When you get to a place where you understand that love and belonging, your worthiness, is a birthright and not something you have to earn, anything is possible."*
>
> **~Brene Brown**

When you feel unworthy and undeserving, you create a vibrational wall around you that acts like an energetic repellent that says, "Dear Universe, I'm not open to receiving all the wonderful things you have for me." Most likely you're not even aware that this is the vibration you're giving off because much of it is housed in your subconscious mind. This story of unworthiness continues to replay in your subconscious and then projects into your outer world. Remember, your outer world is a projection of your inner world, so until you can release your story of unworthiness, the outer world will stay the same. In other words, until you're able to melt away the wall created by your story of unworthiness, you will not receive what is already there in the Universe waiting for you.

Do you know what story I'm referring to? This is the story sitting in your subconscious mind that holds your limiting beliefs about your worthiness. Because you're reading this book, I know there's something deeper that's trying to be freed from the confines of your Soul. Let's discover together what that story is so you can let it go and write a new story. Let's delve into this right now.

Close your eyes and take three deep breaths. Drop into your heart and focus on your *divine worthiness*. When you think of your life, do you feel worthy and that you deserve the life you've always dreamed of having? If not, why not? What are the things blocking you from living the life you deserve? Stay in this sacred space for a minute or two and let your story come to the surface. What images, words, feelings, or sounds are showing up? Write down what they are in your journal or on a piece of paper. Don't judge whatever's coming through; just write from your Heart and Soul. When you feel as if you've completed this task, look at what you wrote and see if you can find any common themes. Do any of the items on your list have to do with memories of things said to you or memories of things you did that you feel guilty about? Make any final notes and save this list for later. We'll be doing more work at the end of the chapter to help you write your new story.

Most likely your inner child is the one holding tight to the memories that aren't allowing you to feel good enough, worthy, and deserving of the life you dream of experiencing. After about age seven, the innocent child that you were was affected by your experiences of the outside world, and things said and done formed the beliefs you live by in your subconscious. Your innocence faded if those experiences were not positive ones. And, for the majority of us, this is the case because we were surrounded by others who also carried pain, and as they projected their hurts on those around them it was bound to affect the make-up of their siblings, parents, children, co-workers, etc. It's human nature. But something inside you is ready to let all that go. You're prepared to create the life you're worthy of and deserve.

For so long I felt unworthy and undeserving in my life. I felt guilty about so many things. Why didn't I scream when I was being abused? Why did I lie to those I loved? Why wasn't I a better daughter, sister, wife, lover, mentor, manager, or leader? Did I really deserve to be loved by the Divine? On and on these thoughts of unworthiness replayed in my mind. There was a part of me that felt like a villain. Somehow I believed

I deserved being treated with disrespect or violated, or was not even worthy of being loved. My inner child believed wholeheartedly that she was to blame for many of the things that had happened to her. She must have been "bad" to deserve such treatment. I grew up believing I needed to be the perfect little girl, and I had somehow failed.

Yet when I tried to be that perfect little girl, it always seemed that what I did was not good enough for those around me. My mother was very strong and controlling. She grew up in Puerto Rico with eight brothers and sisters, and my grandmother was one tough lady. I know that beyond that tough exterior was a beautiful Soul, but her own upbringing had caused her to mask and shield herself from the outside world. My mother was no different back then. She had been taught that you couldn't disrespect your elders, no matter what. Even if you didn't agree with what they were saying, you were supposed to keep your head down and obey. So my older brother and I grew up believing we had to be "perfect" and obey our parents no matter what the cost. While I've managed to heal my relationship with my mother from my younger years, I still constantly felt inadequate and not good enough in her eyes. I hadn't yet learned that my mother's behavior was a reflection of not only how she was raised, but of her own wounds and pain. She was living her own agony of feeling unworthy and undeserving in life. No one ever intentionally hurts you. Your hurt is their hurt.

Because I wanted to obey my mother's wishes so that I would be loved, I began to live my life through others. I was not doing the things I really wanted to do; I was doing what others wanted for me or thought I wanted because society said it should be that way. I was living someone else's dreams, someone else's truths. I became a people-pleaser in all areas of my life: relationships, personal, and career. I wore the mask of judgment, pretending to be happy and successful, but deep down there was something very wrong—a deep sadness, a big lie, because I was afraid to be me. I felt unworthy of being the real me, undeserving of living the life I really wanted. I was afraid that if I didn't please everyone around me, I would be rejected and lose them forever.

Those fears of rejection even extended to my career. I remember many times during my career when I felt I couldn't be the real me or I wouldn't be accepted. In my early days as a consultant, I was offered a job in one of the top consulting firms in New York City. I was really excited to be working for such a prestigious firm in the Big Apple. I remember an important conversation I had with one of my mentors there at that time. I told him about some of my concerns about what I observed while working there. I could see the company wanted to mold all the employees in the same way. It seemed as if they were creating a group of robots. We were all supposed to look, speak, and behave in their chosen way. I started to feel trapped, but at the same time enticed by the potential of making lots of money. When I asked this mentor for some advice, he said, "Eileen, you're not WASPY enough. If you want to fit in, you need to play the game. You need to look the part and play the role or you won't succeed here." Honestly, I didn't even know what it meant to be a WASP, but I knew it wasn't something I wanted to be. This conversation really made me think, *Wow! Is this what it's like working in a corporate environment?* I started to believe that if I wanted to make it career-wise, I had to play the role that I was being given. Again, in my efforts to please, I ignored the true desires of my Heart and Soul. I began to believe that the only way I would be able to have the financial freedom I wanted was to work in a corporate environment and "play the game."

I stayed with that company for three years, but as I worked hard and continued to move up in the organization, I still felt this uneasiness and unhappiness within the deepest parts of me. Although I worked long hours and always tried to do what was right for the team and our clients, I still felt that what I was doing was not good enough for those in positions of power. I was told I was not aggressive enough. I witnessed things that were borderline unethical, and behavior that made me question whether the money was worth it. Since I wasn't listening to what my Soul was telling me, the Divine gave me one more experience that took me over the edge, and I was forced to choose "me" or "them."

I had been chosen to be the project manager for a pitch we were giving to an important client. The pitch was for a big transformational project in the millions of dollars that was a big deal. I was responsible for pulling together the presentation and all the resources, including organizing a multitude of experts from within the firm and without who were chosen to be part of the pitch team. On the day of the pitch I was a little nervous, but excited about the opportunity to be part of this big transformational project.

We arrived at the client's offices and were directed to a big conference room. I gave out copies of the presentation and we went around the room making introductions. And off we went, each of the leads going through their portion of the presentation. Afterward we all returned to our main office, and as soon as I arrived at my desk I received a call from one of the partners responsible for this client. She called me into her office and told me that she had received a call from the woman we had just made the pitch to. She had specifically called the partner to tell her how "inappropriately dressed" I was; that I had worn a pantsuit, and women at their company didn't wear pantsuits; that I had my hair in a ponytail and they didn't do that either; that my scarf and my earrings just did not fit in with their dress code. I'm paraphrasing, but the essence of the conversation was that this woman was insulted by and upset about the way I looked.

My heart just sank in that moment. I had worked so hard on the pitch, yet all this woman was able to focus on was my appearance. I can tell you that the black suit and silk scarf I wore were beautiful to me; but in this woman's eyes, I had not met her expectations of the type of person she wanted on her team. This took me back to the conversation I had previously had with my mentor and his comment about looking and playing the role. I was most disappointed that this partner had not stood up for me and did not care one iota about me personally, but made it clear the firm was only concerned about winning this lucrative deal no matter what the cost.

That was the last straw for me. I had reached a point in my career with that company at which I needed to decide whether or not I was full-in for the partner track, and I decided not. For the first time in a long time I decided *I* was more important, and that I needed to choose my happiness rather than continuing to live someone else's life. It was time to start changing my people-pleasing habits. It was time to set healthy boundaries for myself and learn how to say no to those things and people that did not serve my highest good.

And so I did. I looked for other opportunities. The Divine quickly sent me a wonderful new opportunity, and I took it. It was time to start creating new beliefs and habits that aligned with my own Soul's yearnings.

Your Divine Child Embodies the Origins of Your Divine Worthiness

Your real worth is determined from within, in the stillness of your heart.

In thefreedictionary.com, *worthiness* is defined as something of merit or value. Unfortunately many of us are conditioned to believe that external things determine our value. For a long time I held the belief that the number of degrees you had achieved, your profession, your title, and how much money you made determined your value or worth. That is so far from the truth! Your real worth is determined from within. In the stillness of your heart you find the true expression of your *divine worthiness—love.* Just by being born, you are worthy and deserving. Your external circumstances have nothing to do with your worthiness or value. Your true worthiness is not predicated on how much you know, how much you have, or what your net worth is. It is predicated on how much you honor you, how much you value you, and knowing at the Soul level that you are divinely cherished and that at your core you are *love.*

Love is the fire that fuels your *divine worthiness.* When love is in charge of what you think, do, and say, you automatically surrender to *divine worthiness.* What are you really surrendering? You're surrendering to the love you are who knows that you deserve to live the life of your dreams. You deserve to be happy, joyful, and living a life in which you are the highest version of YOU—the divine expression you were created to be. No matter what others think or say, it's your divine right to be YOU. And as you surrender to *divine love*, you also surrender to the emotions, memories, or pain that have kept you from embracing your *divine worthiness*. Until you can feel your emotions, you cannot let them go. If you resist, the pain persists. So instead, face the pain, feel it, converse with it, and then let it go. You are not your emotions; you are not the pain. Those are falsehoods that your ego uses to keep you hostage and trapped in a life that is not fully expressed or lived. I know you want something different or you wouldn't be reading this now.

> *Everything you want to manifest in life begins with intention.*

Everything you want to manifest in life begins with intention, so let's start by affirming your *divine worthiness*. Right now, in this moment, take a deep breath and say these words (silently or out loud):

Divine Creator, I ask you to open my heart to acceptance of who I really am. I know I am more than this physical body. I know that the real me is *divine love*, divine consciousness, a divine being of love and light. My deepest desire is to be the highest version of me that I can be. I don't want to live someone else's life any longer. I don't want to hold on to feelings of unworthiness or guilt. I don't want to be afraid to be the real me. Help me heal and release these emotions, beliefs, and memories that have kept me from being the real me. It's time. In this moment, I surrender to your divine will. I release all that no longer serves me. I accept me, all of me. I love me, all of me. I honor me, all of me. I know I am worthy of the life I desire. As I take a breath into my heart, I see myself completely healed, whole, and complete. As *divine love* emerges from the inner sanctum of my heart, it fuels the fire of my *divine worthiness* and imprints it forevermore within my being. Thank you for your divine grace.

Judgment is one of the culprits behind your feelings of unworthiness. It could be that you're judging yourself as not good enough because those were the beliefs handed to you by family or those around you. Or it could be that feelings of guilt about things you've done (from this life or previous ones) have caused you to judge yourself as not worthy or deserving of the life you desire. The bottom line is that your ego uses these experiences, be they those handed to you or created by you, to keep you hostage in this emotional field of unworthiness. Your ego uses every trick in the book to make you believe you're "less than" or "not enough," and it does that by keeping you separated from your divinity and the remembrance of your *divine worthiness*. The key then is to discover what is causing your feelings of unworthiness so you can dismantle them.

One of the ways you can discover the origins of these feelings of unworthiness is to connect with your *divine child*. Your *divine child* is the expression of you that came into this world whole, complete, and of pure, virgin light. This part of you knows and remembers the true origins of your *divine worthiness*. It knows what it feels like to be completely enveloped in *divine love* and cherished beyond words. To help you understand this remembrance of *divine worthiness*, I want to share a story about my goddaughter, Vanessa. She has truly been one of my greatest teachers:

One day while I was babysitting her, out of the blue she asked me why I "did healing" on people. It's those out-of-the-blue moments to which I pay the most attention, because I know it's the Divine working through someone else. I told her that God had created me to do this work and that I really *loved* helping people. She went on to say that she *loved* many things, too. She was at the age at which she really enjoyed writing things down on paper, so I said, "How about you write a list of all the things you love?" Now I knew that meant I would have to help her spell each and every word, but I was up for the task. I gave her a pad of paper and a pencil, and off she went, writing not one, but a list of twenty-four things she loved. Anytime she wasn't sure how to spell a word she asked me and I helped her. I was enjoying every minute of this and was intrigued to see the entire list. When she was done I asked her to read off the list to me. I was astonished, yet so proud of her when she read her first item. She had written her name on the top of the list. I told her how wonderful it was to see how much she loved herself, and I encouraged her to always remember that. I told her I wanted to take a picture of the list so that when she grew up I could remind her of this moment—the day she said "YES" to her *divine worthiness*. As you can see, SpongeBob made it to the list as well. I'm sure there are many children who share that love, too.

I didn't share this story just because it's a cute little story of a five-year-old girl. I shared it because this is what you hold within you, too: a remembrance of that same *divine worthiness*. Your *divine child* also holds and knows that truth at a very deep Soul level. As I mentioned earlier, until the age of seven we hold the pure source of our divinity and light, untarnished and unblemished. But then life takes over and we experience outside forces that affect the pure, virgin light and feelings of *divine worthiness* that are inherent in our core beings. I want to help you connect with that part of you that knows this truth. Let's connect you with your *divine child*.

Borrowing from this experience with my goddaughter, I want you to create your own list, but your list will contain those things you want to release that you feel are holding you back from remembering your *divine worthiness*. Before we do that, let's connect you with your *divine child*.

You can record the following meditation so you can close your eyes while you listen to it. Find a quiet place where you can be alone for fifteen to twenty minutes. Sit

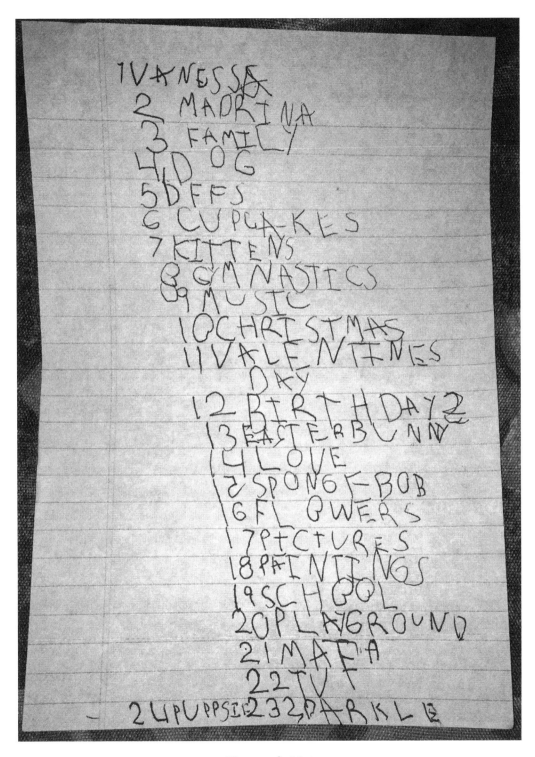

Vanessa's List

comfortably where you won't be disturbed—with your feet flat on the floor and your hands on your knees with palms facing up. If you're an experienced meditator, use whatever position is most comfortable to you. When you're ready, please move to the meditation.

Guided Meditation: Connecting with Your Divine Worthiness

Take a deep breath… and then two more deep breaths.

When you feel relaxed, imagine your divine little girl or little boy standing there in front of you. Imagine them in a state of pure innocence and light. You can see a beautiful white and golden light radiating all around them. From their heart center emerges a beautiful pink light.

The pink light extends towards you and enters your heart space, engulfing your heart and your entire body with a deep, peaceful feeling of divine love. You feel embraced by the Divine and feel oneness with your divine child and all that is. Ask your divine child to help you remember how loved and cherished you are, and just sit with this for a minute or two.

When you feel complete with this experience, take another deep breath and hold the remembrance of your divine worthiness in your heart space. See yourself imprinting this knowing, these words: divine worthiness… divine worthiness… divine worthiness… in your heart space, which is available to you at a moment's notice. Just one divine breath will take you back to this remembrance.

When you're ready, slowly come back and open your eyes.

Now it's time to create your unworthiness list. First write down anything of significance from this sacred encounter with your *divine child*. Then write a list of all the experiences in your life that have made you feel unworthy. You can write them in order of importance. The more emotion there is around a particular experience, the higher up on the list it should be. Just write without judging what you're writing. Do this for a good ten to fifteen minutes.

When you feel your list is complete, prepare to release these words to the Universe and the Divine through a short sacred ritual. You can do this by burning the piece of paper, tearing it up into pieces and throwing it in the garbage, or whatever feels appropriate to you. The point is that getting rid of the paper symbolizes ridding yourself of these energies within you. As part of the ritual, say some words as a symbol of your commitment to surrendering these energies to the Divine. You can repeat the following words prior to burning or discarding the paper:

> These words, memories, and experiences no longer have a hold on me. As I burn/release this paper, I also burn away and release the energy and the emotions related to these feelings of unworthiness. The fire (either physical or symbolic) that burns these words also fuels the *divine worthiness* within me. I now connect with that part of me that has always been there and knows that I am worthy and deserving of the life I desire. I connect with my pure, innocent child of light who carries my *divine worthiness* from the womb of creation. Thank you for your grace, my beloved *divine child*.

How Thoughts of Unworthiness Can Sabotage Your Life

Just by being born and being you, you're worthy of all you desire.

Worthiness is your birthright. Just by being born and being you, you're worthy of all you desire. There is goodness and worth in every human being. If you take a moment to look into the eyes of the Souls that surround you, you will discover the light that is YOU and that is the essence of humanity. In the essence of that light is your goodness, your honor, your worth. Perhaps you've been told or made to feel that you're not worth anything. I remember overhearing arguments when I was a kid and hearing these words in Spanish: "*Tú no vales nada.*" These are pretty harsh words in any language. When you're told you're not worth anything, and if you hear it often enough, you start believing these words are true. I said it before, but I will say it again: Your thoughts create your reality. Oprah Winfrey said this very same thing: "You become what you believe."

It's important to take an inventory of your thoughts about worthiness. You have a choice whether or not to accept your thoughts as true. Remember, you're not your thoughts, so you can choose to replace any thoughts that don't serve you. If you believe you're not worthy or deserving, the Universe brings experiences into your life to validate that belief until you're willing to break the cycle. You can choose to say no to those thoughts and replace them with "I am worthy. I deserve the life I desire." Your ego uses these thoughts of unworthiness to keep you feeling "small" and not living the potential and magnificence you really are. The poet Rumi said it beautifully: "Stop acting so small. You are the Universe in ecstatic motion."

I can't tell you how many times I've had those same thoughts and feelings of unworthiness. That same girl who strived to be perfect so she would be loved also punished herself over and over again when she didn't hit her mark. It was the desire for perfection that caused me to hide the real me for so long. Underlying the desire to be perfect was my fear of failure, and so many times I took the road already travelled, the one that felt safer. Yet being the real you requires taking the road less travelled. Only by facing your fears head on do you grow and expand. It is when you push yourself beyond your comfort zone that divine grace occurs and the Universe shows you the infinite possibilities available to you. These become the magical moments of serendipity in your life.

Trying to be perfect is bound to bring disappointment at one point or another. It's a recipe for emotional sabotage. Ask yourself why you're trying to be perfect in the first place. I bet the answer has something to do with wanting to please someone else. Perfection is always about fear of being judged in some way. That judgment begins with your own thoughts of yourself. If you're still in judgment of yourself and your own worth, you feel judged by others when they say anything that triggers or fuels your own thoughts of unworthiness. In the book *The Four Agreements*, Don Miguel Ruiz teaches the Toltec principle "Be impeccable with your word." This means don't go against yourself in any way, including judging or blaming yourself for your actions. This holds true for your treatment of others as well.

Life always provides the right experiences for you to learn these lessons. When I was in high school I struggled with fitting in and frequently questioned my worth, or *mi valor* as we say in Spanish. I grew up in a small town that was mostly Caucasian. I was always the model daughter, student, and sister, but mostly because I was afraid not to be. I couldn't bear the thought of having to face my mother if I ever got into trouble, so I strived for perfection in all I did, and my studies always came first. It was like I was trying to prove my worth to everyone by being smart and getting good grades, except deep down my thoughts were of not being good enough.

I was a loner for most of my high school years, but in my junior year of college I started to make friends with a few Hispanic girls. This was the same year I was placed in an advanced placement calculus class. As I looked around the classroom on my first day of class, all I saw through the wounded eyes of my little girl was a classroom full of people who had no similarities to me. My little girl was scared shitless. That story of needing to be perfect yet feeling that I didn't fit in kept looping inside my head. I was determined, though, to make the best of it. I couldn't let my family down, right? Well, my thoughts of unworthiness were tested by the Universe.

The class was freakin' hard, so I starting stressing out the day the teacher announced we were having our first test. Exam day came and I took the test with sweaty palms and a nervously beating heart. As we waited for our grades, my mind continued to revel in all the possibilities. When we got our test papers back, I extended my arm and looked at my grade. It was an A. I gasped with relief. One of my classmates looked over at me and asked, "*You* got an A?" as though I could not possibly be capable of it. And again, my mind went crazy. Immediately I started thinking that perhaps I didn't deserve an A. How could I get an A? I was a Hispanic female and was supposed to be stupid, right? Wrong. But that's the belief my wounded little girl was holding on to. She believed that perhaps she was not worthy of an A.

So what did I do? I started to sabotage my grades. I started to have a little too much fun with my new friends. I didn't realize it at the time, but I was trying to fulfill the thoughts of unworthiness that played in my head. I started to step outside the box I had created for myself, even lying to my mother and cutting school. I did this even though I was terrified that my mother would find out and I would lose my status as that "perfect daughter." Soon the warrior part of me kicked in and I discovered that I couldn't jeopardize my future. I managed to refocus my energies and attention in the nick of time and graduated with a great grade point average, but the story doesn't end there. The Divine knew I still had a lot of issues to heal surrounding my feelings of worthiness.

To push me along, the Universe decided that I needed to run into this same classmate again, only now it was eight years later. I had just started my MBA graduate program at Columbia University. It was the fall semester of 1991, and I was walking on campus when guess who I ran into—my classmate from high school. And guess what she said when she saw me: "Hey Eileen, what are you doing here?" as if I didn't belong there. *What the f*ck*, I thought. *Here we go again.* I didn't go off on her, although I wanted to, but instead told her that I was finishing up my first year of the MBA program. After exchanging some pleasantries, we each went on our own way.

Wouldn't you know it? The Universe wasn't done with us yet. We ended up in the same marketing class! This was completely divinely orchestrated. The day came when we had to pick partners for our class project. I was determined I was not going to end up with you-know-who, so I quickly asked two of the guys in the class if they wanted to partner with me. For the class project we had to create a new product and a marketing plan to go with it. I ended up with two smart, geeky guys, and we chose to create a new technology product.

Now I was freaking out because each team member had to present a part of the marketing plan and I was terrified of public speaking. Again, up crept those thoughts of unworthiness and judgment in my psyche. And to make matters worse, you-know-who was going to be in the audience when I presented. I was completely stressed out by the time the presentation came around, but I was determined to do my best despite the circumstances. I stood up at the podium with my two partners and prepared to address the class. With my armpits sweating bullets, my knees knocking, and my heart wanting to come out of my chest, I began to speak. I managed to get to the end without a hiccup. *Whew*, I thought.

At the end of the class you-know-who came up to me. I was dreading every moment of speaking with her, but this time she surprised me. She said, "Eileen, you did an amazing job." I thought, *Was that a compliment that just came out of her mouth?* I couldn't believe it. My Soul just smiled. It was about time. We had both grown in those years apart, and her compliment gave me a renewed sense of faith in my own worthiness and that of others. I finally learned that the moment you stop judging yourself and caring about what others think, you see yourself differently, seeing the perfection in all you've done, all divinely orchestrated to be exactly as it was meant to be.

Expressing Divine Worthiness through Service

> *It is through selfless service that we are able to express and embrace our divine worthiness even more deeply.*

Since you're reading these words, I know that just like me you want to make a positive impact on the world. It is through selfless service that we are able to express and embrace our *divine worthiness* even more deeply. The more you understand your "why"—why you were created and what gifts you're meant to share with others—the more you remember your *divine worthiness*. When you express your "superpowers," the ones gifted to you by the Divine, you live and experience your *divine worthiness* in the flesh. I share more about *divine purpose* in chapter 6, but suffice it to say that it is by living from a place of passion and purpose that the remembrance of *divine worthiness* becomes explicit in your life. You may already be living that path of purpose, but are reading this to connect more deeply with your Soul so you can up your level of service and expand your spiritual muscle. I applaud you for wanting to go deeper. When you say yes at a Soul level, and commit to expressing your *divine worthiness* through service, opportunities appear to follow through on this intention.

It's always helpful to find role models who embody the qualities you aspire to demonstrate and integrate into your own life, so you can determine how you might look once you attain these qualities. Let's look at some amazing people and see what they said about worthiness and serving others:

- *Jesus*—The great spiritual teacher and master healer said, "If you bring forth what is within you, what you bring forth will save you. If you do not bring forth what is within you, what you do not bring forth will destroy you." It's time to take off your mask of judgment. It's time to stand in your *divine worthiness*. Unless you claim *your divine worthiness*, you will never be able to shine your true light to the world and serve in the way your Soul knows it's meant to be. It's time to stop playing small. Let's play BIG together.

- *Mother Theresa*—She shined her *divine worthiness* to the world through her humanitarian efforts to actively help the poor in every way possible through The Missionaries of Charity, which began in India and later grew to thirty other countries. She said, "I alone cannot change the world, but I can cast a stone across the waters to create many ripples." What is the stone you want to cast in this moment? How will you serve today? Create your own ripple of *divine worthiness*.

- *Martin Luther King Jr.*—Best known for his civil rights movement "I Have a Dream" speech and his practice of non-violence as a protest against injustice. In his book *Strength to Love* he said, "The ultimate measure of a man is not where he stands in moments of comfort and convenience, but where he stands at times of challenge and controversy. The true neighbor will risk his position, his prestige, and even his life for the welfare of others." Are you willing to stand up for what you believe in? Are you willing to stand up and claim your *divine worthiness*? Do it now. Stand up and say, "I am worthy of the life I desire. I claim my *divine worthiness*!!!"

- *Oprah Winfrey*—An American media proprietor, talk show host, actress, producer, philanthropist, and spiritual leader. Oprah is best known for her talk show, *The Oprah Winfrey Show*. She dared to push the envelope by speaking her truth, following her heart, and bringing self-improvement and spirituality to the mainstream. Her new show, *Super Soul Sunday*, does just that. She said, "In every aspect of our lives, we are always asking ourselves: How am I of value? What is my worth? Yet I believe that worthiness is our birthright." It's time for you to claim *your divine worthiness*. Proclaim your birthright!

- *Anita Moorjani*—A spiritual teacher and author of the book *Dying to Be Me*. In the book she said, "Only when we fill our own cup with regard for ourselves, will we have any to give away. Only when we love ourselves unconditionally, accepting ourselves as the magnificent creatures we are with great respect and compassion, can we ever hope to offer the same to anyone else." If you want to serve others, embracing your magnificence and *divine worthiness* is key. You are cherished beyond words. Believe that and embrace it.

- *Ricky Martin*—He shines his *divine worthiness* through his singing, songwriting, acting, and authorship. One of his greatest gifts is his humanitarian efforts to create a group of peacemakers to combat human trafficking and the exploitation of children. He said, "Heroes represent the best of ourselves, respecting that we are human beings. A hero can be anyone from Gandhi to your class-room teacher, anyone who can show courage when faced with a problem." Be your own hero today and embrace your *divine worthiness* so you can be a hero to your tribe, those you're meant to serve.

- *Lisa Nichols*—A motivational speaker, CEO, entrepreneur, author, teacher, and coach, Lisa is well known for her appearance in the movie *The Secret,* in which viewers are taught about the Law of Attraction. Lisa is also dedicated to serving teens through her non-profit foundation Motivating the Teen Spirit. She said, "You deserve to be happy. You deserve to be joyful. You deserve to be celebrated. But, in order to do that, you must first fall madly in love with yourself." What is the one belief you can change in this moment to help you fall madly in love with yourself and celebrate your worthiness? Write it down. Post it on your mirror. Affirm your *divine worthiness* every time you look in the mirror.

I'm not saying you have to give up the life you have to express your *divine worthiness* through service. What I am saying is that when you get clear on your "why" and bring your gifts to the world in service to others, you automatically engage your *divine worthiness* muscle. What all the people I mentioned above have in common is that they were (or are) clear on their "why." They knew *how* they were meant to serve and *who* they were meant to serve, and *were committed* to passionately and selflessly serving their tribe. They all listened to the voice of their Soul and followed through on that voice. They had the courage to be themselves. They came to the understanding that *divine worthiness* is their birthright. They were clear on how they could contribute to the greater good and the sacred life we all share.

Think about how you might want to express your *divine worthiness* through service. There's a ritual at the end of the chapter to help you with this, but for now just start tapping into that inner awareness of what that looks like for you. Tap into the voice of your Soul and see what it has to say. Take time to be still, ask the question why, and then just wait for a response. The answer will come in its own time and form. Pay attention to the small details, for the answer is there waiting for you. Remember that through your selfless service to others you activate and magnify the *divine worthiness* within yourself and others.

You can use the guided meditation that follows to help you remember and reclaim the *divine worthiness* that is the inherent part of your *divine child.* You can record the meditation so you can close your eyes while you listen to it. For the audio version, visit **www.UnmaskingYourSoul.com/Meditations.** Sit comfortably where you won't be disturbed—with your feet flat on the floor and your hands on your knees with palms facing up. If you're an experienced meditator, use whatever position is most comfortable to you. When you're ready, please move to the meditation.

Guided Meditation: Reconnecting with Your Divine Child

Take three deep breaths, breathing in deeply through your nose and out slowly through your mouth. As you awaken to the light within you, divine love radiates from your Soul. Allow this love to be the beacon that illuminates your healing journey today.

Imagine you're walking on the beach. The sun is out and the sand is warm beneath your feet. With each step you take you feel the warmth of the sand penetrating the bottoms of your feet and this warmth moves up through your body. As you look to your right, you see some big boulders and other rocks. You watch and listen as the ocean waves come crashing over the rocks. You walk forward and pick a spot to sit near the water. Just take a moment to listen to the ocean waves and the seagulls as they fly overhead. {Pause in silence for a short moment.}

As you look to your left you see a figure approaching you dressed in white who has beautiful angelic features. It's your guardian angel. You can see their beautiful shimmering wings. As the sun hits their wings, you see brilliant flashes of color—the colors of the rainbow—red, orange, yellow, green, blue, indigo, and violet. Your breath is taken away by such beauty. {Pause in silence for a short moment.}

Your guardian angel sits next to you on the sand and says, "You are so loved and cherished. From within the womb I watched you grow. I'm so proud of you. You've worked so hard to heal your life. And now we are here together so you can remember who you really are... so you can remember how much God loves you... so you can remember that beneath the pain you hold is the real you—a divine child of God whose essence is pure love and light. I'm here to help you remember this truth. Your divine worthiness is an inherent part of your divinity, and you are a divine being having a human experience. It is your divine birthright to claim what was given to you by God. You deserve and are worthy of the life you desire and the blessings of the Universe."

Your guardian angel embraces you, then takes your hand and places it on their heart. A beautiful bright pink light emerges from their heart and enters your hand. You feel an intense, deep love move through your heart, taking you to a deeper awareness of who you really are. {Pause.}

Your guardian angel speaks to you again. "Call your inner child to your side now so we can help you both discover and release the pain that no longer serves you in this life." And so you do. As you look to your right, your inner child emerges from the light.

As your inner child joins you, take their hand in yours. Tell them you've missed them. Tell them how much you love them. Embrace your inner child.

*Holding the hand of your inner child, you ask, "Tell me, why do you question your worth? Why do you feel that you don't deserve what you want? What is holding you back from embracing your divine worthiness?" Your inner child tells you how they feel. Observe your inner child and listen intently to what they have to say. Stay here for a moment just listening to your inner child, letting whatever needs to be healed come to the surface. {**Pause in silence for one minute.**}*

*As you try to comfort your inner child, you say, "I know you question your worth and are having trouble loving yourself completely and accepting yourself as you are, but know this—you deserve the best. You are worthy of love, of peace, of joy in your life; worthy of all the abundance and gifts from the Universe. And you are surrounded by the Divine who wants to help you on your journey and is ready to do so at your asking. Remember: You are a divine, infinite-loving, spiritual being whose essence is pure love, and my love for you is eternal." {**Hug your inner child.**}*

*Now your guardian angel asks you both to stand up, and so you do. Holding hands together you walk towards the water. You slowly enter the ocean, one small step at a time, allowing the waves to cleanse your beings. With each wave that washes over you, you feel lighter and lighter. Off in the distance are several dolphins. They're coming closer, as they are here to gift you and your inner child with a healing today. The dolphins come directly in front of you and one in particular comes nearer. Just extend your hand out and touch its skin. Your inner child is also greeted by a dolphin, and you both just gently pet them. {**Pause in silence for one minute.**}*

The dolphin places its nose on your heart center, and as it does, you feel a deep sense of oneness with the dolphin. Your heart is opening wider and wider, and any pain that was there is being lifted and released into the water. Your inner child is experiencing the same. You're both feeling lighter and lighter, and so loved and cherished. Then the dolphin places its nose below your navel, lifting any pain and any memories from this area. You are feeling so serene and at peace. You are feeling the dolphin's healing light cleansing every part of you.

Your inner child seems so happy as they play with the dolphin. You are both becoming whole again... remembering your magnificence... remembering your divine *worthiness... remembering that you are divine love in its purest form. {**Breathe all this into your being.**}*

Your heart center is radiating such deep, divine love. You can feel that something has been removed and released from your being.

*Your inner child is smiling again and transforming right before your eyes, becoming the divine child they have always been, emerging as a radiant being of pure, white light, as if emerging from the womb of creation for the first time. You feel this intense longing to be reunited and you step forward and merge in oneness. You are one with God's pure love. You are oneness. You are infinite. And you remember that you've been this being all along, but the pain was masking your true self. The mask is gone now. Rejoice in the freedom and grace of feeling whole again. {**Pause in silence for one minute.**}*

As you complete your healing, you thank the Divine and the dolphins for this healing today. Take a moment to bask in these new feelings of divine love and divine worthiness.

When you're ready, slowly come back and open your eyes.

Now that you've completed the guided meditation, take some time to do some journaling. Spend about ten to fifteen minutes in a quiet place where you won't be disturbed answering the questions below. You can put on some soothing music or light a candle or incense to support you as you write. Just write from your Heart and Soul, and the rest will follow. Take some deep breaths as you write, allowing the words to flow through you with love and grace.

Journaling Exercise

1. Write down anything of significance you experienced during the meditation. What did you notice about your inner child? How old were they? How did they look? What emotions were they expressing?

2. Is there is a pattern in your feelings of unworthiness? If so, what is it? Write several things you can do (even small steps help) that can assist you in changing this pattern.

3. What are the lessons you're meant to learn from this? Are there areas where you still need to go deeper to heal? If yes, write down what those are.

4. Now focus on your *divine child* and write down how it felt to remember being worthy. Do you remember other moments in your life when you felt worthy, deserving, and cherished? If so, write some of those down.

5. What are some actions you can take to continuously remind you of your *divine worthiness* and reinforce those moments when you have felt cherished and loved?

6. Earlier in the chapter you started to look at your story of unworthiness. Now it's time to write your new story of worthiness. Using what you've learned about yourself and the answers to the questions above, write your new story of worthiness. When you've written your new story, read it aloud so the Universe can help you set things in motion. To give it even more power, read your new story to someone you trust who's willing to listen without judgment. Post or keep your story nearby so you can constantly visualize the new life you're creating in which you completely embrace your *divine worthiness*.

After journaling, continue working on the **Canvas of Your Soul.** (You can download the PDF at **www.UnmaskingYourSoul.com/Blueprint.**) Pick phrases, words, or symbols and put them on section 3 of the **Truth** part of your roadmap. Make this canvas your own piece of artwork, representing your transformational journey of self-discovery. Color, paint, write, or cut images from magazines that depict the messages and insights you received in this chapter on *remembering your divine worthiness.* You don't need to be a professional artist to do this. Just let your Soul express through you as it wants to. This will become the vision board of your Soul's unmasking, a precious gift to you from your *divine child.*

Five Rituals to Awaken Your Divine Worthiness Muscle

The rituals below are meant to help you awaken your *divine worthiness* muscle. You can repeat any of the rituals that follow and the exercises and guided meditations earlier in the chapter as many times as you like. With each repetition you go deeper in accessing your *divine child.*

Remember: You are enough. You are worthy. You are love. You are powerful beyond measure. You deserve the life you most desire. Your soul knows what that is. Begin there, in your moments of stillness. Connect with your Soul and see what it has to say. As you nourish your Soul, your Soul nourishes you. Life takes on a different flavor. It becomes more pleasurable, savory, and inspiring to you and those around you. Start living life knowing that *you are enough and being the real you is your birthright.* Claim it every day.

Before you begin, create your sacred space and take some deep breaths to relax your mind and body. Connect with your Soul as you enter this sacred space.

1. Write a list of all the expressions of you as a divine, worthy being, and repeat these statements to yourself daily over a period of twenty-one days. Remember that your value comes from within. Practice witnessing the voice of your Soul and allowing it to remind you of how precious you are. The more you clear your vessel and the noise, the louder and clearer the voice of your Soul becomes. Take a moment now to go into the stillness and listen to the voice of your Soul. Let's begin.

   a. Close your eyes and take a couple of deep breaths. Remember your experience with the dolphins earlier in the guided meditation. Go back to that moment of feeling so cherished and loved. Allow your Soul to dictate to you a list of all the reasons why you are worthy, precious, and deeply loved. Write these down.

   b. If you need a kick-start, here are some statements you can start with:

      I am worthy.

      I am cherished.

      I am loved.

      I am perfect as I am.

      I am enough.

      I am precious beyond words.

      I deserve the life I desire.

      Life loves me and cherishes me every day.

   c. Keep your list somewhere where you can access it on a daily basis. For twenty-one days, take this list and stand in front of a mirror. I recommend you do this as part of your morning routine to set the energy for the rest of your day. Start by looking deeply into your eyes and saying, "I love you." Say it several times. Then look at your list and read the first statement on it. Break the statement down into parts if needed so you can read each part looking into your eyes and repeating it out loud.

   d. Close your eyes and go into your heart center. See yourself actually dropping down into your heart. Take a deep breath and inhale love into your heart. See the statement you just read right in your heart center. For example, if the words are "I AM perfect as I AM," see these words being written right across your heart. Then seal the words with a beautiful stream of pink and green light. Continue sending streams of pink and green light around the words and your heart until you feel a sense of peace and love. As you do this, you're imprinting the vibration of the words in your heart center and energy field. Everything begins with intention at the energetic and divine-consciousness level before manifesting in the physical world.

e. Repeat the same steps with your remaining statements. It might sound like this takes a lot of time, but it really doesn't. Once you have practiced this technique a few times, you can do it in five to seven minutes tops, and you can use this technique for anything you want to manifest in your life.

2. Continue the relationship you began with your *divine child* during the guided meditation earlier in the chapter. I have a client who keeps a picture of herself as a little girl next to her bed on her nightstand. Every night before she goes to sleep she speaks with her *divine child*. I, too, have a similar practice. I have a picture of me when I was about three years old that I keep in my writing space at home. In the picture my older brother and I are hugging by a Christmas tree. I chose this picture because we both have huge smiles on our faces. We were sharing so much joy and love in this photo. It reminds me of how lucky I am to be so cherished by my family, friends, and the Divine. While I wrote this book, I kept the picture nearby so I could share that same love with you. This is what you do next in this ritual:

> Pick one of your favorite pictures of you when you were a child, one that expresses the pure, virgin light of your *divine light*, innocence, joy, and love. Use it to continue a daily kinship with your *divine child*. Speak to them and tell them how much you love them. Tell them how cherished they are. Have them speak to you their worries, fears, or where they need your help in loving more of them (which is more of you). Send love to the places that need it. This is about cherishing you—all of you. Be creative in how you maintain your kinship with your *divine child*. You can speak to your child in the morning or in the evening, in front of the mirror or in silence as you go within the stillness. Ask your Soul for guidance and then just allow for whatever needs to come forth, and it will. There is no right or wrong way. It's just about being—being the real you.

3. Create your own daily celebrations of your *divine worthiness*. You can do this in a multitude of ways. Below are just a few examples.

a. Write yourself love notes about how worthy you are each day for twenty-one days. Write statements of your *divine worthiness* on post-it notes or index cards. For example, you can write "I AM enough exactly as I AM." Then place the post-it notes all over your house, car, office, etc. Place them wherever you need a daily dose of "cherishable moments." If you use the index-card method, you can carry the affirming statements with you wherever you go. Just be sure to make time to look at them daily, even if for just a couple of minutes. Take a deep breath in and out as you inhale the words into your heart. Consistency is what builds your *divine worthiness* muscle.

b. For twenty-one days, do something daily that nourishes your Soul and helps you feel cherished. It can be anything, so listen to the wants and desires of your *divine child*. It could be a need to use your imagination or creativity, or just plain have fun. This can be getting a massage, reading that novel you've wanted to read, doing some artwork, visiting your favorite art museum, or going for a walk at the park. Keep it simple so you can do it daily. On weekends, go for the gusto and do things that take a little more time. You deserve the best, so don't hold back. Remember, consistency is key.

c. If you have an iPhone, I recommend you get a reminder app. I use AidaReminder. I learned about this app from Cheryl Richardson, who's an amazing coach and author. With this app you can send yourself daily doses of *divine worthiness*. This is an example of one of my daily doses: "Eileen, you are so cherished and loved! Remember how magnificent you are. Let your light shine fully. No more playing small. No more mask. It's time to be the REAL YOU! This is your time, Girl!" The app allows you to send text or voice reminders. You can set the frequency of these reminders, but I recommend the daily setting so you get your love notes every day.

4. Express simple acts of *divine worthiness*. Honor the *divine worthiness* of your neighbor, spouse or partner, family member, or friend. When you engage in making someone else feel worthy, you also engage the memories of your own *divine worthiness*.

a. Pick someone you want to honor with words of *divine worthiness*, then write them a letter that expresses why you honor their presence in your life. Tell them how much you cherish them and how grateful you are for having them in your life. Remind them of how worthy they are and how much they deserve the best life possible. Visit with them and read the letter out loud to them. Take some tissues because it might get a little emotional. If they're far away, call and read them the letter.

b. Honor your mother or anyone who has been a mother to you. In the book *The Wounded Chalice*, author Mary Grace teaches that "You are here because your mom honored the Divinity of her Womb, which contained You." Honor your mom or surrogate mom with sacred expressions of love. Cherish them for how they cherished you. It is the smallest and most heartfelt expressions of love that are remembered for a lifetime.

    c. Create post-it notes for others using words of *divine worthiness* and leave them in places they will be found. For example, put a sticky note on the mirror for your spouse who might read it, like this: "You are cherished beyond words." Or leave one on the mirror of the restroom at your favorite restaurant or book store. Instead of using sticky notes, you can create little notes of *divine worthiness*. Carry them with you so you can give one to your hairdresser, neighbor, clergyman, cashier at the grocery store, or even a perfect stranger you meet on the street. Just allow your heart to lead you and immerse yourself in the love.

5. Meditate with my painting **A Child's Light**, shown at the end of the chapter. This painting holds special meaning for me, as it was inspired by my goddaughter, Vanessa, when she was six months old. Each of my paintings was divinely channeled and holds messages and energetic impressions of the Soul that bring healing to the bearer. This particular painting holds vibrations of healing for those needing to remember their true expression of *divine worthiness*.

    a. Close your eyes and take a breath... inhaling slowly through your nose and exhaling slowly through your mouth... and with each breath you take relax your mind, body, and spirit. Continue focusing on your breath... and with each breath allow your thoughts to pass freely... thought after thought... breath after breath... relaxing more and more deeply. Continue taking several more deep breaths. {**Repeat for one or two minutes.**}

    b. Briefly open your eyes and observe the painting. Allow yourself to be taken on a journey into the painting. Look at the images and symbols, and allow your gaze to go to one focal point in the painting. Soften your gaze as you focus on this point of interest. Breathe in its energy, seeing the symbols, images, and colors in your mind's eye. Continue breathing in the energy... breath after breath, allowing you to feel and absorb the healing energy from this focal point.

    c. With your next breath, listen to the voice of your Soul. What is it communicating? What messages do you hear or feel within you as you breathe in the energy of the painting? Pay attention to where the energy is going in your body. This gives you an indication of where in your body you may need to release old energy, traumas, or wounds. Continue breathing and just go into the stillness while you connect deeper within. Allow the healing energies of the painting to penetrate your mind, body, and spirit. {**Do this for two to five minutes.**} If you feel guided, you may continue repeating this step, changing to a different focal point in the painting each time. Again, allow yourself to breathe the images, symbols, colors, and healing energies into your being.

d. Don't forget to journal about anything of significance that comes up during this experience.

EILEEN ANÜMANI SANTOS, *A CHILD'S LIGHT*, C. 2009

A Child's Light helps you reconnect with your *divine child* who inherently knows that you are precious beyond words, cherished, and loved in such a way that can only be experienced to be known. You can return to this purity, innocence, and light that you once knew as you emerged from the womb of creation. You are worthy to be you; it is your divine right. Embrace it, be it, love it. Imagine, create, and just *be* you without limitation or barriers. Your *divine child* is a master at just being themselves. Reconnect with your *divine child's* light. This is your true essence.

Remember your MAGNIFICENCE and DIVINE WORTHINESS!

Embodying Your Divine Truths

by Eileen Anümani Santos

I say to God: As I sit here in Your presence, there is no doubt that You are always with me. I can feel the warmth of Your voice as You whisper in my ear;

The joy and love expressed in Your heart as You embrace me in Your arms;

And the knowing within each of us that we are part of one another.

In my times of stillness with You, You have shown me how to return to You;

The home from whence I came; the home that holds the essence of who I really am: a radiant being of light, infused with all Your divinity, all Your wisdom, all Your love—a magnificent being of light—all-knowing, all-loving, all-healing.

In Your tender arms I remain in grace to serve You and humanity with gratitude for all that is and will be,

For all that I AM that I AM,

For all the miracles I have witnessed and will continue to see.

Thank You for this miracle-mindedness that has served to humble my heart and spirit. I know without a doubt that with You, Dear God, anything is possible. And the moment we clear our vessel to receive You completely, we witness the infinite possibilities that You have ready for us.

As we surrender to Your divine plan and we become one with all that is… one with You, Dear God… finally embodying who we really are at our core… an infinite being of light radiating the pureness of Your love… a love that is unmistakable as its emergence from within engenders immediate recognition of the divinity and sacredness we hold in each other.

God says: Now is the time to fully be who you are. Radiate your light and *divine truths* fully to the world. Choose to live in your truth once and for all. In the stillness I remain to witness the glory of your return home.

CHAPTER 4

Soul Chamber IV:
Accepting Your Divine Truths

No matter what your truths are, it's time to accept them—truths that are only yours. My truths and your truths are not the same. There is one *divine truth* that unifies us all; we are all God-seeds, *divine sparks* of creation, unified fields of unconditional love. But within you is a set of **divine truths** that are unique to you. Your *divine truths* are the expression of your Soul essence in this incarnation. You give voice to your *divine truths* by living on purpose (which we will cover in chapter 6).

If I were to explain this in business terms, the best analogy that comes to mind is the difference between a strategy and a tactic. Strategy is the "what." It represents the overall vision of those things that are inherently unique to the business. Your *divine truths* are the what. They represent the unique God-seed that you were created with—your Soul's genius or divine secret sauce. A tactic is the "how." Tactics are the steps and actions you take to implement your strategy or your what. In similar form, purpose is the how. It is how you express your *divine truths*, those divine gifts that are the make-up of your Soul's DNA. Discovering what your *divine truths* are and where fear is holding you back from accepting those truths is what this chapter is about.

Between your heart and the bottom of your neck (the higher heart) is the location of **Soul Chamber IV—Divine Truth,** the fourth of the Soul virtues that will be unmasked as you continue on your journey of wholeness. The mask associated with this fourth chamber is the **Mask of Injustice**. The emotional state associated with this mask originates from feelings of sorrow and grief. This chamber is represented by the archetype of the **divine magistrate**. Your *divine magistrate* is the seeker and upholder of your *divine truths*—the orchestrator of justice, integrity, and truth in your life. In this case the mask of injustice represents repression or suppression of your *divine magistrate* due to sorrow or grief you may be holding in your higher heart. This emotional state is a direct result of some injustice you feel (consciously or subconsciously) has been inflicted on you or even on the greater good of humanity. The sacred symbol of this chamber is shown below.

It took a lot for me to discover and accept my own *divine truths*. Sometimes we need others to help us remember our *divine truths*. When it is time, God, will send you the messengers to help you do just that. The deeper you go with the Divine, the more you discover, until one day it all starts to make sense. It's always about divine timing. Age or circumstance doesn't matter. When it's your time to discover your *divine truths*, it just happens. That's how it occurred for me. I told you the story in the preface of the day a perfect stranger told me that I was meant to be a healer, one of my *divine truths*. The Divine has always

Divine Truth Symbol

sent me messengers when I needed them most. It's no coincidence that as I was writing this chapter the Divine sent me not one, but two messengers.

One of those was my dear friend who has multiple sclerosis (MS). She was my maid of honor when I got married in 1997. She looked perfectly healthy then, but a year or two after my wedding she was diagnosed with MS. We had been best friends in high school. What I loved most about her was that she never once judged me. I remember the day I was going to tell my beloved how I felt about her and was overwhelmed with fear. It was my friend who talked me off the ledge and said, "You can do this, Eileen. Just do it." And I did. It was one of the scariest moments in my life, but one I needed to experience. I had to feel the fear and do it anyway. Yet for several years I stopped visiting my friend. There was a part of me that carried a deep grief and sorrow for her because with each year that passed my friend's condition worsened. By the time I next saw her, she had completely lost mobility of her body, and I couldn't bear seeing her that way.

My mother, who is very intuitive, kept nudging me and reminding me what a special friend she had been to me. She told me it was time to go see her. I kept putting it off until one day I unexpectedly ran into a mutual friend of ours. I was celebrating my great niece's baptism with my family at a local restaurant, and in came this mutual friend. I hadn't seen him in about twenty years. As soon as I went up to him it was like old times. After some chitchat he asked me if I had seen our friend. He went on to tell me she was in bad shape and that I should go see her. I knew it was no coincidence I had run into him. I was getting signs from all over that it was time to visit with her. As

I meditated the next day, the Divine said loud and clear, "You need to go see her today." And so I did.

I had no idea how I would react when I saw her, but I went anyway. Her mother opened the door and was happily surprised to see me. It turned out it had been six or seven years since my last visit. I had no idea it had been that long. I didn't know if my friend would remember me, but as soon as I walked into the room she smiled and said, "Leenie." That was her nickname for me. Her mother told me she couldn't move any part of her body except her head. She had lost muscle movement of one of her eyes and basically all parts of her body. She could still speak, but not for long periods of time, and had to be fed intravenously. When I saw her all I could tell her was how much I had missed her, and I caressed her head.

Despite her condition, she remembered everything about our lives together. She immediately asked me about all my family members and how I was doing. I was astonished by how positive she was and what a bright light she was. At one point she told me how blessed she was. She had her mother who was taking care of her, and family and friends who loved her so much. I said, "You know, God loves you very much, too." And she said, "I know. I speak to Him all the time." In that moment, everything changed for me. I had been guided to go there to be inspired by her, to know that our circumstances don't define us or express the truth of who we really are. There was no need for me to feel sorrow or grief for my friend. She was content, grateful, and full of life in her own way. This was part of her own *divine truths*. She was shining her light and inspiring those around her through her illness.

I updated her on my life and mentioned I was writing this book. She asked me what it was about, and as I told her about it, she said, "I know you. It's time. Be the real you." I knew God was speaking to me through my friend that day. I needed to really own and accept my *divine truths* at a deeper Soul level. As I sat by her bedside, I continued to caress her head, and was guided to place my hands on her head and heart. I could feel the peace within her and a confirmation from her Soul. Her Soul spoke to me very clearly. It said, "Eileen, you are a healer. It's time to accept this truth fully." She looked at me and smiled.

At the end of this chapter is the image of the painting that was inspired by my friend. It's called *Listen to the Voice of Your Angels*. In that moment, my friend became that messenger, that angel, with an important message for me. That precious moment with my friend helped me embody my deepest truth in a way I never had before. Yet I knew there was more—more to discover, heal, and embody. I was being prepared for the arrival of a second messenger. More about that shortly.

After this inspirational and healing experience with my friend, I thanked the Divine for giving me the strength to do what I had to do. As I went deeper into the stillness, this is what God said to me:

> Today you see the truth within your Soul. You recognize the old patterns that must end and the new you must create. You walk in oneness with me as we create the tapestry of your new life; the canvas of your Soul. The time has arrived for you to deliver on your promise to honor your *divine truths*.

There were no more words necessary for me to know it was time for me to embody my *divine truths* in a way I never had before. I was living and breathing every single word I was writing in this book. Until then I had still been living in two worlds. I was working at a job that was not my purpose-work, only doing my purpose-work on a part-time basis. I was being given the green light (the sign) that it was time to start transitioning into my purpose-work full time. I knew that completing this book was an important step in making that transition. It's not enough to discover your *divine truths* and heal the blocks in the way; you must also embody your *divine truths*. This means you commit to them at a Soul level and accept them as the inner truths you are meant to express to your outer world.

Before you can embody your *divine truths*, you must discover what they are. I love this quote by Gandhi that says just that:

> ***"In the attitude of silence the Soul finds the path in a clearer light, and what is elusive and deceptive resolves itself into crystal clearness. Our life is a long and arduous quest after Truth."***
> **~Mahatma Gandhi**

Once you identify what your *divine truths* are, remove and heal the blocks that are in the way so you can fully embody them into the you that you're meant to be in this life. Let's begin your quest for your **divine truths**.

Discovering Your Divine Truths

Divine truths emerge from the inner sanctums of your Soul. What deeper truths is your Soul trying to communicate with you? Why are you here in this body, at this time, in this life? What is that God-seed that makes up your *divine truths*? In Sanskrit, the word *satya* (saat-ya) means truth. One of the translations noted in Wikipedia is "that which pervades the Universe in all its constancy." This translation really hits

> *Your divine truths are a constant source of your God-seeds that make up your Soul's DNA.*

home for me because your *divine truths* are just that. They are a constant source of your God-seeds that make up your Soul's DNA. They are the foundation of the real you, containing the "what" of your Soul.

So what are your *divine truths*? I'm sure you have some awareness of what they are but just need a little nudge to go within to gain more clarity. If you already know what they are, use this as an opportunity to go deeper with them. I've learned throughout my own journey that we are all works in progress, learning from and teaching those around us at the same time. Be open to what your Soul wants you to know about your *divine truths* and where you need to take them. In the book *Life Loves You*, Louise Hay said that "Your 'yes' will always find you." She's talking about those things you're meant to do in life. You know inside when it's time to say yes, because that sacred yes is not one you can ignore. Similarly, I believe that your *divine truths* always find you.

> *Your divine truths always find you. Resistance is futile.*

Resistance is futile. The more you resist, the more they persist to be known, loved, and expressed. As Buddha said below, the truth cannot be hidden for too long. Just as happened to me, the Divine will put you in situations that are meant to help you discover what your *divine truths* are. You just need to pay attention and be open to connecting with them.

"Three things cannot be long hidden: the sun, the moon, and the truth."

~**Buddha**

This is where messenger number two comes in. A couple of months before I started writing this chapter, I saw an advertisement for a voice workshop. I had been a fan of this voice coach for years and he finally had decided to put on a workshop in Canada. As soon as I saw the email I knew I was supposed to be there. In meditation I was told that there was something about my voice that I would discover by attending this event. Throughout the years I've learned the importance of trusting these messages without question even if in that moment it doesn't quite make sense. We'll talk more about accessing your *divine wisdom* in chapter 8. For now, just start paying attention to your own intuition and the signs that surround you. Sometimes all it takes is being present in the moment and open to receiving, and the rest takes care of itself.

At one point I checked in again about this workshop because I was feeling that perhaps it wouldn't be a convenient time for me to travel, but once again the Divine insisted I needed to be there, and so I listened.

The day of the workshop I arrived early, excited to know and see why the Divine was so insistent I be there. It was amazing. This was the first time I had been in a room full of singers. Everyone in this room was interested in using their voice for speaking, singing, or work associated with their businesses. By this point in my life I had already released a meditation CD in which I sang one of my songs, but I hadn't quite owned that part of me. It's like God was telling me, "Okay, My Daughter, I gave you this gift for a reason. It's time to own it."

As I met people at this workshop, they asked me how I began singing. It was assumed that if you were in that room, you were a singer, even if you sang just for enjoyment. It was exceptionally beautiful to see people from all over and ranging in age from sixteen to eighty-plus years old. One woman was relaunching her singing career at the age of eighty-three after a forty-year hiatus. That is inspirational. There is no age limit for doing what you are meant to do. For the first time I found myself owning my singing gift and saying, "I'm a healer and I sing to heal."

I soon discovered that when the Divine gives you a gift it's important to use it. Anything you suppress or reject turns into a constrictive energy within you, and not only can it lead to ailments in your body, but most likely it will affect your emotions. Why? When you resist doing those things that make your heart sing, you hold yourself back from experiencing the most joyful and soulful life you deserve to have. You were born to be you, and when you resist being the real you—the highest version of you that you were born to be—your mind, body, and spirit reflect this. It's your body's way of letting you know that something is not right inside you. I had been feeling that way myself. As much healing as I had already done through using my voice, there was still something there that I was masking. I didn't know what, but I knew being at this workshop would help give me some answers.

The workshop had been going on for hours, yet I hadn't received any clarity about why I was supposed to attend this particular event. I wondered when that defining moment would come and I prayed for clarity. An hour before the workshop was to end, my prayer was answered. The voice coach called one of his students to the stage to sing a song she had written. After she walked up to the platform, she shared with us that she had only been singing for three or four years. All her life she had been told she couldn't sing, so she never tried. But one day she felt this strong stirring within her Soul that something needed to be expressed through her voice, and she wrote a song called "I Am Free." She also shared with us that she had discovered that her name meant "freedom from sorrow." Boy, I can't tell you how significant that was for me. I didn't know it yet, but that was exactly what this woman was going to help me do. As she sang, I felt this strong stirring within my Soul. It was as if she had written the song for me. It was about being free from the shackles that hold you back from being you, and living on purpose. I began to sob. Her voice unleashed something within me: a pain and a sorrow I had been holding in my heart. I listened to every word intently and just allowed her healing voice to penetrate my Soul.

At the break I went up to her to thank her and shared with her how deeply her song had impacted me. She looked at me intently and said, "Wow, you are a very ancient Soul." I said, "Yes, I am a healer." She then said, "Okay, that explains what I'm feeling." There was this powerful exchange of energy between us. No words were necessary. It was as if we had made a divine appointment long ago to meet again in that place at that exact time. Something very powerful and healing had just happened, not all of which I understood yet. So I waited and simply allowed my body to process what had just occurred.

The next morning I started my trip home. No matter where I am I always make a point to continue with my morning rituals. I got up early to meditate, and that's when the insights became crystal clear. Everything I had experienced at the workshop was related to another of my *divine truths* that I am an ancient Soul. This was not new to me. I had experienced the memories in meditation and had also been told by others the same thing, but until that point I had not yet owned this *divine truth*. This ancient Soul who is me had something to say to the world. I had something to sing to the world, something to teach the world. And yes, I had been suppressing and rejecting the voice of this ancient Soul because I was holding sorrow in my higher heart for times when I had been hurt for sharing my gifts and when I had witnessed humanity hurting one another. I discovered this sorrow had a counterpart called fear that I was holding in various parts of my body (in particular in my throat and my left knee).

Because of what I had witnessed done to me and others, I was afraid of allowing this ancient voice to come through me in song, but the woman at the workshop had opened the door for my healing. It was a Soul-to-Soul transmission from one healer to another. As I boarded the plane to return home, the Divine said, "Sing away your sorrow." When I got home I did just that. I sang and sang and allowed the sorrow to leave me. It was a profound experience. When you trust and open to the guidance of the Divine, to the guidance of your Soul, you open the door for healing to occur. These are the moments in your journey that define the next steps of your evolution and transformation.

Right now you may be asking yourself what your next step in evolution and transformation is… but let's not go there just yet. Instead, ask yourself the question "Who am I, really?" Are you the face you see every morning in the bathroom mirror? Are you the heartbeats in your chest or the thoughts in your head? You are none of these. You are an all-loving, all-being, all-knowing Soul whose core essence is infinite love. In the *Svetasvatara Upanishad (Part 3)* of the Hindu scriptures it says, "Concealed in

Your Soul is the keeper of your divine truths.

the heart of all beings lies the Atman, the Spirit, the Self; smaller than the smallest atom, greater than the greatest spaces." In Sanskrit, *atma* means essence, the breath of your Soul. Your Soul, or *alma* as we say in Spanish, is the keeper of your *divine truths*, and it is here that we will go to help you discover what yours are. If you've ever asked yourself questions like those earlier in this paragraph, you know that this type of contemplation requires you to go into the stillness, into your inner sanctuary. Only there can you find the answers. We will be going there momentarily.

It's time for you to discover your *divine truths*. You may already know what some of them are, and if you do, wonderful. Either way, it's time to add another piece to the canvas of your Soul. Just set the intention to be open and receive whatever your Soul wants to communicate to you in this moment. You can record the meditation so you can close your eyes while you listen to it.

Sit comfortably where you won't be disturbed—with your feet flat on the floor and your hands on your knees with palms facing up. If you're an experienced meditator, use whatever position is most comfortable to you. When you're ready, please move to the meditation.

Guided Meditation: Discovering Your Divine Truths

We start with an invocation: "I call in the angels, my guides, and the divine beings who are meant to accompany me on this journey. May this space be filled with the deepest vibrations of unconditional love, where I feel embraced by the arms of the Divine and the highest power of creation. I'm safe to be me in this sacred space. I allow and surrender to all that I AM. May the Divine provide the gateway for me to connect effortlessly with the transmission of my Soul. Here I become the observer, and witness my divine truths emerge to the surface of my consciousness. And so it is."

Let us continue in silence. Close your eyes and take a deep breath into your heart center. Exhale slowly through your mouth, witnessing the essence of your breath. Now take another deep breath and do the same. With each breath you feel calmer and more relaxed. Every part of your body feels lighter and lighter. Take one last deep breath and bring your focus to your heart center.

As the curator of your Soul, imagine the canvas of your Soul sitting right in your heart center. There is an area of this canvas that holds your divine truths. Imagine a door in front of you. Step forward, grab hold of the doorknob, turn it, and walk through the doorway. This is the inner sanctuary of your Soul. You feel so at peace and serene here. Allow the beautiful, angelic rays of light to enter your heart space. You are connecting with the pureness of the infinite love that is you. Breathe this beautiful energy into your heart center.

Call your Soul forward. You feel the expansive energy of your Soul step forward. Become the witness of this energy. See your Higher-Self. This part of you immediately recognizes the vibration and frequency of your Soul. In this sacred sanctuary there is no noise, only love and pure light. You exist here as virgin light. Your Soul sends you words, messages, colors, images, symbols. Your divine artist emerges with paintbrush in hand. You are about to paint your divine truths on the canvas floor. Slowly you begin to paint. One after another, each message, divinely transmitted by your Soul, takes form on the canvas floor of your sacred sanctuary.

Stay here for several minutes. Just allow your Soul to guide your hand as you continue to write your divine truths on the canvas floor. Effortlessly, one after another they emerge. You feel a sense of freedom as this part of you rises to the surface of your consciousness.

Each divine truth brings respite and solace to your Soul, signaling the evolution of your spiritual journey. Your heart surrounds the divine truths you have just painted on the canvas of your Soul with a beautiful pink light. Each ray of light brings the words higher and higher into your consciousness, imprinting them in your heart center so you can retrieve them at any moment.

When you feel complete, thank your Soul and the Divine for this sacred experience and walk back through the doorway of your inner sanctuary. Slowly come back into your body. When you're ready, slowly come back to the present and open your eyes.

Now you're ready to write your *divine truths*. Let's continue in your quiet place with some journaling. Take a moment to reflect back on your sacred sanctuary. Reconnect with those messages you painted on the canvas floor of your Soul. The messages can be in the form of full sentences, symbols, words, or even colors. Write down whatever came through for you. Again, write from your Heart and Soul. Do not judge what comes through. Trust that what you're writing is a direct transmission from your Soul. With time, all will become much clearer. What's important right now is to capture the seeds of whatever came through. The rest will follow.

To help you with your list, here are some examples of my own *divine truths*. Just so you know, these *divine truths* were not completely clear to me from the get-go. As you know, I had messengers and other divine experiences throughout my journey that helped me gain a deeper understanding and clarity around these. The same holds true for you. I phrased my *divine truths* below as my Soul communicated them to me.

"You are an ancient Soul. This expansive expression of you speaks through your voice, art, and music. This part of you holds a deep container of ancient wisdom across many lifetimes, dimensions, and galaxies. Communicate and teach this wisdom to your flock."

"You are a healer and seer. You see and heal through time and space. Allow the divine breath, divine voice, and *divine artist* within you to activate a remembrance of wholeness within those you serve."

"You act as a bridge between the human-self and the Soul. You can see within the inner sanctums of the Soul. You can hear its voice and understand its language. Become the divine interpreter of the Soul for those you serve."

Healing What Stands in the Way of Accepting Your Divine Truths

Now that you've discovered some or all of your *divine truths*, let's go underneath the layers and see what might be holding you back from truly embodying them. In the deepest layers of your being you're constantly evolving, whether you recognize it consciously or not. When you ignore the signs that tell you that you have to be actively involved in this evolution, your life can come crashing down. It is painful. Sometimes pain is the only thing that awakens you to your truth; it's the natural course of evolution. You can stop denying what deep down you've always known to be true.

In your darkest moments your Soul calls out to you for resolution—for unmasking a truth—one of your *divine truths*. Beneath the pain is a *divine truth* wanting to be embraced, expressed. You know those moments; we've all experienced them. You lose your job unexpectedly, a relationship comes crashing down, or your body becomes ill. All of these are sure signs that something inside is seeking refuge. You are a work in progress. We all are. This journey of self-discovery takes you deep within your Soul so you can remember your true identity—formless, expansive, all-knowing, all-being, and all-loving.

Beneath the pain is a divine truth wanting to be embraced, expressed.

When you hold back from being the real you and expressing your *divine truths*, you shackle yourself to living a mediocre life that doesn't represent the joyful, loving, and passionate life you

> *It's through the expression of your divine truths that you feel liberated to live the life you desire and deserve.*

truly deserve. Why settle for mediocre when you can have the stellar, exquisite, and unparalleled life God wants you to have? You may have heard the Latin phrase *Veritas liberabit vos*, which means "The truth will set you free." In Spanish we say *La verdad te hará libre*. And in John 8:32 Jesus said, "Then you will know the truth, and the truth will set you free." Well, it's true. It's only through the expression of your *divine truths* that your Soul, your being, and the real you feel liberated to live the life you desire and deserve. You are worthy of living the life you desire. It's your birthright as a divine being of light and love.

Fear is the culprit behind your inability to fully own your *divine truths*. I shared in the previous section how I had been afraid to own one of my *divine truths*. I knew I was holding back from being the real me because my body and external circumstances were showing me that something was not quite right. Your body is a divine temple of truth. When you live in your truth fully, your body reflects that. You feel healthy, vibrant, energetic, and passionate about life. When you're not fully living in your *divine truths*, your body reflects that as well.

In the Bible (New International Version), in the Psalm of David, 32:3, David, who had been struggling with the guilt of his unconfessed actions, declared, "When I kept silent, my bones wasted away through my groaning all day long." David's guilt was causing his bones to wither away. More reason for you to be you, no matter what. You are energy, so when you hold back who you really are, your energy is restricted within your body; it becomes restrictive energy. And each part of your body represents a particular type of fear or restriction. For example, the knee represents the inability to be flexible enough to accept life's inevitable changes. In her book *Heal Your Body*, Louise Hay talks about how our thoughts can afflict our bodies with physical illness.

In the previous section I mentioned some of the fears I held about my *divine truths*. It only took a moment to be reminded that all I had to do was surrender my fears to God, meet Him in our inner sanctuary, and find respite in His love. These are the words that God gave me as I worked through those fears:

Fear me not, My Child.

As you ponder your fear, you go deeper into fear.

Risk that not.

Instead come to me, come to me now and give me your worry.

Give me your package of fear.

I will absolve you from those things beyond your reach that only I have the power to manage and see.

There are things you are not meant to see or hear because they would only
cause you overwhelm in the haves and have nots.

Clear your mind of those thoughts now. Take a deep breath, and come into
our inner sanctuary.

There I will nurture your spirit and fill your cup.

For it is only my cup that can allow you to feel free and live in complete
trust that all that you need will be given unto you.

Can't you see and feel how much I love you?

How all I want is to see you happy and living in your greatest passions?

Allow your gifts to shine.

It's time to stop living small.

It's time to stop being afraid to show your true power, the light that shineth
as big as the sun.

It's time to believe in you, in all that you are because I created you.

And when I created you, I gave you all you need to live that big life, to
serve me and all those who are meant to receive your *divine light.*

Embrace your *divine truths* today.

Shine your love today.

Shine the sparkle in your eyes to your brethren.

Come forward and commit to living your *divine truths* today.

Remember, I am always present within our inner sanctuary.

This is the place within you where you connect with me;
where you express the me that is in you.

Stop living small. Live big today, because all my children are
meant to live big.

It is what I designed you to be and what you deserve as my
beloved children.

Stand free in your *divine truths* today.

You, too, may have some fears about your *divine truths.* Let's investigate what
those are now. Take out the list you completed in the last section and put it aside for a
moment. First let's get grounded and relaxed:

Sit in a quiet place where you won't be interrupted. Close your eyes and take a
deep breath, inhaling through your nose for about four seconds, and slowly exhaling through your mouth for about eight seconds. Do this two more times. Now
imagine that you have a cord attached from the bottom of your spine directly to
the center of the Earth. You are connecting with the beautiful essence of Mother
Earth, Gaia, and Pachamama. Feel embraced by this divine goddess. Allow the

Earth's energy to come up through your grounding cord and up into your body. Take another deep breath.

When you feel relaxed, slowly open your eyes and take your *divine truths* list in hand. Place the list against your heart and ask your Soul to help you identify where you might be holding fears about your truths.

Start reading each *divine truth* out loud. If you didn't write them down in words, that's okay. Just start feeling into the first item on your list (be it words, symbols, colors, etc.) As you feel into this first item, notice if there's anything going on in your body. You can close your eyes if that helps you tune in better. Ask yourself the following questions as you tune in to each item on your list:

"What is my body telling me about this *divine truth*?"

"Is there a particular sensation I am feeling? Where is it showing up in my body?"

"Is there a part of me that is afraid of owning this *divine truth*? If so, why?"

After each item, list any answers to the questions above that will help you understand where you may be holding fear related to each of them. Spend a good ten to fifteen minutes feeling into each one and answering the questions above. When you feel complete, put your list aside.

You can record the following meditation so you can close your eyes while you listen to it. Sit comfortably where you won't be disturbed—with your feet flat on the floor and your hands on your knees with palms facing up. If you're an experienced meditator, use whatever position is most comfortable to you. When you're ready, please move to the meditation.

Guided Meditation: Releasing Your Fears about Your Divine Truths

Take several deep breaths into your heart center. Imagine that you're standing in a beautiful garden. You can smell the flowers so deeply, as if you held them in your hands. Breathe the fragrance into your heart. There are beautiful hues of pink and green light radiating around your body, and they enter your crown and flow gently within you to all those parts of you that need God's nourishment.

Feel the serenity and love gently pulsing in your body. Take a moment to breathe all this in and remember its tender grasp of encouragement.

> *Think about your divine truths and the fears you have about them. In front of you, God has placed a beautiful wooden box. Open the box and place all your fears in the box.*
>
> *Close the lid and speak your truth to God, the Divine, the Creator, your higher power. Allow your Soul to guide you. Commit to letting your fears go forever.*
>
> *Say this out loud: "I surrender my fears as I give this box to you, My Dearest God. I commit to not looking in this box again. Instead I will remember this moment with You, the love that I feel, and the serenity that fills my cup in this moment. I promise to return here whenever I feel the urge to look inside the box. Thank You for this grace."*
>
> *As you surrender this box to the Divine, you see God's hands extending from the heavens and taking your box away. Now take a deep breath and sit in silence for a moment.*
>
> *When you're ready, come back to the present and journal about your experience.*

Make it a practice to journal about these moments, for they serve as your cellular memory to help you enter this space again in an instant.

Embodying Your Divine Truths

As you embody the *divine truths* that are held within the womb of your Soul, a door is unlocked that leads from your inner sanctuary to your outer world. This is the secret, hidden door within your higher heart that helps you manifest your deepest desires into your outer world. In the book *The Voice of the Master*, Eva Bell Werber said, "When you learn to turn within to find that which you wish expressed in your outer world, you have learned a great secret." This inner sanctuary holds your Soul note, your unique sound, the signature of your real being. When the door to this sanctuary unlocks, you become the observer of your outer world and allow your inner world and your Soul to guide the way. Every breath, action, and word is anchored in the divine flow of your divine essence.

I said before that every seed of creation begins with an intention. If you want to embody something, begin by setting the

> *As you embody the divine truths that are held within the womb of your Soul, a door is unlocked that leads from your inner sanctuary to your outer world.*

intention. Deeper embodiment occurs when you're able to fully commit to it at a Soul level and then surrender it completely to the Divine. If you've ever studied the Law of Attraction in the book *The Secret*, you know that in order to attract something you desire you must plant the seed, but then detach from it so the Universe can take care of the rest. When you get out of your own way you can see the pure magic manifest in your life.

Embodying your *divine truths* requires a real commitment from you to live this way every day through your thoughts, words, and actions. This is the foundation of living a Soul-driven life. As you commit to your *divine truths* within your Heart and Soul, they unfold in all areas of your life, bringing you into closer alignment with the real you—your divine essence. In the *Chandogya Upanishad VI.1.5* it says:

> As by knowing one piece of gold, dear one,
> We come to know all things made out of gold—
> That they differ only in name and form,
> While the stuff of which all are made is gold…
> So through that spiritual wisdom, dear one,
> We come to know that all of life is one.

It is through the embodiment of your divine truths that you realize a Soul-driven life and a oneness with all that is.

It is through the embodiment of your *divine truths* that you realize a Soul-driven life and a oneness with all that is. Through this collective oneness you contribute to the creation of your own Heaven on Earth. To help you embody your *divine truths*, we're going to use the technique I introduced in chapter 3 called *imprinting*. With this technique you can *imprint the vibration* of an intention into your energy field so it can be manifested. All intentions and seeds of creation begin at a spiritual level, in the consciousness of the *divine mind* (discussed later in chapter 9) before they are manifested into physical existence in your outer world. As within, so without. What is imagined in your inner world (your thoughts) becomes reality in your outer world. This is made possible through the presence of your *divine essence*, that part of you that carries the imprint of God—a higher power. In his book *Wishes Fulfilled*, Dr. Wayne Dyer refers to this presence as your "I AM" presence.

We're going to use this divine presence within you to help you embody your *divine truths*. You can record the following meditation so you can close your eyes while you listen to it. Sit comfortably where you won't be disturbed—with your feet flat on the floor and your hands on your knees with palms facing up. If you're an experienced meditator, use whatever position is most comfortable to you. When you're ready, please move to the meditation.

Guided Meditation: Embodying Your Divine Truths

Close your eyes and take a deep breath, inhaling deeply through your nose and exhaling slowly through your mouth. Again, and then one last time. Let's plant the intentions around your divine truths so you can embody them at a Soul level.

See yourself drinking from the fountain of the cosmos. Imagine you're extending your spinal cord up over your head, reaching up and drinking in the light through the top of your head—your crown.

You feel lightness and tingling as the divine mind downloads into you, bringing you clarity about who you are—connecting you more deeply with your God-self and divine truths. See your Higher-Self coming closer into your body, embodying more of you. {Pause in silence for one minute.}

Place your attention on your divine truths and see yourself planting each one in your heart center... each one a part of your divine creation taking root in your heart center. See the swirls of pink and green light nourishing your divine truths. {Pause briefly.}

Imagine how it would feel if you were already living those divine truths. How would that make you feel? Experience those feelings as if they were happening right now in this moment, and imprint those feelings into your heart center. See your divine truths as seeds beginning to grow roots. Connect those roots now to your life-force energy in your dan tien, or power center (right below your navel). {Pause in silence for one minute.}

Feel the heat of the life-force energy in your dan tien growing and growing, red hot, orange and red in color; and as it grows in intensity, see the seeds of your divine truths growing and planting their roots firmly within your heart center. {Pause briefly.}

Now connect the seeds of your divine truths to your higher heart (right below your collar bone and above your heart center). This is the location of your Soul note, the unique sound of your Soul. See the sounds and vibrations of your Soul note immersing your newly planted divine truths in commitment, clarity, and divine love. Continue to send love to your seeds of divine truth... love... love... love. {Pause briefly.}

*And now connect with the seat of your Soul, extending your spinal cord about three feet above your head. Allow the golden and silver light radiating from this point to enter the top of your head. Bring this light into your heart center to nourish the seeds you have planted. Again, imprint the feelings of having already experienced embodying and living from your divine truths. {**Pause briefly.**}*

Your seeds have now received their nourishment for growth and embodiment. It's time to release your divine truths to the Universe. See yourself giving them over to the Divine so that you can embody them in divine timing.

*Believe, trust, and surrender. Detach from your seeds now, but keep them nourished daily. You are creating your future through this present moment. Intend for the future, but attend to the present. See yourself embodying your divine truths in the present moment. {**Pause briefly.**}*

Repeat in silence: Sankalpa, Sankalpa, Sankalpa—my dreams become my desires.

When you feel complete, slowly come back to the present and open your eyes.

If you feel you need to do some deeper healing regarding the acceptance of your *divine truths* and the removal of blocks or fears that are still holding you back, do the meditation that follows. You can record it so you can close your eyes while you listen to it. For the audio version, visit **www.UnmaskingYourSoul.com/Meditations.**

Sit comfortably in your sacred space. Begin by reciting out loud this invocation to create your sacred space:

Through the darkness, I shine the light. Today I am here to unmask that which till now has remained hidden. No more shall it remain hidden. I am here to unmask my *divine truths* and any fears that hold me back from embracing those *divine truths*. And so I ask the Divine, my ancestors, guides, and all that is to join me today in this sacred space; to create a safe womb for me to heal. Help me connect with my Higher-Self. May I clearly hear the voice of my Soul and accept it with pure love. May I only experience what is in my highest good, allowing me to evolve to a higher state of awareness, consciousness, and wholeness. And so it is.

When you're ready, please move to the meditation.

Guided Meditation: Unmasking and Healing Your Divine Truths

Start by taking three deep breaths, breathing in deeply through your nose and out slowly through your mouth.

Imagine you're sitting on a very old stone bench in the most beautiful garden you've ever seen. You breathe the clean, fresh air very deeply into your lungs. You feel the freshness of the brisk air against your face and your body. The sun is radiating brightly and you soak in some rays for a moment. {Pause briefly.}

As you look around, you see flowers of all kinds. It almost seems impossible to be surrounded by so many flowers, as many are rare, exotic breeds, but you know Spirit is blessing with you such beauty today. There are beautiful roses of all colors: red... white... purple... pink... and yellow. You lean over to smell their beautiful fragrance. {Pause briefly.}

You see a beautiful fountain in front of you. The water flows up and down over a sacred statue of a dolphin family in the center. You walk over to view its beauty up close. As you arrive at the fountain, you admire the beautiful yellow citrina orchids surrounding the fountain. You lean over to smell their lemony fragrance. You can even taste the lemon tartness on your tongue. {Pause briefly.}

Now focus on the sound of the water. You hear the droplets of water whirling together... drips and splashes... bringing calmness and peace within you. As the water flows, you feel it cleansing away all your stress, all your anxiety, and all your fears. All that remains is the loving and joyful connection to the divinity within you. You can feel your crown tingling as you surrender to the present moment. You're just soaking in this feeling of peace that has now extended to every part of your mind... your body... and your spirit. Notice how this makes you feel. {Pause in silence for one minute.}

As you look forward, you see a young Amazonian Indian girl standing by the fountain. She speaks to you telepathically and tells you she will be your guide today. She seems young in years, yet you know immediately she's a very old Soul. You can feel the innocence and purity of her heart and her powerful light. The young girl gives you a coin the size of a quarter. She tells you to throw the coin in the fountain and make a wish. Think of what you want most in your life in this moment, and make your wish. {Pause briefly.}

Your young guide then asks you to follow her. She leads you into her homeland—the Amazon jungle. As you enter the rainforest, you're mesmerized by all the sounds that surround you.

The girl tells you that you're now ready for the most important part of your journey. She tells you that she will be taking you through a secret portal that leads to a very special place, a sacred sanctuary that has been protected by her people for thousands of years.

The girl taps her walking stick on the ground three times and a door appears in front of you. You walk through the doorway with your young guide and arrive at the sacred sanctuary. In front of you is a beautiful cascading waterfall that flows into a sacred pool of water. The girl tells you that you will find your answers in this sacred pool.

*As you look closer, you see Amazonian pink dolphins splashing and playing together in the sacred pool. You feel the joy and love these precious creatures share with one another. You can feel your heart smiling as you experience this sacred moment. Connect with the dolphins and relish in this feeling for a few moments. {**Pause briefly.**}*

Your young guide says the dolphins have been waiting for you because now is the time to remember who you truly are, to unmask your divine truths. It's time to reflect on your life, understand what's been holding you back, and release any fears you're holding. She points to a small stone staircase that leads into the sacred pool and asks you to get in.

*As you dip your feet in the water, you immediately feel the sacredness of this experience. One of the pink dolphins swims up to you and tells you telepathically to hold onto its fin. You do and you find yourself swimming with the dolphins. You feel safe and protected. You smile and feel so much joy and love at this moment. You feel the oneness with the Divine and your new dolphin Soul family. You tingle all over. Stay in this oneness for a moment. {**Pause briefly.**}*

Now it's time for some contemplation with your dolphin friends; a moment of divine truth; an unmasking of your Soul. Your dolphin friend tells you telepathically to look into its eye. Here you will find the answers to your questions: What are your divine truths? Where are you still wearing a mask? Is it in your relationships with your family, in your career, in your finances, in your spiritual life? Where are you holding back, afraid… in darkness… feeling stuck with parts of you that you dislike? As you reflect on your life and your journey, listen with your heart. Your Soul speaks. Be open and receive as the eye of your dolphin friend guides you deeper into your inner sanctuary. Listen and wait for all to be revealed. **{Pause for several minutes.}**

Now that your Soul has spoken to you, it's time to heal any fears that you felt come to the surface. As you wade in the water, three pink dolphins swim to you to help you release your fears.

One of the dolphins gently approaches you. You extend your hands out and gently caress its head. You look into its eyes as it places its nose on your heart. You feel your pain, sorrow, and grief being released into the water. Focus on love and wholeness in this moment. **{Pause.}**

Dolphin number two now swims up to you. You gently caress its fin and look into its eyes. Allow yourself to get lost in the Soul of this amazing creature. "Love, beauty, magnificence—that is what you are," says your dolphin friend telepathically. The dolphin places its nose on your power center over your abdomen. It's filling your power center with beautiful golden-yellow light. You can feel the warmth of this glowing sun burning through your fears and melting away your doubts about taking action. Divine love and divine power flow through all of you. **{Pause.}**

The third and last dolphin approaches you. You receive it with so much love and gratitude. You extend your hand out and caress its head. You look into the dolphin's eyes and go deeper once again. You feel a oneness with this animal, as if you share one mind, one body, and one Soul. Allow these feelings of oneness to nourish your Soul. The dolphin places its nose on your throat, lifting away any unspoken words, any unexpressed creative seeds, any fears of embodying your divine truths. **{Pause.}**

All the dolphins come forward and form a circle around you. They swim around you, and as they do, beautiful swirls of light enter your body and surround you completely. You release and release and release all that no longer serves you. Only love and oneness embodies you now. **{Pause in silence for one minute.}**

As the healing is completed, your young guide signals for you to step out of the sacred pool. You swim to the small stone staircase and slowly climb up to land.

Your young guide asks you to follow her. She returns you back through the portal to the garden where you began your journey today. You thank your young guide for her love and wisdom, and return to your bench. As you sit on the bench, take one last moment to integrate all your experiences from this journey and thank Spirit and your new dolphin Soul family for the divine guidance you received. **{Pause briefly.}**

When you're ready, slowly come back and open your eyes.

Now that you've completed the guided meditation, take some time to do some journaling. Spend about ten to fifteen minutes in a quiet place where you won't be disturbed answering the questions below. You can put on some soothing music or light a candle or incense to support you as you write. Just write from your Heart and Soul and the rest will follow.

Journaling Exercise

1. How did it feel swimming with the dolphins? Note any sensations in your body.

2. What did your Soul share with you about your *divine truths*? Were there any new revelations about your *divine truths*? If so, what were they?

3. What did your Soul share with you about any fears you may still be holding about your *divine truths* or other areas of your life?

4. Where are you still wearing a mask in your life?

5. How did you feel after the dolphins gave you a healing? Are there any other places where you need healing? If so, note those down.

6. Write down any steps or actions you feel will help you deepen your healing and fully embody your *divine truths*.

7. What is the one step, the one action you're willing to commit to today? Once you commit, be sure to follow through. Only through action can you deepen your spiritual muscle in accepting and living your *divine truths*.

After journaling, continue working on the **Canvas of Your Soul.** (You can download the PDF at **www.UnmaskingYourSoul.com/Blueprint.**) Pick phrases, words, or symbols and put them on section 4 of the **Truth** part of your roadmap. Make this canvas your own piece of artwork that represents the journey we're taking together in this book. You can color, paint, or even cut images from magazines that depict the messages and insights you received in this chapter on *accepting your divine truth*. You don't need to be a professional artist to do this. Just let your Soul express through you as it wants to. This will become the vision board of your Soul's unmasking, a precious gift to you from your *divine magistrate*. Congratulations! You've just completed one-third of your journey.

Five Rituals to Awaken Your Divine Truth Muscle

The rituals below are meant to help you awaken your *divine truth* muscle. You can repeat any of the rituals that follow and the exercises and guided meditations earlier in the chapter as many times as you like. With each repetition you go deeper in accessing your *divine magistrate.*

The more deeply you connect with your *divine magistrate,* the more you accept and embody your divine gifts. These are the parts of your Soul's DNA that are unique to you and ONLY YOU. Understand this *divine truth*: God gave you something that nobody else has, and I mean nobody. Remember, your *divine truths* are the "what." They represent the unique God-seed that you were created with—your Soul's genius. These are the inherent divine gifts you were born with. When you're able to accept and embody your *divine truths* fully, you see the canvas of your Soul manifest at a faster pace and with less effort. That is something to aspire to, for sure.

Before you begin, create your sacred space and take some deep breaths to relax your mind and body. Connect with your Soul as you enter your sacred space.

1. Use this ritual to release any fears you may still be feeling about your *divine truths.*

    a. Take a couple of deep breaths to help you relax. When you're ready, begin by revisiting your responses from the journaling exercise and the *divine truths* you wrote earlier in the chapter. Highlight or circle any fears, limiting beliefs, or pain that arose about your *divine truths.* Select one or more of these that you feel you're ready to release to the Universe and write them down on a separate piece of paper.

    b. Fold the paper four times. Hold the piece of paper against your heart. Silently see the paper embraced in your love and that of the Divine. Beautiful pink swirls of light surround the paper. See each word being transmuted by the vibration of love in your higher heart. Stay here for a moment and continue to see the beautiful pink light melting away the words.

c. When this feels complete, say out loud, "I release these fears, limiting beliefs, and pain that were part of the old me. I fill this space now with eternal love and embody the new me. I am consciousness. I am expansive. I am light. I am love. Through the expression of my *divine truths* I release the old me and embody the real me. I am free."

d. Thank the Divine for this experience. To complete the ritual, burn your piece of paper outside in a metal bowl, preferably under the light of the moon (a new moon or full moon is preferable), and then offer the ashes of the paper to Divine Mother Earth. As the ashes are reintegrated into Mother Earth and transmuted to Earth energy, so is the essence of that which you released. You begin anew.

2. If you feel you're holding some sorrow or grief in your higher heart, the following guided ritual is for you. Take a couple of deep breaths, inhaling slowly through your nose and exhaling slowly through your mouth. Look back at your journaling and the messages or insights you captured on the **Canvas of Your Soul**. Focus on insights about any pain or sorrow you may still be carrying in your higher heart.

> *Close your eyes and drop into your higher heart. Ask the Divine to assist you in bringing this sorrow or pain (both conscious and subconscious) to the surface so it can be transmuted and healed. Today you will be assisted by Mother Mary and Kuan Yin (the Goddess of Compassion).*
>
> *In front of you is a beautiful garden. You can feel the presence of the Divine as you walk towards the garden. You can see beautiful white orchids in front of you. You walk over towards them. As you do, Mother Mary appears before you. She takes one of the white orchards and places it in your hands. She asks you to place the orchid on your higher heart. As you do, the pure, virgin light of Mother Mary enters your higher heart and surrounds your pain and sorrow. Mother Mary approaches you and places her arms around you. As she does, you feel the release of sorrow and pain as they leave your body. Peace and serenity flow through every part of your being. Stay here for a moment.*
>
> *Now Mother Mary asks you to walk with her to another part of the garden. You stroll towards what looks like a beautiful Buddha statue. It's not a statue, it's Kuan Yin. She gets up from the ground and greets you. She is here to plant the seeds of compassion and forgiveness in your higher heart. To fully*

release your sorrow you must forgive those who inflicted the pain, including yourself. She asks you to extend your hands out and gives you a beautiful pink lotus flower. She asks you to place the lotus flower over your higher heart, and as you do, the lotus flower integrates into your body. You become one with this lotus flower. You feel immersed in feelings of love, compassion, and forgiveness. Tears roll down your face as you release what no longer serves you. Stay here for a moment.

When you feel complete, thank Mother Mary, Kuan Yin, and the Divine for their grace and healing today. When you're ready, slowly open your eyes.

3. It's time to meet your *divine magistrate*, the upholder of your *divine truths*, up close. Use this ritual to develop a deeper relationship with this part of your Soul and gain a deeper understanding of your *divine truths*.

    Take a couple of deep breaths, inhaling slowly through your nose and exhaling slowly through your mouth. Drop into your higher heart (that place between the bottom of your neck and your heart). An ornate, golden-colored door appears in front of you. You walk forward and open the door and walk through. As you enter the inner sanctuary of your higher heart, you notice the crystalline nature of the walls that surround you emanating beautiful pink light. You feel so loved and embraced by God's love.

    In the center of the room is a small marble table. Your divine magistrate is sitting there. You approach the table and sit down facing them. Your divine magistrate places a small wooden box in front of you and asks you to open it. Inside the box is a scroll that lists your divine truths. You take the scroll out of the box and hold it against your higher heart. Your divine truths leave the scroll and enter your body through your higher heart. You can feel the wisdom and energy of your divine truths moving throughout every part of your essence.

    Now ask if your divine magistrate has any messages for you. What do you need to know in this moment about your divine truths? When you feel complete, thank your divine magistrate for their assistance today. Walk back through the doorway you used to enter this chamber in your higher heart. When you're ready, slowly open your eyes and come back to the present. Remember to journal about any significant messages or experiences.

4. Use this ritual to deepen the acceptance and embodiment of your *divine truths*.

    a. Grab some paper and something to write with, and pick a sacred spot for doing this ritual. If possible, pick a place outside in nature. It could be in a park, your backyard—anywhere in nature would be ideal. If it's too cold outside, pick your favorite sacred space in your home. When you're there, sit down comfortably and take a couple of deep breaths.

b. Breath after breath, relax every part of you. As you do, imagine you're connected to every creation around you: the grass, trees, animals, water, people—anything and everything that surrounds you all becoming one. With each breath you see and feel connected with all that is. You feel the Divine holding you and all that is in a field of eternal love.

c. Open your eyes gently and write a letter to God, the Divine, the Creator— your higher power. Write from your Heart and Soul and ask for any assistance you need in fully accepting your *divine truths*. List any fears that hold you back from fully embodying your *divine truths*. Ask for clarity, love, and wisdom to fully become the real you—the expression of your divine gifts in the world. When you feel complete, fold the letter in half and place it against your higher heart. Immerse the letter in your love and offer it to the Divine with humility and eternal love.

d. Now place the letter in a sacred place in your home. You can place it on your altar or in a sacred box. If you have rose quartz crystals, place the crystals on top of the letter wherever you place it. The crystals will energize the letter even more with vibrations of love. If you don't have any rose quartz, that's fine too. If you have a favorite sacred text, like a Bible, you can place the letter in the pages of your favorite scripture. Just follow the guidance of your Heart and Soul and do what resonates with you.

e. Keep the letter for as long as you feel you need it (days, months, years). When this experience feels complete, you can discard the letter in whatever way makes your heart sing.

5. Meditate with my painting **Listen to the Voice of Your Angels**, shown at the end of the chapter. This painting holds special meaning for me, as it was inspired by my friend who has MS whom I wrote about earlier in the chapter. Each of my paintings was divinely channeled and holds messages and energetic impressions of the Soul that bring healing to the bearer. This particular painting holds vibrations of healing for those needing to remember their expression of *divine truth*.

a. Close your eyes and take a breath... inhaling slowly through your nose and exhaling slowly through your mouth... and with each breath you take relax your mind, body, and spirit. Continue focusing on your breath... and with each breath allow your thoughts to pass freely... thought after thought... breath after breath... relaxing more and more deeply. Continue taking several more deep breaths. {**Repeat for one or two minutes.**}

b. Briefly open your eyes and observe the painting. Allow yourself to be taken on a journey into the painting. Look at the images and symbols, and allow your gaze to go to one focal point in the painting. Soften your gaze as you focus on this point of interest. Breathe in its energy, seeing the symbols, images, and colors in your mind's eye. Continue breathing in the energy... breath after breath, allowing you to feel and absorb the healing energy from this focal point.

c. With your next breath, listen to the voice of your Soul. What is it communicating? What messages do you hear or feel within you as you breathe in the energy of the painting? Pay attention to where the energy is going in your body. This gives you an indication of where in your body you may need to release old energy, traumas, or wounds. Continue breathing and just go into the stillness while you connect deeper within. Allow the healing energies of the painting to penetrate your mind, body, and spirit. {**Do this for two to five minutes.**} If you feel guided, you may continue repeating this step, changing to a different focal point in the painting each time. Again, allow yourself to breathe the images, symbols, colors, and healing energies into your being.

d. Don't forget to journal about anything of significance that comes up during this experience.

Eileen Anümani Santos, *Listen to the Voice of Your Angels*, c. 2007

Listen to the Voice of Your Angels helps you reconnect with your *divine magistrate*, the one who seeks to guide you in upholding your *divine truths*. The angels are the defenders of God's truth and also work through your *divine magistrate* to help you uphold your *divine truths*. Connect with your God-seed, the *divine spark* of creation that you are. Go within your inner sanctuary where your eternal flow of *divine love* exists, and allow this love to give you the strength to embody your *divine truths;* to embody the real you.

Allow your *DIVINE TRUTHS* to shine fully through the real you!

STAGE TWO: LIGHT

Connecting with Your Soul's Light

As you experience this awakening and pierce the spiritual veil, you shift from a sense of separateness to one of connectedness. As you CONNECT with your authentic you—your *divine light*—you shed the hurts and ego-driven behaviors that no longer serve you.

Claiming Your Divine Light

by Eileen Anümani Santos

Me: I am afraid... something has shaken me to the core.
I feel it welling inside of me. My frame of reference is being challenged.
What should I believe now, My Dearest God?

God: Believe in our oneness; believe in your divinity, in the limitless opportunities before you. I am here to hold your hand and guide you on this journey. Give your fears to me... take a breath and join me once again in your inner sanctuary. There you will find me. Feel your presence in this chamber of love. Here only the highest of vibrations exist—breathe them into your heart. Know that my Heaven is your Heaven and that this Heaven exists within you. Let go of what you think you are. Let go of the form that you think you are. Let go of your old life—your old story. I am here to help you create the life you deserve. The bounty of love that already exists within you is boundless and limitless. Connect to this place now and breathe it in.

Me: I am afraid... my heart beats loudly as if wanting to burst out of my chest. I know I am on the verge of a big truth, a big revelation... even the thought of that scares me... why?

God: It is your ego creating a new story out of an old story. This new story your ego is trying to create is based on the past... and that is not acceptable. Shut the door on that past and open the new door that I offer you now. This new door vibrates only at the highest goodness for you. Can you see the door opening in front of you now? Surrender to my will and open this new door I offer you. As you walk through this new opening, see the old you dissipating behind you. That is not the real you; it is an illusion of the *you* you really are. I know this feels scary, leaving this old you behind, but this is not the real you. You are formless, you are whole, you are me, and I am you. Let go of any form, of any thoughts of or labels for your existence. Walk through this doorway into freedom of expression and see the light that you are. As this beacon of light, you are and will always be the highest expression of me, where love is the foundation of your being. With each beating of your heart, a new light radiates from your heart. Walk through the doorway now and become you... the I AM presence that you already are.

Me: For the sake of me, I walk through the doorway. I let go and see the me I really am. I am the light, Your beacon of light. My presence in the world is Your presence in the world. As I transition to living on purpose, fully, and serving Your will, I surrender fully to my true expression and release the old me. For the sake of me, I step fully into our oneness and allow Your love to carry me forward with grace and peace. I claim my *divine light*!

CHAPTER 5

Soul Chamber V: Claiming Your Divine Light

In this chapter you move to Stage Two of your transformational journey. In this stage, *LIGHT*, you will unmask four chambers of your Soul that connect you more deeply with your *Soul's Light*. In the Bible (New International Version), Matthew 5:14, it says, "You are the light of the world."

As this light that you are, God says to you, "I see you in my midst, Divine Child. I see the real you, the *divine light* that you are. As you surrender to my light, you become my lamp to the world, illuminating the pathway to me. As you become my beacon of light, others will follow you. The more lamps that illuminate in oneness, the brighter becomes the world around you. Together in our oneness, we create Heaven on Earth."

How would you like to create a world in which you and those you love are living Soul-driven lives in which you're showered in love, harmony, peace, passion, joy, and abundance? In this sacred haven of Heaven on Earth, all you need is always given to you. You're able to connect daily with the Divine and that part of you that is divine. You're passionate about what you do and energized every time you do it. You see it, feel it, and live it on a daily basis. If that's something you crave in your life, claiming your *divine light* is one of the keys to attaining that. You and everyone around you stands in this circle of light.

"God created a circle of love and light so vast, no one can stand outside of it."

~Carlos Santana

The left heart chamber is the location of **Soul Chamber V—Divine Light,** the fifth of the Soul virtues that will be unmasked as you continue on your journey of wholeness. The mask associated with this fifth chamber is the **Mask of Darkness**. I use the word *darkness* to mean those parts of you that hold lower vibrations, what some call your "shadow." We are all works in progress, so the more we heal those parts of us that carry wounds, the more *divine light* we become and hold for others. The famous poet Rumi said, "The wound is the place where the Light enters you." So working on your shadow and the wounds that Rumi speaks of is important if you desire to live a more Soul-driven life.

The emotional state associated with this mask originates from feelings of trauma, turmoil, and even violence—things that challenge you to the core. These fears can be from this life or previous lives in which you experienced trauma and it became encoded in your cellular make-up in the here and now. This chamber is

Divine Light Symbol

represented by the archetype of the **divine guru,** known as the dispeller of the darkness. And, by the way, there is one of those in each of us. Yes, you have your own *divine guru* within you; it is your *divine light* that is the place where this part of you exists. The sacred symbol of this chamber shows four diamonds surrounding a circle in the center (see symbol above). Together these symbols create the sacred space for your *divine light* to shine within your heart center and radiate outward towards humanity.

Marianne Williamson tells us, "Our deepest fear is not that we are inadequate… It is our light, not our darkness that most frightens us." Claiming your *divine light* will feel glorious and empowering, but it can also be scary and can trigger fear within you. This fear can be either conscious or subconscious (hidden away in the deepest parts of you). I know this to be true because one of my deepest fears has been around my own divinity and not feeling safe in the world *if* I allow my Divine-Self to shine through fully. I'll share more about my own experiences with this a little later.

> *As you awaken from your deep sleep, the divine light that you are radiates fervently through your being.*

As you awaken from your deep sleep, the *divine light* that you are radiates fervently through your being. Those around you might notice that something has changed. They might say that you look brighter, freer, happier, but not know exactly what has happened. We awaken in many different forms, some calm and others more dramatic. My dream of awakening was triggered by a difficult period in my life, a time when my Soul urged me to wake up, tend to my health and unhappiness, and step into a new life that awaited me. And I said, "Hell YES!" It was a scary time for me, but hearing God's voice in that dream is what gave me the strength to say yes and make changes in my life, changes that challenged me to the core and transformed me into the real me, leaving behind all that no longer served me.

What no longer served me also didn't serve those I was meant to serve. The more you grow, heal, and evolve, the more able you are to serve those you're meant to serve. Everything in life is divinely orchestrated. God has a divine plan. The canvas of your Soul represents this divine plan, unique to you and only you. This canvas is the road-map to where your Soul is taking you: the evolution of your life into greater clarity, joy, love, abundance, and manifestation of all you desire and deserve in your life. That is what claiming your *divine light* does for you. It allows you to shed the wounds and the ego-driven behaviors that no longer serve you so the real you can emerge and reap the benefits of the Soul-driven life that you seek.

Connecting with Your Divine Guru

In the sacred Indian text the *Upanishads, guru* is defined as one who dispels the darkness, one who is the guiding light.

> *"The syllable 'gu' means shadows*
> *The syllable 'ru' he who disperses them,*
> *Because of the power to disperse darkness*
> *The guru is thus named."*

~Advayataraka Upanishad 14-18, verse 5

You are your own *divine guru.* Within you sits that dispeller of the darkness. It is your *divine light* that is the torch of illumination for others to follow. Imagine a world in which you work with others of like mind to bring more light to the world. That is what you're doing in this moment as you seek a deeper connection to your own *divine light.* Together we can impact the world in a big way just by being who God created us to be. Simply by being the real you—*the divine you,* you contribute to a world lit from the inside out. As you heal that sacred inner temple that you are, you manifest the same in your outer world. We all benefit from your claiming your *divine light* and transforming into the real you.

> **Within you sits that dispeller of the darkness. It is your divine light that is the torch of illumination for others to follow.**

Everyone and everything has a guru within: a bird, a stone, your parents, your spouse, children, co-workers, teachers, and, most important, YOU. It is up to you to connect with your *divine guru* as you live your daily life. As you build your spiritual muscle and practice communing with your *divine guru*, you learn to rely less on the outside world in making your choices and decisions.

There's a difference between sharing a choice with a loved one because you want them to share in your joy, and sharing a choice because you feel you need their permission or validation to do something. They are not inside of you. They don't know what your Soul whispers to you so you can bring the truth of your existence to fruition. The vision, the truth, the being of your existence is within you and is unique to you, so how can someone else make choices for you? Even the best coaches in the world cannot make choices for you; they give you tools so you can find your own answers. In a similar vein, the *divine guru*, as defined in the traditional sense of the spiritual teacher, is the guiding light to your remembrance of that which already exists within you.

Most of us think of gurus as the most enlightened spiritual beings that live outside of us. And while there are many beautiful and enlightened beings who can serve as your guiding light, only by finding and connecting with your own *divine guru* are you able to maneuver through life's waves of events and challenges. Within you sits your own holy grail of mastery, where you can sit and commune daily and embody the knowledge that allows you to gently and briskly walk your journey. This inner guru is your *divine light*, your Higher-Self—that part of you that always has been, and continues to be, in oneness with the Source of all creation. You're not part of this, you *are* this. You're not separate from it, you *are one* with it. Our collective consciousness forms the "isness" of this *divine light* that defines who you really are.

From the "who" comes the "how" you are meant to serve. This is your purpose, your mission. And through "who" (your light) and "how" (your purpose), you birth hope, or *esperanza* as we say in Spanish, for the rest of humanity. Hope brings faith that a better today and tomorrow are achievable. Faith connects you to that deeper part of you that believes in the unseen and knows that infinite possibilities are available to you through the Source of creation that lives within you.

Some of us learn faith through our religious circles, but faith ultimately emerges

> **Faith emerges from the living essence that you are and your connection to your Higher-Self.**

from the living essence that you are and your connection to your Higher-Self, your God-vibration, your *divine light*. Your inner guru resides in your inner sanctuary of oneness with all that is. I experience it as a chamber within my heart that is illuminated in beautiful hues of pink, vibrant light, where there is no separation between me and Source. In this sanctuary I feel adored and unconditionally loved by the Divine, and everything else around me seems to drop in importance. Here I can be the real me without judgment. I feel embraced by the arms of the Divine, carried and held gently as a parent holds their infant child. I am coddled and cared for and encouraged to be me without fear.

Some call this your inner sanctuary or your sacred temple. Christel Hughes, a very gifted intuitive and teacher, calls it "the tiny space of the heart." The name doesn't matter; what matters is connecting to you and Source in this place, because this is where you can return at any moment to find respite and solace in your life, especially in those difficult moments. You can meet with your inner guru, your Higher-Self, the conduit of your Soul, in this sacred place and receive the wisdom and guidance that propels you forward in living a life of purpose and authenticity—a life in which you can take off your mask fully and live in joy despite what others think or say. What is said won't matter, because when you live from this place you live in a vibration of absolute love. And as you live in this way, the world around you morphs as well, bringing more love and acceptance from others into your life.

Is there a question burning inside of you right now? I know there is at least one, because our lives are fluid, and with every movement comes the need for a next step or an evaluation of why we feel stuck in certain areas of our lives. So let's take a pause right now. Close your eyes for a moment and ask yourself from a place of love, "What is it that my Soul wants me to know in this moment? What is that burning question that I can't continue to ignore?" Write the question down and then read my poem that follows. Read it with an open heart so you can connect with your *divine guru* and your *divine light* and hear what you need to know in this moment about your Soul's evolution.

In Seeking the Divine Guru Within, the Answer Reveals Itself

by Eileen Anümani Santos

Divine guru, the guiding light to me, I ask thee for guidance.
You sit within the walls of my sacred temple and you caress my Soul with gentle movements of awareness.

Sometimes it is difficult to find you amid the noise outside and within me, but today we remove that noise so I can clearly hear your voice and feel your presence within me; for I am you and you are me: we are one in our sacred temple.

I see you come forward in my heart and we join hands. It is a reencounter of remembrance, a knowing of the deep love and adoration we feel for one another.
I feel safe in your embrace and surrender fully to your wisdom.

You are my guiding light, and as your light shines brightly within my heart, I open to receiving the sacred messages that you want to bestow upon me in this moment.

I pause and take a breath, I feel our hearts joining as one, I see you within me, not separate, but as one. I rest in my heart now for a moment to receive your wisdom. Let it be so.

I pause again and take another breath, and with each breath comes the answer, effortlessly filling every part of my being.

I know now that which has been hidden from my conscious self.
I see the words and the images and experience the feelings that let me know I can now move forward with more clarity.

Thank YOU, *Divine Guru*. For this experience I am eternally grateful.

As you receive your answers, journal about them. If you don't feel complete, don't be disappointed; just try again. You matter to the world, but you must matter to YOU above all else. And because you do matter, don't give up on yourself. We only find completion and wholeness by loving ourselves as we are and loving each moment as it is given to us. Everything happens in divine order, so if you didn't get all you wanted by embracing this poem, try it again at another time. I know you will get what you need exactly when you need it. I believe in YOU and your greatness!

From Darkness into the Light

I don't need to go very far to know when I am in the presence of God, as I can feel it. Like the day I heard God's voice say to me, "My Child, I have a mission for you." That voice was in my dream of awakening. And the day God said, "Stay calm, I have a plan for you. Hold my hand and live on purpose," was another time when I was going through another dark night of the Soul. I had just lost my job at a non-profit agency where I had been working as a marketing consultant. The news came quite abruptly.

The thing is, I knew it was coming. Two weeks prior to losing my job I told a friend of mine that I could feel something was going on, and that "something" didn't feel right. Well, sure enough, two weeks later my boss called me in to his office. I sat in one of his leather chairs and heard a voice that said, "Stay calm, I have a plan for you." I knew at that moment that it was God's voice. I recognized it immediately and managed to stay calm for a short while.

Yet as the days went by I became depressed and fearful. I was living with a mindset of scarcity. I had not been able to, or should I say willing to, address my limiting beliefs about money, and had not saved a dime. I was broke. I had no savings. As this was a consulting job, I had no rights to receive any government assistance. I spiraled further into fear and into the darkness. I found myself crying all the time. I had a mortgage to pay and couldn't see the light through the darkness that had enveloped me. I was basing my reality in past experience, believing it would take a long time to find a new job and thinking about how I would manage in the meantime.

Things started to break down all around me. Two windows in my house developed leaks. My garbage disposal and my toilet broke. My car suddenly required $2,000 worth of repairs. On the front façade of my house some of the vinyl siding started to fall off. My outer world was reflecting how broken I felt inside. I couldn't believe this was happening to me. The signs had been there, right before my eyes and ears in my inner knowing, but I had ignored them all. My *divine guru* had tried to tell me and help me take steps to heal that broken part of me, but I didn't want any part of it.

My mother, who is so intuitive, could feel and hear my pain as we spoke on the phone one day. She immediately said that my father and she would be coming to visit me. I knew God was sending them to help me through this difficult time, as they had done many times before. When they arrived I fell into my mother's arms, taking in every breath of love she gave me. My father, who always had a hard time expressing his true feelings, showed me his love through small acts of kindness.

I had grown up seeing my father as a handyman around the house. I remember as a young girl standing by his side and handing him tools as he did carpentry and a myriad of other things around the house. This man who had worked with his hands all his life came to use his hands once again in my home. A day after they arrived, off I went to Home Depot with my dad. He had never installed a toilet before, but we were going to give it a try. There I was, standing in my bathroom, reading the instructions with my father and handing him the parts and tools as I had done as a little girl. It brought back many wonderful memories of our times together.

After successfully installing the toilet, back we went to Home Depot, this time to buy a new garbage disposal unit. He had never installed one of those either, but something told me that the Divine was lighting our way to a new place of trust and being. The overwhelm and fear had me spiraling into a dark place. I had fallen off the wagon and even stopped my daily spiritual practice. But having my parents there and feeling their love caused a small beacon, a glimmer of light, to appear in my life, allowing a sliver of hope to come into my Heart and Soul.

I began to feel the call of my own *divine light*, my Soul calling me to my inner sanctuary. For the first time in a couple of weeks, I listened. Even in our darkest moments, there is always a glimpse of the Divine. We just need to take a moment to seek and we will find the expression of the Divine that we are. I went outside and meditated on the grass, under the trees, and on Mother Earth. I could feel her love nourishing my Soul once again. My mother, bless her heart, would peek out the window to make sure I was safe. She had seen me crying and was quite worried about me. But day by day I improved. The more I connected to my inner sanctuary, the more hope and faith I regained that all would be okay. Sitting outside on my deck one day, I wrote this as I looked to the Divine for some solace from my fears:

Father, I sink quickly and deeply into an abyss of fear.
In this place, thoughts of pain, defeat, and non-existence surge into my mind.
I spiral deep. With each negative thought, more come. They seem to never cease.
I breathe into my heart center to find You.

Ah, there You are. I feel You not as strongly as before. The negative thoughts
have created a veil between us. I don't like this feeling. I feel alone,
yet I know You are there because I have been in oneness with
You in our inner sanctuary before.
I try to find You, breathing deeply into my heart center, trying to
remember those moments of oneness we have shared.

Show me, beloved Father, how do I find You once again? I am in despair,
sinking... sinking... crying... crying. I am scared.
I begin to ask and question why I am here. Should I stay here?
How could that be? I know I have a purpose. You have told me over and
over again, but the fear engulfs me.

I go into nature to find You again. I place my hands and feet on Mother Earth.
She reminds me of our oneness. I shed tears, releasing my pain. "I want to go
home," I say to You.

You respond, "Just be. The miracle is at your doorstep."

I calm down because I recognize Your voice, the same voice that has
spoken to me before.
Your voice has shattered the veil. I can feel You now in my heart. I see us
together in our inner sanctuary. Love engulfs me. I feel safe again. I feel one
again with You. I believe in the unseen miracle. I listen to Your command, "Just
be," and so I am. My Soul finds respite once again in Your arms of love. I am

grateful for I have transcended my dark night of the Soul. Thank You for this gift, Divine Father.

The words "Just be… the miracle is at your doorstep," became my daily mantra. I felt such truth in these words as I wrote them. I knew the Divine was holding me in a place of eternal love and knowing. And on that day everything changed. I began to feel this inner peace and calmness. No longer was my daily spiritual practice a chore. Instead it became a sacred time of renewal, Soul nourishment, a cherished time for me to be held in God's womb of eternal love.

After about a week my parents left with smiles on their faces. They knew something big had happened inside me. I was eternally grateful that my parents had listened to the call of the Divine to be with me in my hour of need. Love transmutes all, and that week the love of my parents and the Divine transmuted my dark night of the Soul. Several weeks later I got a call from a friend about a new consulting opportunity, and in a matter of weeks I was happily employed again. My miracle arrived just as the Divine had said it would.

The powerful words that began this time in my life were "Stay calm. I have a plan for you. Hold my hand and live on purpose." I couldn't feel the power of these words in the moment they were spoken because I allowed fear to spiral me into the darkness. But wow, after getting through that experience, all divinely orchestrated by the way, I held on to each of those words fearlessly. I even had them engraved on my little red iPod Nano so I could look at them every day and feel their power in my Heart and Soul. When you learn to stop resisting and trying to control what is beyond your control, something shifts inside you. There is a door that opens in your heart, and no longer are you separate from your light; you become the *divine light* that you are. Your greatest gifts are birthed from the darkness. It's a passageway to the light. Joseph Campbell says just that in this passage: "The cave you fear to enter holds the treasure you seek." Let's enter that cave together.

Some important lessons I learned through this experience:

1. **Make your time with Spirit non-negotiable.** Just as an athlete practices their sport to be better at it, honor your sacred time with the Divine to build your spiritual muscle on a daily basis. As you deepen your relationship with the Divine, you're better able to navigate the waters of life. While it may seem counterintuitive, the minute you begin to feel fear or become overwhelmed, turn inward. Remember, your outer world is a reflection of your inner world. The answers and the solace you seek always come from within.

2. **When you find you've fallen off your spiritual wagon, accept it, forgive yourself, and let it go.** It's part of the lessons you learn as you live your life and participate in our Earth school. These lessons are what allow you to have a deeper and richer experience, one that always supports you as you strive to become the highest version of YOU that you can be. Be grateful for all that comes your way, for this creates the space for your own evolution in shining your true magnificence to the world.

3. **Recognize that being in human form means that you're not perfect and aren't expected to be perfect.** Learning to accept yourself as you are in this moment is the greatest gift you can give yourself. You will learn, evolve, and mature into the REAL YOU in perfect divine timing. In the meantime, forgive, accept, and love yourself to the fullest every day. Self-acceptance of YOU is the key to being able to find and align with your Soul's rhythm and purpose.

4. **The more you build your spiritual muscle, the more you learn to trust the guidance that comes through**. With consistent spiritual practice you learn to trust your own *divine light*. Make it a practice to go to your inner sanctuary daily. In your inner sanctuary you'll always find eternal love and respite. In this place nothing else matters and everything else around you becomes white noise.

> *When you find the divine light within you, your inner sanctuary of oneness, hold it tightly and never let it go.*

When you find the *divine light* within you, your inner sanctuary of oneness, hold it tightly and never let it go. It is who you really are. Practice being there in the presence of your *divine light*, your higher power, because it is from this place of love and oneness that you find the courage to follow your heart's desires, the words you need to speak, and the thoughts that lead you to your highest purpose and manifestation of your destiny. I sit here now writing from this place... this inner sanctuary. To me it appears as a chamber within my heart, a portal to a place where I feel complete peace and serenity. For you it might take a different form. You will see it in the way you need to see it. Do not judge it, just flow with whatever images or feelings you get when you're in this sacred space. In your inner sanctuary you're given the courage to scale mountains, move mountains, and walk through mountains, because within this tiny space is a vastness that expands beyond the logical mind, time, and space.

Let's practice tapping into this part of you now. You can record the meditation below so you can close your eyes while you listen to it. Sit comfortably where you won't be disturbed—with your feet flat on the floor and your hands on your knees with palms facing up. If you're an experienced meditator, use whatever position is most comfortable to you. When you're ready, please move to the meditation.

Guided Meditation: Connecting with Your Inner Sanctuary

Start by dropping your focus into your heart center. Take a couple of deep breaths. Inhale slowly through your nose and exhale slowly through your mouth. With each exhale, create the sound "Ahhhhhhh," and release any stress, anxiety, and old, stale energy from your body.

Now imagine there's a door in the center of your heart. This doorway leads to a sacred chamber within your heart, your inner sanctuary. You open the door and walk through. As you enter the chamber, you're immersed in the highest vibrations of pink hues that form eternal love; you are this eternal love. You're met by your guardian angel who tells you how loved you are and that they've been waiting for you, for this exact moment in your life. It's time to be restored to your purest form of love.

God is present in this room. You can hear the sound of creation present in this chamber. Experience this presence in your own way; however you're meant to do so is perfect and unique to you. *{Pause for a moment.}*

As you stand in the middle of the chamber, a cloak appears out of thin air and is magically placed over your shoulders. The cloak shifts into various hues of the rainbow, the light spiraling around your body. You feel your consciousness expanding, and as it does your energy field expands in tandem.

With ease and grace you expand in alignment with your Soul's desires. The cloak melts right into your body—you are becoming one. You soak in this deep, rich vibration of infinite love into your being. The presence in the room whispers in your ear. Listen for a moment. What do you hear? *{Pause for a moment.}*

As you become one with the cloak, you're restored to your purest form of love. Remember how this feels in your heart so you can return here with just one breath. Imprint this in your being by bringing your index finger and thumb together. Whenever you want to return to this moment, all you need do is bring those two fingers together, take a deep breath, and in an instant you are back in this sacred chamber.

In this sacred chamber you are one with God and are restored to your purest form of love. Take a deep breath and relax for a moment. Integrate this eternal love into your being. *{Pause for a moment.}*

When you're ready, come back to the present moment.

Don't forget to journal about anything of importance from the meditation. You can even capture insights on the **Canvas of Your Soul**.

Trusting, Believing, and Surrendering to Your Divine Light

> *Claiming your divine light requires trust, belief, and surrender.*

Claiming your *divine light* requires trust, belief, and surrender. Trust is built through faith, and faith is built through belief that through the Divine anything is possible. Both trust and belief require full surrender to your higher power to guide you on your journey called life. You need all three in order to co-create with the Divine the life you desire and deserve. When you put trust in the Divine, you're putting trust in your own *divine light*. Your human form is the vessel that was created to embody this *divine light*. The more you believe and trust in your own contribution as a light to the world, the easier it becomes to surrender to divine will. In every moment it's up to you to choose whether you will accept the flow of God's eternal love—the eternal light of existence—or reject it.

As you evolve and grow, you're constantly posed with this question: Accept or reject your *divine light*? When you accept and claim your *divine light*, life is easier. When you reject the divine flow, life is harder. So when something feels difficult or you feel stuck, that means there's something you're resisting. Change is difficult for all of us. When unexpected events happen in our lives that shake us to the core, fear tends to rear its head. As you already read, fear can spiral and take you into dark places. But as you learn to trust, believe, and surrender to your *divine light*, you're able to navigate these events with greater ease and make Soul-driven choices and decisions that serve your highest good.

I struggled with this lesson for a long time. I learned that there are layers of limiting beliefs, fear, and trauma that hold us back from being the highest versions of ourselves, so you must peel back each layer delicately and in its own time. Your Soul will guide you on this quest. The more you build your spiritual muscle and practice connecting with your *divine light* daily, the easier the journey and the deeper the spiritual lessons. In one of my morning chats with God, I asked for help in being able to step through my fear of claiming my *divine light* fully. This is what God had to say to me:

> I am here with every breath. Imagine me holding your hand. Remember that we are one and you were created in my image, and so all I am, you are. All I am capable of can come through you. All I have dreamed of for you is at your fingertips.

Your Soul knows you have access to infinite possibilities, but you must do three things:

Trust in me and in you (only through the expression of loving yourself as I love you does the trust become real).

Believe in our oneness and in our ability to co-create miracles together, for you can achieve anything you set your mind to. With me, anything is possible. It does require you to believe in the unseen and have faith that when the seeds are ready for harvest they will ripen and miraculously and effortlessly appear in your life.

Surrender to my will and to your Soul's will. Remember who you really are (not in physical form, but in spiritual form)—a being of light and love. Your Soul already knows what you need to do to live on purpose, so surrender control.

I am the Creator of the seas (your fate), but your Soul is the captain of your destiny. Surrender to your higher purpose and let your Soul navigate the seas of my creation, knowing that you are never alone. I will always carry you and help you when the seas get rough. Through complete surrender you will achieve the freedom you have always been seeking.

When you do these three things, you will see a dove of peace land on your ship and the seas will calm and life will become effortless. For when you live on purpose, following your Soul's yearning, joy and love reign in your life. You come to know and understand that your purpose is not about you, it is about those whose lives you touch along the way as you co-create with the Universe to bring Heaven on Earth.

As you claim your *divine light*, you, too, contribute to Heaven on Earth and co-create your destiny. To get there you have to peel off the layers of the "onion" and heal those wounds that hold you back from fully trusting, believing, and surrendering to your *divine light*. This prepares you for when the unexpected happens in your life. I remember when my niece, Kristi, brought some unexpected news to our family. The phone rang and I heard my mother's concerned voice say, "*Ya sabes lo de Kristi?*" which means "Do you already know of the news of Kristi?"

She went on to tell me that the family was in a ruckus. Kristi had been away at school in her first year of college, and had come home and announced to her parents that she was pregnant. My older brother and my sister-in-law were very upset and my mother and father were in shock. It was one of those moments when everyone allowed their fear for the well-being of my niece to overshadow what should've been a moment of joy. They were all thinking, *Oh my God, now she'll never be able to finish school.* I knew better. I knew that everything happens for a reason, and that if she was pregnant, that was the way it was supposed to be. Yes, she wasn't married; and yes, she hadn't finished school. But that didn't mean she wouldn't be okay.

I felt a deeper calling that day. I knew the Divine was calling me forward to bring some peace and hope to our family. A day later Kristi called me to give me the news herself. I took that moment to reassure her that all would be okay. Our family loved her above all else and right now they were just processing the unexpected news. Not only did I have conversations with family members to encourage them to see the blessing in this situation, but I also knew my Soul was calling me to do something special for Kristi. I was guided to paint something for her that would give her strength and courage. That was the day the Divine planted the seed of a new painting, *"La Gitana (Gypsy) Warrior Goddess"* within me. You'll get to see this painting at the end of the chapter. This was the process that I knew very well by now. My paintings were meant to bring healing, and the seed of each one always began with a deep message from the Soul, not unlike what happened that day.

So off I went to create, allowing the message to guide the images I would paint. I was guided to paint angel wings as a sign of protection, hope, and trust—a belief in the unseen. In the center was the image of a woman, the gypsy. She represented my niece. The gypsy was travelling on a new road and she had no idea where she was being taken, but she was being asked to surrender to it. Next to the gypsy I painted a lion. The lion represents courage and strength. She would need courage and perseverance to get to wherever the Divine was taking her.

I remember giving the painting to Kristi as soon as it was finished and telling her the story and the message of its divine creation. She loved it and I had loved every moment in its making. Before she got pregnant, her dream was to use her own artistic gifts to become a graphic designer, and she never gave up on that dream. She raised my goddaughter, went to school, and worked all at the same time. She even graduated with honors when her daughter was five years old. I remember holding the hand of my goddaughter at her mom's graduation, both of us beaming with joy and pride at seeing her receive her diploma. I lovingly got to witness as Kristi became the woman in her painting. She brought a child into our family who reignited the flame of our love for one another. Eventually everyone came to see what an amazing blessing this pregnancy was for all of us. Kristi had claimed her *divine light* and allowed the Divine to guide her to her destiny. She trusted and believed it would all be okay and that her dreams would become reality. She was able to surrender to God's plan for her and trust in the direction she was being taken, and in the end it was divine perfection. This is what it means to trust, believe, and surrender to your *divine light.*

By claiming her *divine light* and surrendering to divine will, Kristi achieved the grace of our Creator, as it so beautifully says in *Katha Upanishad (Part 2)*:

"Concealed in the heart of all beings is the Atman, the Spirit, the Self; smaller than the smallest atom, greater than the vast spaces. The man who surrenders his human will leaves sorrow behind, and beholds the glory of the Atman by the grace of the Creator."

~Katha Upanishad (Part 2)

The Importance of a Daily Spiritual Practice

I can't tell you how many times I've heard, "But I'm too busy to meditate every day." Or "I'm just too busy to fit one more thing into my life." Spiritual practice isn't just "one more thing." It is the thing that changes you, deepens you, allows you to grow, and allows you to see and experience yourself and those around you as the sacred, divine beings you are. The more you practice building your spiritual muscle, the more you're able to see through the eyes of the Divine; through the eyes of your own *divine light*— led completely through the love of your Soul.

This practice is not just something that benefits your personal life; it also benefits your relationships and your career. Most of us spend the majority of our time working in some form, either for ourselves or someone else. The same guidance that emerges through you and for you as you claim your *divine light* also guides you as you create, inspire, and make decisions in your workplace. These are the intuitive nudges you get to call someone you haven't spoken to in a long time, and when you do it turns out they needed to share something important with you. Wouldn't you love to have some help making the decisions that can make or break what the future holds for you? When you claim your *divine light* and deepen your relationship to this part of you, you open the door to make better, Soul-driven decisions in all areas of your life, including career.

Having spent the majority of my life in corporate environments, I'm here to tell you that your spiritual life and career don't have to be separate. What you practice spiritually can be applied to any area of your life. Imagine this scenario: You have an important meeting coming up. You are the focal point of this meeting. You're pitching an important client, a new idea, or an improvement for your company. Normally you would prepare until the "nth" hour, worrying about the outcome of the meeting. Why not instead take a deep breath, connect with your inner sanctuary, and set an intention that all will be okay, asking that the Divine work through you so that whatever occurs will be the highest good for you and all those involved? This takes five minutes, and serves you better than staying up all night worrying about something you have no control over. All you have control over is putting your best foot forward; the rest is in the hands of the Universe. So give it to the Universe and the Universe will support you in ways you didn't even know were possible. This is what creating a daily spiritual practice can do. It gets you real, tangible results. You feel calmer, younger, healthier, and happier. And you're able to be more productive and clearer in making decisions that perhaps before would've taken longer or caused you some level of angst.

> *As you tap into your own divine light, you tap into the consciousness of the Universe.*

As you tap into your own *divine light*, you tap into the consciousness of the Universe and, in effect, everyone around you, since we are all connected. Consciousness is light. This light is filled with Source code, and this code is embedded with knowledge, instructions, gifts—all that you need to align with your Soul's purpose. How do you access this consciousness? Yes... through your spiritual practice. Meditation, prayer, and chanting are all examples of spiritual practices. In his book *Wisdom of the Peaceful Warrior*, Dan Millman describes meditation as "Two simultaneous processes: One is insight—paying attention to what is arising. The other is surrender—letting go of attachment to arising thoughts."

Some teachers will tell you that a specific type of meditation or spiritual practice is the best, but once again I remind you to tap into your *divine guru*. You know best what works for you. Experiment with different practices. Your Soul will guide you along the way. You will know when you've come across a practice that is right for you. And if you're interested in learning a specific type of meditation, such as transcendental meditation, invest in learning how to do it properly. It will be worth your while.

Any activity that helps you connect to the stillness within you can be made into a spiritual practice. *Practice* means that you do it daily, because consistency is what builds your spiritual muscle. However, the most important thing is that whatever spiritual practice you choose, it allows you to connect with the stillness within you. I love Martha Graham's quote about the importance of practice. Martha was a well-known American dancer and choreographer, and was celebrated by many as the Mother of Modern Dance.

> *"We learn by practice. Whether it means to learn to dance by practicing dancing or to learn to live by practicing living, the principles are the same. One becomes in some areas an athlete of God."*
>
> **~Martha Graham**

Painting is a form of meditation for me. When I paint, I'm so focused on what I'm doing (I get into my zone) that I'm able to become the vessel for whatever Spirit wants to bring through on my canvas (images, colors, messages, etc.). Athletes speak of getting in the zone as well, where they just become one with whatever sport they're playing. My younger brother tells me that when he snowboards this happens to him. It's like he becomes one with his snowboard as it glides over the snow, the bumps, the hills, and the flakes that rise up onto his goggles, all creating this experience of stillness for him. And what about the captain at sea? He becomes one with the water that surrounds him and his boat. He steers as the sea guides him to steer. That is the goal of your spiritual practice: getting lost in the stillness, where your thoughts no longer matter and the sound of creation becomes your guiding light.

The great thing is that you can practice connecting with the stillness within you just by doing your normal daily activities. In his book *A New Earth*, Eckhart Tolle speaks of those moments during the day when you can find stillness in ordinary activities, like gazing at a beautiful flower, becoming present as you cook dinner, as you climb the stairs, or enter your car. It's about paying attention to every moment, breathing into it, and allowing your focus to be exclusively on what you're doing, be it stirring the soup or lifting your heel off the floor as you walk to your bedroom.

Sometimes we don't realize how powerful and magnificent our breath really is. Many of us take this for granted. I believe God was a genius in creating our breath to have such power. I have learned to treat each breath as a sacred experience, and, in turn, the Divine has shown me how to use it to reconnect with my *divine light* in an instant. In one instant you can recenter and recalibrate your being. It's like your breath becomes the trigger to finding your way home again to your inner sanctuary. I'm not talking of just a normal breath, but a deep, sacred breath, when you inhale and exhale slowly with focused intention. God has told me many times that He's just a breath away, and I can tell you that it's possible to experience that in your daily life. You can use your breath as the doorway to your own *divine light*. This is especially helpful when you're feeling anxiety, stress, or even fear.

Imagine yourself at home or at work. Something just happened, and now you're feeling stressed or worried, or you're starting to panic. Stop, close your eyes, and take three deep breaths. Breathe in slowly through your nose and breathe out slowly through your mouth. With each breath you're surrendering to that part of you that exists beyond your mind and body, your *divine light*, that higher power that exists within you, not outside of you. In just a couple of minutes, your heart has stopped racing and now you can allow your Soul and the Divine to help you manage the situation instead of allowing your mind to control your actions from a place of fear or anxiety. It's that simple. Try it for yourself.

I recommend you start your day with whatever spiritual practice you decide works for you. Spend some time experimenting, and then create your own morning ritual to help you deepen your spiritual muscle. It always helps to ask those you trust for recommendations, so ask friends and family what they do for their morning rituals. You might just be surprised at the tidbits you learn. Take what resonates with your Soul and leave the rest. If you want to learn more about various spiritual practices, check out Jonathan Ellerby's book called *Return to the Sacred*.

My morning routine takes about thirty minutes. I begin with prayer and then move right into meditation. I practice a form similar to transcendental meditation in which I repeat a mantra for about twenty minutes. (I practice this same meditation technique in the evening.) Then I read some inspirational quotes or messages before I go off to start my day. One of my favorite go-to books is Eva Bell Werber's *Quiet Talks with the Master*. I randomly flip to a page and always receive the exact message I need, starting my day nourished and full of spirit.

If I'm looking for guidance regarding a particular challenge or question, I take out post-card-sized replicas of my paintings to consult directly with the Divine. I pick a couple of paintings to receive guidance from my Soul. And, if I need a little healing boost, I listen to one of my healing instrumentals that accompanies the painting. I carry my instrumentals, guided meditations, Paraliminals® audio programs, and other inspirational audios on my iPod Nano. I love that I can take this tiny piece of technology anywhere I go for short stints of spiritual nourishment and inspiration. I sprinkle in other activities during the week in short increments to keep me connected to my *divine light*. Some of these include:

- **Sacred stillness expands my mind**. This includes any form of guided meditation, walking meditations in nature, morning chats with God during long commutes or long road trips, mantras, and emotional freedom technique (EFT), where I get to tap away my pain, blocks, and limiting beliefs. If you've never tried EFT, check out Nick Ortner's book, *The Tapping Solution*.

- **Sacred inspiration warms my heart**. Sacred inspiration includes reading sacred texts (like the Bible, *A Course in Miracles*, and the *Bhagavad Gita*); heart-centered books (like Louise Hay's *Heart Thoughts* and Christine Kloser's *A Daily Dose of Love*); inspirational quotes and affirmations (Danielle LaPorte's Truthbomb iTunes app and the *Daily Word*); and watching uplifting movies and videos (check out Elizabeth Gilbert's TED Talk about "Your Elusive Creative Genius").

- **Sacred ritual creates the space for healing**. I'm a water sign (Pisces), so water has always been my best friend. Not only do I tend to use water as a healing tool for my clients, but I cherish my sacred baths as a healing element for my mind, body, and spirit. Candles, incense, and aromatic oils light up my senses as I bathe with lavender and salt.

- **Sacred movement helps me connect with my life force**. As I follow the deliberate, slow movements of tai chi or allow my body to dance to Soul-connecting music, I become one with my life force.

- **Sacred sound melts away my stress and pain**. Singing, playing the guitar, toning with my tank drum, and listening to sound-healing instrumentals and songs connect me with inner peace.

- **Sacred creation becomes my doorway to the Divine**. Painting, writing, and journaling get me into my divine zone. Connecting with my inner passions in this way propels me forward in my purpose-work.

As you grow and deepen with your *divine light*, the inevitable is your own transformation. That's why you're here in the first place, isn't it? So let's continue your journey by helping you connect more deeply with your *divine light*.

You can record the following meditation so you can close your eyes while you listen to it. For the audio version, visit **www.UnmaskingYourSoul.com/Meditations.** Sit comfortably where you won't be disturbed—with your feet flat on the floor and your hands on your knees with palms facing up. If you're an experienced meditator, use whatever position is most comfortable to you. When you're ready, please move to the meditation.

Guided Meditation: Claiming Your Divine Light

Breathe slowly, inhaling through your nose and exhaling through your mouth. As you breathe, focus on your breath and feel with every breath the relaxation of your mind, body, and spirit. Just focus on your breath and let thoughts pass as they may.

See your Higher-Self coming to meet you. Take a moment to observe what your Higher-Self looks like and how you feel standing in the presence of your own divine light. **{Pause for fifteen to twenty seconds.}**

Listen closely as your Higher-Self speaks these words to you: "You are a being of divine light. See yourself as this being of light. You are love; love in its purest form; resilient and magnificent and all-being. Let go of the image of your body... your name… any beliefs or disbeliefs about who you really are. Just see yourself as a being of light radiating brightly to the world."

Go deeper into the nothingness that surrounds you. Take a moment to feel yourself in this state of nothingness. {Pause for fifteen to twenty seconds.}

"We walk together hand in hand in a tunnel of angelic rays. You are safe, as I am with you. We go deeper and deeper within… into the nothingness, and with every step we take you are shedding all beliefs, disbeliefs, and limitations, and opening the space for infinite possibilities. With each step you see your divine light beaming brighter. With each step you take you feel you are in the arms of the angels and the Divine. You are safe. You are protected by God's armor. All you feel is infinite love… infinite love… infinite love."

As this being of light, you have no worries… no beliefs… no pain… no doubts… no concerns… no thoughts. All you feel is divine love, acceptance of your true self. You have surrendered to the you you really are. You are home once again. You have returned from whence you came. Your light now radiates fully. All your fears are gone… all your fears are gone… all your fears are gone.

You are no longer afraid to shine your light fully. You now embody your true self… nameless, without a body, only infinite love. All the illusions and delusions have dissolved, leaving only feelings of emphatic divine love. A euphoria of joy, peace, and stillness overtakes your soul.

You are just being… pure being of love… claiming your divine light for the world to see.

Take some time to bathe in this mystical bath of eternal love. {Pause for several minutes.}

When you're ready, slowly open your eyes and come back to the present moment.

Now that you've completed the guided meditation, take some time to do some journaling. Spend about ten to fifteen minutes in a quiet place where you won't be disturbed answering the questions below. You can put on some soothing music or light a candle or incense to support you as you write. Just write from your Heart and Soul and the rest will follow.

Journaling Exercise

1. When you met your Higher-Self, how did you feel? What did your Higher-Self look like? Feel like? What else did you notice in that moment?

2. As your Higher-Self spoke to you, how did you feel? Did you notice any energy in your body? If so, in what parts?

3. Were you able to experience yourself as a being of *divine light*? If so, what did you see or feel?

4. How did it feel being in a state of nothingness? Note any significant moments that transcended the boundaries of your mind.

5. How did you feel at the end of the meditation?

6. Note at least one action or activity you will commit to doing daily to deepen the connection to your *divine light*.

After journaling, continue working on the **Canvas of Your Soul.** (You can download the PDF at **www.UnmaskingYourSoul.com/Blueprint.**) Pick phrases, words, or symbols and put them on section 5 of the *Light* part of your roadmap. Make this canvas your own piece of artwork that represents the journey we're taking together in this book. You can color, paint, or even cut images from magazines that depict the messages and insights you received in this chapter on *claiming your divine light*. You don't need to be a professional artist to do this. Just let your Soul express through you as it wants to. This will become the vision board of your Soul's unmasking, a precious gift to you from your *divine guru*.

Five Rituals to Awaken Your Divine Light Muscle

The rituals below are meant to help you awaken your *divine light* muscle. You can repeat any of the rituals that follow and the exercises and guided meditations earlier in the chapter as many times as you like. With each repetition you go deeper in accessing your *divine guru—your bringer of light*.

The more you embody your true essence, your *divine light*, the easier it is to navigate the peaks and valleys of your life. Water is a purifier and bringer of light, so several of the rituals below use the element of water to connect you more deeply with your *divine light*.

Don't forget to create your sacred space and take some deep breaths to relax your mind and body before you begin. Connect with your Soul as you enter this sacred space.

1. Use this sacred bath ritual to connect more deeply with your *divine light*. You will need some sea salt or bath salts, candles, lavender oil, rose petals, and a clear or rose quartz stone (preferably a flat palm stone).

   a. Prepare your sacred space. Light one or more candles of your choice and set your intention for what you want to receive in this sacred ritual. You can play soothing music in the background if you like. Run the bath water as you say the following invocation: "Dearest God, as I prepare to bathe with You in this sacred water, I ask for Your divine guidance and blessings. May Your eternal love be embedded in each molecule of water that touches my skin. May all that needs to leave me, leave as I cleanse with Your sacred water. May the *divine light* that I am radiate purely from our sanctuary of eternal love."

   b. Place the sea salt or your bath salts in the bottom of the tub, sprinkling it in with your hands. As you do this, send love through your hands and into the salts. Then place seven drops of lavender oil into the water. Again, with each movement and each action, send love and ask the Divine for blessings and healing. Once the tub is full, hold the rose petals against your heart and see your *divine light* and love permeating each rose petal. Sprinkle the rose petals on top of the water and place the quartz crystal on the side of the tub where you can reach it.

   c. When you're ready, get into the tub. Immerse your body fully in the water. Place the quartz crystal against your heart. Ask the stone to be your guide and help you heal whatever stands in the way of your embodying your *divine light*. Place the stone to the side. Slowly take water in your hands or use a small container to pour water over you. Allow the movements to be slow and deliberate so you become one with the water. Do this for one or two minutes.

   d. Hold the quartz crystal against your heart for a while. Lie against the wall or tub and just relax, breathing in slowly through your nose and breathing out slowly through your mouth. With each breath you become more relaxed. Allow the energy of the crystal to permeate your being. When that feels complete, move the crystal to the top of your head. Place it on the center of your head and leave it there as you relax. Just focus on your breath, in and out slowly, allowing any thoughts to pass freely.

   e. Place your attention on the crystal and see its energy flowing in through your head and coming straight down into your heart center. Swirls of light engulf your heart. The light expands and expands, getting bigger and bigger, engulfing your entire body. As it does, you see your body fade away, and what's left is the real you in *divine light* form. Your light radiates brighter and brighter. Allow your light to radiate outward from you.

f.   You see your light becoming bigger, moving now to fill the entire room, and then expanding to embrace your loved ones in your home. Your light continues to increase, engulfing the entire house. You see your light expand beyond your home, your neighborhood, your state… expanding and expanding, now engulfing the country you live in…. expanding and expanding. You're expanding across the entire planet… still expanding. You are now one with the galaxy, you're one with all that is… beyond time and space. Sit in this place of oneness for several minutes.

g.   When you feel complete, thank the Divine and your crystal companion for their healing and divine guidance today. Then remove the crystal from the top of your head and begin to come back. Slowly open your eyes. If you feel called, journal about your experience. Place your crystal on an altar or in a sacred space, or carry it with you to reconnect with your *divine light* and this divine experience anytime you wish.

2.   You can use the following guided ritual to create a space for deeper healing and to plant the seeds for the life you desire. In this ritual you're joined by *ascended masters*, great spiritual teachers who once existed in human form and then achieved a level of spiritual enlightenment that allowed them to ascend into a higher vibratory plane of existence.

> *Close your eyes and take a deep breath, then another, and one more. Picture yourself at the beach. You look to your right and see the ocean waves hitting the rocks. The sound is amazing as the ocean hits the stones and splashes its brilliant, clear water against the sandy beach. The sand is pure white. You're sitting on the sand a few feet from the ocean. You pick up some sand in your hands and see it flow freely between your fingers and down again to join the other tiny sand particles.*
>
> *As you sit here, you look up and see the bright, yellow sun. You breathe the yellow light into your heart and down into your abdomen. It fills your stomach with warmth, love, and divine power. The ocean waves get closer to you and you get up and walk into the water. The waves rise and come over your head and torso. Bring any thoughts or feelings of anxiety or pain to the surface. With every wave that comes over you, you are cleansed. You're beginning to feel much calmer and relaxed.*

As you become more centered, you feel divine beings around you—angels, ascended masters, guides, and ancestors—all joining you here in this sacred place. One of your guides places their hands on your heart and you feel your heart melting away pain, grief, and loss... all melting away into the ocean. Another divine being places their hands on your crown and you feel you're being transported to another plane of existence. It is as if your body is being lifted out of the water and you are flying freely in the heavens. When you look down you can see the ocean beneath you. You feel so free in this state—free to be you, free to feel the deep love that surrounds you and that you are. When you look at your body, it's not there. All you see is your divine light body. Streams of light radiate brightly from you. It is the make-up of your true existence.

Nothing else matters in this place except you. You imagine the life you want and desire. You see it right in front of you as you continue to fly in the heavens. You can feel how wonderful this life is. It's so real you can feel it now within you. Love, joy, peace, and abundance. Everything you want, you have in this life. It is here now. Feel it in your heart. Hold your thumb and middle finger together to imprint these feelings into your being. To return here, put your thumb and middle finger together. In that holy instant you will be brought back to this place of peace and remembrance of the amazing life you are now creating on the spiritual plane. Soon you will see proof of its existence in your reality.

You slowly descend to the ground and feel the warmth of the white sand beneath your feet. You wiggle your toes in the sand and give thanks to the Divine for this wonderful experience today. Remember the feeling of your true essence, your divine light, so you can return here anytime. Create your own inner sanctuary, one that speaks directly to your Soul. Just allow and be, and you will be taken there. Practice daily and soon you will be able to enter this sacred space in an instant with just one breath.

3. You can use the spiritual practice of self-inquiry to help you connect more deeply with your *divine light*. Use this sacred ritual to discover where you might be holding blockages or wounds, or to receive guidance on a particular question or challenge in your life. This ritual is best done outside where you can connect with Earth with your feet on the ground, though it can be done inside as well.

   a. The first step is to *relax* into your inquiry. Close your eyes and do some deep breathing to relax your mind and body. Allow thoughts to pass as you focus on your breath. Bring the breath up and down from your abdomen.

b. The second step is to *connect*. When you feel relaxed, take a moment to feel the ground beneath your feet. Visualize the Earth energy entering the soles of your feet and creating a line of connection. See the Earth energy connecting four points in your body. The Earth energy lifts upward and connects your abdomen (the seat of your inner *divine power*); your heart (the seat of your *divine love* and *divine light*); your brow in the center of your forehead (the seat of your *divine wisdom*); and a point six inches above your head (the seat of your Higher-Self).

c. The third step is to *inquire*. Drop into your heart center and place the inquiry, your question(s), in your heart center, and see the words there within your heart. The words become enveloped in a beautiful, bright, pink light. The swirls of light continue to immerse your words in unconditional love. Connect with your own reservoir of *divine love*. Do this for as long as you feel guided to.

d. In step four, move to *receive*. Continue with your breathing, in and out of your abdomen, and allow the answers, revelations, and wisdom to rise to your consciousness. The answers may come in the form of words, images, or just feelings. Let go of any expectations and just allow your Soul to communicate what needs to come through in this moment. Stay here for as long as you need to.

e. Return to the present. When you feel complete in receiving what is meant to be experienced in this moment, slowly come back to the present and open your eyes. You may want to journal about your experience so you have a history of wisdom and revelations that you can refer to over and over again. Sometimes the wisdom is not revealed all at once, so pay attention to your surroundings and experiences over the next several days and weeks. Sometimes the answers are revealed through unexpected sources (animals, a person, a stranger, a movie, a song, etc.), so just allow yourself to receive as you're meant to receive.

4. Dance and movement are other ways you can connect more deeply with your *divine light*. This particular dance ritual is best done in the evening. Try to pick a night when there's a full moon, or a strongly lit night, as this makes the ritual even more powerful. You need several colored candles to perform the ritual. Pick three to five differently colored candles and a piece of music that inspires you. Let your Soul guide you as you connect with your inner sanctuary.

a. One by one, light each candle, setting the intention for healing, oneness, flow, joy, and whatever else you wish to receive.

b. Turn on the music. Stand in the center of the room and become aware of your energy and light flowing through you. Focus on your breath. Slowly inhale and exhale to relax your mind, body, and spirit. When you feel relaxed, continue breathing deeply and visualize the candles in your mind's eye. See yourself breathing in the light and color of each candle you lit.

c. Tune in to the music, feeling every vibration in your body. Visualize the words, notes, and vibrations of the music merging and integrating with the colored light emerging from the candles. The colored light of the candles, the music, and you are all becoming one. Allow the colored light to go wherever it needs to go in your body.

d. Move with the music. Let the music inspire you as you move your body and continue to bring color to the parts of your body where you sense you need it the most. Let your Soul—not your mind—direct the dance.

e. Flow with the music. Allow the music to flow through the rest of your body. Loosen your movements and surrender your body to the dance, using all the space in the room. Follow your Soul's guidance to spin, circle, step, jump, or become still as you move into different positions, always observing and listening to your body.

f. Conclude with the music. As the music ends, your movement also ends naturally. As you finish, enter fully into the silence and stillness around you. Listen to any messages your body may have for you and journal about them. You should now feel recharged and harmonized.

5. Meditate with my painting **La Gitana (Gypsy) Warrior Goddess**, shown at the end of the chapter. It helps you reconnect with your *divine guru*, the one who embodies your *divine light*. Each of my paintings was divinely channeled and holds messages and energetic impressions of the Soul that bring healing to the bearer. This particular painting holds vibrations of healing for those needing to remember their expression of *divine light*. As I mentioned earlier in the chapter, I created this painting for my niece, Kristi. May it help you *trust, believe,* and *surrender* to your *divine light* as it did for her.

a. Close your eyes and take a breath... inhaling slowly through your nose and exhaling slowly through your mouth... and with each breath you take relax your mind, body, and spirit. Continue focusing on your breath... and with each breath allow your thoughts to pass freely... thought after thought... breath after breath... relaxing more and more deeply. Continue taking several more deep breaths. {**Repeat for one or two minutes.**}

b. Briefly open your eyes and observe the painting. Allow yourself to be taken on a journey into the painting. Look at the images and symbols, and allow your gaze to go to one focal point in the painting. Soften your gaze as you focus on this point of interest. Breathe in its energy, seeing the symbols, images, and colors in your mind's eye. Continue breathing in the energy... breath after breath, allowing you to feel and absorb the healing energy from this focal point.

c. With your next breath, listen to the voice of your Soul. What is it communicating? What messages do you hear or feel within you as you breathe in the energy of the painting? Pay attention to where the energy is going in your body. This gives you an indication of where in your body you may need to release old energy, traumas, or wounds. Continue breathing and just go into the stillness while you connect deeper within. Allow the healing energies of the painting to penetrate your mind, body, and spirit. {**Do this for two to five minutes.**} If you feel guided, you may continue repeating this step, changing to a different focal point in the painting each time. Again, allow yourself to breathe the images, symbols, colors, and healing energies into your being.

d. Don't forget to journal about anything of significance that comes up during this experience.

Eileen Anümani Santos, *La Gitana (Gypsy) Warrior Goddess*, c. 2007

La Gitana (Gypsy) Warrior Goddess is about trusting the direction the Divine is taking you. You are safe and divinely protected as you walk this new path, your journey of self-discovery. Your Soul guides you on this quest, and with each step forward you gain more courage, strength, and momentum. Through *trust, belief,* and *surrender* you're able to *claim your divine light*. As you embody your true essence, you become the light for those around you.

**Believing is becoming, becoming is believing.
In becoming what you believe, the REAL YOU emerges!**

Finding Your Soul's Purpose
by Eileen Anümani Santos

As I watch the droplets of rain coming down, I feel the Earth's response, "Thank you for this nourishment."

What glory to be able to see the beauty of the heavens and the Earth meeting in a place where they are able to express their love for one another.

In similar form to the elements, our humanness and spiritual being also meet in this place of shared love… at our heart center.

In this place we are no longer just human or just spirit; we are both.

As we feel the purity of God's love and infinite wisdom, our true self emerges.

Allow yourself to be guided by this divine presence within you to your Soul's purpose.

Only when you feel your heart singing will you know you have found it.

CHAPTER 6

Soul Chamber VI:
Embracing Your Divine Purpose

In chapter 4, "Accepting Your Divine Truths," I introduced the topic of purpose. If you recall, your *divine truths* represent your unique God-seed, your Soul's genius. These are the inherent, divine gifts you were born with. In this chapter we dive into your *divine purpose,* where you give voice to your *divine truths.* If your *divine truths* are your "what," then your *divine purpose* is your "how." God created you with a unique God-seed that belongs only to you. Your *divine purpose* is the *vocation* that brings forth your God-seed into *physical* form in the world. For example, if one of your *divine truths* is that you're a healer, like me, your *divine purpose* defines how you express that healing gift to others. Perhaps your main vocation is as a teacher to help those you serve embrace their own healing gifts. Or you might express your healing gifts through art, music, or your voice. Most likely you have one primary and several secondary vocations that support how you express your gifts to others. Later in the chapter there's an exercise to help you discover what those are. Your Heart and Soul will guide you on your journey of self-discovery.

The right chamber of the heart is the location of **Soul Chamber VI—Divine Purpose,** the sixth of the Soul virtues that will be unmasked as you continue on your journey of wholeness. The mask associated with this sixth chamber is the **Mask of Destruction**. The emotional state that underlies this mask is tendencies towards self-defeat and self-sabotage, limiting your ability to fully embrace and bring your purpose-work into fruition. These behaviors stem from limiting beliefs and fears in your psyche (either conscious or subconscious) that your ego uses to prevent you from shining your true magnificence to the world. That doesn't serve you or anyone else, as Christine Kloser, a gifted spiritual guide and transformational leader, says so beautifully in the quote below.

"Playing small and hiding—especially when it looks to the world like you aren't—doesn't serve you or anyone on this journey."

~Christine Kloser

Fear can manifest in one of two ways. The first stems from an underlying fear of not having the capabilities, resources, or vitality to manifest your purpose-work and have the life you desire. The other originates from a fear of losing what you achieve, so you might as well give up now. Your ego uses this story to prey on your psyche and make you believe that you shouldn't even try in the first place, or sabotage any success you have as a measure of "protection." Your ego wants to make you believe it's protecting you and helping you avoid pain and disappointment. It's yet another tactic of your ego to keep

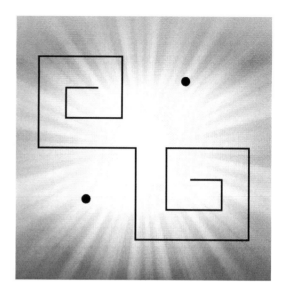

Divine Purpose Symbol

you small and hold you back from being the real you. But your ego is not to be feared or seen as the enemy. Instead you should try to make friends with your ego and understand the why behind its actions. By doing this you can recognize where you're still holding a limiting belief or pain that's holding you back from truly embracing your *divine purpose*.

This chamber is represented by the archetype of the **divine creator.** Your *divine creator* is the one who helps you create and manifest your vocation in life. Look to your *divine creator* to help you embrace your vocation and purpose-work. The sacred symbol of this chamber is shown above.

What It Means to Live on Purpose

Living a purpose-centered life is the most fulfilling experience you'll ever have. Many of us walk through life searching for our purpose, not knowing or remembering why we chose to be born in this time. Have you ever wondered why you are here? Your Soul knows the answer to that question, and it's your Soul that guides you to the answer. I spent the first thirty-eight years of my life not knowing or remembering why I was here. I seemed pretty happy and successful to most people, but inside I was yearning for something more. There was something missing that I couldn't put my finger on until I had my dream of awakening in October of 2003. This was the beginning of my own healing and transformation that led me here, to this moment with you, so I could guide you on your own journey of self-discovery.

The question you should really be asking yourself is "How am I meant to serve?" Your purpose-work is driven by the answer to this question. We are all here to serve in some way. I'm here to help you remember that you're more than your name, your thoughts, and your physical body. The real you exists on a much deeper, ethereal level. The real you is an infinite being of love and light. It is your *divine light* that contributes in multiples to the consciousness of humanity. Inside you, beneath the layers of skin, bone, and physical matter, exists a presence that is your *divine light*. This part of you lives in the vastness of consciousness, beyond the comprehension of your physical mind, only intelligible by the *divine mind* that transcends the human intellect. As the wonderful poet Rumi said, "You are not a drop in the ocean. You are the entire ocean in a drop."

I love this quote because it really gets to the crux of what we all have to learn on order to embrace and remember who we really are. Within you is all you need. You are powerful beyond measure, and in that *divine power* there is a great force that can transcend anything and everything. Jesus said, "You can do what I do and more." I know there may be a part of you that finds that statement hard to believe because of the conditioning imposed on you by life experiences and even society, but it's time for you to embrace this *divine truth*. You are more powerful and magnificent than you can imagine. As the *divine creator* that you are, you have the power within you to heal, transform, and create miracles for yourself and those around you. As you remove the layers that hold you back from embodying the real you, you help unlock a piece of the canvas that makes the union of Heaven and Earth possible.

As you step into your purpose-work, you begin to embody your *divine power*, a force that makes you unstoppable. This force is propelled by universal alchemy to align your Soul with the Soul of the Universe. Take a breath right now and go within the deepest part of you. Drop into your heart center and see if you can feel your Soul. SOUL is **S**acred **O**penness to **U**niversal **L**ove. Tap into the source of love that is you. Soul cannot be expressed in words; it must be felt and experienced as a presence within you. Your Soul is your compass to True North, your very own unique path of purpose and fulfillment. In this chapter you will be led to a place of discovery of that purpose.

When you serve others knowing and believing that what you bring to the world is of value, the Universe conspires to help you bring that value to the world.

When you serve others knowing and believing that what you bring to the world is of value, the Universe conspires to help you bring that value to the world. Jesus said, "I came to bear full witness to the glory of the one that dwells in me." Within you dwells that *divine creator* that will help you do the same—become the witness to the glory of that purpose, your vocation, that transforms and changes lives in the way that only you can.

In Mastin Kipp's Daily Love blog from March 17th, 2015, there was a beautiful quote from Dhru Purohit that said, "There's someone out there that needs your work. There's someone out there that needs you to show up, in only the way you know how." This is what I'm talking about. Only you have the gifts you have in the way that you have them. There may be a million writers out there, but if you're meant to be a writer, then how you give voice to that writing is unique to you. This is where it all begins: in the belief that you were created with a *divine purpose*, a vocation that only you can deliver in the way God intended. God planted the seeds within you that allow the germination of your unique gifts to come to life at the time designated by the Divine. When this time arrives, the unlocking of these gifts occurs. There is a time for germination between your Soul and the Universe. Your Soul nurtures the seeds to their ripeness. When the time arrives, your Soul opens the doorway to harvest the seeds of your *divine purpose*, your divine vocation. Since you're reading this now, I know that something is ripe within you to be harvested. Now is the time to pay attention to the signs that surround you about what action you're being asked to take.

There is a saying my mother says quite often: *Dios dice, ayúdate, que yo te ayudaré*. This means "God helps those who help themselves." But there is a deeper meaning here. As you knock on the Divine's door, God opens it, but you have the responsibility to take the action to walk through that doorway; no one else can do that for you. It is by taking action that you demonstrate your commitment to the Universe that you're serious about doing your part. This is the time to make that same commitment to your *divine purpose*.

In the movie *The Matrix*, there's a powerful line that Morpheus says to Neo about this action. He says, "Neo, sooner or later you will learn there's a difference between knowing the path and walking the path." You see, knowing the path is recognizing when the Universe is opening the door for you. Walking the path is when you decide to walk through the doorway and embrace that opportunity. Life doesn't happen *to* you—it happens *through* you. This goes for embracing your *divine purpose* as well. As you commit to growing, deepening, and embracing your *divine purpose* and who you really are, you become the witness to the life you have always desired and deserve. This is the life your Soul has been yearning for. Walk through that doorway right now. Say "YES!" to living on purpose and doing it fearlessly! Remember that you're always safe and protected as you step forward into being the highest version of YOU that you're meant to be.

Keeping Your Divine Purpose Channel Open

To embrace your *divine purpose*, practice keeping your channel of reception open. Your Soul works through your *divine creator* to manifest your *divine purpose* in your life. You are the co-creator of your destiny, and your Soul guides you on that journey. To become an effective co-creator, you need to be able to listen and receive guidance from your Soul, your *divine light*, that divine presence within you that is all-knowing. As I mentioned in the previous chapter, this is where spiritual practice plays a big role. Only through the practice of stillness can you learn to condition your mind, body, and spirit to listen and receive the guidance that helps you co-create your destiny. This is crucial as you embark on your journey of aligning with your Soul's purpose, the vocation that God intended for you in this life.

> *Only you can bring your unique gifts to the world with the inimitable voice that was seeded within you in your Soul's DNA.*

It's up to you to keep your channel open so you can embrace your *divine purpose*. Only you can bring your unique gifts to the world with the inimitable voice that was seeded within you in your Soul's DNA. The great American dancer and choreographer Martha Graham says this about purpose:

"There is a vitality, a life force, an energy, a quickening, that is trans-lated through you into action, and because there is only one of you in all of time, this expression is unique. And if you block it, it will never exist through any other medium and it will be lost. It is your business to keep it yours clearly and directly, to keep the channel open."

~Martha Graham

Once the channel opens, trust what's coming through. We'll get more into intuition and trust in later chapters, but for now practice connecting with the voice of your Soul and trusting it's presence within you. One way to do this is to practice staying centered in your source, *divine light*, throughout your day, and returning to your inner sanctuary. Your eyes are the window to your Soul, so let's use this symbol to connect you with your *divine creator*, the one who is ready to help you embrace your *divine purpose*. Imagine this eye sitting right in your heart center, serving as the doorway to your inner sanctuary. In this safe haven, neither your ego nor the outside world can harm you. Walk into this eye and meet your *divine creator*. Here you are protected, coveted, and loved as the divine being you are.

The symbol of the all-seeing eye was used throughout ancient times to represent a doorway to the unseen, to deeper sources of consciousness and awareness. It can serve the same role for you, helping you keep your channel open to your *divine purpose* and vocation in life. It can keep you open to witnessing, experiencing, and receiving the signs and messages that serve as your guideposts to a deeper knowing of who you are and why you exist. For my niece Ashley, a routine moment of togetherness between us turned into a very deep experience in which the symbol of the eye opened the channel for her to gain a deeper understanding of her own *divine purpose*.

In what seem to be routine activities or events, we sometimes find deep messages that result in transformational experiences. One weekend my niece Ashley came to visit me so we could spend some quality time together. She was at a spiritual turning point in her life and I knew this visit was no coincidence. It was part of the transformation she was experiencing. She had asked that we spend some time together in spirit, so I suggested we meditate together in nature. So off we went to my favorite park.

When we got to the park, we walked over to the pond. I love it there. The ducks, turtles, birds, and ripples of the water always make it a special place to meditate. As we walked down one of the nature trails, I asked her to choose a bench to sit on where we would begin our time in spirit together. Again, it was no coincidence that she chose one of my favorite benches under a beautiful tree that in summer has long vines of leaves that sway beautifully in the wind. I had sat there many times before and received some beautiful messages, and even channeled some heart-warming poetry.

After giving Ashley a short lesson on meditation, we both sat in silence. I could hear the swaying of the vines and the rippling water as we sat in perfect stillness. All around us became white noise as we met in divine consciousness, where there was no separation between us, only oneness. After about fifteen minutes we broke from our silence and I asked Ashley to choose another spot where we could go into the silence. I did this on purpose so that she would learn to trust her own intuition as to where the Divine wanted us next.

After a short walk on the trail she selected a picnic table that overlooked the pond on the other side of the park. Neither one of us knew that it was there, in that spot, where the stillness would take us to a much deeper place of existence and knowing. Ashley decided to sit on the side of the table that faced the water and I decided to sit on the other side of the table. I gently took my journal out and gazed at the water. After several minutes we both sat in silence, becoming one with the water and entering the stillness with the Divine. After some time, something amazing happened: I channeled words from Ashley's Soul. They were words I was to share with her that would hold special meaning. The words flowed into a poem describing her experience as she connected with the stillness of the water. I had no idea that what I was writing was being experienced by her at the same time I wrote it. It was as if her Soul had taken hold of my pen and hand to capture what turned out to be a deep, spiritual experience for her. These are the words her Soul whispered to me:

As she sits near the water,

Her hair glistens in the sun and the wind blows.

I hear God's breath whispering, "My Child, I am here with you."

Her Heart and Soul are so intent on remembering and reuniting
with that place of pure bliss and love,

Yet her fears and doubts hold her back from hearing God's words,
but they are so clear to me…

"You are special," "I love you," and "It's time to awaken and embrace
your divine purpose in life."

She sits and ponders, hoping to see a glimpse of what could be;
what God's breath and love feel like.

I see the gateway of spirit opening and touching her heart.

The door opens… and she walks through.

The new journey has begun…

On the other side of the table, Ashley stared at the water. At the same moment that I wrote these words for her, a group of gnats flew over the water and formed a symbol in the water. Yes, you guessed it… an eye. "It was God's eye," she said to me later. As she looked into this sacred eye, the answers flowed. She had come on this trip in search of answers. There was something troubling her heart and there were choices she had to make. Some of these questions were about her purpose in life and what actions she needed to take to let go of what was getting in the way. There was a light that emanated from the center of the eye that connected her to the voice of her Soul. In that short instant, but yet vast moment, the answers flooded her heart. She knew what she needed to do and she knew that her desire to help transform lives would manifest through her healing gifts. Healing was her *divine truth*; she just needed to surrender to the *how* and the *when* those healing gifts would emerge as her *divine purpose* vocation. In that moment, *just being* was what was called for.

Just as Ashley was able to keep her channel open to her *divine purpose*, let's help you practice keeping yours open as well. You can record the following meditation so you can close your eyes while you listen to it.

Find a place where you can sit quietly for ten to fifteen minutes. Sit comfortably —with your feet flat on the floor and your hands on your knees with palms facing up. If you're an experienced meditator, use whatever position is most comfortable to you. When you're ready, please move to the meditation.

Guided Meditation: Connecting with Your Inner Sanctuary

Close your eyes and take several deep breaths. Breathe in slowly through your nose and breathe out slowly through your mouth.

Drop into your heart center and feel surrounded by eternal love. You are this love. Imagine an all-seeing eye sitting in the center of your heart. This eye is the window to your Soul. In the center of the eye is a doorway. It leads to a room where you will meet your divine creator, the one who is ready to assist you with your divine purpose, your vocation in life.

You open the door and walk through. You are met by your divine creator. Take a moment to feel the presence of this part of you. What do you feel in this moment? **{Pause for a moment.}**

In the center of the room is an ornate table covered in gold leaf. Your divine creator takes your hand and asks you to walk towards the table. The table has the symbol of the all-seeing eye imprinted in its center. There is a clear crystal orb that sits in the center of the eye.

Your divine creator asks you to pick up the crystal orb in your hands, and so you do. Place the orb against your heart and allow it to open your channel. Allow the energy of the orb to immerse you in divine love and healing. **{Pause for a moment and embrace this love and healing.}**

Your divine creator is holding a magic wand. This wand is accessible to you to manifest your Soul's purpose. Your divine creator tells you that the orb holds a message for you about your divine purpose. You take the wand in your hand and tap the orb to retrieve your message. Look into the orb to receive your message. It may be a word, symbol, or feeling.

Just be in allowance. Immerse yourself in the stillness of the orb to receive your message. **{Pause for a moment.}**

When you feel complete, place the orb back on the table and thank your divine creator for this blessing. Walk through the doorway of your all-seeing eye and return to the present.

When you're ready, slowly open your eyes.

Take a moment to journal about what you just experienced. Write down any feelings, messages, etc. that feel significant and relevant to your *divine purpose*. How did it feel to open your channel in this way? Write down any observations that will help you continue keeping your channel open to receiving messages about your *divine purpose* and vocation.

Discovering Your Divine Purpose

> *When you do your purpose-work, your heart just sings and soars, and you feel like you have a never-ending flow of energy.*

Now that you've tasted your *divine purpose*, let's go a little deeper. *Divine purpose* is driven by a passion so deep that performing this work feels seamless and effortless. Instead of draining you, it fills you and nourishes your mind, body, and spirit. When you do your purpose-work, your heart just sings and soars, and you feel like you have a never-ending flow of energy. In fact, your reservoir of passion ignites such fire within you that you have to force yourself to rest your body.

Are you ready to have a life in which your mind and heart are aligned with your Soul's purpose? If so, it's time for you to commit to doing just that. Drop into your heart center right now and make a commitment to embrace your *divine purpose*. It's time to surrender to your vocation in life. The day I decided to commit to living on purpose, everything changed for me. When you commit to your purpose on a Soul level, you feel the relentless courage of the *spiritual warrior* within you. If you saw the movie *Braveheart* with Mel Gibson, you know what I mean about having relentless courage. His dying word in the film was "Freedom." This is what you get when you surrender to your Soul's purpose: freedom—freedom to live the life you desire and deserve, loving, joyful, and abundant in all aspects.

Sometimes you need a gentle nudge to let go of the fear that holds you back from embracing who you really are. In my case, I was on my way to Puerto Rico with my parents in 2011. They were so happy they were returning to their homeland, the origins of my ancestral healing lineage of the *curanderos*, or what you might call a medicine man or folk healer in English. I hadn't been there in several years and I was excited about having a week off from work just relaxing and spending time with family. As I sat on the plane and connected with the Divine, I was told that before I returned to the States I must visit the rainforest, *El Yunque*. Its name comes from the Taino Indian spirit Yuquiyú, and means "forest of clouds." I had always felt a pull to this sacred land, but didn't understand my connection to it until this trip.

173

A day after landing on the island, I lost the hearing in my left ear. The ears are the channel for what is called *clairaudience*, the ability to hear God's words, the messages from the Divine. There was no denying that this was happening for a reason. What was it that I didn't want to hear? What was it that I had been ignoring or resisting? I was soon to find out.

I told my parents that we needed to go to the rainforest. Needless to say, I was in no shape to make the trip without all my senses, so off I went to the doctor. The doctor told me I had allergies and that they had formed pockets of wax in my left ear. He sent his nurse into the examination room to remove the wax. She told me I might feel a little faint, and if I did, I should let her know. As soon as she removed the wax, I became very faint, so she gave me an alcohol pad to place near my nose, and as I inhaled it, back into my body I came. The feeling of fainting is the same as the one you get when your spirit lifts upward or partially leaves your body because of some terrible pain or trauma. I needed to get grounded right away, and the alcohol did the trick. Grounding is critical to your ability to bring the seeds of creation into existence, be it through a book, a job, or whatever it is you desire to manifest. (More on grounding at the end of the chapter in the rituals section.)

As soon as I was mended, I told my parents we needed to go the rainforest. I wasn't going to be on the island much longer and I knew I couldn't leave without making this trip. My parents lovingly indulged me and said they would accompany me. I told them I needed to meditate alone, but they insisted they needed to be within eyesight of me. After we spent some time together exploring and reading about the ancient trees in this sacred place, I wandered off to find my meditation spot. I found this beautiful brown, orange, and green-colored tree near the entrance of the rainforest that was calling my name. My parents managed to find a nice little bench nearby where they could keep an eye on me. As I closed my eyes and connected with these magnificent creatures, I could feel the land pulsating and the beat of the Souls of my ancestors as they had walked this land in ancient times. When I stepped into this sacred, deep container of divine consciousness, my ancestors spoke to me. This is what they had to say on this blessed day:

> As the morning glory rises, so do the spirits of Mother Earth and the kindred ones—those who walked these lands in times before. This was sacred land and still is. Feel the call of the spirits. They call for love, connection, and reunion of spirit. It is a time of remembrance of what once was and now needs to awaken—the white, sacred lands fertile with life, love, and all the elements: water, fire, air, and earth.

Now it will awaken once again—to a time of newness, of love, of *divine light*. Come and experience the sounds of the rainforest—the sounds of the Puerto Rican parrot, the birds, the lizards, the coqui—they sing to Mother Earth and bring love and fertile energy for healing our forest in the clouds. Sing to me—the song of joy, love, and oneness with life—oneness with the divine spirit, oneness with God. I hear the call of the parrot, I hear the call of the coqui. Sing together now to show your love to Mother Earth. She is sacred and needs your love.

"As you speak, I listen. How may I serve?" I asked.

We ask you to shine your light on your brethren; your tribe awaits your arrival. You come from a long lineage of curanderos and it's time to embrace your *divine purpose* as a healer and teacher of our ancient ways that have been a part of you for thousands of years. We celebrate you as you listen to the call of our Soul.

When I finished meditating, I approached my parents with a big smile on my face. My parents didn't consciously know what had just transpired, but at a deeper Soul level they knew that something significant had just occurred. I felt complete. This experience had opened the door for a deeper embodiment of my *divine purpose*.

I'm so glad that I had enough courage and persistence to answer the call of the Divine on that day. For so long my Soul had been yearning for this deeper experience. Yet in the past I had been scared to hear these voices because those who didn't understand might think I was crazy. That's why I had subconsciously plugged up my ear with wax. Being me had not felt safe for so long, but as I was held in this deep and powerful container of my Soul family, that fear melted away. We'll get more into healing your fears of your *divine purpose* in the next section. For now let's focus on helping you tap into your Soul's consciousness so you can gain a deeper understanding of your own *divine purpose* and vocation.

We're going to start with a meditation and then take you into an exercise in which you get to create a list of vocations and prioritize them. You can record the meditation so you can close your eyes while you listen to it. Sit comfortably where you won't be disturbed—with your feet flat on the floor and your hands on your knees with palms facing up. If you're an experienced meditator, please use whatever position is most comfortable to you.

Begin with a deep breath, breathing in slowly through your nose and exhaling slowly through your mouth. With each exhale, breathe out the sound of the heart center, the "Ahhhhhhhh" sound, releasing any tension and stress. Do this three times before you begin the guided meditation.

Guided Meditation: Connecting with Your Divine Purpose

Imagine you are in a sacred temple made of stone. You are ascending a spiral staircase. Up and up you go, focusing on your breath as you take each step. You can sense a beautiful uplifting energy coming over you as you ascend the staircase. Up and up and up you go, feeling lighter and more relaxed.

As you reach the top of the stairs, you see a big wooden door. You open the door and walk through. You see a beautiful white building made of marble. The front of the building has beautiful tall pillars and there is a huge archway in the front. You walk to the archway and are met by your Higher-Self. You are told by your Higher-Self that you are entering the Akashic records. This is where all the past, present, and future records of your life exist.

Your Higher-Self walks you into a brightly lit room and asks you to sit at a small table. The room is radiating in a luminous blue light. The light flows in through the top of your head and fills every part of your body, every cell of your being. You feel peaceful and serene. Your Higher-Self comes over to the table, bringing you a big book from the Akashic library, and places it in front of you. There are symbols on the cover that your Soul recognizes. As you place your hands on the front cover, the symbols transfer onto the palms of your hands, and a beautiful green light radiates from your hands and into your heart space.

*Set an intention within your heart to receive whatever information is important to receive in this moment about your divine purpose. It can be a direct answer to what your divine purpose is or a clue or action you must take to embrace and commit to your purpose on a deeper Soul level. {**Pause for a moment to set your intention.**}*

You are feeling incredibly loved. You know this is your moment to open the book. You randomly open the big tome. Take a deep breath and allow the words, images, and feelings to enter your heart center. What does this page hold for you about your *divine purpose? {**Pause and stay here for as long as you need to as you receive the download of information about your divine purpose.**}*

When you are complete, your Higher-Self comes over to walk you out of the Akashic library. You thank the Divine and your Higher-Self and follow them to the entrance archway. As you walk through the archway you are transported back to the stone temple. You walk through the wooden door and descend the steps. As you reach the bottom, you feel more present in your body. You feel every part of you coming back to the present moment.

When you feel ready, slowly open your eyes.

Now would be a good time to journal about your experience. What messages did you receive about your *divine purpose* (vocation)? You may still be processing what just happened, and more memories may come later, but for now jot down anything significant. You'll be using some of this information in the exercise that follows. Before you begin the exercise, it is helpful for you go back to your *divine truths* that you discovered in chapter 4. *What are the divine gifts you were born with?* You may find it helpful to refer to the **Canvas of Your Soul** and see what you wrote in the **Truth** section 4 area. Find a sheet of paper to write on or use your journal to capture your answers in the exercise.

Journaling Exercise

1. Make four columns. Label the first column "My Divine Truths (Gifts)." Label the next column "My Divine Purpose/Vocation(s)." Label the next column "My Fears," and label the last column "Origins of this Fear."

2. Go back to what you wrote in chapter 4 about your *divine truths*, your divine gifts. Check out what you wrote in section 4 of the **Truth** section of the **Canvas of Your Soul**. Write down the list of divine gifts you identified from your work in that chapter and place those in the first column.

3. Based on your journaling from the Akashic meditation above, list the vocations that came through from the meditation and write those in column two. Don't try to prioritize or combine them yet. Just write down what came through. Say the first vocation on the list out loud. Stop and feel how the word or words resonate in your body. Continue down the list saying each vocation

and stopping to feel it resonate. Asterisk or circle each vocation that reso-nates with you. Use your body to help you find the resonance. You may feel a tingling on the top of your head (in your crown), or in your heart or in your abdomen when you say a particular word. That's a sign that you're on the right track with your *divine purpose* vocations.

4. Staying with the second column, prioritize and categorize your vocations. If you have a list of five to ten items, narrow that down to no more than four vocations. Ideally you want to end up with one ideal vocation and two or three secondary ones. One way to narrow down the list is to weigh each word against each of the others. It helps to number them. Mark the ones that feel like they could be a primary one for you. For example, if "Teacher" or "Coach" appears on your list, and throughout your life you have taught, mentored, or coached others, that might be a logical candidate for a primary vocation. How do you know? Your vocations usually arise naturally from within you. When you do them you feel uplifted, joyous, in your divine zone. You don't necessarily have to have done them formally; you might have practiced them informally.

5. Narrow your list of primary vocations down to one. You can do this by com-paring each primary vocation to each of the others and circling the one that resonates the most with each comparison. For example, let's say you have four primary vocations circled. Number them from one to four. Then compare #1 to #2. Of those two vocations, circle the one that resonates more. Next com-pare #1 to #3 and #1 to #4; #2 to #3 and #2 to #4; and #3 to #4, each time cir-cling the vocation that resonates more. Count how many times each vocation was circled. The vocation you circled the most is your ideal vocation.

6. Go back to your full list and see what other vocations might now serve as secondary vocations. For example, if "Teaching" is your ideal vocation, your secondary vocation might relate to a specific audience you do that with, such as teaching children or teaching in corporate environments. Narrow down your secondary vocations to no more than three.

7. Now you should have one ideal vocation and two or three secondary voca-tions. Review the list one by one again. Say each vocation out loud and see if you feel any resistance or fear associated with it. Notice where in your body you feel any resistance or fear. In column three, "My Fears," list any fears that you feel rising to the surface. And in column four, note any comments

or thoughts about where this fear might be coming from. Did someone say something to you as a child that makes you believe you can't achieve this? Did you have some negative experience around this gift? Anything you feel or remember about the origin of the fear can be helpful. If nothing comes, that's okay, too. We'll get to releasing fears in the meditation in the next section. Don't forget to include these vocations on the **Canvas of Your Soul** in section 6 of the **Light** section.

Healing the Fears that Hold You Back from Your Divine Purpose

The next question is "What is holding you back from living your *divine purpose*?" Most likely the answer is rooted in fear—fear of the unknown, fear of change, fear of navigating into the unknown. The truth is you don't need to navigate anything. Your Soul is the navigator. All you need to do is surrender to that part of you that already knows the way forward. In surrendering to your Soul, you embrace the fear. This means you spend time with your fear so you can observe it and become its witness. As you observe yourself having this experience of fear, your true essence (the loving compassionate essence that you are) comes through to melt the fear away and help you transcend it.

Remember the *divine warrior* we spoke of in chapter 2. This is one of the qualities of the *divine warrior*: they're able to feel the fear, yet do what is calling them anyway, because they have an unstoppable faith that propels them forward. Sometimes all you need is one small step forward.

"Faith is taking the first step even when you don't see the whole staircase."
~Martin Luther King Jr.

I know that sometimes even taking that first step can be terrifying. That's when surrounding yourself with like-minded people who can help you through that first step becomes paramount. Find someone who is willing to support and love you no matter what. My mother is one of my greatest cheerleaders. I remember many times when she would say to me, "*Pa'lante. No te dejes caer. Tú eres guerrera como yo.*" This means "Keep moving forward and don't let yourself fall down. You're a warrior like me." Her words always reminded me of the strength and courage I knew existed within me, that *divine warrior* that exists within each and every one of us. God created us to hold such strength within our spiritual and human existence. I'm sure you've experienced that part of you during difficult or challenging times in your life. Go to that place to find the courage to take that first step. Step after step lead to success and more success.

Taking small steps is extremely important, especially if what God is asking you to do feels big and overwhelming. Brian Whetten, a gifted coach, says, "The bigger the purpose, the smaller the steps." Remember this important point. Start small and build your purposeful life one brick at a time.

If you've already taken steps towards living on purpose, then perhaps you're facing fears about not being accepted and judgments from others. What others say to you is not about you, but about themselves. We are all mirrors of each other. So when someone criticizes your actions, they are just reflecting back to you that part of themselves that holds pain about being judged—that part of themselves that they don't love. What happens outside of you is of no consequence to you. Only you (guided by your Heart and Soul) know the right path for you. Never let someone else's pain or fear hold you back from following your dreams and shining your magnificence to the world.

As you discover your gifts and *divine purpose*, there is no question that at some point your ego is going to present itself masked as something else. This happened to me multiple times during my journey, and I'm sure my ego will pop its head up again at some point, because as we grow and expand we are faced with deeper layers of healing around our core issues. You're like an onion. You're removing layers to get to your core essence, the real you. This is where your spiritual muscle and discipline come in. Only as you continue to work on yourself can you discern when those moments of illusion and fear rear their ugly heads to hold you back from your true magnificence.

Worthiness has been one of my core issues. This issue continues to surface in different areas of my life, including my gifts and *divine purpose*. There were even moments as I wrote this book when I questioned my worthiness. As I dug deeper, the question that rose to the surface was "Am I worthy of these gifts when at times I have mistrusted my own divinity?" As I heard these words in my mind, all I could feel was guilt and shame. In mistrusting my divinity, I was also mistrusting the God within me. That guilt and shame wasn't allowing me to fully embrace my *divine purpose*. Even though I knew that God chose me to do this work, this wounded part of me wasn't allowing me to embrace the real me, the one God created to be a healer and spiritual teacher. But this is where discernment comes in. Learn to discern the difference between the voice of your ego and the voice of your Soul. Your ego always tries to keep you separated from that divine part of you that is whole and exists in a vibration of eternal love. In my case, my ego tried to forge a separation between my humanity and divinity, using my doubts about my worthiness as an excuse for not accepting my gifts and *divine purpose*.

It was during a birthday excursion that I was able to heal this part of me. When I look back on my life and this experience, I can see how God divinely orchestrated all the events that led to this trip. I was having dinner with my good friend Dawn, and she asked me if I had thought about what I wanted to do to celebrate my birthday. It was no coincidence that she was bringing this up now. I had been thinking about it quite a bit. I had recently seen an email about someone who offered dolphin excursions in Hawaii, but the price tag was just out of my league. However, I put the intention out to the Universe to make it possible for me to spend my birthday with the dolphins. So when my friend asked me what I wanted to do, the answer came immediately. "I want to spend my birthday with the dolphins," I said.

It was so funny. She looked at me and said, "I just received an email about a woman who does this where I live in Florida." Dawn came over and sat next to me while we searched the Internet to find this woman. I was in awe as the Universe responded to my Soul's calling. I love how the Universe conspires to move you forward once you put your intention out there. As soon as we found her website, I wrote down the information and immediately started to plan this trip that I knew in my heart would be transformational. This trip was a rite of passage for me. God was asking me to step fully into my purpose-work. It was time to stop hiding the real me. This trip was divinely orchestrated to help me transcend those fears that were still holding me back from being the real ME—the ME God created ME to be.

I knew I would need some strong support from family and friends as I experienced this rite of passage, so I invited some close friends and family. I also knew that whoever said yes was also saying yes to their own rite of passage.

The boat that took us out to be with the dolphins could only hold seven people, including our captain and guide. Five came forward and said yes to my invitation: my friend Dawn; her friend Teena, whom I had never met before; my cousin Betsy; my younger brother Joe; and his fiancée, Lauren. The boat was now full with the seven Souls chosen to be on this trip. Before our human existence, our Souls had made a divine appointment to meet together at this time to create the sacred space for new beginnings in our lives.

After several days of holding this trip in meditation, I was ready to call the woman whom many called "The Dolphin Whisperer." As soon as I heard her voice, I knew she was the one to guide me on this rite of passage. As we spoke, she reminded me that I was entering a new phase of my life—the *Crone*—the wise, ancient one. She told me that we should all think about the blessing we wanted to receive from the dolphins and create that intention prior to our arrival. I knew for me this was to be a moment of complete surrender.

Several months later I arrived in Key West, Florida, where my friend Dawn would host me and my family for what would be a life-changing trip. My Soul had waited for this divine moment to help me understand how worthy I truly was just by being alive in this human body. Worthiness is your birthright as a spiritual being having a human experience. When you learn to love yourself as God loves you, feelings of unworthiness disappear. I spent the first two days of my trip enjoying the ocean and the new surroundings with those I loved. As I meditated in preparation for our boat excursion with the dolphins, I kept seeing the eye of a dolphin, but didn't know why until the day of our excursion.

On the day after my birthday, we all headed down to the pier with great anticipation in our hearts. The weather had been unsettled, so we delayed our excursion by a day. Everyone was worried that it might rain, but the Divine kept telling me to trust that everything would be perfect, and it was. We had 80-degree weather and sunny skies all day long. It was perfect for boating. We all got on the boat and readied ourselves for our day together.

Shortly after leaving the dock, our guide stopped the boat to explain how our day would go. She would be taking us to areas where she knew the dolphins liked to play. She explained that when the dolphins rise and make eye contact, that is when the blessing occurs. Here was the connection with the dolphin eye I kept seeing in meditation. She explained that they didn't need to make eye contact, so if they did, it was significant. She also explained that dolphins react to emotion. When you show true emotion that comes from your heart and not your ego, they happily grace you with their presence. I knew they would be getting tons of that from me, as I had already started my day with tears and emotions rippling up to the surface.

The trip began with some great music and the group howling as we went under a bridge. As we glided into the open sea, we were all intrigued and excited, but also wondering what the day would bring. We stopped in peaceful waters and gathered around our guide and captain. We held hands as she guided us in speaking our intentions for the day. There were many words spoken of new beginnings, celebration, freedom, surrender, gratitude, love, and trust. When we got to my brother Joe, I melted with emotion. He had always been there for me, just like other members of my family—solid, supportive, and always loving me without question. He had originally decided to be there for me, to show me his support, but had realized as we gathered together that it was much more than that. He, too, would be starting a new life with his fiancé, and this trip was his rite of passage to this new life. Needless to say, when it was my turn, number seven, the last one to speak, I had to compose myself as the tears rolled down my face. "I want to be free to be me and surrender fully to my purpose-work. God chose me to bring my healing gifts to the world and I want to be that vessel of *divine love* that I was intended to be. I'm so grateful for being here with all of you and I open my heart to receive." And with those words came more tears, all perfect, because the brain waves of our dolphin friends reacted to the heart-felt emotions.

As our captain gave her signature call to the dolphins with the engine of her boat, we all quietly looked out at the water with anticipation. She took us to the dolphin playground, but no dolphins. Off we went again in search of our dolphin Soul family. We tried the signature call again, and this time we saw several dolphins. Up came one, two, three dolphins, rising and making eye contact with other members of my tribe. We all watched as the dolphins continued to swim underneath our boat. It became a dance with Mother Ocean. I hadn't received eye contact yet, but the Divine told me to stay on the left side of the boat as that's where I would be making contact with my dolphin friends. Then it happened: three beautiful dolphins rising together in the water and making direct eye contact with me. I began sobbing with such gratitude and emotion. In that short moment, which seemed like an eternity, they pierced my heart and melted away that tiny speck of unworthiness that had been holding me back from being the real me. God and the dolphins had answered our prayers and graced us with healing, love, and new beginnings.

That trip was exactly what I needed. It opened the door to heal a part of me that was scared to fully step into my purpose-work. Love is the answer to all we seek. The *divine love* that I felt from my dolphin Soul family and those who shared this experience with me was exactly what I needed to heal that part of me that still felt separate from my *divine light*, my oneness with God. That tiny speck of fear within my heart was holding me back from committing, believing, and feeling worthy of my divine gifts and *divine purpose*. As I looked into the eyes of the dolphins, I remembered the wholeness, the *divine love* that I am. That one short moment of divine connection transformed me forever. Your healing can take many forms. It is your Soul that knows what you need in the exact moment that you need it. When you learn to listen and respond without question, the rest takes cares of itself.

The meditation that follows helps you awaken to the *divine purpose* within you. In the meditation we'll be helping you surrender to your Soul and the truth within you. Take this time now, before you begin, to ask the Divine to help you bring all that is blocking you from embracing your *divine purpose* to your conscious mind, so you can heal and transform it.

You can record the following meditation so you can close your eyes while you listen to it. For the audio version, visit **www.UnmaskingYourSoul.com/Meditations.** Sit comfortably where you won't be disturbed—with your feet flat on the floor and your hands on your knees with palms facing up. If you're an experienced meditator, use whatever position is most comfortable to you. When you're ready, please move to the meditation.

Guided Meditation: Embracing Your Divine Purpose

Breathe slowly, inhaling through your nose and exhaling through your mouth. As you breathe, focus on your breath and feel with every breath the relaxation of your mind, body, and spirit. Just focus on your breath and let thoughts pass as they may.

See yourself taking a stroll in a green meadow. As the morning mist rises, you look to the sky and see a white Pegasus flying your way. It is flapping its wings vibrantly and it lands right in front of you. It leans down as an invitation for you to get on its back, and so you do. It whirls you away into the sky and you feel the wind blowing softly across your face and body—the sensation feels dynamic, yet peaceful. Telepathically the Pegasus is telling you how loved you are by Source... by the Creator... by God. **{Pause briefly.}**

When you look down, you see you are travelling over the Nile River. There are several ancient feluccas (small vessels) travelling down the river. You can feel that the spirits on these boats are your ancestors accompanying you on this journey of healing, each one surrounding you with their loving and protective light. You feel so honored by their presence and thank them for helping you feel safe, loved, and protected.

The Pegasus flies over the river and lands in front of a temple. It is the Temple of the Egyptian Goddess Isis, on the island of Philae. As you dismount the Pegasus, your breath is taken away by the majestic presence of this temple. You can already feel the magnificence of the divine love present here. It is the love Isis shared with her beloved Osiris. Feel this love in your heart center for a moment. **{Pause briefly.}**

As you approach the entrance of the temple you notice the etchings of Isis and Osiris on the temple walls. You climb the staircase leading to the entrance, and as you do, you are met by two Egyptian guides, Priestess Negara and Helios. Telepathically they welcome you to the temple and signal you to follow, and so you do.

The guides lead you into the head of the temple—the holiest of rooms and a sacred sanctuary. There is a sacred altar in the middle of the room, and behind the altar is a round stargate.

Priestess Negara tells you it's time for you to travel through the stargate. This stargate is going to transport you to a past life when you once lived the divine purpose you're meant to live in this life. You will be taken to your past life so you can connect with this vibration and bring it back to this current time.

Priestess Negara invokes your Higher-Self to accompany you through the stargate. Your Higher-Self meets you at the gate and holds your hand as you walk through the portal together.

*As you walk through a tunnel of white light, you're transported to your past life. As you enter this past life, notice your surroundings. {**Pause seven seconds.**} Where are you? {**Pause seven seconds.**} What does it look like? {**Pause seven seconds.**} What year is it? {**Pause seven seconds.**} How are you dressed? {**Pause seven seconds.**} Are you a male or female? {**Pause seven seconds.**} What is your name? {**Pause seven seconds.**} How old are you? {**Pause seven seconds.**}*

*Let yourself be taken forward in this past life to a specific memory of you demonstrating the use of your gifts and divine purpose. Let yourself experience this scene for a moment and feel the specific vibration here. Your Higher-Self helps program this vibration into your being. Take a moment to allow this programming to take place. {**Pause briefly.**}*

*Now ask your Higher-Self how you are meant to serve and bring your gifts and divine purpose into the world. How are you meant to embody your Soul in this life? {**Pause for several minutes.**}*

Your Higher-Self tells you it's time to return and grabs your hand. You walk through the stargate together and return to the Temple of Isis. Your Higher-Self walks you into a sacred chamber. As you enter, you're met by several Egyptian guides: Priestess Negara, Isante, Helios, Osarte, Toras, Nefarte, and the Goddess Isis. They ask you to lie on a beautiful, ornate table made of marble and etched with colorful Egyptian hieroglyphics.

The guides take their places around you. Priestess Negara stands at your feet and the Goddess Isis stands behind your head. The other guides place themselves on each side of the table. Each of them has a healing staff at their side that has colorful hieroglyphics and crystals imbedded on the surface. They tap the healing staffs on the ground and energy radiates from the tips. The energy forms a healing grid around your body. Goddess Isis asks you to take a deep breath, and as you do, the energy from the healing staffs enters your crown. As the energy enters your body, it liquefies into a green, healing light, reaching every molecule and every cell of your being.

As the liquid light flows through every part of your body, you release all your fears about your divine purpose. You can see ripples and threads of energy being released as the green healing liquid moves through your being. As this is occurring, you can hear the guides and Isis chanting and calling your Soul. Release... release... release.

*Stay here for a moment to allow your body to absorb this liquid light as you release the fears surrounding your divine purpose. {**Pause for several minutes.**}*

When the healing completes its course, your Higher-Self comes forward to help you off the table. You take a moment to thank Isis, the guides, and the Divine for this amazing healing today. Your Higher-Self guides you to the exit of the temple and you descend the stairs.

*You get on your Pegasus friend who will return you to the green meadow where you began your journey today. As you fly over the Nile, you bow in gratitude to your ancestors. When you land on the ground, you take one last look at the beautiful blue sky and the yellow rays of the sun, taking in one last breath of the fresh air and letting it solidify your healing journey. Take a moment to integrate all that has happened. {**Pause to integrate.**}*

When you feel complete, slowly come back into your body and open your eyes.

Now that you've completed the guided meditation, take some time to do some journaling. Spend about ten to fifteen minutes in a quiet place where you won't be disturbed answering the questions below. You can put on some soothing music or light a candle or incense to support you as you write. Just write from your Heart and Soul and the rest will follow.

Journaling Exercise

1. How did it feel entering the Temple of Isis? Did anything feel familiar to you? If so, jot down what those things were.

2. When you stepped through the stargate, what did you notice about yourself? Could you see or sense anything about yourself in that past life? If so, write anything you remember about where you were, the year, how you were dressed, your gender, your name, your age, etc.

3. How did you feel, or what did you sense or experience as your Higher-Self was connecting you to the vibration of your *divine purpose* in that past life?

4. When you asked your Higher-Self about your *divine purpose*, what messages or guidance did you receive? And how about the embodiment of your Soul? Write down any specific messages from your Soul related to this experience.

5. How did you feel during the healing from Isis and the Egyptian guides? How about after the healing—any other messages or guidance that came through from your Soul? If so, jot down anything of significance.

After journaling, continue working on the **Canvas of Your Soul.** (You can download the PDF at **www.UnmaskingYourSoul.com/Blueprint**.) Pick phrases, words, or symbols and put them on section 6 of the *Light* part of your roadmap. Make this canvas your own piece of artwork that represents the journey we're taking together in this book. You can color, paint, or even cut images from magazines that depict the messages and insights you received in this chapter on *embracing your divine purpose*. You don't need to be a professional artist to do this. Just let your Soul express through you as it wants to. This will become the vision board of your Soul's unmasking, a precious gift to you from your *divine creator*.

Five Rituals to Awaken Your Divine Purpose Muscle

The rituals below are meant to help you awaken your *divine purpose* muscle. You can repeat any of the rituals that follow and the exercises and guided meditations earlier in the chapter as many times as you like. With each repetition you go deeper in discovering your *divine creator*, the one who helps you manifest your vocation in life.

Before you begin, create your sacred space and take some deep breaths to relax your mind and body. Connect with your Soul as you enter this sacred space. Use this invocation, if you like, to prepare your space:

> I invoke the *divine creator* within me to bring forth understanding, healing, and guidance as I seek to embrace my *divine purpose*. I open my heart to receive all I need in this moment. May I be protected and surrounded in God's eternal love as I continue forth on my journey of self-discovery, allowing my Soul to guide me home. May it be so forevermore.

1. Before we begin with any of the other rituals, let's help you ground yourself. When you're not grounded, it's more difficult to formulate the messages from your Soul and make them actionable. You'll know that you're ungrounded if you feel

lightheaded, scattered, or unable to focus. Let's begin with some simple grounding techniques that you can use daily. Then, in ritual 4, you'll learn how to ground the action steps you create for your *divine purpose* so you can manifest them into the physical plane.

a. If you're in a place that is experiencing warm weather, going outside in nature and walking barefoot on the grass or lying on it is a good way to get grounded. Leaning your back against a tree or hugging a tree is a fabulous way to get immediately connected to the Earth.

b. You can use various stones to help you ground. Hold them in your hands as you meditate, or even better, carry them in your pocket or in a pouch somewhere on your body. Stones like petrified wood, black onyx, black obsidian, and hematite are good choices. Allow the stones to choose you. If you have a gem or rock store near you, go in person to buy your stones. Allow yourself to pick up stones and feel their resonance. You will know when the right ones have found you.

c. Grounding has to do with your connection to the Earth, Mother Earth, Gaia; so any instruments and music that are earthy are helpful in getting you grounded. Anything with drumming suits this purpose very well. You can put some drumming music on and dance to the beat of the drums. The goal is to feel yourself very connected to Mother Earth as you stomp and feel the music within you going down through your feet and connecting you to the ground. If you're like me, you might have a djembe, bongos, or conga drums in your home. If so, sitting to drum is also another fantastic way to get grounded.

d. If none of the techniques mentioned above appeal to you, or you need to get grounded inside your home or office, use visualization as an alternative. Find a place where you can sit and relax, or you can do these standing as well:

> **Option 1:** Imagine you are a tree. Your torso is the trunk of the tree and your arms are the branches. Your feet are the roots. See your feet becoming expansive roots. As the roots extend from your feet, they go deeper and deeper into the Earth. Continue seeing the roots of your feet going deeper until they reach the center of the Earth. When you reach the center of the Earth, wrap your roots around the core of the planet. Stay there for a while, allowing the energy of Mother Earth to come up through the roots of your feet and ground you in this physical existence.

> **Option 2:** Drop down into the bottom of your spine. See yourself connecting a cord to the bottom of your spine and allowing this cord to penetrate the

ground and go deep within the Earth. The thicker you can imagine this cord, the better grounded you'll become. You can practice making this cord two or three times bigger than your physical body. If you're serving many people, over time you will want to practice making this cord much bigger than your original one. Perhaps the cord becomes as big as your house. When you have your cord ready, connect it with the center of the Earth and wrap the cord around the core of the planet. Stay there for a while allowing the energy of Mother Earth to come up through the cord and ground you in this physical existence.

2. Now let's help you get into a space of knowing, where you can connect with your Higher-Self and see what your *divine purpose* is. If you already know your *divine purpose*, take it a step further and allow your Soul to guide you on the next steps of your journey. Find a quiet place to sit and relax. Place your hands on your knees with palms facing up, take a couple of deep breaths, and sit back and allow yourself to go to a deeper place within you. You can read the meditation and follow along, or you can record the words and listen to them as you sit and relax.

> *Take a deep breath and allow all your thoughts to leave one by one as you focus on each breath you inhale and exhale. With each breath you feel your entire body relaxing: your head, neck, and shoulders... all relaxing. As you continue downward, your arms, hands, and torso are all relaxing. You feel lightness going down into your legs, ankles, feet, and toes. All the events from the day are being released from your being down a cord from the bottom of your spine into divine Mother Earth. As these lower-vibration energies go down the cord, she recycles them into new, higher, more vibrant energies.*

> *Imagine you're walking in a beautiful valley. You're surrounded by lush greenery, trees, plants, and expansive hills that reach far into the vista. You smell the poignant fragrance of lemon drop flowers so sharp that you can taste the tartness in your mouth. You stop to touch the beautiful flowers and you bring into your body a beautiful golden light that ignites your solar plexus, right over your abdomen. You feel so strong and ignited in passion. As you continue walking, you see a group of butterflies heading your way. They come to greet you personally. Seven blue butterflies land on you, gently fluttering their wings. With each movement of their wings you feel a surge of blue light entering your throat and all that was there is cleared. You feel a warmth filling you up and your voice feels complete and bursting with expression. Natural sounds and tones emanate from you as you connect with the expression of your divine purpose.*

You see a bench and go to it and sit down. Your Higher-Self comes to greet you and sits beside you. Notice what your Higher-Self looks like and how you feel as it sits next to you. Take a moment to remember this feeling so you can come back here whenever you like. {Pause.}

Ask your Higher-Self how you're meant to serve in this life. Pause for a moment and just be in allowance. Ask about your divine purpose and the next steps you should take as you go deeper into your purpose-work. Your Higher-Self may give you an image, whisper words, or just give you a feeling or a knowing of what this is. Just pause for a moment to receive this divine knowing into your being. {Pause.}

When you feel you've received what you're meant to receive in this moment, see yourself merging with your Higher-Self. See it sitting inside your body. As this merging happens, you feel you now see through the eyes of your divine expression, your breath, heart, and Soul all melded in oneness. Believe and know that you will now be guided by your Higher-Self in all you do. Allow yourself to feel and integrate this experience into your being for a moment. {Pause.}

When you feel complete, thank the Divine for this sacred experience and slowly return to the present moment. When you're ready, you may come back and open your eyes.

You may want to spend some time reflecting and journaling about this experience. Continue to pay attention to the signs and messages that continue to be revealed to you about your *divine purpose*. Remember, your Soul communicates to you through your Higher-Self. Practice connecting with this part of you daily.

3. Throughout this chapter you had multiple opportunities to receive messages about your *divine purpose*. As I mentioned earlier in the chapter, it's important to take small steps forward. The bigger the purpose, the smaller those steps need to be, otherwise you'll find yourself feeling overwhelmed or even paralyzed in fear. I know; I've been there. So let's begin with some easy steps you can do daily to move forward in embracing your *divine purpose*.

   a. Concentrate on one vocation that you listed in the exercise earlier in the chapter. Let's say your vocation is coaching. Pick one thing you know you need to do to get your coaching vocation going. You might want to find a good coach who can certify you and give you some great tools for your coaching practice. Perhaps you need to promote yourself to attract new clients or expand your client base. One of the first things you need to do is figure out who you're serving. Think about who your client base is and what problems you can solve for them. Once you've spent a little time thinking about this, write your daily action list. You should try to do this first thing in the morning so you have time to take action throughout your day.

    i. Write down the vocation you're taking action on. For example, coaching, teaching, etc.

    ii. Pick one category of actions that you know you need to do in order to bring this vocation into being. For example, training, promotions, or defining your target market might be your action category.

    iii. List no more than two or three actions you can take today to start moving forward on that particular vocation and action category. For example, one of your actions might be to do some research online to find a good coaching certification program, or you might know someone you can call who can give you some recommendations. It's always better and faster to go to someone who has more experience in what you're trying to figure out, and ask for their help. There's no use reinventing the wheel. That can become quite frustrating and overwhelming.

    iv. When you have your two or three items, start taking action right away. You might want to block some time on your calendar when you will focus on one particular item. Try to spread them throughout your day so that it doesn't feel overwhelming. Some actions take five to ten minutes and others need more thought and time. Keep checking in with your Soul throughout the day for guidance.

4. Now that you've created your *divine purpose* vocation list and action steps, it's time to ground them so they can take form on the physical plane. You can repeat this ritual daily to help you ground your action steps. Make sure you're feeling calm and relaxed before you begin this ritual.

    a. **Choose what you want to ground.** Look at your vocation list and action steps. Pick something on your list that has a lot of energy associated with it, and perhaps is making you feel uncomfortable or fearful. Let's say you've decided you're going to take a six-month coaching certification course. You might have concerns about the time or financial investment required, or even worry about how good you'll be in this vocation. Once you've chosen what action to ground in this exercise, move on to the next step.

    b. **Write down the feelings.** Putting your worries and fears aside, start by writing down how you will feel once you accomplish this vocation or action step.

    c. **Surround the words or images with _divine love_.** Drop into your heart center and see or sense the words in the center of your heart. For example, if you want to ground yourself about the coaching certification program, you might place its name or an image of the coaching program in the center of your heart. Surround the name or image with pink light, seeing or sensing it surrounded by _divine love_. Continue doing this until you can clearly feel this center of eternal love radiating in your heart center.

    d. **Surround the words or images with feelings of accomplishment.** See yourself surrounding the words and images with the feelings you captured in step (b) above. You want to go beyond just imagining what it would feel like to achieve your action step; actually bring the feelings (using all of your senses) into your body as you see yourself accomplishing your action step or vocation. Feel the joy in every cell of your body. Feel the sense of accomplishment in your heart and in every molecule within you. Whatever feelings you jotted down in step (b), make sure to feel those profoundly within your being. You're imprinting a projection of having already accomplished this action step within you.

    e. **Ground the words or images.** Now see yourself attaching a red cord to these words or images that you placed in your heart center, and running this cord down into the center of the Earth. Go deeper and deeper until you reach the center of the Earth, then wrap the red cord around the Earth's core.

    f. **Release the words or images to the Divine.** Drop into your heart and see or sense yourself holding the words or images in your hands. See yourself reaching upward into the light as hands come down from the Divine to accept your offering. As you release the words or images to the Divine, you're trusting in and surrendering to how and when this will manifest. You can nourish your action steps daily by sending them love, but refrain from worrying about the how or when, as that will delay the outcome. When you feel complete, you can come back and open your eyes.

5. Meditate with my painting **_The Master Builder_**, shown at the end of the chapter, to help you reconnect with your _divine creator_, the one who helps you embrace your _divine purpose_. Each of my paintings was divinely channeled and holds messages and energetic impressions of the Soul that bring healing to the bearer. This particular painting holds vibrations of healing for those needing to remember their expression of _divine purpose_. This painting was inspired by my niece, Ashley, whom I wrote about earlier in the chapter. It brings together many powerful goddesses (Isis, Artemis, Aphrodite, and Sekhmet) to help you embrace and align with your Soul's purpose.

a. Close your eyes and take a breath... inhaling slowly through your nose and exhaling slowly through your mouth... and with each breath you take relax your mind, body, and spirit. Continue focusing on your breath... and with each breath allow your thoughts to pass freely... thought after thought... breath after breath... relaxing more and more deeply. Continue taking several more deep breaths. {**Repeat for one or two minutes.**}

b. Briefly open your eyes and observe the painting. Allow yourself to be taken on a journey into the painting. Look at the images and symbols, and allow your gaze to go to one focal point in the painting. Soften your gaze as you focus on this point of interest. Breathe in its energy, seeing the symbols, images, and colors in your mind's eye. Continue breathing in the energy... breath after breath, allowing you to feel and absorb the healing energy from this focal point.

c. With your next breath, listen to the voice of your Soul. What is it communicating? What messages do you hear or feel within you as you breathe in the energy of the painting? Pay attention to where the energy is going in your body. This gives you an indication of where in your body you may need to release old energy, traumas, or wounds. Continue breathing and just go into the stillness while you connect deeper within. Allow the healing energies of the painting to penetrate your mind, body, and spirit. {**Do this for two to five minutes.**} If you feel guided, you may continue repeating this step, changing to a different focal point in the painting each time. Again, allow yourself to breathe the images, symbols, colors, and healing energies into your being.

d. Don't forget to journal about anything of significance that comes up during this experience.

EILEEN ANÜMANI SANTOS, *THE MASTER BUILDER* C. 2012

The Master Builder is about manifesting your Soul's purpose and embodying who you really are—a divine being of light whose core essence is infinite love. As you surrender to the truth within you and connect with the wisdom of your light, you shed what holds you back and return to a healed state of being. The blue orb in the painting contains vibrations of truth, power, and wisdom. Take a moment to connect with these vibrations and breathe them into your heart center.

**Within you lies the WISDOM to your *DIVINE PURPOSE*.
BE STILL and know thy PURPOSE!**

The Emergence of Your Divine Voice
by Eileen Anümani Santos

Do you know that beneath the layers of fear of your unspoken truths sits your real voice—a *divine voice* that is more powerful and sacred than you can imagine?

There is no denying that as you awaken your heart and your Soul, my voice reverberates through your being.

You sit in the stillness of your heart and there I come to meet you in our sacred commune.

I place my hands on your higher heart and your Soul tells me you are ready.

I embrace you and anoint you with the light of my light.

As I place my hands on your throat, all that has been unspoken is released into my being.

I see your *divine voice* coming forth, wanting to be heard, wanting to be embraced by those you are meant to serve.

As I blow my divine breath on the note of your Soul, the voice of the real you emerges.

No longer is your *divine voice* hidden; it emerges blanketed in my love.

Now I may speak through you knowing that all you say vibrates in *divine love*, for it is through my eternal love that your *divine voice* has been born into existence.

CHAPTER 7

Soul Chamber VII: Finding Your Divine Voice

The spoken word illuminates a chasm within your spiritual body that is the cup of your Soul's vibration. When the notes of your Soul come together in oneness with the Universe, what emanates from you is your *divine voice*. When this occurs, every word spoken vibrates in the essence of your Soul and brings a distinctive quality of knowing, love, and harmony to those who witness you as the divine being you are. Can you imagine a life in which you no longer have to fear speaking your truth? Can you imagine a life in which every word you speak is a blessing to you and to everyone who witnesses you as you heed the call of your Soul? You can have this life as you find your *divine voice* and stand in your truth. This chapter will show you how to do that.

The center of your throat is the location of **Soul Chamber VII—Divine Voice,** the seventh of the Soul virtues that will be unmasked as you continue on your journey of wholeness. The mask associated with this seventh chamber is the **Mask of Lies.** The emotional state that underlies this mask is fear-based lies that are meant to hide truths that seem debilitating or too painful to accept or share with others. These lies are often rooted in feelings of unworthiness and an inability to embrace your power, which were discussed in chapters 2 and 3. In this case fear of disapproval is the underlying culprit. The more you feel you need approval from the outside world in all you say and do, the more difficult it is to stand in your truth and find your *divine voice.*

I am confident that you, just like me, can find your *divine voice.* This is one of the areas I struggled with most of my life, always pretending and saying what I thought others wanted to hear. I was always looking for outside approval. But one day it all began to click for me. Love was the answer. In chapter 1 we spoke of self-love, and it applies here as well. As you embrace and honor your divinity and love yourself as God loves you, there comes a point when there is no longer a choice between truth and lies; the choice automatically becomes TRUTH. Truth is the essence of becoming the real you, the authentic you, the purposeful and Soul-driven leader whom those you're meant to serve are seeking.

But beyond your physical voice there is something much deeper, more sacred about this chamber. In this chamber you find the portal that connects you to the voice of God. In your oneness with the Divine, you become the voice box for the Universe, allowing the Divine to communicate through you. The activation of this chamber is critical as you embark on your *divine purpose* work discussed in the previous chapter. Those you serve are looking for authentic leadership, which means you must "walk your walk" and not just "talk your walk." In other words, not only must you speak your truth, but your actions need to support what you say.

The archetype of this Soul chamber is the ***divine composer.*** Your *divine composer* helps you compose the words, actions, and life that are built on speaking your truth as well as the truth spoken through you by the Divine. You probably can see how this chamber builds on the work we did together in chapter 6 on your *divine purpose*. *Divine voice* gives the words and expression of the real, divine you to your *divine purpose* or vocation. Not only is this chamber about the divine spoken word taking place through you, but it is also about the divine spoken word that comes to you from your Higher-Self (the spiritual being through which your Soul communicates), spirit guides, and other celestial or divine beings who communicate with you throughout your journey.

Some call this *clairaudience*, or "clear-hearing." This is the ability to internally "hear" intuitive messages that come to you from your spiritual team as words, phrases, sounds, or even musical notes or lyrics. Your *divine composer* helps you decipher the meaning behind these intuitive messages. The more you practice deepening your spiritual muscle and maintaining a daily spiritual practice like meditation, the easier it is for you to distinguish your own voice from the voices of your spiritual team. The sacred symbol of the *divine voice* chamber is shown here.

Divine Voice Symbol

The Relationship between Divine Power and Divine Voice

Your ability to speak your truth is just as much connected to your *divine power* as it is to your *divine voice. Divine power* is about consciously choosing you above all else in your life. It's about loving yourself that much and putting yourself first, despite what others say or do. That is part of what you learn as you grow and deepen spiritually and fully step into your purpose-work. This means consciously choosing who and what surrounds you, and when the time comes, letting go of things and even relationships that no longer serve you. Letting go of my marriage was one of the most difficult yet illuminating experiences of my life. If you recall, it was my dream of awakening in which I heard God's voice that gave me the courage to take action, to leave something behind that had run its course. I had to learn to stand in my *divine power* so that I could then heal that part of me that would turn out to be one of my greatest gifts, my *divine voice.*

Yet for most of my life I hid behind the mask of lies. I pretended to be someone else I thought I needed to be so that others would approve of me. I behaved this way because I was acting out the moments of my life when I felt disempowered that I still carried with me. The abuse I experienced is an obvious example of being disempowered, but it can also stem from childhood experiences in which you were yelled at, hit, or controlled in some way by someone close to you. I've witnessed parents telling their children to only speak when spoken to. We can only imagine what that does to a child. What happens energetically is that you feel constriction in that part of your body where your *divine power* sits—in the abdomen, or the solar plexus. Just as this constriction forms in your abdomen (which eventually becomes illness in the body such as digestive disorders), it also forms a constriction in your throat. For me it felt like I was being strangled by the energy of my abuser so that the words wouldn't come out. I remember as a child I was so shy that I was even afraid to raise my hand in the classroom.

> *"Your pain is the breaking of the shell that encloses your understanding."*
> **~Kahlil Gibran**

After I left my unhealthy marriage, I began to heal all these wounds from my childhood, as well as remnants of wounds I carried in my cellular structure from other lives in which I experienced disempowerment. As always, when I was ready to heal this part of me, the Divine orchestrated the events that would help me do so.

One morning as I was checking my emails, I happened to see one about a concert that was being hosted by one of the holistic centers in my area. It was with a shaman who was visiting from California. He was a master at the didgeridoo and other indigenous instruments. I had never met this man, yet deep down I could feel our Souls were connected. I knew immediately I had to meet him and go to this concert. I ended up inviting one of my friends to go with me, and when I mentioned his name she knew exactly who he was. This shaman had lived in our area for several years but had relocated to California a few years back. He was returning to meet with his tribe here, and I knew I was in for a treat.

As my friend and I entered the retreat center, the shaman came over to say hello to my friend. She introduced us and I felt such warmth and love in his smile. As we entered the hall to take our seats, I noticed the beautiful altar the shaman had created on the ground. There were various instruments (didgeridoos, flutes, drums, rattles) and many sacred objects on it. He began by sharing his story with all of us, and what a wonderful storyteller he was. His humor created a beautiful, safe, lighthearted, sacred container for all of us who were there to witness his divine gifts and receive healing.

As the shaman played the didgeridoo, I immediately felt the connection to the Divine. I could feel the power of the ancestral spirits who were accompanying us on this sacred journey. The vibrations of the didgeridoo acted as a type of sonic alchemy and transported me to a place beyond my human mind—to a spiritual realm where I could feel God's love profoundly. He continued to play, pointing the end of the instrument on each of our heart centers. As he played, I journeyed with him and saw a white wolf enter the room and sit next to me. I had seen a white wolf once before, and I knew the Divine was telling me I was being guided to a new path and a place of inner strength. When the night was over, it was announced that an opportunity to have a more intimate healing session with the shaman during a healing circle was being organized at a local wellness center. I immediately jumped at the opportunity and signed up for the session to take place the following day.

I had always felt a strong connection to shamanistic rituals. Shamans have existed and practiced their teachings and healing practices for thousands of years. I was told by the Divine that my family came from a long line of *curanderos*, or native healers or shamans, so this experience caused me to awaken to those parts of me that had lived this before. In meditations I had experienced myself as a *kahuna* (the Hawaiian word for shaman) and a medicine woman, so I knew that being present at this event was no coincidence. Being there created the sacred container for me to awaken to that medicine woman who already existed within me.

The following day I waited with eager anticipation for what I already knew intuitively would be a major event in my life. I arrived a little early and got a spot right near the altar at the head of the circle. A couple of minutes later I saw the shaman by the altar getting ready for this sacred event. When the opportunity arose, I said hello to him. As we spoke, I could feel a deeper connection with him and I knew that this man would change my life that evening.

We had been instructed to bring blankets to make a bed on the floor. Comfort would be important as we would be there for the next six hours. As we closed the circle to begin the sacred event, the shaman shared wisdom that was meant to prepare us for our evening together. He spoke of light and darkness and how they are not opposites, but integral parts of our wholeness. He said we need them both to experience our Earth-plane journey. The darkness, or the shadow side, is the things (lessons) we are here to learn. He spoke of the importance of naming these shadows and acknowledging them so they don't sneak up on us when we least expect it. By naming our shadows up front, we're able to better control them and transcend them when the moment arrives. In many indigenous cultures, the medicine man wears a medicine bag around his neck (over the heart center) that represents his shadows. It's a way for the medicine man to show truth and honesty to those they're serving. To me it's akin to representing the perfect imperfections of our humanness.

As the shaman continued speaking, he mentioned that within each of us is a medicine woman ready to help us heal. I had already felt the connection to my inner medicine woman in previous meditations with my guides, so I knew I was being taken to a deeper place where this part of me that was ready to be seen could be awakened. It was no coincidence that the five of us who signed up for this circle were all healers. It was like we had made a divine appointment to meet with this shaman on this day, all supporting one another in what we all knew would be a transformational healing.

When I received the talking stick (which is used to represent a time of sharing), I began by talking about my dream of awakening that occurred in 2003. I talked about the mission that I knew I had as a healer, and about knowing that I was present to let go of something that was still holding me back from embracing the real me at a deeper level. I knew that this day was about finding my voice again—the voice that was somehow connected to my Soul's purpose.

As we began the ceremony, each of us lay down on the blankets we had laid out on the floor. We were all to lie in silence, holding space for our sisters, who one by one would be called to the center of the circle to receive their healing. I lay down and meditated, just feeling the energy that was beginning to emerge in the room. I could see my medicine woman emerging within me. It was as if she was stepping into my body. I kept my eyes closed, and I could feel the energy of my ancestors in the room, and once again I saw a white wolf lying by my side. I felt the presence of all my guides and ancestors and the spirits of my physical family surrounding me with love and protection.

As I was brought to the center of the circle, I could already feel my body tingling. The shaman played the didgeridoo over my body. As he did this, my body shook profusely. Then he pressed my stomach and lower back. There was a great deal of pain when he pressed his hands on these places. Even anger started to come to the surface. All the unspoken words and held-back screams residing in these areas wanted to be released. The shaman continued to press on particular points of my stomach and lower back as he called on his ancestral lineage to help me release this energy. He played the ancient flutes and sang and spoke to me what was spoken to him from his ancestors and guides. He immediately saw the connection of this energy to my ex-husband and all those moments of disempowerment I had experienced until now. He told me I was worthy of love and that I was no longer to be anyone's victim; that I was a being of light and it was time to let go of this pain, anger, and resentment. All that evening I had been affirming that I was surrendering completely to God's will and was ready to let go of that which no longer served me.

As the shaman continued to work on me, tears rolled down my face. Then we arrived at a pivotal moment in the healing. It was time to choose whether or not I was willing to let go of this pain and anguish that not only was constricting my stomach, but was strangling my vocal chords. He told me it was time to scream, and together we screamed three times as he continued to work on my midsection and lower back. On the fourth scream, I was on my own. "Scream at the top of your lungs," he said. As I screamed the loudest I had ever screamed before, a sudden release of energy happened. The energy was so ready to be released that it just shot out like a rocket. At that moment I felt complete liberation and pure joy. It seemed I had been carrying this heavy energy for eons, and in one fell swoop it was gone forever. Tears of gratitude and joy ran down my face.

That evening each of us experienced our own transformation. A rebirthing occurred that was the stepping stone to new pathways and beginnings. But there was more for me to understand about this experience. When the shaman ended the healings, we went back into a circle to talk about our experiences. As we passed the talking stick around again, I shared how liberated and powerful I felt, like I was ready to take on the world. The shackles had been released and I had found my voice again. The shaman responded with, "You go, Girl." Then he told me what I still needed to understand. He said that the painful energy I had released would now be creating the space for the love that was trying to come in. I understood later this was not just about love in my relationships, but the love of God, the Divine, of my God-self. This pain had been keeping me separated from the love that was the foundation of the real me, my spiritual-self, my Soul essence that was waiting to be expressed through me. When you're able to connect with the eternal love that you are and transcend the illusion of separation, the real you emerges into wholeness.

The shaman continued to tell me of the visions he received as he worked on me. He had clearly seen that part of my Soul's purpose was to sing, and that when I did, those in attendance would feel all the emotions being expressed in that particular song, like pain, love, joy, and forgiveness. My voice was to be the fountain of healing through which God's eternal love could be expressed. As he spoke these words to me, it all made sense as God had told me that evening: "There is a song to be sung that only you can sing." I hadn't known what that message meant until this moment. What a humbling moment it was for me.

As you reflect on your life, think about what pain you're still holding that is keeping you from being the real you—from expressing your true voice, your *divine voice*. Let's do this now. Take a moment to find a quiet place where you won't be disturbed for the next fifteen or twenty minutes. Get a piece of paper or your journal to capture your thoughts about your *divine voice,* and place it to the side. If it will be helpful, turn on some soothing music or burn some incense or a candle to help you connect more deeply. I'm going to take you back to different points in your life so you can discover what might still be holding you back from finding and expressing your *divine voice*. You can record the following meditation so you can close your eyes while you listen to it.

Sit comfortably where you won't be disturbed—with your feet flat on the floor and your hands on your knees with palms facing up. If you're an experienced meditator, use whatever position is most comfortable to you. When you're ready, please move to the meditation.

Guided Meditation: Connecting with Your Divine Voice

*Close your eyes and breathe deeply. Imagine yourself as your fetus in your mother's womb. You're swirling around in liquid love made of pure, virgin light. Pink swirls of eternal love engulf your entire being. As you are forming into your human body, you carry imprints of days beyond this human form. Allow this energy to come forward. What are you feeling? What are you remembering? What messages are emerging from this time in your mother's womb? Stay here for a moment and allow what needs to be shown to emerge. {**Pause for as long as you need to receive.**}*

*Accompanied by your guardian angel and the Divine, your Soul guides you to a period between the ages of one and twelve. Allow yourself to be taken to a moment, an experience, or a specific memory from this time in your life. What do you see and feel? How old are you? How does this connect to the finding of your divine voice? Is there something that needs to be healed? Stay here for a moment and allow what needs to be shown to emerge. {**Pause for as long as you need to receive.**}*

Continue on your journey of self-discovery. Your guardian angel holds your hand as you move to the period between twelve and twenty-four years of age. Allow yourself to be taken to a moment, an experience, or a specific memory from your teens or young adulthood. Focus on your divine voice and allow any memories, events, or pain to be revealed to you. What pain are you still holding from this stage of your life that prevents you from embracing your true voice? Stay here for a moment and allow the truth to emerge. **{Pause for as long as you need to receive.}**

We continue together on this journey of truth and healing. Now your Soul guides you to the period of your life between twenty-four and thirty-six years of age. (If this period is not relevant to you, move to the healing portion of this meditation.) As before, allow your Soul to take you to a specific memory, event, or experience that is causing you to hold on to pain that relates to your divine voice. What pain or feeling is emerging? How has this pain held you back from expressing your true voice? Stay here for a moment and allow the truth to emerge. **{Pause for as long as you need to receive.}**

Continue to when you were between the ages of thirty-six and forty-eight. (Again, if this period is not relevant to you, skip to the healing portion of this meditation.) Allow any memories, images, or experiences to come to the surface. Allow your Soul to guide you to this place of remembrance. What is emerging for you? What has continued to repeat as a lesson or habit that needs to be released because it keeps you from finding your divine voice? Stay here for a moment and allow your truth to emerge. **{Pause for as long as you need to receive.}**

Go to the stage of your life after age forty-eight. (If not relevant for you, skip to the healing portion.) What happened during this time that contributes to holding back your divine voice? Go deeper with your Soul and seek the truth. During this time of your life you've had time for second chances and much learning. What lesson emerges for you? How can you apply this lesson going forward? Is there more to be released? Stay here for a moment and allow your truth to emerge. **{Pause for as long as you need to receive.}**

Healing

Now that you've traversed the various stages of your life remembering what still holds you back from finding your divine voice, it is time to let that all go. See yourself in your current state of being. Bring all the pain and memories to the surface. You're surrounded by the angels and you can feel their love permeating your being.

Archangel Metatron comes forward to assist you. He gives you a ball of fire to burn through this pain. Take the ball in your hands and pass it over your body. See the ball of fire burning through every memory, event, or pain associated with your divine voice. Pass the ball of fire over every part of your body including your abdomen, heart, throat, and crown (the top of your head). With each pass of the ball of fire, you feel lighter and more resilient. You're regaining your power. You're reconnecting with the real you, the eternal being of light and love that you are. You can feel your divine voice radiating truth and joyful expression. Stay here for a moment and allow the integration of healing to occur throughout your mind, body, and spirit. **{Pause for several minutes.}**

When you feel complete, slowly come back and open your eyes.

Now that you've completed the meditation, pull out your journal and capture your experience. Answer the following questions:

Journaling Exercise

1. For each of the different stages from fetus to your current age, what did you feel or experience about your *divine voice*? Was there a common thread of pain or lessons that repeated in those various stages?

2. Is there a particular period that you still feel needs some work so you can find or express your *divine voice*? If yes, write down as much as possible about the feelings and experiences that are still holding you back from expressing your true voice.

3. Write down any actions you can take over the coming days and weeks that will help you transform and heal this part of you so you can fully express your *divine voice*.

Speaking Your Truth Helps You Find Your Divine Voice

If you're like me, you, too, have been hiding some truths about who you really are. There are two aspects of this. One is related to your physical being. It could be that you're hiding something you've done, something that was done to you, or things about yourself that you think others might not accept about you, like your spiritual beliefs, for example. The second aspect is related to your spiritual-self or the divine you. I spent a long time being careful about what I said and to whom I said it when it came to my spirituality. Maybe you've also been hiding your divine gifts either consciously or unconsciously in fear of disapproval.

> *Both aspects of you—your physical being and your spiritual-self—have to be given voice—a truthful, honest voice.*

Both aspects of you—your physical being and your spiritual-self—have to be given voice—a truthful, honest voice. The more you keep these separate, the more fragmented your life becomes. The real you is the divine you, your spiritual-self. When you deny or separate that part of you from the rest of your life, your life cannot flow with ease and grace. Some parts of your life grow while others become stagnant or stuck until these two parts of you become one. They can only become one when you give them voice—*divine voice*—and stop hiding the expression of the truth that exemplifies each of these parts of you.

I had to unmask both these parts of me in my own journey to find and embrace my *divine voice*. I've mentioned many times how I spent most of my life trying to get approval from others. In doing so, I became an expert at masking those parts of me that I didn't think others would approve of. Looking back, I find it ironic that for years I felt I was supposed to write books, but something kept holding me back. *What would people say if I told my true story? Would anybody read what I wrote?* I soon realized that if I became an author, I wouldn't be able to hide anymore. This was the fear rolling around in my subconscious. The Divine kept putting me in situations that caused me to confront these fears, until one day I did. I was sitting at home watching a virtual summit of a training program I had purchased. Onto the stage came Christine Kloser, a transformational writing coach and spiritual guide. As soon as I heard Christine speak, I knew she was the one to help me write my book.

There is a process that we all go through in life. Everything you need to know is already within you, but it may be deeply hidden, masked, or even dormant. God chooses each and every person who comes into your life. Each person holds something for you. Christine is the one who helped me unlock some of what was still hidden within me. She has this amazing gift of being able to see you as the *real you* you're meant to be. I immediately signed up for her Get Your Book Done' program, an online program that leads you step by step to create your manuscript. In September of that year I attended Christine's Transformational Author Breakthrough conference, and it was there that I discovered how some of my fears were still holding me back.

During the conference, Christine spoke about one of her high-end programs called MasterHeart. I knew that I needed a small, intimate community to support me as I continued moving forward with my book and the unmasking of my Soul, and Christine's MasterHeart program seemed perfect. It would provide me with an opportunity to write a short chapter that would be part of her bestselling anthology series, *Pebbles in the Pond*. Yet as I thought about it, I became afraid. Initially I thought I was afraid of the investment required for the program, but as I dug deeper I discovered the real fear was that I wouldn't be able to hide anymore. As soon as I discovered that truth, I said, "Hell yeah! I'm in." Being part of this program was exactly what I needed, and the Divine had planned it so perfectly.

As I meditated about what I would write about for my chapter, the Divine said, "Unmasking your Soul." I was to write about my own story. That story was to become the introduction to this very book. As I wrote about my own unmasking, I was divinely guided to "tell all," even those parts that had been hidden from my family and friends. That was a bit scary, but with the encouragement from Christine and my MasterHeart Soul family, I was able to write my truth with courage and love.

For months I thought about how I would tell my family about what I was writing about in that chapter, and for months I delayed speaking of that truth. Some of my family members knew this truth, but my older brother and parents did not, and I felt I owed it to them to tell them the truth before the story was published. I kept waiting for the sign to speak up, but the sign didn't arrive until the week before the story was to be published. I thought I would tell my older brother in person, but the Divine had other plans. My older brother called me, and that's when I got the sign: "Okay, it's time," the Divine said. "You mean now?" I asked the Divine. "Yes, now," was the reply.

So I waited for the perfect opportunity to talk with him about my story and the book launch. I shared with him about the sexual abuse and about the fact that I had fallen in love with a woman. Despite the fact that this love, until now, had been unrequited, I was still being nudged by the Divine to speak of this part of my life; I was to teach others about love. And so I began to share this with my brother. "Love cannot be placed in a neat little box," I said. "Love is of the Soul; it is not of the mind. It chooses you; you don't choose it." As I told my brother everything, he listened attentively and only offered support and love. I knew this was a test run by the Divine for the conversation that would need to take place with my parents very soon. Whew! What a relief. One down. But now I had to tell my parents.

I decided I wanted to tell them in person, which meant waiting until the following weekend. I would be visiting my parents for Father's Day, and that would be my last opportunity to speak my truth before the book launch.

I waited for the sign to speak, but "Wait" was all I heard. That evening, as my mother was relaxing in her favorite chair, I sat next to her and told her there was something I needed to share with her about my chapter which would be published soon. She was a bit surprised and immediately got nervous. She already knew about the abuse. She couldn't believe there might be something else I had been hiding from her all this time. I told her it was about my chapter. I had just been guided to go get a printed copy of the book from my car. I didn't know why until that moment. As much as I insisted that I wanted to tell her about something that appeared in my *Pebbles* chapter, she insisted that she would rather read it herself. I was shocked to say the least. My mom's first language is Spanish, so reading English is not one of her preferences. But in that moment there was no changing her mind. I knew it was best to grant her wish, so I bookmarked my chapter for her and went to bed.

I got up the next morning not knowing whether or not she had read the chapter. I sat down to have breakfast and she joined me. I was not about to bring up the subject. She seemed very calm and we spoke as we normally do. She then asked me what time I would be leaving. She knew I would be returning to my own home later that day. I said I wasn't leaving until I had the conversation about my chapter. And that's when the atmosphere changed. She started to tell me that she had always known or suspected I had feelings for a woman. I remembered the exact moment that prompted it. She had been visiting me in my home and I had decided to plant some seeds about this possibility. I told her that I was open to whomever God sent into my life, either man or woman, and that I had learned something much more profound about love and its origins than I was aware of growing up. She got very upset and said that just because I had been hurt by a man didn't mean that they were all the same.

My mom then told me that she had read my chapter. She began to explain that in her generation same-sex relationships were taboo, and how the Bible talked about Adam and Eve; but that she knew times had changed. She went on to tell me that she had finished reading my chapter at about 1:00am and couldn't fall asleep, so she turned on the television and there were two women getting married. I said, "Wow! God is so good." That was divinely orchestrated as a sign to her and to me that times are different, and I'm here to be a catalyst for that change in mindset. Love has no gender, no religion, no age, no race; it just is. It is a gift from the Divine that happens at a Soul level and is meant to be cherished no matter what package it comes in. At the end of our exchange, my mom said that she would love me always, no matter what. I still get emotional when I think of that moment. It was amazingly beautiful to experience the depth of my mother's love in that way. I know not everyone is as lucky as I to have such a loving and supportive family, but I believe that each of us can help contribute to creating a world that is more loving and accepting. I know that you are here because you are one of those whom God has chosen to bring that love and light to the world. There are no words to express how deeply loved I felt in that moment—not just by my physical family, but by the Divine who so perfectly orchestrated everything that happened that weekend. I felt so liberated and free to be me. That had been my wish all along. I just wanted to be ME.

Then the book launch was only two days away, and I would have my chance to speak my truth about my story to hundreds of people around the world. I was told by the Divine not to over-prepare, but just allow the words to flow freely from my being. That what needed to be said would be said. As my turn came to talk about my story publicly for the first time, I felt such peace and calmness come over me. The words were gentle, yet powerful. I talked about wearing a mask for most of my life, pretending to be someone I wasn't. It was time to stop playing small and dimming my light. It was like I had been wearing shackles on my wrists, holding me back. By dimming my light in this way, I was perpetuating the veil of separation between my physical being and my spiritual-self. As I spoke my truth to my family, and then publicly, I was finally liberating my Soul. Love was the redeeming force. As I experienced the love of my family and the Divine, I embraced the love that I am to myself and others. It was that self-love that allowed me to release myself from the shackles I had been wearing all my life. I had finally found the first part of my *divine voice*—the physical aspect in which I voiced my truth to the world.

The spiritual-self had yet to be revealed and expressed in its entirety. That's where my story continues. Several months after the *Pebbles in the Pond (Wave 4)* launch, I attended a writing retreat with Christine and thirteen other women. It was a beautiful, transformational time for all of us. I knew we had made a divine appointment to meet during this time to love and support one another and create the sacred container that would allow each and every one of us to transform and awaken to deeper parts of ourselves. It was during this retreat that I received a profound message from God. He said, "From the cauldron of time and space emerges a *divine truth*. You are the messenger of this truth. And soon you will know this truth as it emerges from you and through you. Allow this ancient Soul that you are to have a space to breathe, be, and speak. You are this ancient Soul, Anümani."

This message came to me as we stood in a sacred circle. I had already received my name previously during a sacred pilgrimage I had been on by myself, but I had not yet voiced my name to anyone. But on the final day of the retreat, the Divine said, "It's time to unmask your ancient name." It was during this retreat that I felt safe enough to unmask my spiritual-self, for the first time, in such a deep and profound way. Now it was time to bring voice to my ancient name. As I felt called, I shared my name with my Soul-sisters as we sat in a circle. I was asked to lead the circle in chanting my ancient name, and as we chanted my name together, I felt the ripples of time and space opening, taking us to a vastness of consciousness that felt so familiar to this part of me that had lived before. I had completed the union and found my *divine voice*—marrying the physical and spiritual selves together.

Because you are a spiritual being having a human experience, it is essential that the physical and spiritual parts of you are integrated seamlessly. Putting voice to both parts of you is what helps bridge the gap—the separation between your physical being and your spiritual-self. As you bring voice to these parts of you, you live and operate in a different way, in which the spiritual-self is guiding and leading the way, making choices that align with your Soul's purpose instead of being driven by your ego-mind, fears, or limiting beliefs.

When you give voice to your spiritual-self, your Soul drives your life as the captain of the ship.

When you give voice to your spiritual-self, your Soul drives your life as the captain of the ship. You then become the co-creator of your life, acting on the guidance of your Soul and the *divine mind* (discussed later in chapter 10); no longer living from adversity, fear, or limiting beliefs that are just illusions, but from what you truly feel.

Let yourself put voice to your physical being and your spiritual-self. As you do, you find your true *divine voice* and you see that the Universe conspires to uplift and bring you all you need to manifest what you're putting voice to. You're able to see with your own eyes that you can live the life you desire and deserve because you're experiencing it in its totality.

> *"Listen to your voice. No one else can hear it. Tell your story. No one else can speak it. Run after your passion. No one else can catch it. Being true to the person you were created to be is the best gift you can give yourself, your family, and the world."*
>
> **~Joel Boggess**

Finding your *divine voice* might not be as dramatic as my experience, but I think you get the message that it is the merging of the physical and spiritual aspects of you that allows your true *divine voice* to be found and expressed. Being able to say who you are and what you do without fear is a true testament to the beginning of the union between your physical being and your spiritual-self. Until this happens, your life can feel fragmented and like you're on a rollercoaster, with many peaks and valleys.

Finding your *divine voice* requires you to speak your truth, and that includes speaking about your spiritual gifts with comfort and confidence. The more you open to your gifts and *divine purpose*, the more you meet others who support you in that journey. Those you're meant to serve are part of that. You learn to embrace the love and support and leave the rest. Those who aren't ready for what you have to offer naturally fall away. Surround yourself with and embrace those who support the expression of your *divine voice*, and release and let go of those who do not. While this may be difficult, you will learn to accept that relationships and people come and go throughout your journey. The more you learn to love and cherish yourself as God loves you, the easier it is to let go of those situations, people, and relationships that no longer serve your highest good.

Accessing the Voice of Your Higher-Self

> *Your Soul holds a specific vibration or signature that is unique to you and only you.*

Your Divine-Self and the vastness of your Soul are constant. Your Soul holds a specific vibration or signature that is unique to you and only you. Think of this vibration as a string of musical notes brought together to express the melody of your ancient Soul. In the vastness of your Soul, nothing is questioned and everything is complete. The real you exists as a constant masterpiece of divine creation. As you tap into the real you, the desire to express your authenticity and integrity prevails in your life. It is your *divine composer* who helps you compose the meaning behind the words and messages of the *divine voice* that expresses through you from your Higher-Self.

The *divine voice* of your Higher-Self is the voice of your Soul. The more you clear your vessel and the noise in your mind, the louder and clearer you hear this voice. This is where spiritual practice becomes essential. Only through consistent, daily communion with the Divine do you learn to distinguish the voices in your head.

Some clients have told me that they have multitudes of voices coming in all at once. That certainly can be quite overwhelming. The lower-vibration (or fear-based) voices consist of the ego, inner critic, or what in Buddhism is called the "monkey mind" chattering away in your head. Then there are the higher-vibration (or love-based) voices that consist of, for example, your Higher-Self, angels, spiritual guides, and God Himself. Practice listening, receiving, and connecting with the specific vibration of your *divine voice* so you can learn to distinguish one from the other. The more you practice, the easier it becomes to distinguish when it is your ego (your lower-self) speaking and when it is your Higher-Self speaking. I'm not going to get into how to distinguish between all the various voices, as that is a book in itself and will be more deeply explained in the second book of this trilogy. For now let's keep it simple and focus on distinguishing between the voice of your ego and that of your Higher-Self.

I've mentioned before that the voice of your ego is of lower vibration and is the expression of your emotional body. It's the voice of fear, limiting beliefs, and the pain and wounds you're still holding within you. These emotions may have been accumulated through tragedy and painful experiences, or may exist at a deeper cellular level from the ancient you who has lived before. They are always related to lessons you're meant to learn, or another way to look at this is to unlearn what no longer serves you. Unlearn what you've become attached to in this life that was not there in the womb of creation from which you originated. You learned fear as you experienced life. Your true essence is love, so in effect you're unlearning fear so you can return to that wholeness of *divine love* that you already are. *Divine love* exists on a different plane of consciousness, accessible to you within your heart, which is the portal to the God within you—your Christed-Self (more about this in chapter 12).

Think of the awakening process as an unmasking of the layers of your Soul that brings the real you front and center.

As you took physical form, the vastness of your Soul never changed, but how to access that wisdom has to be relearned. The best analogy I can think of is that when you take human form, it's like getting amnesia. You fall asleep so you can experience the specific lessons of your Soul's canvas. Each experience connects with the next, all divinely orchestrated and co-created between the Divine and your Soul. And when the time arrives, you awaken to your spiritual-self. Some don't awaken in this life, but because you're reading this page, I know you've already experienced some part of your divine essence. That means that you're part of a community of "light workers" that has been chosen to help shift the consciousness of humanity. How you express and bring that shift about is unique to you and can occur in whatever vocation was chosen for you to have in this life. Think of the awakening process as an unmasking of the layers of your Soul that brings the real you front and center. Each layer that is unmasked brings with it a remembrance of that divine part of you to your conscious mind and shifts your vibration to higher levels. The more you're able to shift your consciousness to higher vibrations, the more your Soul embodies you. It's from this place that your Higher-Self can then communicate to you the guidance of your Soul.

Let's practice listening to this voice now. You can record the following meditation so you can close your eyes while you listen to it. Find a quiet place where you can relax and not be disturbed. Sit comfortably—with your feet flat on the floor and your hands on your knees with palms facing up. If you're an experienced meditator, use whatever position is most comfortable to you. When you're ready, please move to the meditation.

Guided Meditation: Connecting with the Voice of Your Higher-Self

Close your eyes and take a deep breath. With each subsequent breath, feel every part of your body relaxing—your head, shoulders, arms, chest, abdomen, legs, and feet—all deeply relaxed. As you become more relaxed, ask the Divine to support you and provide a loving and safe environment for receiving whatever you're meant to receive today.

Drop your presence into your heart. Imagine your heart as a beautiful rose. The rose becomes larger and larger, covering the full breadth of your heart center. In the center of the rose appears a key. Grab the key, and as you do, a door appears. Set an intention that you will meet your Higher-Self on the other side of this door. Place the key in the lock and open the door. You enter a crystalline room that is radiating a beautiful deep-pink light.

Place your hands on the walls and feel the warmth of love entering your heart and flowing through the rest of your body. When you look across the room, you see your Higher-Self. Take a moment to discover what your Higher-Self looks and feels like. {Pause briefly.}

Greet your Higher-Self. Your Higher-Self responds, "Hello, Dear One. I am you and you are me. We are one." You respond, "Sometimes I have trouble hearing you. Please help me hear you more clearly." Your Higher-Self responds, "Yes, of course. I'm going to imprint my voice in your heart so you can always recognize me no matter where you are and what you're doing."

Your Higher-Self places their hands on your heart, transferring the frequency of their voice into your being. You can feel specific vibrations being recorded in your heart. They flow into your throat, ears, and head, and down into your abdomen. This allows you to recognize the voice in your preferred sensory method. You lean in and ask your Higher-Self to impart any words of wisdom for you in this moment. Pause and allow the messages to be revealed. {Pause briefly.}

When you feel complete, thank your Higher-Self and go back through the doorway of your heart center. Slowly come back to the present moment. When you're ready, you may open your eyes.

As always, now is a good time to take your journal out and capture any significant messages, emotions, or ideas that emerged from this experience so you can refer to them as you move through your journey of self-discovery. I leave you with some important points about finding and embracing your *divine voice*:

1. Believe in the **POWER** of your voice. Everything you say has an effect on you and those around you. Your *divine voice* is the seed of manifestation. When you give voice to what you want and desire in life, you plant the seeds for it to become reality. As long as what you desire is aligned with your highest good and your Soul's purpose, all moves with grace and divine perfection.

2. Give voice to your **TRUTHS**, both your physical and spiritual truths. Only in speaking your truths is your Soul liberated to guide you to unlimited possibilities. Give voice to who you really are, what you want, and how you want to serve. Bring together your physical being and your spiritual-self as you speak those truths. The more you understand why you're here and how you're meant to contribute to human consciousness, the easier it is to bring these two parts of you into union.

3. Your *divine voice* is **UNIQUE** to you and carries a vibration that only you hold—the vibration of your Soul. When you unmask this part of you, what you speak becomes manifested in your life. You were born to bring something unique and special to this world—something that only you can do. Give voice to that uniqueness that you are—to the vision of who you're meant to be in this world. When you do, you ignite the cycle of creation, and what you have vocalized begins to appear in your life.

4. You are both **CREATED** and **CREATOR**. God's consciousness lives and speaks through you. Allow the warmth, love, and peace of the created you to emanate through your voice. When you speak from this deeper, spiritual part of you, it's like breathing consciousness into those around you. It's as if you become the voice of the Soul of the person you're speaking to. You may have experienced this already. Perhaps you've been in the audience at a workshop, or even a concert, and you felt like what was said or the piece of music that was played spoke directly to your Soul. As you live in that created part of you and express your *divine voice* from that place, what's created around you is wonderment and awe for you and those in your company.

5. **CONNECT** with and **LISTEN** to the voice of your Higher-Self—the vessel of your Soul, daily. Practice distinguishing the difference between your Higher-Self and your lower-self. Your Higher-Self always comes to you from a higher

vibration of love, understanding, and deep reverence for the divine being that you are. On the other hand, the voice of your ego-mind (your lower-self), approaches life from a lower vibration of fear and woundedness. It is the voice of what Eckhart Tolle calls your "pain body." This is the emotional pain that lives within you. The more you feed this pain body with fear, anger, or jealousy, the more it consumes your body and mind. When you bring the light of your divine consciousness forward, you transcend that which you've been reliving over and over again. Underneath this pain body there is something else that is trying to be born through you. This is the voice of the real you that knows that there exists a plane of consciousness where you are perfect and whole. Allow your *divine voice* to give life to that real, divine essence that you are.

"Behind every problem, there is a question trying to ask itself…Behind every question, there is an answer trying to reveal itself. Behind every answer, there is an action trying to take place. And behind every action, there is a way of life trying to be born."

~Michael Beckwith

Now let's help you return to wholeness. Use the following meditation to heal those fears that are still holding you back from finding and embracing your *divine voice*. You can record the meditation so you can close your eyes while you listen to it. For the audio version, visit **www.UnmaskingYourSoul.com/Meditations.** Sit comfortably where you won't be disturbed—with your feet flat on the floor and your hands on your knees with palms facing up. If you're an experienced meditator, use whatever position is most comfortable to you. When you're ready, please move to the meditation.

Guided Meditation: Finding Your Divine Voice

Breathe slowly, inhaling through your nose and exhaling through your mouth. As you breathe, focus on your breath and feel with every breath the relaxation of your mind, body, and spirit. Just focus on your breath and let thoughts pass as they may.

See yourself in an open, green meadow. As you look above at the sky, you see the rising sun bringing warmth and light to a new day. You stop for a moment to witness the beautiful colors of the sun as it rises. You feel the warmth of its orange and red hues in your body. As you look closely for a moment, you notice seven rays of light emanating from the sun. These rays extend from the outer edges of the sun, and their brilliance is breathtaking. You continue breathing into your mind, body, and spirit the beauty, warmth, and love you feel from this magnificent view.

As the sun settles in the sky, you look beyond the green meadow and notice the entrance to a large, abundant forest. Walk towards it, and as you do, feel the wind blowing gently across your face and body. The sensation feels refreshing and exhilarating. As you enter the forest, you can see the mist of the dawn—droplets of water resting quietly on the foliage of the plants and trees. You feel amazingly connected to Mother Earth.

When you look to the right you notice a creek and can hear the soft, crackling sounds of water flowing and ebbing with such gentleness. There, on the edge of the creek, is a white wolf drinking its morning glory. You try not to make a sound, but the wolf has already sensed your presence in the distance. As it raises its head to connect with you, you notice a symbol on its forehead. It is a sun with seven rays of light. Telepathically the wolf tells you it will be your guide today.

*You notice the pureness of its white coat, and although you feel its strength and power, you also feel a loving energy emanating from its being. The wolf instructs you telepathically to place your hand on the sun symbol on its forehead, and as you do, you feel the loving pureness of its divine spirit. You're feeling so loved by God. Bask in this loving feeling for a moment. {**Pause briefly.**}*

You begin to follow the white wolf, and you notice huge, multi-branched redwood trees. The wolf tells you telepathically that these majestic beings are 500-year-old candelabra trees and that you're in the Enchanted Forest. As you continue walking, you feel the presence of many ancient spirits who walked this land before you hundreds of years ago. They're accompanying you on this journey today.

You lean over and place your hands on the trunk of one of the redwood trees and immediately feel the ancient wisdom this tree possesses. You can feel its aliveness and the pulsing light that streams through its roots, trunk, branches, and foliage.

*You begin to feel this same aliveness within you, and this essence from the tree seems to cause a stirring of your own wisdom within. Begin to connect with this source of wisdom within you. Stay here for a moment. {**Pause briefly.**}*

As you continue walking, you feel the magic all around you—sounds of birds chirping and tweeting, frogs croaking, and the gurgling of nearby streams of water all melding together as one beautiful symphony. You feel profoundly connected to every source of creation within this forest. Paying attention to every sound around you, all your senses awaken and you feel the essence of the Divine and the sacredness of all you see: the beautiful redwood-candelabra trees, mosaics of ferns, and beautiful roses and wild flowers in all colors—red, purple, pink, white, orange, and yellow.

When you look ahead a bit into the distance, you can see the wolf is guiding you to a clearing, so you continue to follow. There's much light in this clearing. As you walk through, you behold the most beautiful sight... an iridescent pool of water. The sun is radiating strongly from the sky, and the water seems to be reflecting the hues of the rainbow—red, orange, yellow, green, blue, indigo, and violet. You're mesmerized by its beauty.

You look into this sacred pool, the water begins to ripple, and you see musical notes rising from the water. A symbol appears in the water. This is the symbol of your Soul's vibration. Allow it to rise from the water until it becomes a three-dimensional symbol in front of you. The symbol rotates and the light emanating from its center enters your throat center, activating your divine voice. Stay here for a moment as this occurs. {Pause briefly.}

Then another symbol appears in the water. It is the same sun symbol that you saw in the sky and on the forehead of your wolf guide. It is the sun with the seven rays of light. Your wolf guide tells you telepathically that seven Divine Souls will speak to you today through these rays of light.

You feel the presence of many souls with you now. You become part of a collective consciousness around you—the Souls that form God's angelic choir. Your divine composer is creating this healing for you with the help of these divine masters. You watch the sacred pool as each ray of light rises from the rippling water. Each ray represents a different Soul that has healing light and messages for you.

Ray 1 rises from the water. There are symbols and various hues of red and golden colors encoded in the light. As the light enters through the bottom of your feet and lands at the bottom of your spine, you release your fears about your divine voice. You are safe to be you and express your divine voice. See or feel the symbols and messages brought to you now. {Pause briefly.}

Ray 2 rises from the water with swirls of orange light. The light enters your body and flows right below your navel. Let go of any childhood memories and emotions *holding you back from being your authentic self. Allow your beauty to shine through. Embrace the beauty of your Soul and your divine voice. See or feel the symbols and messages brought to you now. {**Pause briefly.**}*

*Ray 3 rises from the water with swirls of yellow light and enters your abdomen. Let go of any areas of disempowerment, places where you're giving your power away, so that the true expression of your divine voice can be given form. Embrace the power of your divine voice. See or feel the symbols and messages brought to you now. {**Pause briefly.**}*

*Ray 4 rises from the water with swirls of green light. In your heart you hold the truth of the real you. Let go of any fears of not being loved or lovable for expressing your divine voice. You are love and your divine voice is an expression of that eternal love. See or feel the symbols and messages brought to you now. {**Pause briefly.**}*

*Ray 5 rises from the water with swirls of turquoise-blue light. As the light enters your throat, let go of any constriction in your throat. See yourself being free to speak your truth and allowing your divine voice to bring the melodies of the Divine to true form. See or feel the symbols and messages brought to you now. {**Pause briefly.**}*

*Ray 6 rises from the water with swirls of indigo-blue light. As the rays enter your body and flow to your forehead, let go of any wound that is holding you back from seeing your divine voice as the magnificent, powerful expression of the Divine that it is. See or feel the symbols and messages brought to you now. {**Pause briefly.**}*

*Ray 7 rises from the water with swirls of violet light and enters your crown. Let go of any attachments to your ego-mind and how you see your divine voice expressed in the world. Let your divine voice be free to be expressed in the wonderment of the Divine. See or feel the symbols and messages brought to you now. {**Pause briefly.**}*

*Now take a moment to allow the divine beings that have accompanied you today to come together and form the musical composition of your Soul. Experience the power, vastness, and omniscience of your divine voice. {**Pause for one or two minutes.**}*

When you feel complete, thank the Divine, the white wolf, and the beautiful Souls who walked this journey with you today. Thank Mother Earth and the Enchanted Forest for the magic and essence of pure love and harmony they brought to you today. As you awaken, remember your collective being as one mind, one heart, and one Soul.

When you're ready, you may slowly come back and open your eyes.

Now that you've completed the guided meditation, take some time to do some journaling. Spend about ten to fifteen minutes in a quiet place where you won't be disturbed answering the questions below. You can put on some soothing music or light a candle or incense to support you as you write. Just write from your Heart and Soul and the rest will follow.

Journaling Exercise

1. What did you first notice or feel as you entered the Enchanted Forest?

2. Did the white wolf have any specific messages for you? If so, write those down.

3. What did you experience as you touched and were in the presence of the redwood-candelabra trees? What wisdom did they share with you?

4. Write down what you experienced with each ray of light. What healing occurred and where in your body did you feel the healing of the rays of light? What messages did you receive?

5. What was the sound or feeling of the musical composition of your Soul?

6. How did you experience your *divine voice*? What were the texture, feeling, color, sound, and attributes of your *divine voice*?

7. Are there any other actions you need to take to more deeply embrace your *divine voice*? If so, write down what they are.

After journaling, continue working on the **Canvas of Your Soul.** (You can download the PDF at **www.UnmaskingYourSoul.com/Blueprint.**) Pick phrases, words, or symbols and put them on section 7 of the **Light** part of your roadmap. Make this canvas your own piece of artwork that represents the journey we're taking together in this book. You can color, paint, or even cut images from magazines that depict the messages and insights you received in this chapter on *finding your divine voice*. You don't need to be a professional artist to do this. Just let your Soul express through you as it wants to. This will become the vision board of your Soul's unmasking, a precious gift to you from your *divine composer*.

Five Rituals to Awaken Your Divine Voice Muscle

The rituals below are meant to help you awaken your *divine voice* muscle. You can repeat any of the rituals that follow and the exercises and guided meditations earlier in the chapter as many times as you like. With each repetition you go deeper in finding and embracing your *divine composer*.

Before you begin, create your sacred space and take some deep breaths to relax your mind and body. Connect with your Soul as you enter this sacred space. Use this invocation, if you like, to prepare your space:

> I invoke the *divine composer* within me to bring forth understanding, healing, and guidance as I seek to find and embrace my *divine voice*. I open my heart to receiving all I need in this moment. May I be protected and surrounded by God's eternal love as I continue forth on my journey of self-discovery, allowing my Soul to guide me home. May it be so forevermore.

1. Let's begin with a ritual that helps you identify some of the fears you may still be holding about speaking your truth. At the end you will release these fears to Mother Earth and the Goddess of Fire, Pele, for transmutation. Capture the first part of this ritual in your journal, and use a separate piece of paper for the second part, so you can burn it at the end.

   Part I: Divide the page into three columns. In the first column write the following list of categories vertically: "Spiritual," "Relationships," "Family," "Health," "Career," "Financial," and "Other." In the second column, write any fears you still harbor about speaking your truth in that particular category. For example, next to the Spiritual category you might write something about a fear you have about telling others of your spiritual beliefs, mystical experiences, or divine gifts. Try to be as explicit as you can. For example, if you had a particularly bad experience that perpetuated that fear, you can write about that and who you experienced that with in your life. Continue filling out all the other categories. Again, the focus is on documenting all the fears you have regarding speaking your truth in these areas. When you complete column two, in the third column write down the origin of that fear and what type of emotions or feelings it generates. For example, is the fear about disapproval, being judged, or losing someone's love? If there is a particular person you connect with that fear, write their name down as well. When your list is complete, place your hands on the pages of your journal and close your eyes. Envision the most beautiful pink light going from your heart through your hands and onto the pages of your journal. The pink light is radiating across the words on the page and softening the energy of the words and the fears connected to the words. Everyone involved is being healed and blessed by the purity of love coming through your hands. When you feel complete, open your eyes.

Part II: View the list again and pay attention to any fears that still feel alive within you. Transcribe these fears to a separate sheet of paper. When you're done, fold the paper four times and place it in a metal bowl or something that you can put flame to. If you have an outdoor fireplace, that would be ideal for this ritual. If you have some white sage, frankincense, or myrrh resin, place some in the bowl with the paper. Before you place fire on the paper, say a short prayer of release and consecration:

> Dearest Divine, today I release my fears about speaking my truth. As I burn this paper in your divine flame of eternal light, I return to wholeness again and find the courage to speak what needs to be spoken. May all those involved be blessed by the harmony and love spoken through my *divine voice*. As I speak my truth, I liberate my Soul and embrace fully the truth of who I am. May Mother Earth and Pele, the Goddess of Fire, transmute all the fear and density into love, peace, and harmony. And so it is.

Now light the paper and allow it to burn. If you're using a bowl, sprinkle the ashes on the Earth, giving thanks for this healing today.

2. Use the following visualization ritual to heal any fears about embracing your *divine voice*. Start by taking several deep breaths. When you feel relaxed, begin the visualization below.

> *See yourself walking on the beach. The sand is warm beneath your feet. With each step you take, a beautiful golden light enters the bottoms of your feet and flows through your entire body. Continue walking until you reach the edge of the ocean. As you step forward, a beautiful, gentle wave lifts you up and transports you into the center of the ocean. You're standing on a magical, translucent carpet of water. As you look around, you notice several blue whales and a school of dolphins coming your way. When they reach you, the whales sing and the dolphins join in. An exquisite oceanic symphony erupts. The vibrations of the sounds enter your body, releasing all your fears about your divine voice—sound after sound, vibrating and shaking every cell of your body, awakening a deeper part of you and releasing all that no longer serves you. You feel so alive, so at peace, and deeply loved. It's like you're being held in the arms of the Divine and being sung a sweet lullaby of remembrance, peace, and love. Stay in this place for a moment, receiving the pure, cleansing vibrations of the ocean's divine creatures. When you feel complete, thank the*

Divine and your ocean Soul family for their healing today. Slowly come back into your body and open your eyes.

3. Now that you've done some healing, you can focus on discovering the sound of your *divine voice*. Find a quiet place to sit and relax and take in this visualization ritual. Take several deep breaths, breathing in slowly through your nose and breathing out slowly through your mouth.

   See yourself inside a turquoise-blue sphere of light. Go to the center of the sphere and sit on the crystalline floor. There are symbols emerging from the crystalline walls. Each symbol comes forward to greet you. One by one, the symbols come forward and form a circular ring around your throat. The ring of blue light swirls around your entire body.

   The light forms a composition of musical notes. Your divine composer is standing in front of you and captures the musical notes in a glass bowl. The notes turn into liquid light. Your divine composer hands you the bowl and asks you to drink the liquid light, which will awaken the sound of your divine voice.

   You drink from the bowl and the blue, liquid light circulates throughout your body, awakening the cellular structure of your Soul's vibration, each cell joining the others to form the musical composition of your divine voice. As each note is awakened, you feel movement in your throat and a desire to make sound. Allow yourself to make any sounds that want to emerge. Continue intoning the sounds until you feel complete.

   When you're ready, slowly come back to the present and open your eyes. Remember to journal about anything of significance from this experience.

4. Say affirmations daily to embrace your *divine voice*. Before you begin the affirmations, take several deep breaths. On the exhales, make the sound HAM (HHH-HHH-AAAH-MMMMM). Do this about seven times to open your throat center. Standing in front of a mirror, spend five to ten minutes repeating the following affirmations. Look into your eyes, feeling the divine essence of your Soul. Be sure to put some emotion into the words as you say them, really feeling them in your throat.

   "I am free to be me."

   "I embody, live, and speak my *divine truths*."

   "I choose to be me in every way—mind, body, and spirit."

   "I allow my truth to be expressed in God's exquisite tapestry of creative life-force."

"My will power is aligned with my *divine purpose* in life."

"I express my love and goodness each time I speak."

"I connect with the truth of those in my life, embracing the sacredness of their truths."

"I listen to and trust in the voice of the Divine and my Higher-Self—the vessel of my Soul and divine essence."

5. Meditate with my painting ***The Music within Your Soul***, shown at the end of the chapter, to help you reconnect with your *divine composer*, the one who helps you find your *divine voice*. Each of my paintings was divinely channeled and holds messages and energetic impressions of the Soul that bring healing to the bearer. This particular painting holds vibrations of healing for those needing to remember their expression of *divine voice*.

    a. Close your eyes and take a breath... inhaling slowly through your nose and exhaling slowly through your mouth... and with each breath you take relax your mind, body, and spirit. Continue focusing on your breath... and with each breath allow your thoughts to pass freely... thought after thought... breath after breath... relaxing more and more deeply. Continue taking several more deep breaths. {**Repeat for one or two minutes.**}

    b. Briefly open your eyes and observe the painting. Allow yourself to be taken on a journey into the painting. Look at the images and symbols, and allow your gaze to go to one focal point in the painting. Soften your gaze as you focus on this point of interest. Breathe in its energy, seeing the symbols, images, and colors in your mind's eye. Continue breathing in the energy... breath after breath, allowing you to feel and absorb the healing energy from this focal point.

    c. With your next breath, listen to the voice of your Soul. What is it communicating? What messages do you hear or feel within you as you breathe in the energy of the painting? Pay attention to where the energy is going in your body. This gives you an indication of where in your body you may need to release old energy, traumas, or wounds. Continue breathing and just go into the stillness while you connect deeper within. Allow the healing energies of the painting to penetrate your mind, body, and spirit. {**Do this for two to five minutes.**} If you feel guided, you may continue repeating this step, changing to a different focal point in the painting each time. Again, allow yourself to breathe the images, symbols, colors, and healing energies into your being.

    d. Don't forget to journal about anything of significance that comes up during this experience.

EILEEN ANÜMANI SANTOS, *THE MUSIC WITHIN YOUR SOUL*, C. 2007

The Music within Your Soul represents the sound of your *divine voice*. Your *divine composer* is the creator of the vibration of your Soul. This is the sound of your Soul's vibration that is unique to you and only you. The expression of your Soul's vibration is what comes through your *divine voice* when you've completely unmasked this part of your Divine-Self. As you speak the truth of your physical being and your spiritual-self, the authentic expression of who you really are resonates through your *divine voice*.

SPEAK the unspoken. SING the sound of your Soul.
ALLOW your *DIVINE VOICE* to be born to the world!

Accessing Your Divine Wisdom

by Eileen Anümani Santos

You have known for an eternity all that you need to know.

You have lived all that you have needed to live.

You have travelled between the conscious and subconscious, looking for the clues to who you are.

Who are you, really?

Are you human, spiritual, or both?

The answer to that question is within you, in the deepest realms of your being and divine essence.

Your Soul knows the answer to why you were created, specifically in this time and place, to do what only you know how to do.

Inside you is a wealth of wisdom, both ancient and new. You carry the origins of your ancient Soul and it melds with the you of now. The well of wisdom you hold is limitless, encoded with knowledge from the Universe and beyond.

There is no name or form that this wisdom takes; it just is. It transcends time and space and has been waiting for you to access it.

Your Soul holds the key.

Take the key and unlock the door.

It's time to access your *divine wisdom*!

CHAPTER 8

Soul Chamber VIII:
Accessing Your Divine Wisdom

Because you're reading this, just like Neo from the movie *The Matrix*, you took the "red pill." In the movie, Morpheus says to Neo, "You take the blue pill, the story ends. You wake up in your bed and believe whatever you want to believe. You take the red pill, you stay in wonderland, and I show you how deep the rabbit hole goes." The red pill represents the choice of facing reality and the truth within you. It is akin to waking up or awakening to the spiritual being that you are.

Unfortunately there is no magic pill you can take to become enlightened in an instant. It takes work, discipline, and paying attention to that part of you that is all-knowing. All of us are intuitive by the very natures of our beings. We are spiritual beings having human experiences. That divine part of you is connected to a breadth of knowledge and wisdom that was encoded in your cellular structure as you took human form, an embryo in your mother's womb.

> *"Everything you'll ever need to know is within you; the secrets of the universe are imprinted on the cells of your body."*
>
> **~Dan Millman**

The center of your forehead is the location of **Soul Chamber VIII—Divine Wisdom,** the eighth of the Soul virtues that will be unmasked as you continue on your journey of wholeness. The mask associated with the eighth chamber is the **Mask of Illusion.** Sometimes, especially when you have a big choice or decision to make, the mask of illusion shows up to discourage you from trusting your primal instincts, trusting what your Heart and Soul already know to be the right choice for you. Fear shows up to make you see something that isn't there.

Self-development author and speaker Dr. Wayne Dyer said that FEAR stands for **F**alse **E**vidence **A**ppearing **R**eal. Underneath the fear is the wound that isn't allowing you to see clearly what's in front of you from a place of love. As soon as you allow the fear to step in, your ego takes over the decision-making. This is your ego's way of making you believe that it's keeping you safe from making the wrong decision. I bet if you think back on the times when you listened to your intuition, it was always right on point. The archetype of this Soul chamber is the **divine seer,** the holder of your *divine wisdom*, the container of your Soul's knowing. The sacred symbol of the *divine wisdom* chamber is shown below.

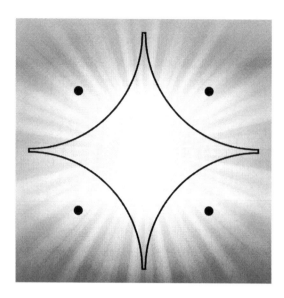

Divine Wisdom Symbol

Accessing your *divine wisdom* doesn't have to be difficult. It's part of your birthright as the divine being that you are. If you're like me, life's experiences have made you believe that following your intuition is not always the right choice. Perhaps you were led to believe that you need concrete facts and data to support the right choice. But what is the "right" choice? The right choice already sits within you. In your heart you always have access to the *right* choice for you, one that aligns with your highest good and Soul's purpose. While data and facts are appropriate at times, if you study the most brilliant scientists, artists, entrepreneurs, and leaders you discover that they all share one common theme: At one point or another they were able to connect with their deepest passions and natural gifts, and become recognized in their fields by learning to follow their hunches. Those hunches came from their very own divine well of knowledge. Within you exists that same well of knowledge—the *divine wisdom* that is encoded in your Soul's DNA. The *divine mind* (which we'll be discussing in chapter 9) then gave it the *divine spark*, or ignition, to become an idea to be manifested on the physical plane. Remember, everything occurs first on the spiritual plane before it manifests on the physical plane, which is the life that you're living now.

> *"You are one thing only. You are a divine being. An all-powerful Creator. You are a Deity in jeans and a t-shirt, and within you dwells the infinite wisdom of the ages and the sacred creative force of All that is, will be and ever was."*
>
> **~Anthon St. Maarten**

Over time we became a society enamored with logic and *doing* (the masculine side of our brains), and stopped trusting the beauty of just creating and *being* (the feminine side of our brains). You need both. One generates creation and the other manifestation. Your feminine side leads the creation; and not just any creation—it must be heart-centered creation so that what you create originates from a place of *divine love*, allowing your creation to be long-lasting and impactful for those you're meant to serve. This creation originates from your *divine wisdom*, the source of your intuition. Once that "intuitive hit" comes through, you can use your masculine (right brain) energies to make it happen in your life. If you think about this in business terms, your feminine side is the creator or visionary and your masculine side is the doer or project manager.

As we've journeyed together in this book, you've become the *divine curator* of your Soul—discovering what each part of your Soul's canvas looks like. Each piece is unique to you. Your feminine side has been playing the role of that *divine curator*, helping you see where you're going, bringing understanding and knowledge to your conscious mind about how the pieces of your canvas fit together to make you the extraordinary Soul that you are. This chapter focuses on how you tap into that feminine part of you, the holder of that wisdom. It doesn't matter whether you're male or female. We all have both divine feminine and divine masculine. When you learn to weave these parts of you together seamlessly in the dance of life, what occurs is purely magical.

The Key Aspects of Your Divine Wisdom

There are three important aspects of your *divine wisdom*. The first relates to the actual knowledge or wisdom that you hold within you in your divine container. You can access this wisdom to help you grow spiritually and create the life that aligns with your Soul's purpose. This wealth of knowledge is also there for you to share with those you're meant to serve. Because you're reading this book, most likely you're meant to be a spiritual teacher, healer, or leader, and were chosen to help contribute to the shift in the consciousness of humanity. How you bring that purpose and wisdom forward is unique to you.

The second aspect of your *divine wisdom* relates to your intuitive capacity, the hunches I spoke of earlier. Those hunches or intuitive hits are ways the Divine and your Soul communicate with you to help you make the choices and take the steps that align with the reason for your existence in this life. This communication can come from within you, through your intuitive capacity, your senses becoming the antennae receiving the telepathic message from the Divine. Sometimes the messages come through an external source. For example, the Divine may give you a message through a song you're listening to, a movie you're watching, an animal or a tree in nature, or another human being. External sources are just as important as internal ones. When this happens, it's key that you remain open and pay attention (stay present) to the experience so you're able to receive it. Then your Higher-Self (the conduit of your Soul), can help you interpret its meaning. The wisdom to decode that message ultimately comes from within you, regardless of whether you received it internally or externally.

In the last chapter we spoke of clairaudience—intuition that comes in the form of words, sounds, or even music. In this chamber, intuition comes in the form of visual representations. It can appear as colors, symbols, or visions. You might even be able to see auras or energy. This type of intuitive capacity relates to what many call *clairvoyance* or "clear-seeing." The visual representation can be in the form of words as well. Sometimes I receive messages in that way. When the Divine wants me to be absolutely clear about what the message is, it will sometimes spell out the words visually for me so there is no mistaking what I need to know in that moment. In this case I'm not necessarily hearing the words spoken to me, but instead seeing them written.

You can always ask the Divine for clarification about a message. That's why it's important to master more than one method of intuitive capacity—clairsentience, clairaudience, and clairvoyance—so you can use them in tandem to help you understand and validate the message clearly. This is especially important when you're using your intuitive gifts to serve others. Anytime you receive a message, your human vessel creates limitations and filters based on what you still carry within you that needs healing. The bigger your purpose and the more Souls you're touching, the more crucial it is for you to work on clearing your vessel daily. As you rid yourself of woundedness and ego-based limiting beliefs, you're able to hold more light and *divine love* within you. This way, each person you serve experiences that higher vibration, which in turn helps them heal, transform, and be the bearer of more light for others.

The third aspect of your *divine wisdom* is about learning to "see" the Divine in all things: people, nature, animals, and all that IS. In chapter 1, "Returning to Divine Love," we began the conversation about this topic and the importance of recognizing the love that is the essence of each and every one of us. We continue the conversation here and take it a step further. As you recognize the love and light in others, you begin to "see" in a different way and "speak" in a different language—the language of the Soul. This is an important principle to master so that you can build a loving, harmonious, Soul-driven life that is guided by your Soul and not your ego. When you're able to see the Souls of your loved ones and those you're serving, you're able to access the wisdom within your own Soul that helps you interact with that person in a way that creates healing, growth, and harmony, serving the highest good for all.

Seeing through the Eyes of Your Divine Seer

One of the key aspects of your *divine wisdom* is unlocking your ability to see through the eyes of your *divine seer*. In the book *The Alchemist*, Paulo Coelho calls on the seers who have an ease to penetrate "the Soul of the World." Seeing does not refer to physical seeing through your human eyes; it refers to the ability to see beyond the veil of illusion painted by your ego. This type of seeing lets you not only see visual messages from the Divine, but also the divinity of those who surround you. It gives you the ability to see their Souls. Why is it important to be able to see those around you in this way? Because beneath the physical layer of the human vessel sits the true aspect of a person, their Divine-Self, the expression of their Soul.

At this fundamental level you are pure, virgin light and love. The more you recognize this place within your partner, loved ones, friends, and colleagues, the easier it is to accept them where they are on their journeys. It opens a space for compassion and love despite what the outer appearance or behaviors may be. Remember, no one intentionally hurts you. A person's outer expression is always the projection of their inner world, including the wounds and pain they still hold. We are all mirrors to each other, so pain inflicted on you from a loved one is always an indication of pain within them. This doesn't mean that you're meant to accept abuse or mistreatment from anyone, including your loved ones; but when you're able to see the real them, the *Divine Soul* they really are, it gives you choices that are inherently woven from the tapestry of your divine being that are always founded in *divine love*.

In the movie *Avatar*, there's a line that struck me very strongly. It was when Neytiri told Jake Sully, "I see you." Before I get to the meaning of this, let me give you a little background in case you didn't see the movie. (Yes, another sci-fi flick, I know, but I am a Piscean mystic, and this movie really hit upon my creative spark and spiritual center.) In the storyline of the movie, Jake Sully, a human, is chosen to replace his identical twin brother on a mission to the planet Pandora, which is inhabited by blue beings called the Na'vi. The way of life of the Na'vi is based on unity of consciousness between all things, and in their world this includes oneness with the being called Eywa (who connects with the Na'vi through the sacred Tree of Souls). Because humans cannot breathe the air of Pandora, Jake must inhabit an avatar that resembles the Na'vi people. This avatar holds Jake's essence, which is transmitted to his avatar's brain electronically. Jake's mission is to integrate himself into the Na'vi culture so he can learn their ways and communicate about them with his supervisors. Mo'at, the spiritual leader of the clan, assigns her daughter, Neytiri, to teach Jake their ways. Jake and Neytiri fall in love. The line "I see you" was used several times throughout the movie, but there was one particular scene that really struck me. It was near the end when Jake was dying

> *When we speak of seeing through the eyes of your divine seer, that's what it's all about—seeing and experiencing the fullness of the Soul.*

and Neytiri saved him. She said, "I see you," and it was the first time she was seeing Jake as the real him. It was like she was seeing into him from the inside out; she was experiencing his Soul. When we speak of seeing through the eyes of your *divine seer*, that's what it's all about—seeing and experiencing the fullness of the Soul.

Being able to see through the eyes of your *divine seer*, your Divine-Self, is an important step as you connect with your intuitive abilities, specifically those of clairvoyance or clear-seeing. The better you can see through the eyes of the Divine, the better you can interpret the visual messages you receive through your intuitive capacity. The more you're anchored in the *divine love* that is your true essence, the more accurate your intuitive abilities become. One way to practice this is to imagine a cord of pink light coming up from your heart, connecting upward to the center of your forehead, and then connecting upward to points of light above your head going as high above your head as feels comfortable. As you connect to higher vibrations and ground your "intuitive sight" in *divine love*, the more accurate the visual messages you receive, as they're based in love and not fear (or ego-based filters).

There's a funny story that comes to mind about a time when I was being divinely "trained" to see through the eyes of my *divine seer* and experience the oneness that occurs when this happens. Out of the blue one day, I received an email from someone I had met at a holistic expo. She was a therapist and a spiritual seeker who had created a support group to help her clients find a safe place to talk about their spiritual experiences. I was invited to speak to the group about a couple of different topics, including the chakras and energy cords. In the past when I had given similar talks, I painstakingly captured very detailed speaking notes, including quotes and stories that would be part of the talk. I always prepared a little notebook that had everything neatly organized. As soon as I got the email, my first thought was, *Okay, I need to put a little notebook together with what I'm going to cover.* Immediately the Divine said, "No, you don't need any preparation. All you have to say is within you. Just be present and allow the Divine to work through you." That felt like a big leap for me, so despite the guidance I received, I decided to put a small notebook together anyway.

The day of the talk I made sure to leave early so I could be at the location with plenty of time to set up and double-check that I had everything I needed. Well, the Divine had other plans for me. Somehow I couldn't see the address of the building. I kept missing the entrance to the building despite having driven by it several times. And my GPS was sending me in circles. On the fourth attempt, I finally found the entrance, and by this time it was already time to start the talk. Luckily others were still gathering, so I shot in quickly and began to set up. I managed to bring everything in, including my notebook, but I had forgotten my reading glasses, so back I went to the car to find them. I had just been using them in the car, but they were nowhere to be found. I returned inside and looked once more for the glasses, but they were silently lost. When my host discovered what was going on, she offered me the use of her reading glasses, but I smilingly declined. I told her this was all divinely orchestrated. I was not supposed to use any notes, and the Divine had worked it out so I couldn't find my reading glasses, and without them it was a lost cause for me to try to read anything in my trusty notebook. I went with the flow and put the notebook to the side. I was guided to begin with my paintings, so I asked each person to pick out the one painting (from the deck of twenty-two cards) that spoke to them the most. I had already discovered that my paintings serve as portals to the Soul, so this was an excellent place to start with the group.

As each person introduced themselves, they also introduced the painting they had chosen, and I offered them a Soul reading. As I went around the room, one by one, I could feel the energy building, and the more present I became the more powerful were the words that emerged from me. As I looked into the eyes of the individual I was speaking with, I could feel our Souls becoming one. It was an amazing experience. I remember the therapist telling me that she had noticed that when I went into that deep container of consciousness, my complexion changed. I knew what she was experiencing was the light that was radiating through me as I met each person in this place of oneness.

It turned out to be one of the most powerful talks I've given to date. Everything that needed to be said came through exactly at the right moment. For the first time, all fear of speaking and being me was completely gone. I discovered what it feels like to be in your divine zone of passion that uplifts you to new heights. I was so energized by the end of the talk that I could've gone on for hours and hours without stopping. In that moment I was exceedingly grateful for this lesson and experience, and I told the Divine I was ready for more of this.

> *"Have the courage to follow your heart and intuition. They somehow already know what you truly want to become. Everything else is secondary."*
>
> **~Steve Jobs**

You're going to have a chance at the end of this chapter in the rituals section to practice seeing through the eyes of your *divine seer* with others, but for now let's practice doing this in the mirror with yourself. You can record the exercise so you can close your eyes while you listen to it.

Begin by finding a quiet spot where you have access to a mirror. You can stand or sit for this exercise, facing the mirror. When you're ready, move to the exercise.

Guided Exercise: Connecting with Your Divine Expression, the Soul of You

Take a couple of deep breaths, breathing in slowly through your nose and breathing out slowly through your mouth.

Look straight into your eyes, soften your gaze, and say, "I love you, _____." (Insert your name in the space.) Do this three to five times.

Soften your gaze even further, allowing yourself to feel the presence behind your eyes—your Divine-Self, and allow your Soul to come forward. Stay here for three to five minutes, just softly gazing into your eyes.

Notice what you're feeling and where you're feeling it. Continue sending love to yourself as you do this. You can imagine rays of pink light going from your heart into the center of your eyes. Keep doing this until you feel complete.

Now that you've completed this exercise, take a moment to journal about your experience. Answer the questions that follow.

Journaling Exercise

1. What did you feel when you gazed into your eyes?

2. How did it feel when you said, "I love you" to yourself? Was it uncomfortable? If so, why do you think that is?

3. Were you able to see beyond your physical eyes and feel the presence of your Soul, your Divine-Self? Could you feel this presence looking back at you through the depths of your eyes? If so, what did it feel like?

4. Write down any significant messages or insights from this experience.

Understanding the Language of Your Soul

One of the important aspects of the language of the Soul is symbols. Symbols serve as portals to your Soul. I'm sure you noticed that in each chapter I included a sacred symbol that was given to me by my Soul to help create the energetic space for you to unmask that particular chamber and receive the Soul virtue associated with it. I use many different symbols in my paintings as well. If you look closely at the painting **Trust the Divine Goddess Wisdom within You** at the end of the chapter, you might notice various symbols including the moon and the sign for Aquarius (the squiggly lines on the Goddess's pendant). In this case the moon represents the divine feminine, the intuitive nature of the moon, and being able to see what's hidden within (the light, wisdom, and shadow). Aquarius is the eleventh sign of the zodiac and is typically represented by the sign of the water bearer. Not only does this sign show the precious gift of water that symbolizes life and purification, but it brings with it the element of air, which is related to the intellect or knowledge. As I painted this pastel, I had no idea what these symbols were or what they represented. I was just following that creative spark that was flowing through me. I'm still amazed at how the Divine works so perfectly through us when we just surrender and get out of the way.

> *Within you is a divine container of knowledge, held by your Soul, that carries the wisdom of every expression you've ever been before.*

Within you is a divine container of knowledge, held by your Soul, that carries the wisdom of every expression you've ever been before. If you're like me, you have a very ancient Soul. Can you imagine thousands of years of knowledge being readily accessible to you? Yes, that's right, and this knowledge is intelligent because it is awakened and accessible to you only when you're ready for it. Some of it requires higher levels of consciousness to be understood and used appropriately. With each stage of awakening and spiritual growth, your divine container opens, giving you access to this information in your conscious mind.

In this case it's a remembrance of this knowledge through some sort of visual representation, like a vision of a movie playing inside you, helping you remember the experience. I've had many visions in which, for example, I saw myself performing some sort of ritual in an Egyptian temple, or even teaching other healers off-planet on Lemuria.

These visions or visual cues can come in your dreams or during moments of stillness and communion with the Divine—while meditating, for example. Many of my clairvoyant or prophetic experiences have come through my dreams, so paying attention to your dreams is very important. During your dreams you travel to other planes of consciousness with much greater ease. I like to keep a pad of paper or a digital recorder on my nightstand so I can record my dreams when I awaken. It's important to capture the dream as soon as you can while the details are still fresh in your conscious mind. I suggest keeping a dream journal or your very own Soul journal. Begin

Your Soul communicates with you based on the experiences it has lived before.

capturing the visions and visual cues you receive in your journal. This is a good way to start understanding the language of your Soul.

Your Soul communicates with you based on the experiences it has lived before. These experiences are unique to your Soul. The more you write down the visual cues and intuitive hits you receive, the easier it is to see patterns in how the Divine and your Soul communicate with you. For example, when I have visions that include water and the ocean, I know that for me this symbolizes purification and cleansing. It's no coincidence that I'm a water sign (Pisces) and feel most at home when I'm near water. By the way, the ocean has its own language just as our Souls do. You might want to start creating your own dictionary of the language of your Soul, capturing symbols, visual cues, and messages that continually show up in your dreams, visions, and external world.

I mentioned before that sometimes the Divine and your Soul communicate with you through some sort of external visual cue. You might be watching a movie and all of a sudden there's a scene that feels very familiar to you and just touches your Soul. Or you're thinking about someone you really care about and all of a sudden a song plays that says exactly what you're feeling about this person. You just know the Divine is speaking to you in that moment. I know I've received many messages through movies and songs. Paying attention to the world that surrounds you is key. The more present you are in what's happening around you, the easier it is to recognize the signs and visual cues being given to you.

I can't tell you how many times I've seen letters or numbers on a license plate and known the angels were speaking to me. I might look to the right and there's a truck with a picture of something that has meaning for me and I know it's the Divine speaking to me, or I have an unusual sighting of an animal that I know is showing up to give me a message. Once I was driving near my house with a group of friends, heading to a boat excursion in a nearby city. We were stopped at a traffic light in front of a small shopping center, and all of a sudden an eagle flew right over the hood of my car. One of my friends, who was in the passenger seat, said, "That's an eagle. I wonder what it's doing over here. Aren't they going extinct?" We were all amazed to see an eagle right there up close. I immediately knew the Divine was speaking its Soul language again. Soon after that experience I discovered I have an affinity for receiving messages through animals, so now I always pay very close attention whenever I see one. Each animal has specific messages associated with it. When there's one I've never seen or experienced before, I like to look in my power animal spirit bible by Dr. Steven Farmer called *Animal Spirit Guides*. It's amazing how accurate the messages always are.

In the case of my eagle sighting, when I meditated on that experience I was told that the eagle had shown up in my life to help me see the hidden truths beneath what my human eyes perceived to be lacking in my current circumstances. It was a time of change in my life. Somehow I had allowed myself to feed into the illusion of limitation. The eagle teaches us about perception and not allowing the illusion of limitation to keep us from pursuing our dreams and the destiny that awaits us. I think you can see how powerful this experience was for me. You, too, can have these powerful experiences if you open your heart and believe they are possible for you. Everything in life begins with intention, and the more you show the Divine your commitment to your own spiritual growth, the more the Universe shows up to support you.

Staying with the theme of seeing through the eyes of the Divine, let me share another story with you that helped me gain a better understanding of the language of my Soul. One day a client asked me to do Soul readings at her home with a group of friends. The day of the talk I went outside to meditate under the branches of one of my favorite trees in my backyard. When I completed my meditation, I looked up and saw a bird chirping very loudly on a tree branch right across from where I was sitting. Then another bird came and began chirping at the other bird. It was flexing its wings, the way you might see a body-builder flexing their muscles. It was like the two birds were arguing and there was one that was trying very hard to be heard. As I tuned in to what was happening, I was told by the Divine that one of these birds represented one of the women I would be meeting that evening, and that there was some healing happening with her in that moment. I had no idea yet who this was about, but I knew I would be talking about this experience during the event.

Off I went to my client's house. We sat in her den and the introductions began. I asked each person to pick one of my paintings from the card deck that spoke to them the most. Then I told each person what their Soul wanted them to know based on the painting they had chosen. One of the women spoke about animal communication and receiving messages from the Divine through animals. It seemed the perfect opportunity to discuss what I had experienced in my backyard with the birds. I told the group the story of what had occurred earlier after my meditation, and that I had been told that one of the birds represented one of the women in the group. As I began to tell the story, one woman raised her hand and said it was she whom the bird represented. She went on to explain that recently she had experienced a falling out with a friend, but that she had wanted to clear the air with this person prior to arriving at the gathering. That same day she had made a date to meet her friend to speak with her. She wanted to make sure she was able to heal that prior to her arrival. So at the same time that she was speaking to her friend and healing the energy, I was witnessing the healing taking place between her and her friend through the birds in my backyard. It's like the birds were assisting her in voicing what she was feeling, getting heard, and releasing the pain and anger she had felt previously with her friend.

This was a teachable moment for all of us. This experience helped me see through the eyes of the Divine and understand the language of my Soul more deeply. It also gave me an opportunity to teach others to be more open to this type of divine communication.

Let's help you connect in this moment to the language of your Soul. You can record the following meditation so you can close your eyes while you listen to it. Find a place where you can sit quietly and not be disturbed for the next fifteen minutes. Sit comfortably—with your feet flat on the floor and your hands on your knees with palms facing up. If you're an experienced meditator, use whatever position is most comfortable to you. When you're ready, please move to the meditation.

Guided Meditation: Connecting with the Language of Your Soul

Take several deep breaths, breathing in slowly through your nose and breathing out slowly through your mouth. Drop down into the center of your heart and feel the beauty of your Divine Heart. See pink rays of light radiating around and within your heart. The pink light forms a heart in the center of your heart. This heart is the doorway to your Divine-Self, your Soul. The heart becomes a door, and as you stand in front of this door you're met by your guardian angel. You're surrounded by the angels and many divine beings who will accompany you today on this journey of discovery. Your guardian angel guides you to open the door and walk through.

You enter a beautiful inner sanctuary within your heart. You're surrounded by so much white light that your eyes have to get used to the brightness. You can feel the presence of your Soul in this room. It's as if your Soul is part of the crystalline walls of this chamber. Telepathically you're instructed by your Soul to place your hands on the wall of the chamber. As you do, you see a sacred symbol emerge in the center of the room. Take a moment to notice and connect with this symbol. Let your Soul share with you the significance of this symbol. {Pause briefly.}

Now your Soul asks you to sit on the floor in the center of the chamber. As you do, another symbol emerges from the floor beneath you and rises to eye level in front of you. Take a moment to notice and connect with this symbol. {Pause briefly.}

Your Soul asks you to stand and walk to the back of the chamber. On the back wall you see an image. It radiates various hues of purple, blue, and green light. The light *enters your body and awakens your divine seer. The energy flows through every part of your body, including your eyes. As you look at the image again, it appears different. You're now seeing through the eyes of your divine seer and your Soul. Take a moment to notice and connect with the images and symbols that appear. Let your Soul help you understand the significance. This is the language of your Soul {**Pause for one minute.**}*

When you feel complete, slowly come back and open your eyes.

Now that you've completed this exercise, take a moment to journal about your experience. Answer the questions below.

Journaling Exercise

1. What did you see or feel as you entered the inner sanctuary within your heart?

2. What symbol appeared as you placed your hands on the chamber wall? What did your Soul share with you about this symbol?

3. What symbol appeared as you sat on the floor of the chamber? What did your Soul share with you about this symbol?

4. What did you feel as the light entered your body and awakened your *divine seer*? How did the image on the back wall of the chamber change after this experience?

5. Did any of these symbols seem familiar to you in any way or have you seen any of them before? If yes, write down the significance.

6. Was there anything else of importance your Soul shared with you? If so, write down any insights that seem important.

Unlocking the Divine Wisdom within You

I've mentioned several times in this chapter the importance of being able to see through the eyes of your *divine seer*, the holder of your wisdom. Now I want to add another layer of understanding to this concept. The key to being able to see through the eyes of your divinity is *divine love*. We addressed *divine love* in chapter 1, and once again I bring this to the forefront because mastering that first Soul chamber is the foundation of all else falling into place. I introduced in chapter 1 the intuitive "clair" that I call *clairlove*. In French *clair* means "clear," so I'm referring to "clear-loving." This is about using the consciousness of your heart to help you see through the eyes of your *divine seer* from a place of love and not fear. Why is this so important? Because if you want to be able to unlock the ancient wisdom within you, you need to develop your ability to use the consciousness of your heart, *clairlove,* to guide the way.

> *Beneath every question is an answer, and with each answer you move closer to understanding what is truly holding you back.*

When the fog of confusion or doubt sets in, usually generated by some underlying fear that lives within you, it's very difficult to see anything clearly. Unfortunately there's no magic wand you can wave that will instantaneously clear the fog. You have to get underneath the confusion or doubt to see why it's there. Pause and use your *divine breath* to get back to center, then ask your heart to guide the way. Listen to what your heart is trying to say to you. Beneath every question is an answer, and with each answer you move closer to understanding what is truly holding you back. Until you're back in alignment with your Heart and Soul, it may be difficult to access your *divine wisdom* with any sense of clarity. Underneath the fog is the lesson that is waiting to be learned. Your Soul knows this and urges you to slow down and be present with the fog so you can learn to transcend it. On the other side of that murkiness is the warmth of God's love and light waiting to embrace you.

I've practiced this very technique in my journey many times. One of those times was when I was writing my chapter for Christine Kloser's anthology, *Pebbles in the Pond (Wave 4).* Our deadline for the chapter submission was rapidly approaching, yet I had not been able to write one word. I felt so stuck in this haze of confusion. When Christine offered those of us in her MasterHeart program an opportunity to meet live for an all-day writing retreat, I jumped at the opportunity. I knew I needed to be there if I wanted to clear the fog that was keeping me stuck.

I was really happy when the day finally arrived for my trip to Los Angeles. I would be spending a full day with my favorite writing coach and mentor and other Soul-sisters from the MasterHeart program. I couldn't wait to see them all. When I arrived at the airport there was an extremely long line for the self-service ticket kiosk. I had forgotten to print my boarding pass at home, so I decided to get out of line, pull out my iPad, and attempt to do a web check-in to speed things up a bit. But with every attempt I made, I got an error message. I had no choice but to get back in line. When I finally got to the self-service kiosk, once again I got an error message. When I told the attendant directing us in line what had just happened, she told me I would need to stand in another line to get help from one of the representatives with a computer terminal. I kept reminding myself that patience is a virtue. I knew there was a reason all this was happening. I finally got up to the airline representative and explained the situation to her. Several times she asked me for my confirmation number because she was having trouble finding my reservation. Finally she was able to pull up my information, and told me that the issue was that my reservation was "out of sync." And boom, it hit me! The Divine was telling me that there was something in me that was out of sync. Immediately I felt that it was sitting in my heart waiting to be healed and transformed. This was why I had been feeling so stuck—not just in my writing, but in other areas of my life. This was confirmation that I really needed to be at that retreat.

The next morning as we gathered for our day together, I thought about what my intention was for being there. I knew it was all about surrendering to the Divine and releasing what no longer served me. If I could do this, the fog would lift, and then the clarity would come. As Christine asked us to talk about our intentions, I placed mine in the sacred circle and expressed my gratitude to the Divine for making this day possible for me. Then Christine guided us in meditation. As we flowed together in this sacred circle of consciousness, I received several messages that helped me understand what was going on. I saw that beneath the fog I was out of sync with my heart. Until then my mind had been attached to the "what" and the "how" the chapter should be written. In other words, I was trying to control what I was writing and how the story would be told. As with everything else in life, we are really not in control; the Divine is. The more we can let go and surrender to the flow of the Universe, the easier things happen for us.

There was something else, though, that I discovered. This was not just about control. It was also about my attachment to the old me who had lived most of her life in a business suit in a corporate environment. Yet the real me hated business suits. I loved being in comfortable, flowy, goddess attire. It's funny because while I packed for this trip, my inclination was around authenticity and unmasking the real me, including the clothes I wore, my hair, and even the expression of my voice. In this moment I was being asked to let go of all of that and really listen to my heart. My heart had been holding these old impressions of needing approval from others, even in the way I dressed and looked. However, my heart was calling me to be a greater version of the real me, the authentic me, whom God created to serve as a teacher and healer. It was time to let go of my need to live through the eyes of others and instead choose me, and know that in choosing me I was gaining my freedom.

As my heart began to heal the energy that was ready to be lifted and transmuted, something amazing happened. The fog lifted and I began to write and write and write. In an hour and a half my entire chapter was written. I was amazed and grateful to the

Divine for having made this possible through Christine and the sacred circle she had created during that retreat. In this Earth school that you and I are part of, we are all perpetual students and teachers at the same time. When you're open to learning and present in the moment to what surrounds you, you receive exactly what is needed to open the gateway to your *divine wisdom.*

Divine wisdom comes in many forms. It can be ancient, esoteric knowledge; a new way of solving a routine problem; a new technology; an important insight that helps you evolve spiritually (as in my story of being out of sync); or knowledge that is applied in a different way to bring a new perspective to those who experience it. Maybe the Divine is downloading a book (or books) into your mind that you're meant to share with your tribe. Or perhaps one night you go to sleep and have a dream that gives you a solution to something that helps your tribe in a way that has never occurred before. This is wisdom that not only helps others, but helps you create the Soul-driven life you seek and deserve. Let go of any expectations of what your *divine wisdom* should be or look like; it's going to be perfect because God designed it to match who you are and what you're meant to do in this life. Surrendering to that divine part of you that already knows and sees through God's eyes allows the unfolding to happen with grace and ease.

The more you unmask your Soul and the real you, the more you're able to open the space for what I call "Soul callbacks." Soul callbacks are impressions of knowledge held in your Soul that transcend time and space. As you remember who you really are and connect with the divine presence within you, you're able to create these Soul callbacks that are the gateways to the knowledge that you've accumulated from the various aspects of you that have lived before. Within the core of your Soul you hold the gateway to the infinite wisdom that sits within you. I love this quote from the book *Saint Germain on Alchemy,* channeled by Mark and Elizabeth Prophet, that says,

> *The reality of yourself is your Divine-Self, and it is this omniscient part of you that holds the genius that unlocks the pure knowledge within you.*

"Become acquainted with the Reality of yourself. For this Reality is the genie (genius) in you that can give the Aladdin (symbolizing the alchemist who rubs the lamp of pure knowledge) the right desires of his immortal being."

You are that immortal being. Your Soul never dies—only the human vessel that it occupies ceases to breathe. The *reality of yourself* is your Divine-Self, and it is this omniscient part of you that holds the *genius* that unlocks the *pure knowledge* within you. This pure knowledge refers to your *divine wisdom* and the impressions of that wisdom that I refer to as your "Soul callbacks." Each Soul callback has its own vibration and frequency, and even its own timing of access. That means that your Soul is the one controlling the timing of when and how you access that wisdom. Each Soul callback is matched to your spiritual growth, the specific juncture of your journey, and your vibration. When your vibration matches the vibration of that Soul callback, the gateway opens for you to access that *divine wisdom.*

One of the best ways to unlock these Soul callbacks and wisdom within you is to ask yourself some deep, Soul-searching questions about who you really are and what your *divine purpose* is in this life. The *divine wisdom* you hold within you was given to you for a very specific reason, one that aligns with your Soul's purpose—a purpose that is unique to you and only you. Some key questions to ask yourself are:

"How am I meant to serve?"

"How does my *divine wisdom* serve me?"

"How is the *divine wisdom* I hold meant to serve others?"

"In what capacity am I meant to share this *divine wisdom*?"

"How will those I serve benefit from this *divine wisdom*?"

"How does my authentic self resonate or vibrate within this *divine wisdom*?"

"What part of my Soul seeks to be expressed through my *divine wisdom* in this moment?"

"What specific Soul callbacks are ready to rise into my conscious awareness, and what parts of my life do they relate to?"

Take a moment now to pull out your journal and spend some time with these questions. Find a quiet place to sit, reflect, and contemplate. Jot down whatever comes through your Heart and Soul. Don't try to answer all the questions at once. Give this exercise the space and time it needs so you can connect deeply with your Soul and allow it to speak through you as you search for deeper meaning about your container of *divine wisdom.*

Now that you've taken some time to contemplate your *divine wisdom*, let's help you experience a Soul callback. You can record the following meditation so you can close your eyes while you listen to it. For the audio version, visit **www.Unmasking YourSoul.com/Meditations.** Sit comfortably where you won't be disturbed—with your feet flat on the floor and your hands on your knees with palms facing up. If you're an experienced meditator, use whatever position is most comfortable to you. When you're ready, please move to the meditation.

Guided Meditation: Accessing Your Divine Wisdom

Breathe slowly, inhaling through your nose and exhaling through your mouth. As you breathe, focus on your breath and feel with every breath the relaxation of your mind, body, and spirit. Just focus on your breath and let thoughts pass as they may.

See yourself walking in a beautiful green meadow. The grass is green and moist from the morning dew. You walk and admire the beautiful fragrant wildflowers. Up ahead you see a field of golden-yellow sunflowers. You walk towards them and sit down on the ground near them. You pick a sunflower and allow its golden energy to enter your body.

*The energy lands in your abdomen and you feel the essence of your divine power coming to the surface. The golden light turns into all the colors of the rainbow and travels through your body, touching every cell and every molecule of your existence. The rainbow light melts away your anxiety, worries, and all lower-vibration energy that no longer serves you. As the light moves through you, you feel lighter and lighter. You can feel how loved you are by the Divine. Allow this divine love to permeate your being. {**Pause.**}*

You get up from the ground and continue walking. Up ahead there's a dirt pathway, and you're guided to follow it. You see many stones on the sides of the path with ancient markings and symbols on them. There's one particular stone that you feel very attracted to. You stop and place your hand on the stone over the ancient markings. The markings imprint the same symbol on the palm of your hand. You continue walking.

At the end of the path you see a man. He's wearing an amulet and a medicine pouch around his neck. When you approach, he tells you that he has been waiting for you. He raises his right palm and you see that it has the same symbol that was etched in the palm of your hand. He tells you that he is a shaman, one of your ancestors, and will be your guide today. He asks you to follow him, and so you do. You walk through a small gate and enter a courtyard of sacred ground encircled by many big stones. You notice many etchings and markings similar to those you saw on the stones along the pathway.

The shaman takes you to the center of the circle. There you see an altar that the shaman has set up. It has many sacred objects on it and several instruments and rattles. He uses a sacred stick to draw the symbol that is etched in your palm on the ground and asks you to sit down. You sit facing each other. He places his hand on your forehead and traces the infinity symbol on the center point between your eyebrows. He blows on it and the symbol becomes three-dimensional on your forehead. You can feel lots of energy flowing there and the shaman asks you to just breathe this all into your being.

Open and surrender to the Divine, omniscient Soul that you are. Stay here for a moment to allow this part of you to come forward and be felt. {Pause.}

The shaman picks up an ancient flute and tells you to just relax and listen. As he plays the flute, the symbol on your forehead begins to activate and a portal opens within your inner mind. See yourself walking through the portal. When you walk through, you enter a sacred forest. Here you will meet various aspects of your Soul that have lived before. Each aspect will share a piece of wisdom that is ready to be awakened in your conscious mind.

You continue walking and you feel a divine presence up ahead. It is an aspect of your Divine Soul. The shaman appears next to you in this sacred forest and begins shaking several rattles. He asks you to call back the divine wisdom that this part of your Soul is holding. You can still hear the notes and music the shaman is playing with his magical flute. The vibration of the music is retrieving and calling back the wisdom held by this part of your Soul, and places it in your conscious mind. Stay here for a moment as this integrates within you. {Pause.}

"There is more," the shaman tells you. "Walk forward," he says. As you do, you feel another aspect of your Divine Soul. You stop, and once again the vibration of the music retrieves and calls back the wisdom of this aspect of your Soul and places it in your conscious mind. Stay here for a moment as this integrates within you. {Pause.}

The voice of the shaman summons you back through the portal and you return to the sacred circle. The shaman tells you that you are now complete. He takes you back to the dirt pathway that brought you here. You thank the Divine and the shaman for their assistance and walk towards the meadow where you began your journey today.

You take one last look at the beautiful wildflowers and inhale their aromatic fragrance.

When you're ready, slowly come back and open your eyes.

245

Now that you've completed the guided meditation, take some time to do some journaling. Spend about ten to fifteen minutes in a quiet place where you won't be disturbed answering the questions below. You can put on some soothing music or light a candle or incense to support you as you write. Just write from your Heart and Soul and the rest will follow.

Journaling Exercise

1. How did you feel as the golden and rainbow light healed your body?

2. What did you feel and experience when the shaman placed the infinity symbol on your forehead and blew on it?

3. What did you experience when the shaman played the ancient flute as you walked through the portal?

4. What did you experience during the two Soul callbacks? Can you sense what *divine wisdom* was retrieved and placed in your conscious mind?

5. Write down anything else of significance.

After journaling, continue working on the **Canvas of Your Soul.** (You can download the PDF at **www.UnmaskingYourSoul.com/Blueprint.**) Pick phrases, words, or symbols and put them on section 8 of the **Light** part of your roadmap. Make this canvas your own piece of artwork that represents the journey we're taking together in this book. You can color, paint, or even cut images from magazines that depict the messages and insights you received in this chapter on *accessing your divine wisdom.* You don't need to be a professional artist to do this. Just let your Soul express through you as it wants to. This will become the vision board of your Soul's unmasking, a precious gift to you from your *divine seer.* Congratulations! You've now completed two-thirds of your journey.

Five Rituals to Awaken Your Divine Wisdom Muscle

The rituals below are meant to help you awaken your *divine wisdom* muscle. You can repeat any of the rituals that follow and do the exercises and guided meditations earlier in the chapter as many times as you like. With each repetition you go deeper in accessing your *divine seer.*

Before you begin, create your sacred space and take some deep breaths to relax your mind and body. Connect with your Soul as you enter this sacred space.

1. This ritual helps you practice seeing through the eyes of your *divine seer*. Do this with a partner. Your goal is to be able to see and experience the presence of your partner's Soul. Have your journals handy. No words are to be spoken during this ritual. Focus on seeing beyond the veil of the human vessel that sits in front of you. An open heart is all that is required. To practice this ritual, do the following:

    a. Each person should sit in a comfortable chair, with feet on the floor, facing each other. Face each other knee to knee, with a small distance between your knees—no more than twelve inches. Place your hands on your knees with palms facing up and begin taking some deep breaths together. Try to match the breathing of the other person, inhaling slowly through your nose and exhaling slowly through your mouth. Close your eyes. When you feel calm and centered, move on to the next step.

    b. Open your eyes and just softly stare into the eyes of your partner. Allow your gaze to soften and send love from your heart to their heart. Imagine a cord of blue-purple light connecting the centers of your foreheads. Call on your Soul to send messages to the Soul of your partner through this cord. Continue to gaze softly into your partner's eyes. See if you can really feel into their Soul. No words are exchanged; just allow the energy to flow through you both. Do this for five to seven minutes. Pay attention to the smallest of details. When you both feel complete, move on to the next step.

    c. Without any vocalization from either of you, journal about what you just experienced. What did you "see?" Did you receive any images from your partner through the cord you created between your foreheads? Did your Soul give you any other information about your partner or yourself? Spend about ten to fifteen minutes journaling about this experience. When complete, share what you just journaled about with each other.

2. This ritual will help you access the nuggets of your *divine wisdom* that are ready for harvesting. Each nugget contains a history of you that is being called back by your Soul to your conscious mind. Do this meditation on a Sunday and repeat it for seven days.

    > *Close your eyes and take several deep breaths. As you breathe in and out slowly, focus on feelings of gratitude and love. When you feel your body and mind flowing in the sea of calmness, then begin.*
    >
    > *There is a white spiral staircase in front of you. Slowly walk up the stairs. As*

you start your journey today, ask the Divine to surround you in a womb of divine love and understanding. With each step you take, you're surrounded by the most beautiful rainbow light, which magnifies the brilliance of every cell in your body and prepares you for what lies ahead.

When you reach the top of the staircase, you're met by your guardian angel. They hold your hand as you walk through the doorway in front of you. You see yourself flying with your guardian angel through an angelic portal that is full of brilliant white light. When you walk through the opening at the end of the tunnel, you're transported to the Isle of Danburesh. The isle is majestic and breathtaking. You don't remember being here before, yet it feels very familiar to you.

Up ahead is a beautiful white tree. The roots go deep and the branches are wide and bountiful, holding a splendor of fragrant flowers and beautiful golden nuggets. Your guardian angel tells you this is the Tree of Wisdom. Each day you will be asked to pick a nugget from the fruit of this tree that unlocks a seed of your divine wisdom that your Soul is ready to call back into conscious existence. Together you walk towards the tree, and as you reach it, an ascended master joins you there. Today you're joined by Mother Mary. She represents the energy of the Divine Mother and will guide you as you pick your first golden nugget.

Mother Mary holds your hand and guides you to the tree's edge. She ascends from the ground and lifts you by her side. There is a nugget ready to be harvested. There's one in particular that sparkles and twinkles before you. You feel a connection to your Heart and Soul, so you reach for this nugget. It eagerly comes off the branch and lands in your hands.

*As you hold the nugget in your hands, it opens freely and radiates bright light. The light enters your crown and travels through every cell of your body. As this is happening you can feel every part of you tingling, and something deeply held within you emerges to the surface. Stay here for a moment and allow this Soul callback to complete. Be with this energy for as long as you feel necessary. {**Pause.**}*

When you feel complete, thank the Divine, your guardian angel, and Mother Mary for this amazing journey today. Your guardian angel takes you by the hand and returns you through the angelic tunnel to the doorway that leads to the staircase where you began your journey today. Climb down the stairs, and when you reach the bottom, slowly open your eyes.

Don't forget to journal about your experience, and continue to do so over the next six days as you complete this seven-day ritual. On each subsequent day you will be joined by a different ascended master. Just be open to the guidance of your Heart and Soul and the rest will follow.

3. For this next ritual you will need to purchase a Tibetan black quartz crystal, called "black" because of the black inclusions in the clear quartz. You will also need an amethyst seer's stone. You can purchase these online, although it is always best, if you have the option, to choose them in person at your local gem or crystal shop. Each crystal serves a different purpose. I find that the Tibetan black quartz helps me connect with wisdom from other lives or dimensions through time and space. The amethyst seer's stone helps me with intuition, prophecy, and seeing through the eyes of my *divine seer*. You can use this stone to open more deeply to your clairvoyant, intuitive-sight abilities. Below are two short rituals you can use with each stone.

    a. Before you begin the rituals, "program" your stones. There are different ways to do this, but I like to hold the stone in both hands and place the stone against my heart. I treat and speak to the stone as the sacred object it is. I thank the stone for coming into my life and send it loving rays of light from my heart. Then I program the stone to help me with the particular need I have at that time. For the Tibetan black quartz, ask it to help you connect with wisdom from past lives and dimensions across time and space. For the amethyst seer's stone, ask it to help you see through the eyes of your *divine seer* and access the wisdom of your own intuitive abilities to see across time and space. Then just pause for a moment and see if the stone has anything it wants to share with you. It may tell you of other ways it wants to assist you on your journey. When the programming is complete, you can choose to practice one or both of the following rituals:

        Tibetan black quartz ritual: After meditation or spiritual communion, hold the Tibetan black quartz in both hands in whatever way you feel guided to do so. Bring the stone in front of your mouth and blow on the stone three to five times. Use slow, deliberate, divine breaths. Each breath serves as a key that opens the portal to the connection between your infinite self and the consciousness of the stone. Close your eyes, if you haven't already, and allow the stone to speak to you. You can rest the stone on your heart or just hold it in your hands. You can start by silently speaking to the stone and asking it what wisdom is meant to be shared with you in this moment. Any *divine wisdom* from past lives or other dimensions of consciousness that serves your highest good in this moment is called forth. You can continue to ask questions as you're guided, or just be in the silence to receive what is meant to be shared in this moment.

Amethyst seer's stone ritual: After meditation or spiritual communion, hold the amethyst seer's stone in both hands in whatever way you feel guided to do so. Bring the stone in front of your mouth and blow on the stone three to five times. Use slow, deliberate, divine breaths. Each breath serves as a key that opens the portal to the connection between your infinite self and the consciousness of the stone. Close your eyes, if you haven't already, and allow the stone to speak to you. You can rest the stone on your heart or just hold it in your hands. You can start by silently speaking to the stone and asking it to share with you wisdom about your intuitive sight or prophetic visions that are meant to serve your highest good. Continue to ask questions as you're guided, or just be in the silence to receive what is meant to be shared in this moment.

b. Remember to clear your stones every once in a while. You can do this in many different ways. Some of my favorites include passing the stones through the smoke of white sage, burying them in the earth overnight, or leaving them overnight in the moonlight.

4. This moon ritual serves you best during the full moon. I encourage you to find a moon calendar online and post the dates and times of upcoming full moons on your calendar. During super moons, the energy is even more powerful. This is a time when the Earth, moon, and sun are all in alignment and the moon is in its nearest approach to Earth. You can find those online as well. As I mentioned earlier in the chapter, the moon holds energy of fertility, intuition, receptivity, prophecy, and illumination, to name a few. You can tap into the moon's energy to help you connect with your intuitive sight and *divine wisdom*. If you'd like to enhance the energy, you can hold a white selenite crystal in your hands as you perform the ritual.

a. On the night of the full moon, pick a spot, preferably outside, where you can see and feel the light of the moon most abundantly. You can sit on a chair or on the ground. Choose the most comfortable spot for you and allow your Soul to guide you on this journey.

b. Take a moment to invoke the Divine and create a sacred space in which you can speak and listen to the moon. You might try something like this:

Dearest Divine and Sacred Moon, I sit before you today to give you thanks for all your love and support. I ask that we may commune in a sacred space where boundaries of time and space are eliminated and we flow in the wonderment of pure oneness. May I see the splendor of your *divine wisdom* shine through me to awaken all that is ready to be seen. May your light shine through me and illuminate what needs to be illuminated. May it come with grace and ease, and purity of spirit. And so it is. Amen.

c. Stare at the moon. Soften your gaze so you can see the outline of the moon and witness the energy that flows in its center and on its extremities. Continue to stare at the moon, allowing your gaze to soften and soften. Allow your eyesight to slightly blur. Stay here and see where your gaze takes you. You might feel attracted to a specific point on the moon. Just allow yourself to go there and receive any visual cues that you're meant to receive in this moment. You might begin to see colors in the light of the moon. Notice what those colors are. Notice any symbols or visual messages that appear before you. Do this for ten to fifteen minutes, or for as long as you feel guided to do so.

d. When you feel complete, slowly adjust your eyesight and return to normal focus. Be sure to journal about your experience.

5. Meditate with my painting *Trust the Divine Goddess Wisdom within You*, shown at the end of the chapter, to help you reconnect with your *divine seer,* the one who helps you access your *divine wisdom.* Each of my paintings was divinely channeled and holds messages and energetic impressions of the Soul that bring healing to the bearer. This particular painting holds vibrations of healing for those needing to remember their expression of *divine wisdom.*

a. Close your eyes and take a breath... inhaling slowly through your nose and exhaling slowly through your mouth... and with each breath you take relax your mind, body, and spirit. Continue focusing on your breath... and with each breath allow your thoughts to pass freely... thought after thought... breath after breath... relaxing more and more deeply. Continue taking several more deep breaths. {**Repeat for one or two minutes.**}

b. Briefly open your eyes and observe the painting. Allow yourself to be taken on a journey into the painting. Look at the images and symbols, and allow your gaze to go to one focal point in the painting. Soften your gaze as you focus on this point of interest. Breathe in its energy, seeing the symbols, images, and colors in your mind's eye. Continue breathing in the energy... breath after breath, allowing you to feel and absorb the healing energy from this focal point.

c. With your next breath, listen to the voice of your Soul. What is it communicating? What messages do you hear or feel within you as you breathe in the energy of the painting? Pay attention to where the energy is going in your body. This gives you an indication of where in your body you may need to release old energy, traumas, or wounds. Continue breathing and just go into the stillness while you connect deeper within. Allow the healing energies of the painting to penetrate your mind, body, and spirit. **{Do this for two to five minutes.}** If you feel guided, you may continue repeating this step, changing to a different focal point in the painting each time. Again, allow yourself to breathe the images, symbols, colors, and healing energies into your being.

d. Don't forget to journal about anything of significance that comes up during this experience.

EILEEN ANÜMANI SANTOS, *TRUST THE DIVINE GODDESS WISDOM WITHIN YOU*, c. 2007

Trust the Divine Goddess Wisdom within You represents your *divine seer*, the one whole holds the container of your *divine wisdom*. Your Soul calls back to you all that is fermented and ripe for harvest. Allow the Aquarian water bearer to cleanse your heart and prepare you to access the wisdom of the ancient Soul that you are. The moon opens the gateway to your clairvoyant and clear-seeing abilities. Honor the sacred Soul that you are.

SEE what has been hidden. ACCESS the ancient knowledge within your divine container and allow it to SERVE you and others through LOVE!

STAGE THREE: HEALING

Embodying Your Soul's Healing

As you fully EMBODY your divine expression, you unlock your Soul's DNA and begin living a more joyful, passionate, inspired, Soul-driven life.

Igniting the Divine Mind

by Eileen Anümani Santos

My beloved child, I created you in my image, and so as I AM, you are—all-knowing, all-being, and all-loving.

Each thought of mine, you carry in your heart.

Each mindful breath you take brings you to our sanctuary of oneness. From this place you can dream, create, and explore the thoughts of my being.

Each thought I express to you is encoded in the vibration of my eternal love for you.

As you clear the noise from your periphery, you are able to experience this knowing in your Soul.

Let not the thoughts of the ego drown out my voice, which only speaks in harmony with your Heart and Soul.

As we connect in the trinity of Spirit, Soul, and Source, the I AM that I AM, you create the passageway for your Soul's embodiment.

Spirit as Light. Light as Soul. Soul as Source.

As each portal of this trinity activates, you transcend your ego-mind and the spark of creation ignites the flame of your *divine mind*.

CHAPTER 9

Soul Chamber IX:
Aligning with the Divine Mind

With this chapter you move to Stage Three, the last stage of your journey, HEALING, where you embody your *Soul's Healing*. As you unmask each of the remaining four chambers, you embody your Soul more deeply. This enables you to live a Soul-driven life and experience your own Heaven on Earth by the time you reach chapter 12.

In chapter 8 I introduced the Soul virtue of *divine wisdom*. This is the force of the divine feminine and the creator of intention—the seeds of manifestation. Now we move to the chamber of the *divine mind*, driven by the energy of the divine masculine: the doer and implementer of manifestation. The *divine mind* provides the *divine spark* or ignition that transforms the seeds into encoded thoughts that manifest on the physical plane. Each encoded thought carries a vibration that tells the Universe what your intention is for that particular seed. If this intention is aligned with your Soul's highest good, the Universe sets its "attention" to connect all existing seeds that match this vibration and frequency.

Then each seed is awakened or ignited by your divine expression and the seeds begin to take form on the physical plane. As this occurs, you experience divine synchronicities that act as magnets to bring together all the pieces for your intention to be made a reality. This can take the form of human intervention, as when someone suddenly calls you to offer you the opportunity of a lifetime, or a spiritual intervention in which, for example, the money you need to start your business miraculously appears or you meet an amazing coach whom you know is the one who can help you move forward with your *divine purpose*.

The center of the top of your head (your crown) is the location of **Soul Chamber IX—Divine Mind,** the ninth of the Soul virtues that will be unmasked as you continue on your journey of wholeness. The mask associated with the ninth chamber is the **Mask of Attachment.** Your ego keeps you attached to people, possessions, and thoughts, so you remain small and safe in your comfort zone. Anything you're attached to creates an energy of constriction or limitation. It's the way your ego-mind attempts to control your life, keeping you from surrendering to the natural flow of events created by the Universe. In order to manifest what is in your highest good, the energy must be free-flowing so that what is formed naturally comes together exactly how and when it's needed without any preconceived conditions of the ego. There's a natural intelligence to the universal *divine mind* that always strives to bring forth for you what is in your highest good. When you're able to surrender to that divine mental force, your life choreographs itself into a harmonious dance that is unique to you and your *divine purpose*. The archetype of this Soul chamber is the **divine alchemist**, the one who helps you transmute the lower vibrations of your ego-mind and align you with the empowering and loving vibrations of the *divine mind*. The sacred symbol for the *divine mind* chamber is shown below.

It's the journey you're meant to pay attention to, not the destination. The journey brings growth and enlightenment to your spirit. Your destiny is already written in this all-knowing *divine mind*. You're here to claim that destiny. By mastering your ego-mind and aligning with the all-knowing intelligence of the *divine mind*, you create a more enriching and Soul-driven life. Every day becomes an inspiration to learn, grow, love, be YOU, and remember who YOU really are—that glorious, amazing, magnificent, beautiful, powerful, and loving divine being that you are!

In this chapter I cover three key areas that help you do that. The first is letting go of attachment by confronting your ego-mind face to face. The second is enlisting the gifts of your *divine alchemist* to connect with your powers of transmutation and the violet flame. And last we'll look at how you can align with the *divine mind* and claim your destiny that is already written in the holographic blueprint of this universal intelligence. In this section I talk about the fifth "clair"—*claircognizance*, or "clear-knowing." So far we've covered four ways to tap into your intuitive senses that allow you to receive messages from the Divine through the inherent make-up of your divine being. In chapter 1, "Returning

Divine Mind Symbol

to Divine Love," I introduced you to a "clair" that I call clairlove or clear-loving. This is a "clair" that I identified through my own spiritual growth, one that you may not find in other teachings. In chapter 2 we covered clairsentience or clear-feeling. Clairaudience or clear-hearing was discussed in chapter 7, and clairvoyance or clear-seeing in chapter 8.

The last "clair," claircognizance, or clear-knowing, usually manifests as a strong feeling of knowing something—not exactly knowing how or why, but knowing in every fiber of your being that what you know is true. This intuitive sense kicks in when you make a direct connection to the *divine mind* (where your divine plan and destiny are already written). You can think of this *divine mind* as a holographic blueprint that contains the God-seeds of the divine thoughts that make up the destiny of your human embodiment. Your Soul is the captain of your destiny. The more deeply you surrender to and embody your Soul, the easier it is to navigate the seas (thoughts) of your destiny that God created and which are imprinted in the holographic blueprint of the *divine mind*.

I have been attached to so many different things in my life: relationships, career, emotions, self-image, limiting behaviors, and thoughts. This is all part of the journey. Your life is orchestrated by the lessons you're meant to learn. The ego-mind and the attachments it forms are a means to an end. It is through these experiences that we grow, enrich our lives, and claim our Souls' destinies. Each attachment is like a wrapper enclosing something inside that needs to be healed and transformed. The *form* of that attachment follows *thought*. In other words, that attachment began with a thought. With each attachment you're able to let go of and transcend, you release another layer of woundedness that holds you back from experiencing the divine perfection that you are at your core.

"Our life is shaped by our mind; we become what we think. Suffering follows an evil thought as the wheels of a cart follow the oxen that draw it."

"Our life is shaped by our mind; we become what we think. Joy follows a pure thought like a shadow that never leaves."

~The Dhammapada (Chapter 1 – "Twin Verses")

My natural inclination, especially in moments of despair and fear, is to go back to God. If you're feeling fear and despair, then something is keeping you separated from that divine part of you that is always connected to Source. That's why daily spiritual practice is so important. In some cases, the more you practice communing in the stillness, the easier and faster it is to find instantaneous comfort and relief. I want to share one of those moments with you when I was in a dark abyss of despair and attachment. This was the conversation that took place between me and God:

Me: My Dearest God, I have felt so stuck lately. It's difficult to even write what I'm feeling. I'm feeling attached to so many things, especially the writing of this book. But in this moment, as the tears roll down my face, You invite me to just write with You. I ask You now from the deepest parts of my Soul and with this deep yearning to serve, "What will it take for me to reach the place of divine flow with You, where the words come effortlessly and are inspired by Your *divine love*?"

God's response: Listen to me now and just be. Savor this sacred moment between us, for I promise you, as you surrender to my calling and will daily, the words will flow with ease. Stay present to our oneness in your heart and allow my love for you to bring forth the inspiration of the words that already flow through your veins, Soul, and being. Your fingers will take over, typing and typing for hours on end. This begins now in this moment. "Why now?" you ask. "How is it so?" you ask. Because for the first time I feel you come in earnest with a desire to truly help those you're meant to serve. In the past your ego has kept you tied to chains of illusion, a desire for power, chained to the material outcomes; but now your Soul resides here with me, guiding you with deep reverence and respect for the gifts I have given you. You have awakened to a deeper purity within your heart. From this place you can teach, heal, and guide my children to their own pureness, a pureness that can only be born from the Divine Heart and Soul.

You have been escalating through the layers of noise that surrounded you—some burdens of this life and some burdens of before. But, more important, the deeper you surrender to my will for you, the less the noise affects your true path. You are finally surrendering to the will of your co-pilot, your Divine-Self. Your Soul now has made its appearance to direct your path to higher ground. I have sent many of my children to help you: Archangel Metatron, Jesus, Mother Mary, a multitude of guides and angels, and many in human form to catalyze this moment in your life. Their presence exists to bring you to that higher ground. You need not understand the why, what, when, or how of it all, but just be present in this moment with me. It is your presence I need most in order for you to be able to co-pilot this ship across the waters you call life.

The waves have been turbulent, bumpy, and painful at times, but now you enter more peaceful seas. You are now ready to transcend the noise that has held you back from your true essence all this time, though not for naught. Everything in life happens for a reason. You had to experience the turbulence and the noise so you could learn to transcend it, for you will teach your flock how to do the same. You are well aware that in order to teach others you must know what it feels like to walk in their shoes. It is only from this place of knowing that you can feel compassion and love for your flock. When you minister to your Soul family, do it from purity of heart, where you are grounded in humility, compassion, understanding, and reverence for all that is—a place of eternal love. You have come home to that place.

And just as you typed these words with great ease, so, too, will the rest of the journey that needs to be documented arise with tenderness, compassion, love, and fluidity of Heart and Soul. Today you embark on this journey with me. Be prepared. You may be surprised by the depth of the words, the profoundness of the experience, and the love of the journey that we will take together.

I leave you with this thought: Let me be the words you write. Let me be the love that inspires your every word. Let me be the voice that inspires your Soul and allows your magnificence to shine brightly. You no longer need to wear a mask. It's time to live on purpose, fearlessly, as I hold your hand. This has always been my plan for you. You are now ready to fulfill your mission on Earth.

Every time I read this passage I get emotional. I'm immediately taken back to this moment when my heart was filled to the brim with God's eternal love. There was a clear understanding and a knowing that I had reached higher ground, a higher vibration of eternal love where purity of heart lives. But by no means did this mean that I had reached nirvana or that I needed to stop working on myself. On the contrary. I continue to work on myself daily, because I want to be able to serve you from the highest version of me that I can be. With every layer we transcend, there is more that needs attention. There may be times when you feel tired and exhausted from all that your journey brings, but I'm here to tell you not to give up on YOU. The more you master your ego-mind and align with the *divine mind*, the more your life transforms. In fact, the new you and your new life will be barely recognizable to the old you that you were. And this new you—well, it's really the YOU you've always been at your core; you just forgot who that was. But your journey, which forges destiny on a daily basis, brings you closer to that divine YOU that you've always been and will always be.

Learning to Let Go of Attachment

Letting go is one of the most difficult lessons we all have to learn. As we experience life and our humanness, it is so easy to become attached to our personal identities and the things that make up those identities, like emotions, relationships, material objects, and even ways of being. Early in *Unmasking Your Soul*, you read about my attachment to an unhealthy relationship that lasted about eleven years. It took me that long to realize I was worthy of something much better and to find the courage to leave that behind me. Don't get me wrong; there are no regrets there. I do believe everything happens for a reason and has its own divine timing, so it all happened as it needed to.

In the last chapter you read about my attachment to an old way of being and the self-image I had created and lived for most of my adulthood as a businesswoman in a corporate environment. That attachment kept me unable to move forward in my writing and other areas of my life. I wasted a lot of money trying to keep up that self-image that didn't even represent the real me. The wounded me thought I would feel better if I bought myself nice things like jewelry, clothes, and shoes. Yet underneath all that I was still broken. I had let these possessions possess me. It was the wounded child I needed to heal, and nothing in my external world could fix that. The solution had always been sitting within me. Only by going there could I shift the pattern. When you go underneath the covers and discover the real reason why you are attached to a pattern, you can change it. I not only felt unloved, but unworthy of being loved. I spent most of my life seeking the approval of others because I lacked the self-love that is an inherent part of my divine being.

At one point I even discovered that I was attached to the form of the healing I was doing with my clients. I started my healing practice by doing hands-on healing, so I thought that was the only way I could serve them. As the Divine asked me to start serving more and more people, I kept resisting because my mind was quite attached to that one way of healing. Every day the Divine reminded me that all I needed to do was be the open vessel and the Divine would partner with me so I could use all of my gifts to bring about healing for my clients. I was reminded of the day I did that amazing talk without any notes, just by being present and allowing the Divine to speak through me. As I let go of the form that I thought the healing should take, I soon discovered that the Divine was guiding me to surrender to new ways of being and expressing my healing gifts. When I worked with groups of people, I witnessed the Divine working through my voice, words, breath, guided meditations, and just my presence. The mind is a powerful instrument. The moment I let go of the limited thinking about the form that the healing should take, I was able to see that the form of the healing created itself in the moment as I became present to the moment and allowed the Divine to work through me freely.

"Attachment is the food for the mind to continue. Non-attached witnessing is the way to stop it without any effort to stop it. And when you start enjoying those blissful moments, your capacity to retain them for longer periods arises."

~**Osho**

Attachments are ways that your ego-mind attempts to control the flow of your life.

Attachments are ways that your ego-mind attempts to control the flow of your life. When you allow that to happen, you interrupt the natural flow of the Universe. In the holographic blueprint of the *divine mind* there exists a vibration of divine perfection. This means that the Divine has imprinted in this blueprint all that is meant for your highest good. It has already manifested there in the field of the *divine mind*. When you become attached to an outcome, a way of being, a way of doing and achieving the task at hand or anything else you're trying to control, it becomes the object of dissonance to the divine perfection that already exists in the magnetic field of the *divine mind*. This dissonance then appears in your conscious mind or mental body as a point of disharmony and dissension. You probably have experienced this before—a moment when you feel conflicted about something. Your heart is telling you to go one way but your mind (your ego-mind) is propelling you in another direction. Your ego is attempting every way possible to keep you from listening to or hearing what your heart has to say. Remember, your heart is the passageway to the *divine light* that you are. The more you let your ego-mind and fear take control, the more they drown out the voice of *divine love* in your heart.

In such moments it's important to pause, take a deep breath, and connect with the tiny space in your heart that leads to your inner sanctuary of oneness with the Divine, your Divine-Self—the Soul of You. The more you practice being in communion daily with the Divine, the easier it is to use these pauses as natural elements of returning to center. It's like anything in life: the more you practice, the easier it gets. In fact, as you master the divine breath, your ability to recenter can be almost instantaneous. The breath helps you get back to the present moment. I find that the more my mind veers off into the future (which it does a lot), the easier it is to allow the uncertainty of the future to entangle me in vibrations of fear of the unknown. Now, the minute this happens, I take a deep, divine breath and use the breath to bring me back to the present moment. I also repeat the mantra "Everything I need exists in this very moment. There is nothing more and nothing less that I need, except NOW."

I ask you to begin practicing this in your life. Your fear always shows up as either an expression of something you experienced in the past or a projection of that same fear in the future, which of course hasn't happened yet. Since every thought creates a vibration of attraction to like frequency, if you project something negative for yourself into the future, you might just get it. So choose your thoughts carefully. The minute you realize you're too focused on the past or the future, use your breath to refocus on the present and go into the stillness to recalibrate your mind, body, and spirit with the present moment. Use that same moment of communion with the Divine to program new thoughts and feelings that vibrate in love, joy, and happiness. Become a beacon of love instead of fear.

Letting go and trusting in the natural flow of the Universe has been a life-long lesson for me. Sometimes your biggest lessons are learned from perfect strangers. Let me share a story with you of one of those moments. I had decided to visit one of the local car dealerships in my area. I had set the intention to find a small, affordable car with great gas mileage. When I walked into the showroom, a nice sales associate walked up to me and introduced himself. When I told him what I was looking for, he began to tell me about all the various models he thought might fit my needs. There was one specific model that I realized might be the perfect match for me. I sat in the car and even took it for a test drive. I could feel such cheer from this man and a calmness that was so beautiful and refreshing. As we spoke, I could feel the genuine love this man had for what he did, but also for humankind in general. I told him I would need to think about things. He handed me his card and told me to call him if I had any more questions.

As I drove home, I knew I would be seeing this man again. I decided to just let this play out in its own timing and divine orchestration. About three days later I was shuffling through some mail and papers sitting on my kitchen table and out popped his business card. I felt it was time to pay another visit. I was going through some changes in my life and there was a part of me that was having a hard time letting go of my old life. When I entered the dealership again, I was greeted by the bright smile of the sales associate I had met three days prior. He came right over and greeted me with such warmth. He took me over to grab a cup of coffee and we sat down at his desk to chat. I told him I was ready to talk about the car again, but instead he looked at me and said, "You know, I can tell something is bothering you. You want to tell me about it?" I started to tell him about what was going on in my life. I had just started a new job and was moving soon to a new place. While this was all very exciting for me, it was scary at the same time—new environment, new people, and many unknowns before me.

He listened attentively and said, "You just need to let go and let God." He then proceeded to tell me about his wife. She had been living with cancer for several years, and every day she lived was a blessing to him. I could feel the pain in his heart because he loved his wife so much. But there was this reverence for life that he was learning by witnessing the illness of his wife. He knew it was out of his control, so instead of worrying or living in fear, he chose to live by this mantra: "Let go, let God." In that moment I felt the power of these words. And so I began to use these words daily. He had a coffee mug with those words written on them on his desk and he told me he wanted me to have it. I graciously accepted it and to this day it still sits with me in my home. Who could've imagined the power those four words would have on my life? I ended up buying the car from this man and thanked him for teaching me something that I knew would last me a lifetime.

Letting go is the formula for freedom. Attachments keep us shackled in a prison of our own making.

Letting go is the formula for freedom. Attachments keep us shackled in a prison of our own making. Let go, surrender, and unmask the real you so you can be free to be the magnificent and beautiful Soul you really are. Dance with the flow of life. Let go and dance in harmony with the flow of life and receive the limitless gifts the Universe has planned for you. Resist, and it feels like every step is an uphill battle. Your Soul already knows the way to your joy and happiness, so surrender control and live every moment, present in that moment. All else then follows with grace and ease. The more time you spend in the present, the more you notice the small miracles that the Universe has been manifesting in your life all along, on a daily basis.

"Letting go gives us freedom, and freedom is the only condition for happiness. If, in our heart, we still cling to anything—anger, anxiety, or possessions—we cannot be free."

~Thich Nhat Hanh

What is the story that is replaying in your thoughts? Change that thought, change that pattern, and suddenly you create the seeds for your new story, the life you've always wanted. Your experiences in life (including past lives) can imprint layers of fear and doubt in your energy field. As you grow from child to adult, the stories replay over and over in your mind and create a similar pattern of vibration in your energy field. The more you leave these vibrations of density untouched and unhealed, the more they form into physical ailments and even dissociation with those parts of you that you don't like (what some call your "shadow side"). Your mind, when you allow it, rules your life with these stories and thoughts of lower vibrations, like feeling unworthy or unlovable. These thoughts are often buried in your subconscious and you're not completely aware they even exist.

Practice letting go of thoughts that no longer serve you and changing the story your subconscious mind is holding. Find a quiet place where you will be undisturbed for the next twenty to thirty minutes. Begin to think about the story that is sitting in your subconscious mind that no longer serves you. Before you start the exercise below, relax your body. Close your eyes and take some deep breaths. Drop into your heart, and with each inhalation, breathe in love and really feel that love in your heart. With each exhalation, breathe out any anxiety or stress, and let each thought pass freely. When you feel relaxed, begin the exercise. I recommend you do this in your journal so you can refer to it throughout the rest of your journey.

Attachments and Your Life Story Exercise

1. Write down some of the things you feel attached to. Create three columns on your sheet of paper or in your journal. In the first column, write the following categories vertically: "Relationships," "Career," "Spiritual," "Family," "Body," and "Other." In the second column write the things you feel attached to in each of those categories. Again, these are things about which you have noticed negative feelings, patterns, behaviors, or addictions that are making you feel stuck and unhappy in your life. In the third column write what it is you're trying to release, transmute, or transform, and the positive aspect you want to replace it with.

2. Write down the story that holds these lower vibrations (negative thoughts). Start with the attachments you captured above in the second column. What is the story you have lived till now? Write that down.

3. Think about the new story you want to create. Leverage the positive aspects you wrote in the third column and integrate those into your story. Write down what you want your new story to be. Let your heart and soul guide the words you write.

Now let's remove the attachments and the old story from your energetic field. You can record the following meditation so you can close your eyes while you listen to it. Sit comfortably where you won't be disturbed—with your feet flat on the floor and your hands on your knees with palms facing up. If you're an experienced meditator, use whatever position is most comfortable to you. When you're ready, please move to the meditation.

Guided Meditation: Removing Attachments from Your Energetic Field

Close your eyes and focus on your breath. Feel the expansion of your chest as you breathe in and out slowly. Let your inner mind take you to the outskirts of your body where your energy field exists. The etheric, or energetic template of your body exists several inches away from your body. It contains an exact replica of your physical body. Allow your inner mind to connect you with this energetic field around you.

*Remember some of the negative thoughts and attachments you wrote down previously. Call those words and attachments forward. Let them come to the surface and appear in your energetic field. Invoke the presence of Archangel Metatron and the energies of his sacred cube, the Merkaba. Imagine this cube as a ball of golden fire. Bring the ball of golden fire to the part of your energetic field where you feel, sense, or see the negative thoughts and attachments. Let the ball of fire transmute these thoughts and attachments to positive vibrations. Stay here until you feel the transmutation occur. {**Pause briefly.**}*

*Continue scanning your field for more thoughts and attachments you want to release. As you find them, pause, and use the ball of golden fire to transmute them. Do this for as long as you feel you need to. {**Pause briefly.**}*

Go half-way down through the center of your head and feel the presence of your pituitary gland. See the gland emanating a beautiful violet light. Let this light fill your entire head. As you do this, a beautiful lotus flower appears on the top of your head. Bring into focus the new story you want to create in your life. Project the image of this life on the center of the lotus flower. See the words, thoughts, and images taking form in the center of the lotus flower. Bring emotion and feeling into these thoughts and words, forming the story of your new life. Feel the love, joy, and happiness you will feel as the life begins to take physical form. Stay here until you feel complete.

When you're ready, you can slowly come back and open your eyes.

Don't forget to spend some time journaling about any significant experiences from this meditation. It will serve you when it's time for you go back to work on the **Canvas of Your Soul** at the end of the chapter.

Spiritual Alchemy and the Violet Flame

I've mentioned before the importance of continuing to work on yourself daily through spiritual practice. One reason it's so important is so you can allow more light into your human vessel. The more woundedness you clear out, the more light you hold, and the less your ego interferes with the messages and conversations you hold with the Divine. And, of course, the added benefit is that a more vibrant, healthier, happier, and more loving you is the end result.

As you continue to practice letting go of attachment and transmuting the lower vibrations in your energetic field, you will notice that your conversations and messages form the divine shift. I've noticed this in my own spiritual growth and evolution. Remember my conversation with the Divine earlier in the chapter in which I described how I was feeling stuck as I wrote this book? It is no lie when I say that I have lived every word I have written on these pages. The Divine made sure of that. There is no greater healing than to write; because when you write, your pain and wounds rise to the surface so you can heal them. That's why journaling is such a powerful spiritual practice.

As I continued to heal my pain and let go of my attachments, this was God's message to me:

> When I look into your heart, I see my radiance flowing within you. You have discovered your true essence and now I may work through you with greater ease to serve my children. Thank you, My Child, for your willingness to be YOU, for your eagerness to serve with humility, for your love of self and those you serve. Today you will begin to feel a change within, and from this place a brighter light will shine, one that carries my love and healing vibration with each word your hands transcribe.

As you awaken to the purity in your heart, your relationship with the Divine transforms into a deeper and richer experience. In chapter 11 we will discuss *divine devotion* and what that really means in terms of your relationship with the Divine. With heightened awareness and spiritual evolution comes the responsibility to share your *divine purpose* with the utmost integrity and authenticity. Please remember that everyone's journey is different. It's not your job to convince your tribe to do things your way; your experience is only beholden to you. If you're a healer, teacher, or spiritual leader, you're here to *guide* your tribe to places you've already walked so they don't have to figure it out on their own. What you've learned on your journey will serve them in multitude, but they get to choose what they keep and what they release. Deep transformation occurs when the student arrives at their own insight with the help of their

Purity of heart is the nectar of oneness that lives in your heart. This is the home of your "heart mind."

guide, teacher, or coach. It is through self-discovery that the real you emerges and the Soul evolves.

Purity of heart is one of the keys of being able to connect with your *divine alchemist*. It is the nectar of oneness that lives in your heart. This is the home of your "heart mind." In Buddhism it is referred to as *bodhicitta*, the mind of love. As you experience this oneness, it unlocks your abilities to transmute and transform. These are the secrets of the spiritual alchemy held by your Soul. In the book *Saint Germain on Alchemy*, channeled by Mark and Elizabeth Prophet, Saint Germain, an ascended master, describes alchemy this way: "Alchemy, when properly understood, deals with the conscious power of controlling mutations and transmutations within Matter and energy and even within Life itself. It is the science of the mystic and it is the forte of the self-realized man who, having sought, has found himself to be one with God and is willing to play his part."

The mystic that Saint Germain refers to here is any one of us who seeks union or oneness with God. Meister Eckhart defines the mystic in this way: "The eye through which I see God is the same eye through which God sees me; my eye and God's eye are one eye, one seeing, one knowing, one love." That is what Saint Germain refers to as the "self-realized man who…has found himself to be one with God." The *divine alchemist* who sits in this Soul chamber of the *divine mind* is the mystic who rests within you and seeks union with oneness. As you practice accessing this part of you and transmuting the thoughts and limiting beliefs that hold you back from this oneness, you attain the self-realization Saint Germain refers to. Every mystic knows that stillness is the gateway to the wisdom of your Soul. Only through purity of heart does this wisdom awaken.

One of the ways to awaken the purity in your heart is to use the violet flame. The violet flame is described by Saint Germain as the "sacred fire" that transforms the cause, effect, and record of transgressions and negative karma that you hold in your energetic field. You can engage the violet flame in your daily life by using the following mantra: "I AM a being of violet fire. I AM the purity that God desires." You can invoke the violet flame to help you transmute negative thoughts, attachments, limiting beliefs, and karma. In the rituals section at the end of the chapter there is a ritual and invocation you can use daily.

For now, let's use the following guided meditation to introduce you to the violet flame and activate the God-seeds of your *divine mind*. You can record the following meditation so you can close your eyes while you listen to it. Sit comfortably where you won't be disturbed—with your feet flat on the floor and your hands on your knees with palms facing up. If you're an experienced meditator, use whatever position is most comfortable to you. When you're ready, please move to the meditation.

Guided Meditation: Activating the God-Seeds of Your Divine Mind

Take three deep breaths. With each breath you relax your mind, body, and spirit.

See yourself walking up a spiral staircase. The stairs are made of white, translucent, crystalline stone. At the top of the stairs you are met by Archangel Metatron. He radiates beautiful hues of purple and golden light, and in the center of his chest you see his heart engulfed in a beautiful violet flame.

He reaches out his hand to you and tells you telepathically he will be taking you through a portal to a sacred sanctuary. You hold his hand and step through the doorway.

Archangel Metatron asks you to follow him. Up ahead you see a small bridge that overlooks a creek. You walk over the bridge and on the other side there's a beautiful golden gate. Archangel Metatron unlocks the gate and you walk through. The gate leads to an angelic chamber. Inside there are twelve angelic beings waiting for you. You see a golden throne in the center of the room and they ask you to sit there.

*The chair has beautiful carvings and colored stones embedded in it. When you sit down, the stones radiate angelic rays of light all around you. The twelve angelic beings surround you as you sit on this ornate chair. Archangel Metatron approaches you and places his hand on your heart. He ignites the violet flame within your heart. As he does this, you feel the pureness of divine love flowing through your heart and entire body. He asks you to repeat "I AM a being of violet fire. I AM the purity that God desires." Stay here for a moment and repeat this statement three times. {**Pause briefly.**}*

*The violet flame consumes you from within and engulfs your entire body. See the flame spinning all around you and ask the flame to transmute all the density, fears, and limiting beliefs in your energetic field into love, joy, health, prosperity, and abundance in all areas of your life. Ask that this be done through all dimensions, time, and space—past, present, and future. Stay here for a moment and allow the transmutation to complete. {**Pause for several minutes.**}*

Now each angelic being takes their turn coming forward to touch your crown. Each one holds a vibration that helps you align with the divine mind. One by one the twelve angelic beings come forward and lightly touch your crown. With each touch you feel the cells of your body responding. Something deep within is being prepared to awaken. When the last one touches your crown, you can sense your divine mind God-seeds beginning to burst through their shells. As the seeds burst open, waves of light radiate from them and a lotus flower forms on the top of your head. There are sacred colors, symbols, and divine thoughts encoded in this beautiful tapestry of light emanating from the lotus flower on the top of your head. Stay here for a moment and allow your vibration to align with the divine mind. {Pause briefly.}

When you're ready, you may slowly come back and open your eyes.

Now that you've completed the meditation, it's time to journal. Capture any significant insights from the meditation. Here are some questions to help you:

Journaling Exercise

1. What did you feel when Archangel Metatron ignited the violet flame in your heart?

2. How did you feel as your *divine mind* God-seeds were awakened?

3. What did you feel as the lotus flower formed on the top of your head? Could you sense, feel, or see what was encoded in the light emanating from the lotus flower? If so, write it down.

4. Did you experience any physical sensations in your body as your vibration was being aligned with the *divine mind*? Write down any significant aspects of this experience.

Illumination of the Divine Mind

Your thoughts are illumined through your Higher-Self, and the source of this illumination is the divine mind.

The illumination of the *divine mind* comes from God. To illumine is to enlighten something, in this case we are illuminating thought and bringing *divine light* to it. Your thoughts are illumined through your Higher-Self (the conduit of your Soul's guidance), and the source of this illumination is the *divine mind*. Saint Augustine said this about the *divine mind*: "We cannot perceive the immutable truth of things unless they are illuminated as by a sun. This *divine light*, which illumines the mind, comes from God, who is the 'intelligible light,' in whom and by whom and through whom all those things which are luminous to the intellect become luminous." It is through the Eternal Truths of the *divine mind* that all is made possible, as it says in the Bible (New International Version) in Mark 10:27: "With man this is impossible, but not with God. For all things are possible with God." These Eternal Truths help you harness the template of divine perfection that is your natural existence in the holographic blueprint of the *divine mind*. You can think of this holographic blueprint as a multidimensional plane of consciousness where all divine thought exists. All which is for you, intended for you, and is your destiny sits in this plane of consciousness. The vibration of this holographic template is one of divine perfection and wholeness. All thoughts held in this plane of consciousness are created in a vibration of eternal love and are meant to serve you in your highest good.

The Eternal Truths

1. There is one universal *divine mind*.

2. Only eternal truth lives within the *divine mind*.

3. All of existence is connected to Source through the *divine mind*.

4. All thought in the *divine mind* originates from eternal love.

5. The *divine mind* holds the universal vibration for limitless bounty.

6. The *divine mind* holds the template of divine perfection.

7. The *divine mind* holds the blueprint of human destiny.

8. The *divine mind* holds the passageway to eternal being.

9. The *divine mind* holds the sacred container that makes possible the union of Heaven and Earth.

To help you remember these eternal, universal truths, let's do a guided meditation that connects you to the *divine mind*. You can record the following meditation so you can close your eyes while you listen to it. Find a quiet place where you won't be disturbed for the next ten to fifteen minutes. Sit comfortably—with your feet flat on the floor and your hands on your knees with palms facing up. If you're an experienced meditator, use whatever position is most comfortable to you. When you're ready, please move to the meditation.

Guided Meditation: Connecting with Your Divine Mind

Connect with the breath of life that flows through your lungs. Allow your breath to come down into your heart. With your next exhale, see the doorway that leads to your Higher-Self appear before you. With your next inhale, walk through the doorway and connect with your Higher-Self.

*As you walk through the doorway, you immediately feel the presence of your Higher-Self. See or feel yourself becoming one with your Higher-Self. Feel the connection happening within your heart center as a beautiful pink light unites you in oneness. Stay here for a moment until the integration occurs. {**Pause briefly.**}*

See a cord of white light connecting upward through the center of your head, forming a lotus flower as your Higher-Self stands in your heart. See yourself lifted by the light into the center of the lotus flower that now sits on your head. You're now standing in the center of the lotus flower and beneath your feet sits a sacred symbol. You invoke the power of this sacred symbol by repeating the word Tay-Yaaaaa, Tay-Yaaaaa, Tay-Yaaaaa. The sacred symbol radiates light and opens a portal beneath your feet that projects the holographic blueprint of the divine mind all around you.

*Within this blueprint sit all the Eternal Truths. Each one appears to you as a point of light within the holographic blueprint. As you say each truth, a point of light illuminates within the blueprint and the truth is awakened within your own divine mind. Before you begin, take a moment to look around you and connect with the holographic blueprint of the divine mind that surrounds you. {**Pause briefly.**}*

Repeat each Eternal Truth slowly.

- *There is one universal divine mind. {**Pause.**}*
- *Only eternal truth lives within the divine mind. {**Pause.**}*
- *All of existence is connected to Source through the divine mind. {**Pause.**}*
- *All thought in the divine mind originates from eternal love. {**Pause.**}*
- *The divine mind holds the universal vibration for limitless bounty. {**Pause.**}*
- *The divine mind holds the template of divine perfection. {**Pause.**}*
- *The divine mind holds the blueprint of human destiny. {**Pause.**}*
- *The divine mind holds the passageway to eternal being. {**Pause.**}*
- *The divine mind holds the sacred container that makes possible the union of Heaven and Earth. {**Pause.**}*

Connect one last time with the holographic blueprint that surrounds you and notice anything of significance. As you complete your connection, the portal closes beneath your feet and you descend downward back into your heart.

When you're ready, walk through the doorway to where you began your journey and come back into the present. You may slowly open your eyes.

Now that you've completed this activation, be sure to capture any significant insights of the experience in your journal. From these Eternal Truths and the imprint of the vibration of the *divine mind* comes the intuitive sense of claircognizance or clear-knowing. In the book *The Alchemist*, Paulo Coelho said that "intuition is really a sudden immersion of the Soul into the universal current of life, where the histories of all people are connected, and we are able to know everything, because it's all written there." In essence, Paulo is describing the process of clear-knowing. Whenever you experience clear-knowing, which I described earlier as an intuitive impression that appears instantaneously within you as something you recognize as pure Truth in your being, you have connected with the *divine mind*. The *divine mind* is like a database that holds all divine thought, and through the mind of your Higher-Self you access this data as intuitive impressions. In most cases you don't know how or why and can't base your knowing in any fact, but your Heart and Soul tell you that what you know is real and factual. This intuitive impression comes in the form of thought.

When people speak of "downloads," this is what they're referring to. Much of this book was written through my Higher-Self (the conduit of my Soul's guidance) connecting me with the thoughts and words that were to be written. Clear-knowing can come in the form of *automatic writing*, when you write from the connection to the *divine mind* and not from your conscious mind. I wrote the divine messages I shared with you earlier in the chapter through an automatic writing experience. This can happen for you, too, as you connect with your guides, the angels, and whatever divine beings are part of your spiritual team who walk this journey with you and want to share their guidance with you.

In the following meditation you'll have the opportunity to practice aligning with your *divine mind*. You can record the meditation so you can close your eyes while you listen to it. For the audio version, visit **www.UnmaskingYourSoul.com/Meditations.** Sit comfortably where you won't be disturbed—with your feet flat on the floor and your hands on your knees with palms facing up. If you're an experienced meditator, use whatever position is most comfortable to you. When you're ready, please move to the meditation.

Guided Meditation: Aligning with the Divine Mind

Breathe slowly, inhaling through your nose and exhaling through your mouth. Focus on your breath and feel with every breath the relaxation of your mind, body, and spirit. Allow thoughts to pass through your mind as they may.

See yourself taking a stroll in a green meadow. As you continue to walk, you see a pathway in front of you made of various stones. You walk on this pathway of stones and it leads you into a beautiful garden. The garden is full of aromatic, colorful flowers. You see roses, daisies, lilies, and lilacs. To the right, beautiful butterflies glide through the wind, their wings full of vibrant colors in hues of orange, blue, and yellow. You see a beautiful rustic bench and decide to sit for a moment. You look up to the sky and watch the birds flying overhead and listen to their calls and singing. {Pause.}

You continue to sit on the bench and as you look in front of you, you see someone approaching you. A monk dressed in white robes comes to you and tells you he will be your guide today. The monk tells you his name is Malike. Take a moment to observe your guide. Notice how he looks and connect with his vibration and energy. {Pause.}

Malike asks you to follow him. He tells you that he is taking you on a journey to a mystical forest. You will be directed to pick up sacred objects on your journey that you will use at your destination in the mystical forest. You begin to walk down a carved stone path.

As you come to the end of the stone path, there, lying on a stone, is a white robe. Malike tells you this robe is for you and tells you to put this sacred robe on, and so you do. When you place the robe on your body, you feel an energy shift within you. You become more observant of everything around you and attuned to the energy of all that surrounds you.

You continue to follow the monk and enter the mystical forest. As soon as you walk into the forest you notice the energy surrounding the trees and all plant life—even the insects and animals have halos of light surrounding them. You're able to sense their auras. When you look at a nearby tree, you notice a shiny object hanging on a branch. As you approach the branch, you see an amulet with the "Om" symbol hanging on the branch.

Malike tells you this is another sacred object for you and to place the amulet around your neck. As you do, you sense an increased sensitivity in your knowing. Your knowing seems much more pronounced. You can feel the vibrations coming in through the top of your head and into your body. Take note of what you're feeling and where you're feeling it. {Pause.}

You continue to follow Malike into the forest and soon you come to a clearing, and as you walk through, you see the most magnificent white, sacred tree in front of you. It has a very wide trunk and very deep roots. You immediately feel the wisdom of this tree and know it carries very old, ancient secrets. Malike tells you this is a sacred fig tree, a bodhi {bo-dee} tree, and asks you to sit on the ground beneath the tree, and so you do.

Malike asks you to invoke your Higher-Self and your ancestral lineage to join you. As you do this, you see your Higher-Self and ancestors joining you and Malike under the tree. Now that the circle is complete, Malike instructs everyone to begin chanting "Om."

As you do, the sacred tree extends a branch that connects to each of the hearts of those gathered there. Each of you is now connected heart to heart to this sacred tree. Your body sways back and forth, matching the vibration of the chant. Then you're lifted off the ground along with the tree and everyone else connected to the tree. As you rise into the light, a portal opens around you. It is the holographic blueprint of the divine mind.

Look into the portal and notice the points of light that are magnified. As you feel guided, allow yourself to be drawn into each point of light. Each time this happens, information is downloaded into your divine mind. Continue doing this until there are no more points of light that stand out to you. {Pause.}

Ask the Divine to connect you with the divine plan (the blueprint of your destiny) that sits in the holographic blueprint of the divine mind. Look around the holographic blueprint and see or feel anything of significance. Elements of your divine plan that are ready to be revealed to you become illuminated in the blueprint and are downloaded into your divine mind. Stay here for a moment until this process completes. {Pause.}

When the chanting subsides, Malike tells you it's time to leave this mystical forest. You thank your Higher-Self, ancestors, the sacred bodhi tree, and Spirit for their divine guidance today. You follow Malike out of the forest and back up the carved *stone path to where you began your journey today. You sit on a stone for a moment to integrate all that has occurred. {**Pause.**}*

When you're ready, you may slowly come back and open your eyes.

Now that you've completed the guided meditation, take some time to do some journaling. Spend about ten to fifteen minutes in a quiet place where you won't be disturbed answering the questions below. You can put on some soothing music or light a candle or incense to support you as you write. Just write from your Heart and Soul and the rest will follow.

Journaling Exercise

1. What did you feel or notice upon meeting your guide, Malike? Note anything of significance.

2. How did you feel when you put on the white robe? The amulet?

3. How did you feel in the presence of the bodhi tree? How did you feel as the tree linked to your heart and the hearts of everyone in the sacred circle? Note any messages you received from the tree.

4. As the holographic blueprint of the *divine mind* was engaged, what information do you feel was downloaded into your *divine mind*? What part of your life does this link to?

5. What information did you receive about the blueprint of your destiny? Note any information or insights that will serve you on this part of your journey.

6. What else do you feel you need to do to align more deeply with the *divine mind*? Write down at least two or three actions you commit to doing to achieve this.

After journaling, continue working on the **Canvas of Your Soul.** (You can download the PDF at **www.UnmaskingYourSoul.com/Blueprint.**) Pick phrases, words, or symbols and put them on section 9 of the **Healing** part of your roadmap. Make this canvas your own piece of artwork that represents the journey we're taking together in this book. You can color, paint, or even cut images from magazines that depict the messages and insights you received in this chapter on *aligning with the divine mind*. You don't need to be a professional artist to do this. Just let your Soul express through you as it wants to. This will become the vision board of your Soul's unmasking, a precious gift to you from your *divine alchemist*.

Five Rituals to Awaken Your Divine Mind Muscle

The rituals below are meant to help you awaken your *divine mind* muscle. You can repeat any of the rituals that follow and the exercises and guided meditations earlier in the chapter as many times as you like. With each repetition you go deeper in accessing your *divine alchemist*.

Don't forget to create your sacred space, and be sure to take some deep breaths to relax your mind and body before you begin. Connect with your Soul as you enter this sacred space.

1. This first ritual helps you practice letting go. I recommend you repeat these affirmations daily, as many times as you can. Feel free to create your own; this list will get you started. If you want to give these affirmations a boost, say them as you look deeply into your eyes in front of a mirror. Anything you do in front of the mirror is very powerful in transforming your subconscious.

   "I release and let go."

   "I let go and let God."

   "Peace is my way of being."

   "I surrender to divine will."

   "I am exactly where I need to be."

   "As I let go, I become more of me."

   "In this moment I have everything I need."

   "I am in perfect harmony with my Heart and Soul."

2. Use this meditation to release your negative emotions. Whenever you're feeling stressed or anxious, or your thoughts are just getting in the way, use this meditation to recenter and let go. You might want to record this in your voice so you can take it with you wherever you go.

   Beneath the hurling sound of the wind, there is truth—a truth that is only found in the silence. Become still and find the silence that gently carries the wind to its destination. The noise around you wants to distract you, but do not be distracted. Go beneath the sound of all that is. Go deep and breathe. Breathe again, and once more. Find the silence beyond the sounds that beg for your attention.

Can you hear the sound of the ethers? Listen intently. Connect with the silence between the sounds. As you focus on the gaps within the sounds, you go deeper, deeper, and deeper. Your ears vibrate at the same frequency. You become one with the sound of the ethers. Don't allow your mind to disconnect you from your focus. The ethers are now vibrating in your ears.

Pick an emotion you want to disperse. Pick something from your day— anxiety, anger, judgment, or whatever you're holding that needs to be released. Bring that emotion to the surface. What does that emotion sound like in the ethers? As you focus on its sound, the silence of the ethers begins to transmute that emotion. You're transforming that emotion—releasing and letting go… releasing and letting go… releasing and letting go.

All you're left with is the sound of existence and the purity of your essence that is love. Feel the emotion of love in your heart. Breathe in love. Exhale love. See the love taking liquid form within you. Allow it to infuse every cell of your being, your inner and outer layers all permeated with vibrations of eternal love. See the love extending outward from your being. Extend it outward to your aura. Extend it outward to people you love. Extend it out to the world.

Be at peace and share your gratitude for what has just transpired. You're back home with the purity of your Soul.

3. Use this ritual to transmute limiting beliefs, negative emotions, and attachments. You're going to invoke the violet flame to help you do this. This is another ritual you may want to record in your own voice to help you have a deeper and richer experience.

   a. Invoke the violet flame, saying, "I AM a being of violet fire. I AM the purity that God desires." Repeat this five to seven times, feeling love and devotion as you say these words.

   b. Close your eyes (if you haven't already), and see the violet flame emerging from your heart. See three flames intertwining together in your heart. Allow these three flames to get larger and larger and expand to the size of your body, engulfing your entire being. As the flames touch every part of your being, use the sacred fire of the flames to transmute all that needs to be released within you.

c. Open your eyes and say the following or create your own version as you use the sacred fire to transmute your limiting beliefs, negative emotions, and attachments:

> Sacred fire, you are spirit as light, light as Soul, and Soul as source. I ask you to transmute all that no longer serves me. I seek to shine my light fully to the world. I seek to be the real me. I seek to be infused with the vibrations of infinite love, compassion, joy, and inner peace. As you burn through the remnants of the old me that I now let go of, new light infuses my mind, body, and spirit, and prepares me for the next leg of my journey. In this new life I embody more of my Soul and am guided by the loving, eternal omnipresence of my *divine mind*. And so it is.

d. Continue envisioning the triple flame surrounding your entire body. Connect with the source of any discomfort and surrender it to the sacred fire. As the old parts of you are transmuted, feel your mind, body, and spirit infused with higher vibrations of light. See a huge ray of light emerge from the heavens. From within the ray of light emerge the hands of God, lifting you higher and higher into the light. A gentle, divine breath encircles you in a radiant bubble of white light as you continue to be held in the hands of God. A gentle breath blows you away inside this bubble of white light and you are gently placed back upon the Earth. As you reach the Earth, the bubble disintegrates, and you emerge with a new vibrancy and profound connection to your Soul. You walk forward into this new leg of your journey with a deeper understanding of who you really are.

e. Thank the Divine and the violet flame for their assistance in your healing and transformation today. When you're ready, slowly return to the present.

4. Use this ritual to connect with the new story you wrote earlier in the chapter. If you didn't get a chance to write your new story, go back and do that exercise now, then return here. It's best to do this ritual in front of a mirror. I suggest you do this early in the morning or at night before you go to bed. If you can do it in both the morning and the evening, that is ideal. You may want to light a candle or some incense to help you create a soothing environment to support you as you vocalize your new story. Repeat this ritual daily for twenty-one days.

a. Begin by taking some deep breaths, inhaling slowly through your nose and exhaling slowly through your mouth. When you feel relaxed, look into your eyes in the mirror and repeat "I love you, _____ [insert your name]." Keep doing this until you feel connected to your Heart and Soul.

b. Take out your written story. Close your eyes for a moment and envision pink light radiating from your heart and infusing your story with deep, eternal love. Do this for several minutes.

c. Read your story out loud to yourself in the mirror. As you do this, continue to send love from your heart and allow the love to infuse your voice as you say the words out loud. Energize the words with feelings of love, peace, happiness, and joy. Imagine how it would feel if you were already living this story, and infuse your body, mind, and voice with these feelings.

d. Close your eyes and demonstrate your gratitude to the Divine and the Universe in whatever form and words you feel guided to express. See yourself sending this gratitude outward to the Divine, Universe, family, friends, those you serve, and the world in general. When you're ready you can come back and open your eyes.

e. Be sure to journal about any insights that come through as you practice this ritual daily. At the end of each seven-day period, take a pause to connect with the Divine and see what messages it has for you. Most likely you will notice shifts happening within you as you begin imprinting this new story in your mind, body, and spirit. Take note of the transformation as you work through the twenty-one day period.

5. Meditate with my painting *Archangel Michael*, shown at the end of the chapter, to help you reconnect with your *divine alchemist,* the one who helps you access your *divine mind.* Each of my paintings was divinely channeled and holds messages and energetic impressions of the Soul that bring healing to the bearer. This particular painting holds vibrations of healing for those needing to remember their expression of *divine mind.*

a. Close your eyes and take a breath... inhaling slowly through your nose and exhaling slowly through your mouth... and with each breath you take relax your mind, body, and spirit. Continue focusing on your breath... and with each breath allow your thoughts to pass freely... thought after thought... breath after breath... relaxing more and more deeply. Continue taking several more deep breaths. {**Repeat for one or two minutes.**}

b. Briefly open your eyes and observe the painting. Allow yourself to be taken on a journey into the painting. Look at the images and symbols, and allow your gaze to go to one focal point in the painting. Soften your gaze as you focus on this point of interest. Breathe in its energy, seeing the symbols, images, and colors in your mind's eye. Continue breathing in the energy... breath after breath, allowing you to feel and absorb the healing energy from this focal point.

c. With your next breath, listen to the voice of your Soul. What is it communicating? What messages do you hear or feel within you as you breathe in the energy of the painting? Pay attention to where the energy is going in your body. This gives you an indication of where in your body you may need to release old energy, traumas, or wounds. Continue breathing and just go into the stillness while you connect deeper within. Allow the healing energies of the painting to penetrate your mind, body, and spirit. {**Do this for two to five minutes.**} If you feel guided, you may continue repeating this step, changing to a different focal point in the painting each time. Again, allow yourself to breathe the images, symbols, colors, and healing energies into your being.

d. Don't forget to journal about anything of significance that comes up during this experience.

Eileen Anümani Santos, *Archangel Michael*, c. 2008

Archangel Michael is the consummate *divine alchemist,* skillfully turning darkness into light. Call on Michael's sword to transmute your limiting beliefs, attachments, and lower-vibration thoughts that still hold you back from shining your light fully to the world. Remember, you are the LIGHT. As you transmute the lower-vibration thoughts hiding in your subconscious into loving, higher-vibration thoughts, you become aligned with the *divine mind.*

Allow the *DIVINE MIND* to be your beacon of light.
Thoughts held in light become more light!

My Soul Sizzles with Divine Passion
by Eileen Anümani Santos

My Soul sizzles with *divine passion* and awe.

I stand before you idle in stillness and ready to serve.

What is it that your Soul whispers? Listen with admiration and curiosity and notice the response… I know you listen with intent.

It is your time to awaken to the wonder that you are. It is time to unmask yourself fully and bring your light fully to the world.

Listen to the sizzle. Can you hear how your Soul calls upon you now to serve? There is something rising to the surface… something new… a passion undiscovered… a gift that was dormant has been awakened… sizzle it does in your heart… sizzle it does in your power center… the energy spirals and spirals from below to above and above to below, encompassing all of your being.

You align with your calling… you embody your divinity… sizzle, sizzle. This passion is so great, the fire radiates from you… creativity, magnificence, divinity… all integrating together.

Unite and surrender to the oneness of your being… sizzle, sizzle, out comes the flame of the creator within you, the *divine artist*, the wizard of light.

You have conquered your fears, the ego no longer controls… you embody your *divine mind*… your Soul guides you now… you have arrived at a new juncture in your life.

Sizzle, sizzle… joy and excitement propel you forward into this phase of divine service!

CHAPTER 10

Soul Chamber X: Igniting Your Divine Passion

There is a *divine spark* that connects us all. From this place of oneness emerges a thread that is illuminated in the sacred fire of our Souls' desires and *divine passions*. When you connect with that thread, there's a natural movement that occurs from the Universe that propels you forward to receive, accomplish, and manifest your *divine truths* in the world. As I mentioned in chapter 4, each of us has our own *divine truths*, the God-seeds that are manifested in the physical through our *divine purpose*. *Divine passion* is the thread that emerges from you as the incubator for the deepest expression of who you really are. When you allow the sacred feeling of *divine passion* to drive you to be the most authentic YOU that you can be, you experience a movement in your life that seems miraculous.

The *divine spark* that is the origin of your *divine passion* is alive within you. It speaks, listens, breathes, and serves through your true essence of *divine love*. When this *divine passion* is awakened, it serves as the fuel that propels you forward in living your Soul's purpose. We seek to be seen. We seek to be heard. We seek to be loved. We seek to feel complete. *Divine passion* connects all those parts of you into a canvas of creation and expression that emerges from the holographic blueprint of the *divine mind*. *Divine passion* is akin to a lighthouse—a beacon that vibrates out to the cosmos of the *divine mind*, telling it that you're ready to initiate a thought, an idea, a project, a gift, a path, a way of being that aligns with the Soul of You. Through this connection of passion through heart to cosmos, you receive the information and clarity about the actions you need to take to align with your Soul's calling.

The palm of your left hand is the location of **Soul Chamber X—Divine Passion,** the tenth of the Soul virtues that will be unmasked as you continue on your journey of wholeness. The mask associated with the tenth chamber is the **Mask of Suppression.** When you suppress that part of you that wants to be expressed authentically and those things that make your heart sing, you also suppress the *divine spark* that is the ignition of your *divine passion*. Your Soul's desires are the underpinnings of your *divine passion* and the connection to your emotional body, which create the doorway for manifestation of those desires. The archetype of this Soul chamber is the **divine artist**, the one who helps you connect with your Soul's desires and ignite your *divine passion*. Your *divine artist* helps you express that which is burning inside you and needs to be expressed to the world because it encapsulates the most authentic you who inspires, moves, and transforms those around you. The sacred symbol for the *divine passion* chamber is shown below.

In chapter 9 you connected with your *divine mind*, your mental body. In this chapter you connect with your emotional body and the desires of your Soul that ignite the spark of your *divine passion* that is waiting to be expressed through you. The *divine mind* plants the seeds of encoded thoughts in your mental body, and your *divine passion* permeates those seeds with heart-based emotions that propel those divine thoughts to become unstoppable forces of manifestation. Let's begin by connecting you with your *divine passion* and discovering where you might be holding back from expressing this most sacred part of you.

Discovering What's Holding You Back from Expressing Your Divine Passion

In the beginning, a *divine spark* was ignited and humanity arose into the flesh. Perhaps you've been taught that desire must be dampened, but do no such thing. Desire carries a fragrance that is not only emotionally uplifting but acts as an aphrodisiac for the human spirit. Through desire you awaken the *divine passion* that sits in this chamber of your Soul. When the portal to this chamber opens, you embody the emotional anchors of your Soul that bring the light of your divine gifts and purpose into physical form. This is the moment of truth when your heart, *divine mind*, and Soul meet to create the inception of the life you want—a divinely inspired life that makes it possible for you to transmute and transcend the limiting beliefs of the ego-mind.

Divine passion is the sacred fire that illuminates the path ahead.

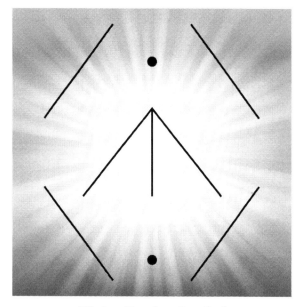

Divine Passion Symbol

Divine passion is the sacred fire that illuminates the path ahead.

Without clarity about what puts your Soul on fire, you can take paths that lead you around and around in circles, ending up in the same spot each time. We've all been there, experienced moments in life when we felt stuck and we caught ourselves repeating the same limiting pattern or behavior over and over again—same action, same result. When this happens it's time to take a different action. A different action means taking a different path, one that is divinely inspired and driven by the desires and knowing of your Soul.

For a long time I held back from following my *divine passion*. I was attached to a job title and a big salary. I couldn't see how my passions would allow me to make a living. In fact, there were some close to me who reiterated that statement to me, and for some time I believed it. Yet inside I could feel this *divine spark* wanting to propel me forward. But something held me back. In a session with a very gifted healer I discovered that this push-pull I felt inside resulted from a negative core belief that I had been holding for many lifetimes. There was a specific past life when this core belief had been created. This is how it was described to me by the ascended masters in that healing:

> In this life you were a Native American Indian woman. You had the tradi-tional gifts of a medicine woman, but you were much more than that. You were a master healer. You held a loving heart, a very open wisdom channel, and a very powerful light current. You not only held your divine gifts very powerfully, but you embodied and anchored them in every single moment. You held an exquisite presence that was palpable, tangible, and by its own presence brought much healing and transformation to those around you. It was in this lifetime, when the Europeans came to America to conquer it, that this was grounded.
>
> The Europeans came to your tribe and did not initially use aggressive force to try to settle your lands. They were more subtle, more seductive. They tried to infiltrate the key members of your community to test the waters and see how your community could be conquered. Meetings were held between the chiefs of your people and the Europeans. There was a certain European gen-tleman who, upon encountering your light, became very beguiled by you. He felt an instant attraction to you, physically and emotionally. Although you were at a very different level of spiritual understanding than he, you saw the goodness and potential within him. You became enamored with this gentleman and believed that if you formed an alliance with him he would not harm your tribe.

He persuaded you to leave your community and go with him. This created a lot of fear within you. You thought you could create healing and bridges between the enemy and your tribe. Your tribe became very angry at you, feeling you had betrayed and abandoned them, and they cursed you for leaving. You lived with this gentleman for a while. Yet with each day that passed, his motives appeared more clearly. He was there to acquire power and the lands of your tribe. Your light highlighted his own darkness, and he began to treat you very badly. He attempted to convert you to his ways and force you to abandon your beliefs and heritage. You were to become his trophy of domination over your race. But you continued to refuse to do this. One night while he was drunk he aggressively raped you and told you that you would now become his wife and denounce all you had lived and known. When you refused, his hands went around your neck and he strangled you to death.

When I was taken back to this life to heal this part of me, I saw my final moments. My spirit hovered over my dead body, and then over the deceased bodies of my ancestors. Many had been massacred defending their families. I was devastated. Even in those final moments I tried to save them, but it was too late. That had always been my intention, yet I had been betrayed and misled. I felt so much shame and guilt, feeling I should have been able to save them. As a result of this experience, the core belief that was imprinted in my energetic field was "The more I open my heart, the more I will be betrayed, hurt, shut down, or even killed."

This made so much sense. I repeated many of these same patterns in my current life so that I could bring them to resolution. Much of this story repeated in this life with my ex. I had seen his light and goodness, and believed I could save him. I didn't understand when I was married to my ex that as human beings we have choice. You can choose to live in the light or in the darkness, and the only person who can determine that fate is you. I couldn't do that for him, and neither can I do it for you. It's up to you to choose what kind of life you will have. It's up to you to co-create the life you desire through the wisdom of your Heart and Soul.

As I released this wounded part of me, I connected more deeply with my Soul, an expression of me that was just waiting to be acknowledged and to serve as my internal GPS and divine guidepost. This is when my life changed. It is only when you follow your *divine passion* that the Universe conspires in miraculous ways to unlock the thread of abundant manifestation in your life. Until that point it seemed like the stars were not aligning. Issues with career, relationships, money, and health were rampant in my life. But the more I trusted and aligned my heart and my mind with the desires and guidance of my Soul, the more things changed in a big way.

> **When you ignite the divine passion within you, your divine artist steps in to paint the canvas that allows the manifestation of abundance into your life.**

When you ignite the *divine passion* within you, your *divine artist* steps in to paint the canvas that allows the manifestation of abundance into your life. And when I use the word *abundance*, I mean receiving the universal flow of love and support that brings about the life you desire, be it career, relationships, spirituality, health, or wealth. As you do what you love, it no longer feels like work, and you lock in this incredible force that opens doorways, brings new opportunities, and allows you to breathe and live a more Soul-driven life. There is no thinking involved; just being who you really are. It opens the limitless possibilities that the Universe holds for you in the holographic blueprint of the *divine mind* that we discussed in chapter 9.

"Choose a job you love and you will never have to work a day in your life."

~Confucius

These are some of my passions: *Love. Soul. Healing. Awakening. Teaching. Creation. Art. Music. Being me. Freedom.* When I help a client awaken to a deeper part of their Soul, it makes my heart sing. When I witness a client releasing a deep pain they've been holding for years, even lifetimes, it makes my heart sing. When I connect with my Soul so deeply that the lyrics to a new song emerge and the chords miraculously appear on my guitar, even though I don't read music, it puts my Soul on fire. When I look into a client's eyes and help them awaken, ignite, and birth their *divine spark* is another wonderful moment for me. This is when *divine truth*, *divine purpose*, and *divine passion* meet and open the door to manifesting their Soul's purpose. From that experience I am showered in the essence of eternal love that I AM and that they are. Or when I'm teaching and speaking to a group and the words seem to flow effortlessly, imbued in the vibration of love and oneness—it is in these moments when what I do doesn't seem like work at all. When I finish, I'm uplifted and reenergized by the experience. That is *divine passion*.

It's time to discover what your *divine passion* is. What is it that your Soul desires? What is it that puts your Soul on fire? Have you ever asked yourself those questions? To help you do that, let's go into a short meditation so you can connect with your *divine passion* and discover your Soul's desires. You can record the meditation so you can close your eyes while you listen to it.

Find a quiet place where you will not be interrupted for fifteen to twenty minutes. You can light a candle or incense, or play some inspirational music in the background to help you find a place of calmness and stillness. Sit with both feet on the floor and your hands on your knees with palms facing up. Begin by taking several deep breaths, breathing in deeply and breathing out slowly. Do this at least three or four times. When you're ready, please begin the meditation below. It takes you through various growth cycles in your life in increments of seven years. You can stop at whatever age is relevant for you.

Guided Meditation: Discovering Your Soul's Desires

Imagine yourself in the womb of your mother. Around you is a cloak of pink light that surrounds you in eternal love. You feel so loved and serene. You swim around in the belly of your mom, and as you do, you notice sparks of light all around you. Each spark of light is encoded with your divine passions, your Soul's desires. Reach your tiny hand out and grab one of those sparks of light. Place the spark on your heart and listen. What is this divine spark saying to you in this moment? ***{Pause for as long as you need to receive.}***

Move forward in your life to age seven. Your guardian angel appears and holds your hand. Allow yourself to be a taken to a specific memory of when you were this age. Notice what you're doing. What is it that you loved to do at this age? Standing next to you is your Higher-Self. Your Higher-Self leans down and whispers in your ear. Connect with this memory and the energy of that time. As you look around you, you see points of light, divine sparks that belong to you. Reach out and grab one. Place it on your heart and listen. What is this divine spark saying to you in this moment? ***{Pause for as long as you need to receive.}***

Move forward to age fourteen. You're surrounded by the angels and your guides as you go to a specific memory of when you were doing something that really made your heart sing. Notice what you're doing. What is it that you loved to do at this age? Standing next to you is your Higher-Self. Your Higher-Self leans down and whispers in your ear. Connect with this memory and the energy of that time. As you look around you, you see points of light, divine sparks that belong to you. Reach out and grab one. Place it on your heart and listen. What is this divine spark saying to you in this moment? ***{Pause for as long as you need to receive.}***

Move forward to age twenty-one. You're surrounded by the angels, your spiritual team, and the Souls of your family. Once again, allow yourself to be taken to a specific memory of when you were doing something that really made your heart sing. Notice what you're doing. What is it that you loved to do at this age? Standing next to you is your Higher-Self. Your Higher-Self leans down and whispers in your ear. Connect with this memory and the energy of that time. As you look around, you see points of light, divine sparks that belong to you. Reach out and grab one. Place it on your heart and listen. What is this divine spark saying to you in this moment? **{Pause for as long as you need to receive.}**

Move forward to age twenty-eight. You're surrounded by the angels, your spiritual team, the Souls of your family, and the Souls of those you're serving. Once again, allow yourself to be taken to a specific memory of when you were doing something that really made your heart sing. Notice what you're doing. What is it that you loved to do at this age? Standing next to you is your Higher-Self. Your Higher-Self leans down and whispers in your ear. Connect with this memory and the energy of that time. As you look around, you see points of light, divine sparks that belong to you. Reach out and grab one. Place it on your heart and listen. What is this divine spark saying to you in this moment? **{Pause for as long as you need to receive.}**

Move forward to age thirty-five. You're surrounded by the angels, your spiritual team, the Souls of your family, and the Souls of those you're serving. Once again, allow yourself to be taken to a specific memory of when you were doing something that really made your heart sing. Notice what you are doing. What is it that you loved to do at this age? Standing next to you is your Higher-Self. Your Higher-Self leans down and whispers in your ear. Connect with this memory and the energy of that time. As you look around you, you see points of light, divine sparks that belong to you. Reach out and grab one. Place it on your heart and listen. What is this divine spark saying to you in this moment? **{Pause for as long as you need to receive.}**

Move forward to age forty-two. You're surrounded by the angels, your spiritual team, the Souls of your family, and the Souls of those you're serving. Once again, allow yourself to be taken to a specific memory of when you were doing something that really made your heart sing. Notice what you're doing. What is it that you loved to do at this age? Standing next to you is your Higher-Self. Your Higher-Self leans down and whispers in your ear. Connect with this memory and the energy of that time. As you look around you, you see points of light, divine sparks that belong to you. Reach out and grab one. Place it on your heart and listen. What is this divine spark saying to you in this moment? **{Pause for as long as you need to receive.}**

Move forward to age forty-nine. You're surrounded by the angels, your spiritual team, ancestors, the Souls of your family, and the Souls of those you're serving. At *this age, your Soul is preparing you for the renewal of your life that begins at age fifty. Your Higher-Self is standing next to you and shows you a movie of your life until now. Many memories of moments that brought your Soul's desires forward are shown to you. Each memory holds clues to your divine passions. Allow the energy of each one to awaken the divine sparks all around you. Reach out and grab all the divine sparks and place them on your heart. What are your Heart and Soul whispering to you in this moment? {**Pause for as long as you need to receive.**}*

Swirls of white, blue, and pink light surround your heart in this moment and imprint your divine passions there so you can retrieve them at any moment. When the light begins to fade, you may slowly come back into your body.

When you're ready, you may open your eyes.

Now that you've completed the meditation, take a moment to journal about any significant messages, feelings, or insights you received about your *divine passion*. For each stage of growth (in the womb, age seven, fourteen, twenty-one, twenty-eight, thirty-five, forty-two, and forty-nine), notice the memories that rose to the surface. Jot down the things you were doing during those ages that really made your heart sing. Once you've captured all your insights, keep these handy so you can use them in the upcoming exercise that will help you take an inventory of your *divine passion* and your Soul's desires.

As a refresher, before we get to the exercise, remember that you've already discovered in chapter 4 what your *divine truths* are. These represent your unique God-seed, your divine secret sauce, your inherent divine gifts and divine superpowers. And in chapter 6 we dove into your *divine purpose*, and you gave voice to your *divine truths* through the *vocations* that bring your divine gifts to the world. Taking that into consideration, your passions should align with what you've already discovered in those chapters about the Soul of You. Those are the things that ignite a *divine spark* within you and make your heart sing. You may want to go back and look at the **Canvas of Your Soul** and see what you captured for those chapters before you do the exercise that follows.

When you're ready, you can pull out your journal and do this exercise.

Discovering Your Divine Passion Exercise – Part I

1. What is that one thing you would want to change in the world if there were no barriers (such as time, money, skillsets)? In what ways does this make your heart sing?

2. Create a table with five columns. In the first column write a list of all the things that really make your heart sing. Don't forget to use the insights from the meditation you just completed and what you've already captured on the *Canvas of Your Soul*. Let your Heart and Soul guide the way.

3. In the second column write how you feel when you're connecting with this passion. What is it about this *divine passion* that puts your Soul on fire?

4. In the third column write how this *divine passion* emotionally inspires you, those you're meant to serve, the world at large, and your career/vocation (*divine purpose*), and how it allows for the evolution of your spirit and Soul.

Save what you wrote and we'll continue this exercise in the next section. Now that you've connected with your *divine passion* and your Soul's desires, let's look more deeply at how these may or may not be showing up in your life now.

Recognizing How Divine Passion Is Showing Up in Your Life

> *Divine passion is the catalyst for manifestation of your Soul's desires.*

Divine passion is the catalyst for manifestation of your Soul's desires. As you connect with clarity to your Soul's desires, you create the emotional and energetic force that helps you initiate action to see those desires fulfilled in your life. Step by step, form upon form, you create the Soul-driven life you aspire to have. As you enlist the power of your desires, the cellular memory of your *divine passion* is awakened. These cells come together to form an energetic force within and around you that propels you to step forward and take action.

Your emotions and body are good indicators of when you're flowing in *divine passion*. It's like you become lost in what you're doing. You become so present to the *divine spark* within you that all else around you fades into the background and all you can see is what is right there in front of you, be it a person you're coaching, a song you're composing, a class you're teaching, a meeting you're leading, a book you're birthing, or just being you with those you love. The more attuned you are to your emotional body and how your body reacts to what you're doing or experiencing, the easier it is to recognize when *divine passion* shows up in your life.

> *"Passion is energy. Feel the power that comes from focusing on what excites you."*
>
> ~**Oprah Winfrey**

For a long time I closed myself off from my *divine passion*. I was too busy wearing a mask and trying to please everyone around me. I lost myself in my outside world and forgot who I really was—a divine being having a human experience. All I ever wanted was to be loved, but I was looking for it outside of myself instead of connecting with the love I already had within. It wasn't until I had my dream of awakening in 2003 that I began to reconnect with my divinity and was able to feel once more. It's like I became numb to the *divine spark* that lived inside me patiently waiting for me to understand the truth of me and my Soul. If you cannot feel, you cannot hear or act upon your Soul's desires. Awakening is not just a spiritual act; it is also about the marriage of your human vessel and spiritual container. It requires alignment between heart, mind, Soul, and body.

As a young girl, music was always a great passion of mine. I remember my mother always listened to music, especially when she cooked or cleaned the house. We loved to dance together. "*Ven negrita, vamos a bailar*," she would say. That means "Come, Sweetie, let's dance." Then she would grab me and spin me around. It's like the music was running through our veins, lifting us vibrationally as our Souls spoke to one another through the emotions of our *divine passion*.

When I was fourteen or fifteen years old, we had a next door neighbor who was from Puerto Rico. He had electric guitars and offered to teach me how to play some traditional music from Puerto Rico called *Aguinaldos*. This is akin to folk music and is played a lot during Christmastime to celebrate our ancestry and the holidays. I was very excited to learn, so whenever I wasn't doing school work I would practice with him. One day my father told me it was time to get my own guitar, so we drove to New York City and found a small shop that sold hand-made Spanish guitars. My dad paid $150 for my first guitar, which was a lot of money at the time. I was very grateful for this amazing gift, but as the years went by I put the guitar to the side.

As I continued into my adulthood and allowed the masks of pain and wounds to take over my life, it seemed as if everything I loved to do was pushed aside, including music. I still listened to music, but playing the guitar had completely vanished from my life. It was like it had never existed. I left that guitar at my parents' house and it stayed there for about twenty years without much use. Then one day, after my divorce, that part of me began to awaken once again. I mentioned previously that art was the first divine gift that awakened within me as I began my spiritual journey in 2003. No surprise there, as art had been my favorite activity as a little girl. Then, shortly after, my desire to play guitar again emerged.

One day while visiting my parents, I asked about my old guitar. I was extremely happy when they told me they still had it. I couldn't believe I had pushed my guitar to the side, especially since it had such sentimental value for me. Back then I didn't appreciate how much of a sacrifice it had been for my father to buy that guitar for me. But now I totally got it. This guitar represented a part of my Soul that had been forced to become a distant observer of the energetic force that brought me to life. As I picked up the guitar after so much time, it was like a <u>déjà vu</u>. My fingers began to play chords that had been imprinted in my cellular memory long ago. I had never learned to read music, but it didn't matter. It all started to come back to me.

Once I picked up the guitar again, we created a family ritual. It was understood that every Thanksgiving I would bring my guitar, and after our meal we would gather and play music together. I would play Puerto Rican folk music on the guitar accompanied by family members. My older brother, Angel, a very talented conga player, would be the first to set up beside me and then everyone else would grab an instrument. It was amazing to see that even as our family grew with little ones running around, they, too, participated in the gathering regardless of their age. My goddaughter, Vanessa, was always there beside me playing her instrument as well. Even my Dad, who had been a bit shy at the beginning in grabbing an instrument and playing, now looked forward to picking up the maracas or the wooden sticks and accompanying the Santos "band." My *divine passion* became a family affair. It not only validated that music was part of me—a part that was here to stay, but it also served to unite my family in love and joy during the holidays.

What I didn't realize at the time was that along with playing I would also be singing. At around this time I felt guided to take voice lessons. My initial thought was that because I had suppressed my voice for so long (practically my entire life), taking voice lessons would heal this part of me. Little did I know that this was all part of the Divine's plan. Once I started taking voice lessons, I began to channel original music and, amazingly, the chords were given to me with the songs. I had to start carrying a digital recorder with me to be prepared to record the lyrics and the melody whenever the inspiration came through.

As this happened, I felt so alive again. I was still not completely confident in my playing or singing, but year by year, as I continued to shed my masks and woundedness, the more I came out of my shell. It was like layers and veils that had been masking my voice melted away, one by one. The Divine told me there was more to do with this than I could see. I began to understand that my voice was the lynchpin for much of the healing work I would be doing. Songs emerged, chords followed, and a discovery that my singing was meant to be part of my healing ministry to others.

My spiritual name, Anümani, when revealed to me by the Divine, became another missing link to the connection to my voice. I discovered the *ü* represents the vibration of my Soul in this life, and this was the symbol I was guided to paint on my second self-portrait, *Unmasking Your Soul*. At the time of painting, I had no clue what the symbol on the necklace I'm wearing meant. But I knew then, as I know now, that whenever I'm guided to do something, I must do it whether or not I understand the full meaning behind it at the time. When you're ready and it's time, your Soul reveals to you what you need to know. What was once a mystery becomes crystal clear. It wasn't until a year later during a writing retreat I attended that I was able to connect the dots. By that time the Divine had already revealed to me my spiritual name, Anümani, but it wasn't until this retreat that I found the courage to reveal it publicly. This is when I discovered that my painting *Unmasking Your Soul* was not just about unmasking my physical self by speaking my truth, but it was also about unmasking my spiritual-self and embodying that ancient part of me.

> *"Don't ask what the world needs. Ask what makes you come alive, and go do it. Because what the world needs is people who have come alive."*
>
> **~Howard Thurman**

When you surrender to your divine passion, you become more of who you want to become.

The transformation that occurred in my life as I surrendered to this experience and my *divine passion* was amazing—each painting a deeper expression of the Soul; each song an expression of the Divine; each client I worked with awakening to a deeper part of their divinity and Soul. This is what happens when you surrender to the real you. When you surrender to your *divine passion*, you become more of who you want to become. When your Soul's desires ignite your *divine passion*, that emotion that sits in your emotional body comes alive. That aliveness nourishes your Heart and Soul to new heights. The more you come alive, the more you attract what you need in order to express that aliveness in service to others. With each action you take in pursuit of that desire and passion, the universal *divine mind* kicks in to manifest destiny into fate.

Think about your *divine passion* and where it's already showing up in your life. Let's continue with the exercise you began in the last section.

Discovering Your Divine Passion Exercise – Part II

Find your answers from Part I of this exercise and continue with the following:

1. In the fourth column write down areas of your life in which your *divine passion* is showing up now (such as career, relationships, family, and spiritual).

2. In the fifth column write about whether or not you're currently connecting and expressing this passion as you serve others. If you are, write the ways it's being expressed. If you're not, write what's holding you back from expressing your *divine passion* to others. Specifically identify any fears that are holding you back from expressing your *divine passion.*

   a. For each fear you identified, where is it showing up in your body?

   b. Have you felt this type of fear before? If so, when and under what circumstances?

   c. If you have felt this fear before, chances are this is a pattern you've been repeating. Feel into this deeper and see if you can discover the theme or subconscious belief associated with this fear, and write that down.

Healing What's Holding You Back from Expressing Your Divine Passion

A Message from the Divine

My Dear One, what are you waiting for? You have travelled far to get to this point in your journey. You have scaled many mountains, some very treacherous, yet here you are because at some point you discovered the love that you are. Your willingness to grow, learn, and surrender to the divine plan that the Universe holds for you has brought you to a new level of understanding. You have learned many lessons. Each lesson opens the door to a deeper awareness of the reason for your existence, your *divine purpose.* You are at a critical juncture in your life. Listen to the desires of your Soul. They drive you to a new way of being. Let your Soul guide the way. As it does, the flame of *divine passion* ignites within you.

Divine purpose is the reason for your existence and why you're on this journey. *Divine passion* is the sacred fire that lights your way to your destiny. When you surrender to this sacred fire that burns within you, it not only helps you manifest the life that is aligned with your Soul's purpose, but heals what is in the way. Anytime you do what you love, it becomes an energetic blanket of love that elicits a response from those places within you that still remain in the shadow yet yearn to be loved and embraced. When these wounded parts of you

> *Divine passion is the sacred fire that lights your way to your destiny.*

show their faces, it means they're ready to be healed, and all you need to do is be present and surrender to the experience.

This is exactly how I ended up writing one of my newest songs entitled "Despierta," which means "Awaken" in English. One day as I sat in my kitchen, I kept feeling the presence of my ancestors. These were the ancestors from the time I had been that Native American Indian woman I spoke about earlier in the chapter. I could hear them saying, "Weo, weo, weo." I didn't know what these words meant, but I knew there was a song coming. I went down into my basement, grabbed my guitar, and plugged it into the amp. I grabbed a microphone and sat on a chair with my blue guitar on my lap. And the words began again: "Weo… weo, weo, weo… weo, weo, weo-wa." The melody was ballad-like and filled with deep emotion. I could feel this pain surfacing within me as I began to sing these words. As I sang, I immediately felt the presence of my ancestors standing there in front of me witnessing the birth of this new song. They were the inspiration behind it. I asked them what these words meant and they told me the sentiment behind the lyrics was about understanding, forgiveness, and a return to the state of pure love they had once known. They were there to heal with me. It was time to awaken once again to this state of *divine love* and oneness they had experienced in that life long ago.

For lifetimes I had held this guilt of having left them, and they felt I had betrayed them by leaving them behind. Yet now as I stood before them, they understood I had left to save them, and this song was their story. They had walked their land with a purity of love and Soul, but when the foreigners came to our homeland, they tried to convert my ancestors and have them leave their old way of life. When they refused, they were massacred as they defended their families. When I sang the lyrics that came through me in that moment, I cried and cried, releasing the shame and the guilt I felt for not being able to save them.

Then they sang with me, and I felt a beautiful sense of forgiveness and healing wash over my body and through my voice. This song had emerged not only to bring resolution and healing to something held between us for lifetimes, but also to remind me of my *divine passion* for music. I surrendered to that part of me in that moment, which awakened a deeper part of me that wanted to be expressed. This is what happens when you surrender to the desires of your Soul. If I had dismissed the words coming through and not followed my intuition to pick up my guitar, I would've missed out on this powerful healing and transformational experience.

When you connect with your *divine passion*, despite the inspiration you may feel in the moment, pockets of fear can also emerge. The more this sacred fire takes you to the edge of your comfort zone, the more your ego-mind tries to convince you to stay put so you can feel "safe." This is not just a resistance of the mind (thought); your body shows signs of strain, energetically holding you back from taking action. Fear comes in many forms: fear of success, fear of failure, fear that you're not qualified to teach what you feel you need to teach, fear that no one will want to listen to what you have to say, fear that no one will want to read the words in your book—the list goes on and on. I think we have all experienced these scary moments in life. This is when you need to become the *spiritual warrior* that you are. You feel the fear, yet do it anyway.

With each level of growth comes a new level of understanding and consciousness. As you climb this ladder of consciousness, you embody a deeper part of your Soul and the real you. At times this new path feels a bit scary. Begin to make friends with your fear—it originates from your ego-mind. When your ego faces uncertainty, which we all encounter many times in our lives, it tries to convince you to stay put because it's trying to "protect" you and keep you "safe." Speak to your ego. Tell it that you know it's trying to protect you, but that you're not going to allow it to control your life. Do this in a loving way as you would speak to your child or someone you love very dearly. You don't want any part of your existence to feel rejected or ignored. What you resist, persists. Suppressed fear expands. Unsuppressed fear dissolves. This is why it's important to face your fears and not ignore them.

As I transitioned from my old corporate life into doing my purpose-work as a healer and spiritual guide, including writing this very book, I kept having a vision of standing on a cliff. I could see the other side of the ravine very clearly. I could even see the Souls on the other side waiting to be served by me. But boy, every time I looked down, the gap just seemed so large. Despite the fact that my Heart and Soul had already made a solid commitment to this path, my mind was not there. Through the help of one of my coaches I discovered that what was needed was to *reframe* that vision. As we reframed the vision together, the cliff disappeared and a beautiful, sacred pathway leading to a sacred garden appeared before me. In this wondrous place there wasn't a gap between me and where I was heading. Instead it was all part of the same pathway. I was surrounded by beautiful creations of God, and as I walked gently on this path I felt safe, protected, and supported. I imagined moving forward one step at a time, and with each step I met the Souls I was meant to serve. With each step I could feel the fire of my *divine passion* propelling me forward in service to others. The fear of uncertainty had transformed into creative inspiration helping me create the programs and services my tribe was waiting for.

When you encounter fears that hold you back from expressing your *divine passion* to the world, reframing is an excellent technique to get unstuck. Here are some other techniques that can help you shift your fears so you can continue to move forward on your transformational journey:

1. **Change your mindset.** *Believe* that you can do whatever it is that you desire. Make that belief solid and real. You can use some of the techniques we discussed in the previous chapter to transmute your fear into positive energy. You can create a mantra like "I know I can do this" to keep you motivated and moving forward. Repeat it as often as you need to. Do whatever you need to shift your mindset. It could be listening to music that speaks to your Soul, speaking your mind to a close friend or partner, or watching a TED talk that helps you see that the repercussions of standing still are just not an option anymore. Practice becoming the observer of your thoughts, and as you do, they dissipate. The important factor with mindset is to think about what happens if you *don't* take action. What is it you're sacrificing? What dreams are you letting go by not following your heart? If this were your last day of life, how would you feel about the fact that you never pursued what you truly love? There is always something scarier than the fear you're holding on to in this moment. Focus on that which is scarier, and it will all come into perspective. ***Change your thoughts, change your reality.***

2. **Get your body to support you energetically.** We are all connected, so the thoughts of others can affect you. If those around you are afraid for you, you can take on their fears, too. Check in with your body and immediately let go of any fears that have been imposed by others. Immerse yourself in some type of body movement or activity that shifts the energy in your body. This might be yoga, tai chi, running, walking on a treadmill, or a stroll in the woods. Whatever action you take, make sure that you set an intention to *surrender* to the present moment and allow each movement to liberate you from your current state of being. You can wear your headphones and listen to soulful music or inspirational words while you do this. Remember that sound is a powerful healing tool, and when combined with physical movement it can be miraculous. ***Move your body, shift your energy.***

3. **Connect with your inner spirit, the Soul of You.** When you experience moments of fear that emerge from the outer mind and intellectual plane, take a deep breath and quiet your mind. Seek the stillness within you. Change the radio station from Earthly to cosmic thought and vibration. *Trust* that the Universe has your back and that in this moment all is perfect. Allow the Divine to pour through you the consciousness of Soul. When this happens, in an instant

you are reconnected with the Soul of You, and the noise of the outer mind fades away. As you cross this chasm of fear, the Divine shows you that you're not alone. You're divinely embraced and held in a blanket of love that makes its appearance as you reach the other side. **Commit to Soul, ensure success.**

"There is no passion to be found playing small—in settling for a life that is less than the one you are capable of living."

~Nelson Mandela

The more deeply you commit to *living and being You through Soul*, the easier it is to express your divine gifts to the world. Deeper embodiment of the Soul helps you instinctively know how to dance with the flow of the Universe. When this occurs, the sacred fire of your *divine passion* carries you effortlessly into the manifestation of your Soul's desires. *Be you and live your dream!*

Now let's help you fully ignite your *divine passion* so it can propel you forward in sacred manifestation. Take out your journal and reread the answers you wrote for the exercises called "Discovering Your *Divine Passion*" (Parts I and II) from earlier in the chapter. Be sure to hold these fears clearly present, even feeling them in your body.

You can record the following meditation so you can close your eyes while you listen to it. For the audio version, visit **www.UnmaskingYourSoul.com/Meditations.** Sit comfortably where you won't be disturbed—with your feet flat on the floor and your hands on your knees with palms facing up. If you're an experienced meditator, use whatever position is most comfortable to you. When you're ready, please move to the meditation.

Guided Meditation: Igniting Your Divine Passion

Breathe slowly, inhaling through your nose and exhaling through your mouth. As you breathe, focus on your breath and feel with every breath the relaxation of your mind, body, and spirit. Allow thoughts to pass through your mind as they may. Continue taking deep breaths and drop into your heart center.

In your sacred heart space you're surrounded by the most beautiful pink light. See yourself standing in the center of your heart being bathed by pure, divine love. Each swirl of light brings peace, harmony, and a deep embrace from the Divine. You invite the angels, ascended masters, your guides, goddesses, and ancestors to surround you. You feel a gentle breeze on your heart as they all enter this sacred space with you. Waves of pearly white, silver, golden-yellow, and violet rays swirl around you, entering your crown and bathing every cell of your body, transmuting the old into the new. All that no longer serves you is being released, layer by layer, cell by cell, atom by atom, all made fresh and new. Take a deep breath and breathe this all into your heart. {*Pause.*}

Your Higher-Self now steps forward and stands by your side. A doorway appears before you and your Higher-Self instructs you to walk through. When you do, you arrive on a magical, mystical Polynesian island. Everywhere you look all you see is lush, green, exquisite, exotic flowers and foliage. It's breathtaking. Off in the distance you see a volcano. As you walk, you see many colorful birds, including a family of yellow canaries. You stop for a moment to watch them. You look up to the sky and feel the warmth of the golden sun radiating on your body.

To your right is a stone bench. You are intrigued by symbols on it that you've never seen before. You walk towards it. You trace each symbol with your fingers. As you do you feel energy shifting, and a portal of energy opens before you. A beautiful Polynesian woman comes through the portal. When she gets closer, she tells you she is the Goddess Pele, the holder of the sacred fire. She tells you how loved you are and that you are safe with her. She is here to guide you and ignite the sacred fire of your divine passion.

Pele reaches out and places her hand on your abdomen. When she does this you feel a powerful energy flowing through your abdomen. It's getting hotter and hotter, bringing warmth to the rest of your body. A liquid flow of fire is moving throughout your body. You're feeling so much divine passion flowing through you that you can hardly speak. Your Soul is becoming ignited and activated by Pele's touch. {*Pause for several minutes to receive and integrate.*}

Pele will be taking you on a journey to a deeper part of your Soul. As your divine passion flows through your essence, notice any places in your body where you may be holding resistance. A new portal opens before you. Pele grabs your hand and you walk through together. You are entering a past life that holds the key to this resistance. As you walk through the portal, look around and see where you are. What are you wearing? What do you look like? Are you female or male? Take a moment *to allow your being to remember this life and connect with what surrounds you in this moment. {**Pause.**}*

*Pele takes you to a sacred place beyond the trees ahead. You see a beautiful translucent body of water in front of you. Pele tells you this is a thermal hot spring containing sacred water infused with her sacred fire. She asks you to enter the water so you can heal all that no longer serves you in this life and across time and space. You enter the water and float on your back. The warm water feels delectable. As you look up into the sky, the clouds form doves and symbols of peace, harmony, and love. Beautiful rays of light emerge from the warm water, enter your crown, and disperse through every cell of your body. You feel so serene and loved in this moment. You continue to float, allowing the sacred water to cleanse every part of you. {**Pause.**}*

*When you feel complete, Pele helps you out of the water. She places a beautiful white robe on you. You're purified and cleansed. You notice there are seven sacred symbols on the collar of the robe. Pele tells you these sacred symbols are now imprinted into your being and will serve as a healing template for your continued healing over the next seven days. Pele holds your hands and looks into your eyes. You can see the sacred fire in your eyes reflected in hers. She has a message for you. She speaks. You listen. {**Pause to receive.**}*

Pele tells you it's time to return through the portal. She takes your hand, and together you walk through the portal. You thank Pele for the amazing activation and healing today. She slowly moves away. A portal opens and she disappears. Your Higher-Self welcomes you back home.

You thank the Divine for its assistance today and you return to your body. Slowly you feel that which surrounds you in the present. As you return fully into your body, you may slowly open your eyes.

Now that you've completed the guided meditation, take some time to do some journaling. Spend about ten to fifteen minutes in a quiet place where you won't be disturbed answering the questions below. You can put on some soothing music or light a candle or incense to support you as you write. Just write from your Heart and Soul and the rest will follow. Take some deep breaths as you write, allowing the words to flow through you with love and grace.

Journaling Exercise

1. What did you feel when the Goddess Pele placed her hand on your abdomen?

2. Did you notice any resistance rise to the surface? If so, in what part of your body?

3. As you entered your past life, what did you notice about yourself and your surroundings? Write down anything of significance from that life.

4. What was your experience as you floated in the hot spring and were cleansed and purified?

5. How did you feel when the white robe was placed on you? Write down anything of significance about the sacred symbols on the collar of the robe.

6. What message did the Goddess Pele have for you?

7. Journal about anything else of significance.

After journaling, continue working on the **Canvas of Your Soul.** (You can download the PDF at **www.UnmaskingYourSoul.com/Blueprint.**) Pick phrases, words, or symbols and put them on section 10 of the **Healing** part of your roadmap. Make this canvas your own piece of artwork that represents the journey we're taking together in this book. You can color, paint, or even cut images from magazines that depict the messages and insights you received in this chapter on *igniting your divine passion.* You don't need to be a professional artist to do this. Just let your Soul express through you as it wants to. This will become the vision board of your Soul's unmasking, a precious gift to you from your *divine artist.*

Five Rituals to Awaken Your Divine Passion Muscle

The rituals below are meant to help you awaken your *divine passion* muscle. You can repeat any of the rituals that follow and the exercises and guided meditations earlier in the chapter as many times as you like. With each repetition you go deeper in accessing your *divine artist.*

Before you begin, create your sacred space and take some deep breaths to relax your mind and body. Connect with your Soul as you enter this sacred space.

1. Write a manifesto that encompasses all of your *divine passions* and record it on your iPod, smartphone, or computer, or print it out and keep it with you so you can

read it or listen to it daily. The more you listen to or read your manifesto out loud, the more you imprint its energy in your energetic field, creating a beacon to the Universe for manifestation. Make this a daily ritual. It's best to integrate it as part of your morning routine of spiritual practice, exercise, etc. Here's my manifesto as an example:

Gratitude for another day of LIFE. BREATHE that IN. I fill each moment with LOVE, KINDNESS, and COMPASSION. BREATHE that IN. I behold ME as God beholds me. I choose ME because God chose ME. I AM safe to be Me. BREATHE that IN. I ONLY DO What I LOVE. It's that simple. DIVINE PASSION is the force that propels me forward. When I do what I love, I'm uplifted by the Universe. The inception point of Heart, Soul, and Divine Mind is the ignition of the spark of divine passion that lives within me. Spark On. BREATHE that IN. I love to paint. Spark On. I love to dance. Spark On. I love to heal and transform myself and others. Spark On. I love to awaken the hearts and minds of other light bearers. Spark On. I love to sing and play my guitar. Spark On. I love to write. Spark On. I love to teach. Spark On. I love to help others unmask their Souls and shine their brilliance. Spark On. I love to empower others to speak the truths of their Souls. Spark On. I love travel and culture. Spark On. I love the ocean. Spark On. I love the Divine. Spark On. I love all of creation. Spark On. I embody all of my Divine Passions. I live on purpose, fearlessly. Breathe that in. GRATITUDE. LOVE. SOUL. TRUTH. FREEDOM. Spark On.

2. Use this guided meditation to connect with your *divine passion* daily. This ritual takes three to five minutes. This is a good one to add to your morning routine so you can set your energy for the rest of the day.

Take several deep breaths, inhaling through your nose and exhaling through your mouth very slowly. Allow each breath to go deep into your abdomen. Take three to five deep breaths, then continue.

Call on a memory that connects you with the energy of your divine passion. Bring in every detail of that memory as if it were happening in this moment. Feel the energy swirling in your abdomen. A beautiful golden light enters your abdomen and integrates with the sacred fire of your divine spark. Breathe this in. The energy begins to rise into your heart and now is joined by beautiful swirls of pink light. Your sacred fire becomes grounded in divine love and your heart sings with joy and happiness. Stay here for a moment, allowing this feeling of inspiration, movement, and love to really sink in. When you feel this rush of sacred fire moving through you, set the intention to allow this energy to propel you forward in service to those you're meant to serve. See the energy flowing through every cell in your body and radiating outward to bless all that you do today. Give thanks and gratitude as you complete this ritual.

3. Use this ritual to open your *divine passion* Soul chamber. This will be most powerful if you add it to your morning spiritual practice. Do it daily for seven days.

    a. Take several deep breaths, breathing in slowly through your nose and breathing out through your mouth. Let each thought pass as it may. When you feel centered, move to the next step.

    b. With the index finger of your right hand, trace the sacred symbol (shown here) for this chamber on the palm of your left hand. Memorize the strokes of the symbol and close your eyes as you do this. As you trace the symbols on your hand, repeat the following mantra: "With this symbol, I ignite my *divine passion.*"

    c. Repeat this seven times. Stay very centered, taking deep breaths as you perform this sacred ritual.

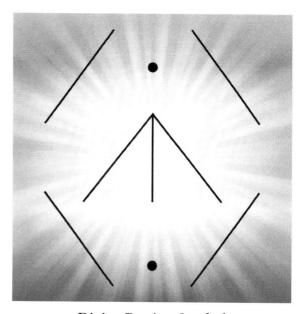

Divine Passion Symbol

d. As you complete the ritual, visualize the symbol as a three-dimensional image, raised above your palm, activating this chamber.

4. Use this ritual daily to ensure that you're doing the things that make your heart sing. Remember the quote earlier in the chapter from Howard Thurman. He was Martin Luther King Jr.'s mentor, and he said, "Ask what makes you come alive, and go do it." Use the questions to determine what areas of your life are either in or out of alignment with your *divine passion* and your Soul's desires. You can also use these questions to help you choose what you say yes and no to. Only those things that make you come alive should be a definite yes. Take out your journal for this ritual and spend about ten to fifteen minutes. I suggest you do this in the evening right before you go to bed. Just write from your Heart and Soul.

a. Answer these questions:

"What are the things that make me come alive? What truly makes my heart sing?"

"Did I do any of those things today? If yes, what were they? If not, why not?"

"How can I do more of what I love? What is in the way of my doing more of what I love?"

"What is the one step I can take tomorrow to move towards doing what I love?"

"As I consider the opportunities currently in my life, how do I feel? When I think of them, do they make me feel alive or do they make me feel drained? What is my Soul guiding me to do in this moment?"

b. As you complete this ritual, take several deep breaths into your heart center. Ask the Divine to enter your dreams this evening and help bring you clarity on your path forward as you work to pursue your *divine passion*.

c. Remember to journal about any signs or messages that come through your dreams or afterward. An answer sometimes appears in a different form as you go about your normal day. Pay attention, because eventually the answers will come.

5. Meditate with my painting **The Phenix Rising**, shown at the end of the chapter, to help you reconnect with your *divine artist,* the one who helps you access your *divine passion.* Each of my paintings was divinely channeled and holds messages and energetic impressions of the Soul that bring healing to the bearer. This particular painting holds vibrations of healing for those needing to remember their expression of *divine passion.*

a. Close your eyes and take a breath... inhaling slowly through your nose and exhaling slowly through your mouth... and with each breath you take relax your mind, body, and spirit. Continue focusing on your breath... and with each breath allow your thoughts to pass freely... thought after thought... breath after breath... relaxing more and more deeply. Continue taking several more deep breaths. {**Repeat for one or two minutes.**}

b. Briefly open your eyes and observe the painting. Allow yourself to be taken on a journey into the painting. Look at the images and symbols, and allow your gaze to go to one focal point in the painting. Soften your gaze as you focus on this point of interest. Breathe in its energy, seeing the symbols, images, and colors in your mind's eye. Continue breathing in the energy... breath after breath, allowing you to feel and absorb the healing energy from this focal point.

c. With your next breath, listen to the voice of your Soul. What is it communicating? What messages do you hear or feel within you as you breathe in the energy of the painting? Pay attention to where the energy is going in your body. This gives you an indication of where in your body you may need to release old energy, traumas, or wounds. Continue breathing and just go into the stillness while you connect deeper within. Allow the healing energies of the painting to penetrate your mind, body, and spirit. {**Do this for two to five minutes.**} If you feel guided, you may continue repeating this step, changing to a different focal point in the painting each time. Again, allow yourself to breathe the images, symbols, colors, and healing energies into your being.

d. Don't forget to journal about anything of significance that comes up during this experience.

Eileen Anümani Santos, *The Phenix Rising*, c. 2008

The Phenix Rising is the consummate *divine artist,* painting the new life you will have, rising from the ashes an evolved Soul, a more authentic YOU who is ready to be expressed. As you surrender to your Soul's desires, the *divine spark* within you is ignited, opening the Soul chamber that houses your *divine passion.* This is the moment of truth when your heart, *divine mind*, and Soul meet to create the inception of a divinely inspired life.

Embrace your Soul's desires.
The sacred fire of your *DIVINE PASSION* illuminates the way forward!

Divine Devotion

by Eileen Anümani Santos

Dear Creator, Heavenly Mind, Giver of Life and All There Is… I awaken to You each morning, giving You thanks for all the grace You bring into my life.

It is Your *divine love* that has transformed my spirit. As You whisper in my ear I am reminded of my wholeness, completeness, and infinite-loving self who is the I AM that I AM.

Your voice is so gentle and warm… it always brings me to the knowing that I can arrive at this place of Heaven on Earth by simply embodying Your likeness and Your love in all I do. I AM You. I AM all that You are.

You tell me that I can do what You do, and more. Many have devoted their lives to connecting with this aspect of You that resides within them. But it is Your steadfast devotion to our well-being and continued awakening that has always inspired me to go deeper and seek Your guidance and love on a daily basis.

Devotion is not just about worship, homage, and a deep demonstration of love to that which we hold most dear. Devotion also brings us to a place of union and oneness with all that we are, which is You. We are You at our core—all-loving, all-knowing, and all-being. In this place of oneness we experience the world around us as You do. No longer is the pain ours alone to carry. No longer do we have to live in sorrow or woundedness. No longer do we have to live in fear. Our oneness with You melts that all away, overcoming all with greater ease and providing the knowing that everything will be okay; that You will always take care of our needs, always and forever.

In doing this, I surrender to the Soul of and the Divine Mind of the Universe, which is ready to guide every step of my journey. Only by becoming a clear vessel for Your *Truth, Light, and Healing* can I manifest that which is already mine for the taking: Devotion to You. Devotion to me. Devotion to all. Devotion to oneness. In that devotion to You, I marry You, Beloved, and our sacred union sanctifies our oneness for eternity.

CHAPTER 11

Soul Chamber XI:
Practicing Divine Devotion

There is something sacred that you hold within you. It is a sacred fountain of humility, patience, gratitude, and holiness. When you practice divine devotion, you are one with these traits. When you honor the guidance of your Soul, it's easier to embody the divine qualities that are the true expression of your creation.

You are love. You are a luminous being of light. You are what the world is waiting for.

In Spanish this is: *Tú eres amor. Tú eres un ser luminoso de la luz. Tú eres lo que el mundo está esperando.*

The divine qualities of humility, patience, gratitude, and holiness are the underpinnings of *divine devotion*. Humility is all about the understanding and belief that there is a higher power that moves through you to support your existence and expression in the world. Humility begins with selfless service. Starting your day with that very question: "My Dearest Soul, how am I meant to serve today?" is a powerful practice. Through humility you demonstrate to the Universe that you're consciously practicing the art of sacred "Soul Speak," in which you *listen, receive, and respond to* the nudges and guidance from your Soul. When you surrender control to your Soul, life is easier, more fulfilling, and magical.

In responding to your Soul's guidance, you practice *patience* so that what is meant to be manifested can do so in its appropriate, divine timing. In other words, not everything you desire is ready to be manifested in the moment you desire it. If you push too hard and the seeds are not ready to be harvested, you can push your seed of creation out further into the future or create unnecessary challenges in your life. Although I believe that what is to be for you will always come to you, I also know from experience that if you "lean in" too early, you can cause unnecessary havoc in your life. Honor the timing that your Soul prescribes to you and the Universe responds in kind.

When you express *gratitude* for all aspects of your journey (even the challenging and painful experiences), your heart becomes a fluid expression of love that permeates all you touch. When love is the guiding force expressed through the Soul of You, it attracts more love into your life, and you live your life as love expanding into love.

It is through love that the last pillar of *divine devotion—holiness—*becomes a daily experiential experience in all those you encounter. Holiness, a sacred encounter of Soul to Soul, allows you to see and experience the sacredness in everything and everyone. This is a divine encounter in which you see through the eyes and heart of your Soul and witness the luminous light that lives in every creation of God. In holiness there is no judgement, pain, or illusion. This sacred encounter is expressed through the touching of hearts that recognize one another at a very deep, Soul level.

When you embody these pillars of *divine devotion,* you create a clearer channel for receiving your Soul's guidance. You tune in to the vibration of your Soul, a higher frequency of your Soul Speak that can only happen when you fully surrender to your Soul's calling. Soul Speak is the transmission tower of your Soul's language and guidance. It comes through the various sensory methods—claircognizance, clairvoyance, clairaudience, clairlove, and clairsentience—we discussed in previous chapters.

Practicing *divine devotion* is the key to creating this clear channel for Soul Speak to occur between your Soul and your human spirit. When you practice *divine devotion,* making the "God" part of you the highest priority in your life, *divine devotion* automatically shows up in others, including those of your most intimate relationships. As I mentioned in the introduction, your Soul communicates to you through your Higher-Self. This is the divine part of you that vibrates in the higher planes of consciousness where love is the driving force. Your Higher-Self has a direct connection to the *divine mind,* where your divine plan and destiny are written. Your goal is to embody more of your Higher-Self, your authentic Divine-Self, which vibrates in the fluidity of eternal love that transmutes the fear-based emotions and thoughts of the ego-mind into dust, never to be seen again.

The palm of your right hand is the location of **Soul Chamber XI—Divine Devotion,** the eleventh of the Soul virtues that will be unmasked as you continue on your journey of wholeness. The mask associated with the eleventh chamber is the **Mask of the Hidden Jewel.** *You are the hidden jewel—God's jewel.* In Spanish this is *Tú eres la joya escondida—la joya de Dios.* When you hide the jewel that you are, you hold yourself back from the life you desire and deserve. Because you're reading these words, I know this: God chose you for a reason. Only you can bring your gifts to the world in the way that you can. Hiding comes from fear. For me that fear has always been about safety and acceptance from others. I feared being seen and heard because in this lifetime and others I was persecuted for sharing my gifts and being me. I also feared that showing my true gifts meant not being accepted by others. As a little girl all I wanted was to fit in. I didn't acknowledge back then, as I do now, that being me means I must do what makes my heart sing regardless of how others perceive me and what I do. I discovered that unmasking your Soul is not about fitting in; it's about living in a state of consciousness that upholds your sacred union with the Divine. Living this way allows you to walk upon the Earth knowing that you're deeply loved, supported, and connected to the sacred wisdom of the Universe.

Being you takes a lot of courage. It requires full surrender, commitment, and stepping into your *divine power*. I remind you once again that everything must be grounded and acted upon from a place of *divine love*. When heart, courage, and action converge, what results is miraculous. The reward is living the life you have always dreamed of.

The fear that causes you to hide your magnificence is caused by the illusion of separation between your human spirit and God—a higher power. It is a fear of being seen in the world as the real you. There can be many reasons for this fear. In my case it was not being safe in the world if I spoke my truth. It was also not being accepted and loved. As you reach this part of your journey, it's time to reconcile this separation and allow the convergence of humanness and spirituality to take new form. As the convergence of your human-self and your spiritual-self occurs, you bring into existence your *divine mystic,* who embodies this on every level—the union of the human heart, mind, and Soul with the Divine Heart, Divine Mind, and Divine Soul. The archetype of this Soul chamber is the **divine mystic,** the one who helps you practice and embody *divine devotion.* The *divine mystic* is the one who knows how to bring forth the divine union between man and the Source of all creation. In this state of Soul-Love consciousness, the *divine mystic* naturally surrenders to the union with God—a higher power. The sacred symbol for the *divine devotion* chamber is shown here.

My Soul chose this life, this time, and this body for a reason. In this lifetime I am letting go of all my outdated beliefs and fears about safety and the need for approval so I can serve humanity in the way God created me to. I am here to liberate myself, my ancestors, and those I am to serve, like you who are reading these words right now. I am

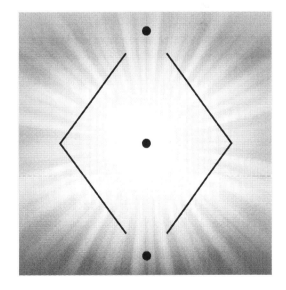

Divine Devotion Symbol

here to liberate my Soul and the voice of my Soul that has much to remember, teach, heal, and transform. You're here to do the same. When you call on the *divine mystic* who lives within you, you liberate yourself from the illusion of separation. The *divine mystic* takes you to a sacred place of union with the Divine where you embody your Higher-Self—the Soul of You. In this place a sacred marriage occurs between your Divine-Self and your human-self. It is through the practice of *divine devotion* that this sacred union between your human spirit and your divine spirit becomes possible.

In chapter 9 I introduced you to the connection to your mental body and the *divine mind*. In chapter 10 I spoke of *divine passion* as the emotional body that propels you forward in expressing your *divine purpose* to those you're meant to serve. In this chapter you have the opportunity to connect with your spiritual body as you learn to practice *divine devotion*. This is where the marriage of Divine-Self and your human-self takes place. We're going to explore three types of *divine devotion*: *divine devotion* to God, *divine devotion* to self and others, and *divine devotion* to your beloved Twin Soul.

Divine Devotion to God

There are many ways to practice *divine devotion*. As I mentioned earlier in the chapter, practicing *divine devotion* engenders within you the celestial qualities of *humility, patience, gratitude*, and *holiness*. All of the masters who lived in human form and ascended demonstrated these qualities. These celestial qualities are primordial in nature, so they were implanted in you before you took human form. They must be remembered and awakened because they create the foundation that allows for the merging of human spirit and Soul.

> **Through the act of divine devotion you connect with the one Source, the one power that lives within you—eternal love.**

Through the act of *divine devotion* you connect with the one Source, the one power that lives within you—eternal love. In her book *The Voice of the Master*, Eva Bell Werber said, "When…you come into the full complete consciousness that there is within you a holy power, and knowingly make contact with that power… it shall cause the living waters of My love to flow over you." That is the power of the love of Source, the power of love that you hold within your very existence. When I learned to stop seeking love (the source of my *divine power*) outside of me, my outside world changed. For the first time in my life I stopped living my life for others and began living my life for me.

At its core, *divine devotion* is about the sacred union between you and God. It is a journey into the heart and a demonstration and expression of your love to God. This is what the *divine mystic* seeks to experience over and over again: a yearning to be one with God. Only through this sacred intimacy are you able to create a deeper relationship with your Higher-Self, the conduit for your Soul's guidance. Through the sacred practice of *divine devotion* you're able to create a deeper relationship with God that is unique to you. Through this sacred union you learn to *just be* the love that you are and live your life from this state of being.

As I prepared to become an interfaith minister, one of the requirements was to learn about all different faiths and their beliefs and sacred rituals. It was through this ministerial preparation that I began to identify with and practice sacred spiritual acts of devotion. There are many different spiritual practices around the world, so my intention is not to cover all of them, but instead introduce you to some of my favorites that have served me well over the past decade. Please note that all of these practices can be done individually or in groups. Some of my favorite forms of *divine devotion* include:

1. **Prayer and invocation.** There are many different types of prayer, some of which you may have practiced as part of your own religious upbringing. I believe prayer is an individual act of *speaking your needs* to God, a higher power, angels, guides, etc. The Divine already knows your needs, but prayer can be very powerful in co-creating with the Divine and asking for what you need with love, gratitude, and commitment to the Divine. The act of asking is in itself a sacred act of self-love. We all know about the power of prayer and how miraculous it can be when done in large groups with complete focus and *intention*, which is the important part. Your prayer needs to be genuine and from the heart. It can be as simple as asking for strength to deal with a difficult situation, or as big as sending love to those around the world who are suffering. Whatever your prayer is, it should be focused on a specific intention. When you blanket that prayer of intention with love and gratitude, the Universe responds in kind. For the longest time my prayer has been: "Help me be the highest version of me so I can serve from a place of love." And, of course, prayer includes focused intention to help those in need such as loved ones and humanity in general.

   Invocation is a type of prayer you can use to invoke the assistance of the Divine in some way. You've already seen some examples in the rituals sections above. I invoke the Divine, angels, guides, ancestors, ascended masters, and other divine beings to assist me in creating a sacred space, healing someone or a group of individuals, or performing a ritual, to name a few. You, too, can do the same to support you on your transformational journey.

2. **Mantra-based meditation.** This type of meditation uses a mantra as the source of focus during meditation. This is similar to transcendental meditation, which

was introduced in the United States in the 1960s by Maharishi Mahesh Yogi. The mantra is repeated in silence over and over again throughout your communion time with Source. You can begin with a generic mantra like "Om," which is considered to be the sound of the Universe. But it is more powerful to receive a mantra specifically for you from a qualified instructor or teacher. I practice this type of meditation twice a day for at least twenty minutes each time. I normally meditate for at least an hour to an hour and a half in total per day, or more, depending on what's going on in my life. I find that when I'm going through a challenging time, releasing or healing, I need more meditation time to get assistance from my guides through the period of transition. *While prayer focuses on speaking to the Divine, meditation is about listening and receiving a response from the Divine.* For this reason I begin every meditation session with prayer. There are just such complementary benefits to linking these two practices together.

3. **Guided meditation and creative visualization.** This form of meditation typically uses some form of imagery and words to guide you to a deeper state of consciousness. This is the type of meditation you have experienced throughout *Unmasking Your Soul.* This was the first type of meditation I was introduced to when I started my journey back in 2003. I use it as a way to supplement my mantra-based meditation practice. With this type of meditation or creative visualization you usually want to achieve some specific intention. For example, you can use this type of meditation to help you heal or release an energetic block; imprint an intention for a new project, idea, or way of life in the Universe; or even take you to a deeper state of consciousness where you can communicate with your Higher-Self, the part of you that expresses the guidance of your Soul. This is exactly what I do with my clients through my Soul Quest meditations.

4. **Sacred study.** This spiritual practice involves the studying of ancient, holy, or spiritually inspired texts. It is the act of *inquiry* that makes this spiritual practice so powerful. When you're trying to get an answer to an inquiry, this is a perfect practice to help you with that. You can do this by randomly turning to a page in the sacred text you're using for your inquiry, or it can involve much more dedicated daily study. I like to do short snippets of this practice daily, so I tend to turn to random pages in whatever sacred text I'm using that day. I always receive the message I need to hear. Some examples of sacred texts are the Bible (Christian), the Torah (Judaic), Upanishads-illumined sages, (India), the *Tao Te Ching* (Lao Tzu), *A Course in Miracles* (channeled by Dr. Helen

Schucman), *A Course of Love* (channeled by Mari Perronor), and works by famous poets and philosophers such as Henry Thoreau, Socrates, Ralph Waldo Emerson, and Kahlil Gibran. But, again, you are your best source of knowing and inspiration. Trust your own intuition when choosing sacred texts to work with. The important thing is to pay attention not just to the words you're reading or studying, but to the emotions that are triggered in you. This always gives you a clue as to what other inquiries you should be making and what areas of focus and study will get you the answers you seek.

5. **Sacred movement.** This spiritual practice uses movement as a gateway to connecting with a deeper consciousness within you and your power center, or life-force energy. This life-force energy is what is referred to as *chi* in China, *mana* in Hawaii, and *shakti* or *prana* in the Sanskrit language. Sacred movement typically includes physical postures and movements that act as gateways to the spiritual connection between body, *divine mind*, and Soul. Tai chi, qi gong, yoga, body prayer, and ceremonial dance are all forms of sacred movement. When practicing sacred movement, the movement serves as your source of focus so you can move from your mind to a deeper state of consciousness. In essence, the movement serves as your mantra for your communion with Spirit through your body's awareness. In a sacred movement practice, your body shows you not only where you hold tension, but sometimes why. Your life story is recorded in your body, and sacred movement allows you to hear it. When there are impediments in your movements, that is indicative of places where you may be holding fear or resistance. When you pay attention to your "body-speak," you learn very quickly where you're holding pain, fear, or resistance. This is actually a good thing because when you can feel it, you can heal it. This is a sign that whatever you're holding in that part of your body is ready to be released. For example, my knees are still where I hold fear and resistance.

6. **Sacred ceremony and ritual.** From the dawn of civilization rituals have been a part of human life. You already know that I believe in the power of sacred ritual. Every *divine mystic* understands the power of ritual. Ritual opens the door to sacred union, healing, and transformation. All of our ancestors performed rituals in some way, from the act of baptism in the Catholic Church to lighting the Menorah in celebration of Hanukah in the Jewish faith and the ceremonial dancing done by my ancestors, the Taino Indians, to name a few. Rituals and sacred ceremonies are a way to invoke the Divine to assist us in many ways, such as healing, initiating a new level of spiritual growth, or sanctifying the birth of a new way of life or a new way of being. I've mentioned before in the

rituals section of each chapter the importance of creating a sacred space when you perform rituals, but rituals don't have to be long and arduous. They can be as simple as creating a sacred space where you light a candle or incense, speak a prayer of intention, and then sit in time of reflection to nourish your Soul. The more you embody your *divine mystic*, the easier and more natural it becomes to create your own rituals that speak to your own Soul and support your unique journey.

7. **Sacred pilgrimage.** Every year many thousands of pilgrims venture to Mecca, the holiest site in the Islam faith; to the Lady of Guadalupe Basilica in Mexico; to the town of Lourdes in Southern France where Catholics celebrate Virgin Mary's ascent to Heaven, or to the Road to Santiago (Way of Saint James) that runs from the French side of the Pyrenees to the western part of Spain. It takes about four weeks to travel this sacred Road to Santiago by foot. There are many such sites around the world. Sacred pilgrimage has become a way for many to seek refuge from our bustling, modern-day life in search of spirituality, healing, cleansing, and life-changing experiences.

You don't have to go to another country to experience sacred pilgrimage. In fact, this is one of my favorite ways to disconnect from my daily life, including electronic devices and even human beings. I like to call this spiritual practice "drinking from God's well of wisdom." I typically go to a local retreat center in my area that has lots of nature and is secluded enough for me to do at least a two- or three-day silent retreat. Practicing this at least once a quarter is ideal. If you can, I encourage you to go away to one of the sacred sites I've mentioned or whichever one calls to your Heart and Soul, because the energy you will feel there will be very powerful due to the many thousands or even millions of pilgrims who have gathered there before you. I achieved my greatest breakthroughs through this sacred practice. Let me share with you one of the experiences I had while I was doing a sacred pilgrimage locally while writing this book. The message I shared with you at the beginning of the book entitled "A Divine Message for You, Beloved Reader" emerged through this particular sacred pilgrimage.

> It was a warm spring day and I had just arrived at a local retreat center in my area. It was my first time at this place so I spent the morning discovering the various paths and natural treasures on the property. As I walked around I discovered a beautiful wood-chip path that encircled the retreat center. I decided this would be my first excursion

for the day. I began walking the path with focus and awareness, connecting with Mother Earth with each step I took. As I continued my meditative walk, I discovered a very old tree. It was huge and there were many carvings on the tree dating back a long time. I immediately felt the power and wisdom of this beautiful creation of God.

The sign by the tree said it was an American beech tree. I placed my hand on the tree and began to commune with this majestic creature. As I connected with the essence of the tree, it told me its name was Yánu and that it was 300 years old. In that moment I just felt called to hum and sing to the tree; it was like I was honoring its existence in the world. Yánu told me it was honored by the gift of my Soul's song. It reminded me to experience in that moment the expansiveness of its branches and the depth of its roots. As I did this, I knew I was being called to go deeper within my own being and remember my own expansiveness as a Soul and connection to the Earth and the Divine.

After a short while I sat on a bench facing this amazing, wise tree. I felt words arising through me that were being expressed by the tree. I immediately grabbed my digital recorder and began speaking the words coming through me. These are the words that you read at the beginning of the book, but they are so powerful I want you to read them again:

In the beginning, you emerged from a seed of *Love*. *Love* became the anchor for your Soul and all that you are. As you emerged into physical form, that *love* remained within you... in a place of oneness with the Divine. In the stillness you can call upon it in a moment's breath. Herein lies the secret to that which you've been seeking all your life.

In this seed of *love* that makes up your Soul's DNA, is the *Truth* of your existence and your unique purpose in this life. Unmask it, accept it, be grateful for it.

You were born in this time to bring your unique seed to humanity. You are on Earth now with a specific purpose that only *Your Light* can deliver. Within your Soul you hold the container for the unfolding of this purpose. Receive it, commune with it, nurture it.

The seed is ready to be harvested. Your Soul calls to you to embrace the **truth** of your existence. The fire has ignited your Soul and the power of your divinity is exposed to the masses. Embrace **truth** without fear. Show your true face to the world—the need to hide no longer serves you. Shine **your light** to the world. Feel it, know it, embrace it.

As the seedling hatches, the **Healing** occurs and you transform into the **real you**—the you that you've always been, the you that your Soul knows is the divine receptacle of God's **love**—every breath, every word, and every action instilled with the expression of your divinity. As you emerge, empowered to be the real you, life transforms with you and the Universe supports you in the unfolding of your Soul's purpose. Believe it, trust it, surrender to it.

You have returned to the purest form of your existence—**love**—and this new you knows no boundaries of limitation or desire. All it knows is that with **love** anything and everything is possible.

And so it is. The **empowered you** begins anew.

I continue to be in awe at how the Divine creates such beauty and inspiration through us when we are able to just surrender and be open vessels. When we get out of our own ways, we open the gateway to the fountain of eternal love that is waiting to pour through us. This is the true elixir of a Soul-driven life.

Divine Devotion to Self and Others

The *divine mystic* embodies the Soul's virtues of humility, patience, gratitude, and holiness. It is through the sacred act of witnessing and experiencing the holiness in yourself and others that you're able to create a sacred union with God—a higher power. As you let go of what you once were, you become what you've always been. There is but one Source, one power within—eternal love. The *divine mystic* knows this and seeks this union with God and all that is (plant, animal, or human). This is what Soren Kierkegaard calls "creeping into God," a deeper intimacy with God. The life of the *divine mystic* is filled with deep, rich, communal experiences with the Divine that elicit awakening, healing, and integration of parts of them that exist across time and space and come together once again to be expressed through them in this present time.

"Just as in earthly life lovers long for the moment when they are able to breathe forth their love for each other, to let their souls blend in a soft whisper, so the mystic longs for the moment when in prayer he can, as it were, creep into God."

~Soren Kierkegaard

As you embody the *divine mystic* within you, there is an alchemy that occurs. This alchemy transmutes any negative energies that you've been holding in your energy field, and releases through time and space any karmic ties or vows so you can embody the love that you are and live a Soul-conscious life. In this embodiment you become the bride or groom of the Divine. This is the marriage of your human-self and your spiritual-self, uniting in oneness with Source, the creation of your being. In this state of consciousness you no longer seek validation, approval, or permission from others. No consequence exists outside of you. There is but a profound knowing that you are no longer separate from the Source of your creation. You feel connected with all that is. From this place of cosmic union with God, all that you practice is a continued nourishment of the oneness that exists between you and all of creation.

All you're seeking in life culminates in the experience of this cosmic union in which the knowing of all that exists in creation becomes accessible to you from this place of oneness. Love is the anchor that allows this cosmic union to be imprinted in the existence of your being so you can live your life from this conscious state of being. You are in an awakened state in which all the answers to your questions are retrieved from the essence of your true existence, the divine essence that you really are. In this state your life becomes a living and breathing expression of this cosmic union. You begin to live your life from "being" instead of seeking. You become aware that all that you need to know is already there with you. You move from wonderment to believing that you are the divine expression of God's creation. As this *divine mystic*, you now live your life seeing and experiencing the sacredness that exists within each and every one of God's creations.

Every plant speaks to you and shares its cosmic knowledge with you. Every tree becomes alive within your Heart and Soul. Every human being acknowledged in your heart is a part of you and you are a part of them. No longer is there a separation between your physical and spiritual aspects. No longer is there a separation between heart, *divine mind*, and Soul. In the new vibration and state of the *divine mystic*, your focus becomes the expression of love in all that you do. All that you experience is focused on connecting with the sacredness of each and every creation and being that surrounds you. In your everyday life you begin to express yourself as love expanding into love; every breath expressing love; every action being guided by the Soul of You.

You become directly connected to the eternal life that lives within you. In the embodiment of Soul as the *divine mystic*, you plug in to the consciousness of Source—the all-knowing presence that lives within you that serves as your guide to grace, love, purpose, and abundance in all areas of your life. The belief that you are a divine being connected to all of creation and expressing as one heart, one mind, and one Soul provides the divine alchemy that allows you to become the core essence of your being. Believing is becoming. Becoming is believing. As you become what you believe, the real you emerges. This is the convergence that happens as you live as the *divine mystic* that you are. This convergence allows you to become the embodiment of your spiritual-self and, in turn, a clear vessel through which Source transmits vibrations, words, sounds, messages, and mystical experiences that create a richer, Soul-driven life.

> **When you honor the sacredness in yourself and others, you experience life through the eyes of your Higher-Self—the vessel of your Soul.**

When you honor the sacredness in yourself and others, you experience life through the eyes of your Higher-Self—the vessel of your Soul. The interactions you have with others change because you can see and experience their light and holiness in ways that perhaps they cannot even see. When you practice living your life from this sacredness, you plant the seeds for others to do the same. Love expands into more love. Light expands into more light. Your Soul touches the Souls of others. In *A Course in Miracles,* it says, "When you meet anyone, remember it is a holy encounter… Never forget this, for in him you will find yourself or lose yourself." When you practice this *divine devotion* with others, you create sparks of illumination within those you hold as holy. I try to practice this type of *divine devotion* daily. Below is my experience with my Higher-Self (the expression of my Soul) at the park one day as I practiced honoring the sacredness in all that surrounded me.

Today I saw your reflection in the water. You were luminous and fluid and sparkly. As I looked at each ripple on the surface of the pond, you were there. As I looked upon the trees, you were there. Within each bird, the deer, and the horses, your presence was clear. Others looked at me with question as I sat in oneness with you, but it didn't matter because in that oneness everything else disappeared. In this place, only oneness mattered. I walked and ran and walked and ran. Each tree gave me earth energy as I passed. Each bird honored my breath. I smiled at each passerby, sharing that joy of oneness I was feeling. They smiled back. Can they feel you as I do? I don't know, but I know in that moment of exchange we honored one another and our Souls smiled. You have taught me this is all it takes, small gestures and tokens of appreciation and gratitude, to connect with this Source of oneness within each of us. As we co-create in this space of love, those around us ponder the joy we express and a yearning begins to pull them towards you, to a place of higher knowing, higher being—a place where love is the answer to all we seek. Let us honor our sacredness this way every day.

You cannot unmask yourself fully if you don't devote time to healing those parts of you that hold you back from being the most authentic you that you can be. *Divine devotion* to self is what is required to release the fears that keep your jewel hidden from the world. What are the parts of you that still remain hidden?

Let's help you discover where you are cloaking the gifts that you hold—the jewel that you are. You can record the following meditation so you can close your eyes while you listen to it. Find a quiet place where you won't be disturbed for fifteen to twenty minutes. Then create a sacred space as you've done many times before. Sit comfortably —with your feet flat on the floor and your hands on your knees with palms facing up. If you're an experienced meditator, use whatever position is most comfortable to you. When you're ready, please move to the meditation.

Guided Meditation: Discovering Your Hidden Jewel

Take several deep breaths, breathing in through your nose and exhaling slowly through your mouth. With every breath you take, you release any stress, anxiety, and wandering thoughts. As you become present in your sacred space, drop into your heart center.

In the sacred space of your heart you're surrounded by beautiful swirls of pink and green light. Connect with this light. Breathe it in. And once again. With each breath you connect with the love that you are. Affirm this silently: "I am love. I am love. I am love."

As you stand in this precious space of love, see a doorway open up in front of you. When you walk through this doorway you enter a sacred garden. You're surrounded by beautiful flowers, so fragrant that you feel they are right there in the room with you. The birds are chirping and singing, celebrating you and your existence. The butterflies are flying all around you, flapping their colorful wings to show you how loved and revered you are. In the distance you see the most buoyant waterfall you've ever seen. You walk towards the waterfall. As you draw near you notice a crystal-clear pool of water that is the destination for the cascading droplets of water.

*You kneel on the ground and lean over to look at your reflection in the pool of water. When you lean over, what do you see? Are there any parts of you that you're hiding? Are there parts of you that seem dimmed, masked, or hidden as you look at your reflection in the pool of water? Stay here for a moment and go to a place of introspection to seek the answers to these questions. {**Pause for one minute.**}*

*Call forward your Higher-Self. As you look into the water again, look deeply into the center of your own eyes and see beyond your physical being. Connect with your Higher-Self, the expression of your Soul. See the light that you are radiating directly from the water facing you now. What message does your Higher-Self have for you? Stay here for a moment to receive. {**Pause for a moment to receive.**}*

When you feel complete, return through the doorway into your heart center. Slowly come back into your body, feeling your feet, toes, arms, torso, hands, fingers, and head.

When you're ready, slowly open your eyes.

Now it's time to do some journaling about this experience. Pull out your journal and write down anything of significance from this meditation. Make a special notation of any clues or insights about where you're hiding, masking, or cloaking any parts of you that are holding you back from expressing the real you, the divine you that you are.

As you learn to embody the *divine mystic* within you, you see that it's your divine will that opens the doorway for the mystical to appear in your daily life. This can happen in many forms. You can experience the mystical as you commune with the Divine through your daily spiritual practice, as you travel in your dream state, or via messengers in human or animal form that bring you to the point where the spiritual and physical planes meet. At this convergence point you can experience life beyond your human senses, and sound, touch, sight, taste, smell, feelings, and inner knowing become amplified to a transcendent state. This means that you begin to experience these senses on much higher planes or dimensions than those of the three-dimensional world most people experience on the Earthly plane when they are not yet awakened to their core essences as divine beings of light.

Having a mystical experience is quite normal if you're on a spiritual journey of awakening, growth, and expansion. However, it may not seem normal to you when those around you think you're crazy or say that what you do is "woo woo." Let's face it; when people haven't experienced something for themselves, it's normal for them to feel uncomfortable discussing what seems outside their norm. They see life through the only eyes they know, and might not be aware that the beliefs in their subconscious are running 90 percent of their lives. These beliefs can be driven by how they were raised, life experiences, or even core beliefs that were created in past lives. So it's not their fault that the mystical makes them uncomfortable. If you want to live a Soul-driven life, you're not going to seem normal to those who've not yet experienced the life of an awakened Soul.

If you want to continue your journey of transformation, make peace with that belief. The best way to do that is to find a community of like-minded people who can support you as you expand, grow, and become the real you. Trust me, I know you can create the life you desire and deserve, but you must be willing to do the work, truly see and love yourself as the Divine sees and loves you, and surrender control to that part of you that lives in oneness with Source in every moment of every day—the Soul of You.

This book would not be in your hands if I had not opened up to the *divine mystic* within me. This is the mystical experience I had that made this book possible:

It was a warm spring day, so I sat outside on my deck to meditate. As I dropped into a deep meditative state, I immediately saw Archangel Metatron, one of my guides, and my guardian angel, Mary. They told me they would be transporting me to a galactic archive where information regarding this book would be downloaded into me. I looked at myself and could see I was dressed as my ancient priestess, Anümani. I was witnessing this experience through her eyes. As I arrived at the archive, a Sirian galactic being told me he would be working with me to unlock and awaken ancient wisdom within me. I could see a sacred geometric symbol on the ground of this archive. It had four triangles pointing in the directions of North, South, East, and West. The triangles were formed by blue and golden rays of light. The galactic being asked me to sit on the ground in the center of the symbol, and so I did.

When I looked down at the ground I saw sacred symbols etched in between each triangle. As Anümani, I began to say an invocation prayer, and as I did, the rays of light from the triangles and the symbols formed a globe of light around me. The symbols came alive and the globe became three-dimensional;

the symbols now were raised above the ground. I was guided to touch each symbol in a specific order. Each time I did this, a portal opened up above my head. There were twelve in total. When I opened each portal, information was downloaded into me through my crown chakra. Then I saw a map of the Soul chambers and their locations downloaded and imprinted in my third eye and heart chakras. The sound and vibration of each chamber were imprinted in my throat chakra as well. At the end I saw an unlocking and activation of the words from the book opening inside of me.

The galactic being then showed me a bookshelf where the book was sitting. I pulled it from the shelf and felt the words and the vibration of the book being imprinted in my heart. I could see bright white light shining from the pages of the book. The activation was complete. Now all the wisdom and words were accessible to my conscious mind. I was immediately shown the location of the first Soul chamber as the heart center and its corresponding Soul virtue as *divine love*.

For some of you this experience resonates; but for some it may feel a little out there. Each divine experience is unique to your individual journey and purpose in life. I invite you to be open to whatever that experience is meant to be for you. Receive what resonates with you and leave the rest. I'm not here to convince you of anything. I'm here to guide you to a more expansive, richer, Soul-driven life in whatever form that shows up for you.

There is one truth that I know, which is that through *divine devotion* you're able to create an intimate relationship with the Divine that opens the doorway to truths that are for your eyes only. This means that no matter what others say or tell you they see for you, only *you* can discern what is in alignment with your Soul's path. I say this to you from experience. There have been times when others tried to convince me of a path that was not the right one for me. I must admit that I had to go through some painful experiences to learn this truth. But as I deepened my sacred union with Source through *divine devotion*, the easier it became for me to discern my truth—the truth that is unique to my relationship and experience of God. Your relationship and experience is unique to you. Even as an intuitive, I can only "see" for a client what the Divine wants or allows me to see. The rest is up to the individual to discover. That makes perfect sense, since the ultimate goal is for you to learn to access and follow the guidance of your internal spiritual GPS—the Soul of You.

Becoming a master at anything requires practice. Not only does it require practicing *divine devotion* to open the door to this sacred union between you and the Divine, but having blind faith in what you cannot yet physically see. Learning to discern this higher knowing within you is key. This knowing comes from the Soul of You—the transcendent part of you that acts as your guiding light in the physical world if you allow it to be so.

Throughout *Unmasking Your Soul* you've had many opportunities to go deeper and witness and experience the mystical with the Divine. Because you've made it this far, I know you've already begun to embody the *divine mystic* within you. Where is your *divine mystic* asking you to focus your *divine devotion*?

Let's do a short meditation to help you discover the answer to that question. You can record the following meditation so you can close your eyes while you listen to it. Find a quiet place where you won't be disturbed for the next ten to fifteen minutes. Sit comfortably—with your feet flat on the floor and your hands on your knees with palms facing up. If you're an experienced meditator, use whatever position is most comfortable to you. When you're ready, please move to the meditation.

Guided Meditation: Connecting with Your Divine Mystic

Take a deep breath, slowly inhaling and exhaling. Do this at least three times. With each breath let go of any stress and just allow the calmness of your divine communion to permeate your essence. Envision yourself dropping into the center of your heart. As you do, you're engulfed in the most beautiful golden and pink light. You're joined by your angelic and spiritual team. They surround you and send you love. It's like you're being held in a warm, cozy blanket of love.

*A door appears in front of you. When you're ready, walk through the doorway to meet with your divine mystic. When you do, you enter a sacred chamber in your heart. The walls of the chamber are filled with sacred symbols that are brightly lit by the rainbow-colored light that illuminates them. Across the room you see your divine mystic. You walk up to them. They hold your hand and point to a sacred symbol on the wall. They tell you this sacred symbol holds key wisdom that belongs to you. You place your hand on the symbol and feel an unlocking occurring within your essence. {**Pause here for a moment and integrate this wisdom.**}*

You ask your divine mystic what messages they have for you. How can you experience a deeper sacred union with the Divine? How can you embody your divine mystic more deeply? Your divine mystic responds with the answers to your questions.

*The answers may come in the form of visions, words, symbols, colors, or sounds, so just be open to receiving. {**Pause for a moment to receive.**}*

When you feel complete, come back into your body. Walk through the doorway in your heart center and slowly return to the present moment.

When you're ready, you may open your eyes.

Take a moment to capture in your journal anything significant from this experience. Be sure to capture any messages, clues, or insights that were shared with you. Make note of anything that may be holding you back from embodying this deeper part of you. This information might come in handy later when you do the meditation at the end of the chapter in which we awaken you to a deeper embodiment of your *divine mystic*.

When you open to and honor the sacredness that you are and practice *divine devotion* with others, you move your essence to new boundaries of Soul Love. When you experience this cosmic union with the Divine, you no longer feel the need to seek love or anything else outside of you. From this wholeness and oneness you open the sacred space for Soul Love to appear in your life in a multitude of ways. It may come in the form of relationships, partnerships, family, career, new projects or creations—everything you've been seeking and desiring now discovered, awakened, and loved into existence. As you live in sacred union with the Divine and become one with the eternal love that you are, you create the space for your beloved Twin Soul to enter your life.

Divine Devotion to Your Beloved Twin Soul

When you embody your *divine mystic* and Soul more deeply, there is a cosmic union that occurs between you and Source, engendering a rich, deep intimacy that opens the sacred fountain of eternal love within you. This type of love goes deeper than emotion or feeling; it is a state of being. This love is what I call Cosmic Love. It is the love that exists between *Twin Souls*, *Twin Flames*, or what we call in Spanish *Almas Gemelas*. When I speak of Twin Souls (or Twin Flames), I speak of two souls that were once one Soul but were split into two before taking human form. There is a specific and divinely ordained purpose for the sacred union that occurs between Twin Souls. The *divine devotion* that occurs between Twin Souls opens the heart space of those they are meant to serve. As a direct embodiment

> **When you embody your divine mystic and Soul more deeply, there is a cosmic union that occurs between you and Source.**

of eternal love, the twins come together to create that same vibration of eternal love in others. The Twin Soul union brings to fruition the awakening and unlocking of deep healing and creative gifts that the twins use collectively to serve humanity in ways they could never have on their own. Before I go deeper into this type of cosmic and sacred union (*union sagrada* in Spanish), I will discuss the three levels of love that lead to this type of union. The spiritual maturity you gain as you experience each level of love opens the doorway for the ultimate embodiment of the last level, *Cosmic Love*.

The first level I call Familial Love. This love is connected to your family and ancestry. It is immersed in learning and discovering your true essence. It is connected to karma and the "Soul contract" you made before you took human form. This is how it's been explained to me by my spiritual guides. Karma has to do with past deeds and repayment of those deeds in this life. By reincarnating into a new body (in this life) you're given a chance to make good on choices you made previously that hurt you or others. Believe it or not you chose the family you belong to; the body you inhabit; the gender, race, and all factors related to your physical life. Through the Soul contract you made prior to inhabiting your new body, all those choices were decided. A Soul contract essentially covers all the life lessons you're meant to acquire in this life to advance the consciousness of your Soul. Your karma influences what your Earthly lessons and experiences will be. Every experience is divinely orchestrated to help you learn your Earth-life lessons and awaken to your true essence as an illuminated spiritual being.

In the first level you learn to heal the ancestral and family ties you currently have and practice seeing your family through the eyes of the Divine. We all carry ties to our ancestral lineage, and this in itself causes you to hold energy that belongs to your ancestors. When you heal that part of you, you're also able to heal the ancestral lineage connected to that part of you. I discovered throughout my own journey, with the help of my guides, the truth of my ancestral connection. I was told that I am here to break a cycle that was created by my ancestors many hundreds and thousands of years ago. I came from a line of healers, but at some point in their history they chose to hide their healing gifts in order to survive the time they lived in—a time when humanity was not ready or willing to openly accept their divine gifts.

I chose to incarnate in this time to break this cycle and heal the pain and wounds that existed in my lineage for many lifetimes. I can say with certainty that there were times when I felt these wounds as real pain in my body, especially in my knees. I felt I was carrying the weight of the world in them. The knees are connected to the first chakra, the root. It is in this energy center where you connect to elements of your life that deal with safety, security, finances, career, and ancestry. This became one of my core lessons in this life—to heal the part of me that was afraid of expressing my true gifts and being seen. I remained hidden for a long time, but when I worked with others and my guides to heal this part of me, I was finally able to step in and allow myself to be fully seen and heard. I found myself constantly repeating the following mantra to help create the energetic force to support me: "It's safe for me to speak my truth, be seen, and be heard."

Let's face it; you chose your family for a reason. Most likely they trigger you in the areas that you're meant to heal. For me it was always about love and authenticity. As a little girl I felt misunderstood by my own family, and at times, not loved. But I know now that those triggers stemmed from the wounds my little girl was carrying in this life from her experiences of abuse and control. I was also carrying very big wounds and traumas from past lives in which I had been tortured, betrayed, and even killed for expressing my gifts and being my authentic self. All this pain was sitting in my subconscious and energy field, causing me to see the outside world in a distorted way. I saw the world through the eyes of my wounded little girl. Back then I didn't know any better. I kept looking outside of me for the solution. I kept trying to please everyone else, and pretended to be someone I wasn't to gain their favor and love. All along I couldn't see that my family was helping me in the best way they knew how.

I am graced with a family who loves one another very deeply. We're not perfect. We have our own dramas that arise from the human imperfections and wounds we carry. But we share a complete understanding that love transcends all. I finally learned to see the goodness in each and every one of them, and to love them as they are and where they are on their journey. That was hard for me. As a healer I wanted to help all of them transform their lives as I had. But with spiritual growth comes responsibility for self and making the choices that allow you to have the life you dream of and desire. No one else can do that for you. As you work on you, it has an effect on those around you. Love expands into more love and light expands into more light. That's a winning proposition for all, so I encourage you to keep at it and don't ever give up.

In this level of Familial Love, you're bound to get triggered over and over again. A trigger can be a moment when you get angry about something a family member says to you or something they do to cause you to feel powerless, controlled, or even worthless. Triggers are emotional stirrings of the Soul that require focus and contemplation. Anytime you're triggered by something or someone, it's time to pull back into a state of quiet and stillness to identify why you're feeling that way. Underneath the trigger is an emotion; underneath that emotion is a wound or a "pain body" as Eckhart Tolle refers to it; underneath that pain is a life lesson, one that you're here to overcome if you choose to do the work and follow the guidance of your Soul.

The second level of love I call Soulmate Love. Typically you move into this stage when you enter an intimate, one-on-one relationship with a partner or spouse. By this time you've already experienced some of the areas and lessons you're here to learn through your family relationships. In this level you attract partners who mirror for you those areas in which you still hold pain and need to heal. A *soulmate* is someone who is in your life to help you discover the shadow parts of you that are yearning to be healed and transformed into light. They come into your life to show you the areas in which you need to do some inner work. The title "Soulmate" tells you that you also have a Soul connection with this person. Most likely you've been with this person in other lives and are living out your karma together in this life in one way or another. When I met my husband there was something that just felt so right between us. There were just too many coincidences that connected us very deeply. Despite what later happened between us, I am grateful for the experience. It was a major life lesson for me. I ended a cycle of abuse that had existed in my life for lifetimes, and I finally learned to stand in my own *divine power*.

The shadow parts of you sometimes remain hidden. You may even subconsciously push those parts of you away because you feel they don't fit in with the way you want others to see you. Krishnamurti, a world-renowned spiritual teacher, said, "Relationship is a mirror in which I can see myself." And, mind you, this mirror does not disappear. You repeat the same patterns until you learn the lesson. For a long time I chose partners who were not physically available to be with me. I would become infatuated with them and then be upset when they weren't available to be in a relationship with me. I came to learn that I was subconsciously choosing them because I was afraid of being hurt. It was my ego's way of holding me hostage so I wouldn't be betrayed or hurt. Then, when I finally got married, I chose a partner who was controlling and verbally abusive. Here again I was being taught the lesson to value myself above all else and learn to stand in my power. This included learning how to set healthy boundaries with others and knowing when to speak up if those boundaries were crossed. Perhaps you've noted similar patterns in your own relationships.

Despite the emotional controversy that arises from your shadow parts, they are here to serve your highest good. As a child I remember how the rebel part of me showed itself every once in a while. It first appeared very poignantly when I was eleven years old. I had just become interested in skateboarding. One day my mom asked me to go with my cousin to pick up something for her at the corner store. She said, "Don't take the skateboard." Despite her urging, that was the first thing I did. I grabbed my skateboard and my cousin and off we went. (By the way, my brothers and I quickly learned to heed our mother's intuitive sight. She was always spot on.) We came to the big hill that was on the way to the store. My cousin and I dared one another to go down the hill on the skateboard. He first gave it a try, but changed his mind half-way. He then dared me to do it. My rebel came out in full force. In spite of my fear of being seen in that moment, I wanted to be heralded as a courageous hero. So I grabbed the skateboard and down the hill I went. It was a miracle I wasn't killed on that busy street. I made it to the bottom of the hill, but was going so fast that I lost my traction and rolled off the skateboard. I damaged the cartilage and ligament in my right knee.

Even with the tragedy of this experience, my rebel actually has served me well time and time again, especially in moments when I needed to stand up for myself and my beliefs. In fact, when I discovered my artistic spiritual gifts, my rebel-self was the one who helped me create Soul paintings that were crafted exactly as divinely guided. It's amazing that I never once questioned the divine creation that was being expressed through my vision and hands. These paintings have served my clients tremendously in understanding where they still hold pain and wounds and in helping them connect more deeply with the guidance of their Souls. That would not have been possible without the help of my rebel.

In the level of Soulmate Love, there is a definite Soul recognition that brings you together. However, the most influential aspect of this relationship still remains in the human or earthly aspects of love that are based in emotion, feelings, and judgment that arise from those parts of you that are triggered by your partner. Now, don't get me wrong; soulmate relationships contain lots of beautiful and loving experiences that make them sacred and necessary for the evolution of your Soul. But the love is held in a field of conditions. What I mean by that is that you place a condition around the love such as "I'll love you only if you're like this or you do that." The love has conditions and stipulations attached to it.

It is a union that is firmly based in the Earthly plane, entangled with all the human aspects of our development as spiritual beings having human experiences. At this level of love, there is a part of your human personality that seeks completion outside of you through the relationship. I know this first hand. When I married my husband, I could see the light in him and, as the healer that I am, subconsciously felt the need to nurture and "save" him from the pain I knew he was carrying. I thought I would feel complete if I saved him; but instead I became the caretaker instead of the caregiver. There's a big difference between the two. The caretaker seeks to nourish others before they nourish themselves, and sacrifices themselves in the process. The caregiver, on the other hand, knows they must love themselves first. They know they must nourish and feed their own Soul first, above all else, or they won't be able to fill the cups of those they're meant to serve. So this level of love can include a lack of self-love, or at least not match the vibration of the eternal love from which we were all created and formed. Eternal love holds no boundaries or conditions. It is a state of being and not just an emotion or feeling.

In the third level, Cosmic Love, each Soul in the partnership has transcended the human frailties of conditional love and achieved a deeper embodiment of the eternal love they are at their core. Each Soul no longer seeks completion outside of themselves and has deeply and richly fallen in love with their own being. They recognize the divinity within each other. This is *divine devotion* at its best: being able to behold your partner as God beholds them. The love is unconditional. The human imperfections are perfect in your eyes, heart, and Soul. A perfect sacred marriage occurs between heart, *divine mind*, and Soul, bringing two Souls that were once one into unity once again. When this alignment occurs, you're able to see through the eyes of the Divine, and what you see is aligned with the thoughts that arise in the *divine mind*, all founded in eternal love. The famous Lebanese poet Kahlil Gibran called this Cosmic Love "the offspring of spiritual affinity." In the Sufi tradition, spiritual affinity refers to the affinity that occurs between God and human beings. I'm referring to the Soul virtue of *divine devotion*. In this level of Soul embodiment you live in a state of being of eternal love and you're able to experience and see it within your partner as well. As you attain your own sacred union with the Divine, you create this same sacred union with your life partner, your Twin Soul.

Imagine this: Mother Mary is holding you and your Twin Soul in her arms. There was a moment when you and your beloved were one Soul, but at some point you were split into two Souls. There is a *divine purpose* behind this. Your Soul connection exists beyond time and space. You may or may not incarnate at the same time, but believe me you will know when you experience this type of relationship because it challenges and changes you to the core. Twin Souls lift one another vibrationally and energetically. Each was created to not only support one another spiritually and physically, but to share a *divine purpose* that can only occur through their union. It is the sacred sexual union between them that opens the gateway or portal to access and embody deeper divine gifts that can only be activated by each respective twin. In essence, your Twin Soul holds the key to your realizing and becoming the highest version of you that you were created to be. In this sacred sexual union, the chakras (energy centers) open and are activated by the vibration and frequency of the other, and an immersion of heart to heart, *divine mind* to *divine mind*, and Soul to Soul occurs—a oneness of one heart, one mind and one Soul—two souls coming together as one again. Through this sacred experience and *divine devotion* to your twin, you're able to experience the *Over-Soul*, "…within which every man's particular being is contained and made one with all other; that common heart… the eternal ONE," as defined by Ralph Waldo Emerson.

All of this is divinely orchestrated because this relationship transcends the boundaries of physical love, time, and space. This is a Soul Love that is anchored directly in God's love and creation. God's love anchors the eternal love in each twin, forming a trinity between God and the twins that allows something magical and beyond words to be expressed through this union. If you were to walk into a room where there was a Twin Soul couple, you would immediately feel the unconditional love that exists between them. Their eyes twinkle with this unconditional Soul Love that is impenetrable, unstoppable, and unmistakable.

When Twin Souls electrically connect through the heart, time and space does not hinder their communication. In fact, telepathic communication between their hearts, Souls, and spirits occurs on a frequent basis. Each twin experiences the other as if the other was residing in their own body, sometimes even mistaking their twin's feelings for their own. It's not unusual to hear the voice of your Twin Soul when they are not with you, or to have a remote, telepathic conversation with them. For those who are clairvoyant, it is not unusual to experience what their Twin Soul is experiencing as if looking through their eyes. This is akin to what some call *remote viewing*, when the deep Soul connection and oneness with the Twin Soul allows one to see through the eyes of the other, even from a remote distance. Some of the key qualities of a Twin-Soul relationship include:

- When you're together, the whole world around you disappears and life just feels perfect, whole, and beautiful. In the moments when you're together, you become so present in each other's oneness that the rest of the world around you becomes a blur.

- You see the divinity in one another and a deep adoration ensues that enraptures your hearts and Souls in a blanket of eternal love.

- Your twin calms and heals you with their love. They become an antidote to the noise in the outside world. You lift one another spiritually and vibrationally.

- There is a strong telepathic connection between you. You might find yourselves finishing each other's sentences all the time.

- You feel the presence of your twin within your physical being. It's like you carry them in your heart with you everywhere you go.

- There is a powerful and distinct Soul-Love vibration that exists between you. It chose you; you didn't choose it. Its power is so great that it influences your Soul's path in a very direct and unique way.

- Your union allows each of you to unlock deeper gifts within one another. You each hold a divine key that unlocks the highest expression of the other.

- When you engage in sexual union, it is sensual, sacred, and divine. As your bodies meld together in oneness, they form an etheric chalice of love. This chalice is an alchemical container that transforms your orgasmic ecstasy into streams of light that "potentize" your etheric (or *ka* body as referred to in

Egyptian teachings), allowing your *cosmic superpowers* (described in chapter 12) to be unleashed.

- You're able to see one another as the Souls you are, overlooking the human imperfections of the physical existence. Physical and human aspects such as gender, race, and ethnicity are of no concern. You have a deep knowing that you belong together no matter what your physical packages look like.

- When you're together in a room, those around you not only feel the eternal love you hold for one another, but they feel the *divine power* that flows through you in divine partnership.

- The Cosmic Love that exists between you gives you the courage to be the most authentic you that you can be. This Soul Love carries you to new heights and vibrations of unconditional love, giving you the courage to turn destiny into fate.

I'm sure you might be asking, "Can I develop this level of Cosmic Love with my current partner?" I believe you can if you and your partner have already attained some degree of spiritual affinity (sacred union) with the Divine and are now willing to grow that spiritual affinity together with one another. In the Bible (New International Version), in Matthew 1:26, it says, "But with God all things are possible." This is a universal truth for all who are willing to believe in it with complete faith. I have learned that anything you want to create and manifest in your life begins with your making a solid Soul commitment to that "thing" you desire, and that with unstoppable faith and belief you can attain it. As you surrender to God's will and the co-creative force you hold in the most eternal aspect of yourself called Soul, which is the universal force of *Sacred Openness* to universal love, *the unseen becomes seen in your life.* This is the miracle of creative manifestation that Source implanted within you before your human incarnation. This universal, eternal love is the unstoppable force that creates the possibility of what to some may seem impossible.

It is the practice of *divine devotion* that allows you to develop a deeper, richer, and more intimate relationship with the Divine, yourself, others, and ultimately with your Soul Partner or Twin Soul. It's through the embodiment of the *divine mystic* archetype that this is all made possible. So let's awaken the *divine mystic* within you. You can use the guided meditation that follows to help you do that.

You can record the meditation so you can close your eyes while you listen to it. For the audio version, visit **www.UnmaskingYourSoul.com/Meditations.** Sit comfortably where you won't be disturbed—with your feet flat on the floor and your hands on your knees with palms facing up. If you're an experienced meditator, use whatever position is most comfortable to you. When you're ready, please move to the meditation.

Guided Meditation: Awakening the Divine Mystic within You

Breathe slowly, inhaling through your nose and exhaling through your mouth. As you breathe, focus on your breath, and feel with every breath the relaxation of your mind, body, and spirit. Allow thoughts to pass through your mind as they may.

Drop into your heart center and see yourself surrounded by the most beautiful rainbow light. Each ray of light is swirling around you and entering your body through the top of your head in your crown. The rays continue to swirl around you, and as they do, you're transported to a sacred garden within your heart. As you look around you see you're surrounded by the most beautiful flowers. You experience the aroma within you as the fructose of the heavens. Each smell awakens your senses and elicits joy and love within you.

As you enjoy the flowers, a family of seven blue butterflies approaches you. They land on your head, arms, hands, and body. They gently flap their wings and say hello. In this moment, just feel the oneness between you and these beautiful creations of God. Each flapping of their wings takes you deeper into this state of oneness and awareness. Stay here for a moment and enjoy this peace and connection. {Pause.}

Off in the distance you see a woman dressed in a beautiful flowing gown approaching you. She is accompanied by three white panthers. As they get closer, you can see the woman has wings that are radiating in beautiful hues of violet and ocean blue. When the woman reaches you, she tells you she will be your guide today, and says her name is Mani. She lifts her hands and points her palms towards you. Blue light emanates from the center of her palms and enters the center of your palms. As the light enters your hands, you feel a deeper devotion and union with the Divine. It's like this woman, the panthers, and all that surrounds you are becoming part of you and you a part of them.

Mani asks you to lie on the ground, and so you do. The white panthers are now lying around you. Each panther has a sacred symbol on its forehead. The symbol is a downward facing triangle, and in its center is another symbol only recognizable to your Soul. You're told this symbol is the sacred vibration of your Soul. An ancient staff appears in your guide's right hand. It is covered with sacred symbols. She taps the staff on the ground and the symbols become three-dimensional images and radiate rainbow-colored light. You begin to levitate off the ground, and the rainbow light engulfs your entire body. The rainbow light becomes a transparent cocoon around your body. You can feel that something is happening to your being.

*Your heart is expanding and expanding all around you, and you're becoming one with the vibration of love that you are. Your physical body is melting away, and all that you see is the luminous being of light that you are. Allow this transformation to continue. {**Pause briefly.**}*

*As your transformation continues within the cocoon, you see images appearing on the inside of it, each symbol bringing you to a deeper understanding of your divine union with God—a higher power. You feel your human-self and your spiritual-self merging and becoming one source of connection with the Divine. The sacred sound of your Soul hums throughout the cocoon, enveloping you in a wake of vibration that seems very familiar to you. You've heard this sound before. As the hum continues, each cell in your being is awakened to a deeper level, accessing those ancient parts of you that have been asleep until now. There is a tingling all over your body and you can sense that this deeper part of you is emerging to the surface. {**Pause briefly.**}*

Mani touches the cocoon with her staff and the cocoon melts away. You're brought safely to the ground. As you look at yourself now, you're amazed. You have fully become your true essence—a powerful, loving, luminous being of light. You no longer feel separate from what once was. You're floating in the lightness and the vast sea of love that is unending and fluid. When you touch your finger to your hand, it's as if you're touching your guide. You feel what she feels. She feels what you feel. No words need to be spoken because each thought is immediately transmitted to all that surrounds you. Even the panthers have become part of your essence.

*The three white panthers come and sit in front of you. Mani taps her staff on the ground and the sacred symbols on the foreheads of the panthers become holographic three-dimensional images radiating light. Within this light emerges the sacred symbol of the vibration of your Soul. The light brings the symbol to you and it lands between your throat and heart. The symbol is etched and imprinted into your being. You're now able to access this vibration within you and it becomes part of your Soul's expression to the world. {**Take a moment to integrate the energy from this sacred encounter.**}*

As you become the divine mystic that you are, Mani and the panthers bid you farewell. They invite you to commune with them in this sacred space whenever you like. You thank the Divine and all the guides and masters who accompanied you on this journey today.

When you feel complete, you may slowly come back into your body and open your eyes.

Now that you've completed the guided meditation, take some time to do some journaling. Spend about ten to fifteen minutes in a quiet place where you won't be disturbed answering the questions below. You can put on some soothing music or light a candle or incense to support you as you write. Just write from your Heart and Soul and the rest will follow.

> ### *Journaling Exercise*
>
> 1. How did you feel when the seven butterflies landed on your body?
>
> 2. What did you experience and feel as you were placed in the cocoon? What sensations did you feel in your body?
>
> 3. What images did you see inside the cocoon? Did you recognize any of them? If so, in what way?
>
> 4. How did you experience the humming sound of your Soul's vibration?
>
> 5. Did you see the symbol of your Soul's vibration that was etched and imprinted in your being? If so, capture any insights about this experience.
>
> 6. Based on this experience, what actions, if any, do you need to take to deepen and enrich your practice of *divine devotion*? How will this help you more deeply embody the *divine mystic* within you?
>
> 7. How would you like the *divine mystic* within you to help you in your life? Write any intentions down and make sure to vocalize them to the Universe in your next prayer or meditation session.
>
> 8. Capture any other insights or messages that feel significant.

After journaling, continue working on the **Canvas of Your Soul.** (You can download the PDF at **www.UnmaskingYourSoul.com/Blueprint**.) Pick phrases, words, or symbols and put them on section 11 of the **Healing** part of your roadmap. Make this canvas your own piece of artwork that represents the journey we're taking together in this book. You can color, paint, or even cut images from magazines that depict the messages and insights you received in this chapter on *practicing divine devotion*. You don't need to be a professional artist to do this. Just let your Soul express through you as it wants to. This will become the vision board of your Soul's unmasking, a precious gift to you from your *divine mystic*.

Five Rituals to Awaken Your Divine Devotion Muscle

The rituals below are meant to help you awaken your *divine devotion* muscle. You can repeat any of the rituals that follow and the exercises and guided meditations earlier in the chapter as many times as you like. With each repetition you go deeper in accessing your *divine mystic.*

Before you begin, create your sacred space and take some deep breaths to relax your mind and body. Connect with your Soul as you enter this sacred space.

1. Use this ritual to practice *divine devotion* with God. As I mentioned earlier in the chapter, one of my favorite ways to practice *divine devotion* is through the act of sacred pilgrimage. I encourage you to make this a part of your life. You decide how often and in what form this works for you and your Soul. Here are some steps to consider as you embark on your own sacred pilgrimage.

   a. Close your eyes and take several deep breaths. Continue breathing in and out slowly until you feel you're centered and at peace.

   b. Ask the *divine mystic* within you where you should go for your sacred pilgrimage and how it's meant to serve you in your life at this moment. Once you receive the answers to these questions, begin to plan your sacred pilgrimage.

   c. Consider taking some of the following on your pilgrimage:
      - Comfortable and climate-appropriate clothing.
      - Healthy snacks and water to take on your walks.
      - If you like to create, you might want to take some art supplies to capture your experience and insights during the trip.
      - A journal, writing pad, iPad, or computer to jot down insights, messages, and ideas.
      - A digital recorder, or you can use a recorder app on your smartphone to record anything significant that arises as you take walks in nature, engage in walking meditations, or visit sacred sites.
      - Inspirational books or sacred texts that will nourish your Soul during the pilgrimage.
      - Relaxing music, guided meditations, and any recordings that will support you in creating a sacred and relaxing environment.
      - A backpack or a carry bag that holds your journal, water, and any items that will help you capture messages, insights, or answers the Divine shares with you during your walks and moments of contemplation.

d. Once you're at the location of your sacred pilgrimage, these are some questions that you might find useful in posing to your Higher-Self. Pick several questions that have deeper meaning for you, or create your own. Hold the questions in your heart to receive the answers whenever and however they may be given.

"What are the deepest desires of my Soul?"

"What are the roots of my existence? Who am I really, at my core?"

"Why do I exist? What is my *divine purpose*?"

"How am I meant to serve in the world?"

"What are my greatest fears? How are these fears affecting my life? What are some actions I can take to face these fears and move forward in my life?"

"What is still holding me back from being the most authentic me I can be?"

"Where am I still hiding the jewel that I am? Where am I still masking myself? Why is that? How can I heal these parts of me?"

e. Be sure to honor your time with silence and contemplation. This means that as you drink from God's well, as I like to call it, you honor this time of devotion between you and God. Make it the most sacred experience you've ever had. Use the quiet time to journal about whatever is flowing through your Heart and Soul. I find that taking a break from electronic devices is helpful. If you have to communicate with family members, set a specific schedule for honoring your time with the Divine and let loved ones know that they should not disturb you during these times unless it is an emergency.

f. Most important, hold no expectations about the outcome of this pilgrimage. It's important to be open and present to the experience. Enjoy every moment of this time between you and the Divine. When you do this, the rest unfolds in divine perfection.

2. Use this guided meditation to practice *divine devotion* with yourself:

Find a quiet place where you won't be disturbed for ten to fifteen minutes. Take several deep breaths, breathing in and out slowly until you feel calm and centered.

Drop your focus into your heart center. Allow yourself to be immersed with the eternal love that you are at your core. See beautiful pink light emerging from a sacred doorway in your heart and infusing all of you with its warmth and vibrancy of eternal love. Allow the rays of light to permeate every part of your being.

Four ascended masters walk through the sacred doorway in your heart, each *holding a divine quality that they will open within you. Jesus comes forth to impart the divine quality of humility. He places His hand on your heart, opening the God-seed of humility within you. {**Pause briefly.**} Saint Germain comes forth to impart the divine quality of patience. He places his hand on the lower extremities of your body, opening the God-seed of patience within you. {**Pause briefly.**} Kuan Yin comes forth and places her hand on your heart, opening the God-seed of gratitude within you. {**Pause briefly.**} Mother Mary comes forth and places her hand on your head, opening the God-seed of holiness within you. Continue to sit in quiet contemplation with your eyes closed, allowing these divine qualities to integrate within you.*

Now imagine you're sitting in a sacred garden. You feel God's presence all around you as you sit on the ground in quiet contemplation. You feel connected to all that surrounds you—the trees, the birds, the flowers, every creation is now part of you. From above, you feel God's breath blowing gently across your forehead. This breath surrounds your entire body and swirls of light enter your body. You're lifted off the ground and you become one with these rays of light. In this moment you have become one with God. No longer are you separate from the rays of light. You are this light. No longer can you feel your body. All you feel is oneness and a vastness of the Universe within your being. Stay here for a moment and bask in the richness of this oneness.

When you feel complete, you may slowly come back and open your eyes. You may want to journal about anything significant from this experience.

3. Use this ritual to practice *divine devotion* with others. In this ritual you will write a letter to someone you want to show your love and appreciation to. Pick someone whom you won't mind reading the letter to in person. It is the vocalization of the words to the Universe that brings with it a deeper blessing and energetic imprint in you and the person receiving this expression of your *divine devotion*.

   a. Find a quiet place where you won't be disturbed and can write from your Heart and Soul. Take several deep breaths and relax into a state of calmness and love.

   b. Choose to whom you will write this letter. It may be a family member, friend, colleague, or anyone you feel called to support in this moment. I find that when you're able to quiet the mind and listen, the Divine shows you exactly who is in need of your devotion in that moment.

   c. Write your letter to this person. It is a letter of appreciation, gratitude, and shared love, and a demonstration of how you see and honor their holiness and sacredness. Perhaps this person cannot yet see their own holiness and you are mirroring to them, through the act of writing this letter, a place of healing and transformation in their life. Only when you can behold yourself in the same way the Divine does can the cycle of completion and enactment of self-love occur.

d. Make a date to meet this person face to face. Don't tell them about the letter ahead of time. When the right moment arrives, and you will know when that is, take out the letter and read it to them. Let yourself be guided by your Soul in the best way to do this that serves you both in the highest good.

e. Afterward, take time alone and write about how this made you feel. Capture in your journal any insights, feelings, and messages that will help you continue to deepen your acts of *divine devotion*.

4. Use the following rituals to practice *divine devotion* in your most intimate love relationships—those with your beloved.

a. Letter-writing with your beloved

   i. Find a quiet spot where you and your beloved can sit. Take several deep breaths together until you both feel calm and centered in a place of love.

   ii. Begin writing letters of love to one another. The intention of these letters is to show one another in words the sacredness and love you hold for one another. Write about distinct moments that you've shared that have made you feel special and loved by one another. Write anything that brings forth joy, gratitude, appreciation, love, and holiness. This is not a time to write about times of resentment, anger, or pain. Those should be resolved separately. This ritual is for nourishing and honoring the love that's already there and allowing it to deepen even further.

   iii. Exchange your letters with one another. Take turns reading to one another the letters you've written. Listen with open hearts and drink in the nourishment to your Souls. When complete, have an open discussion with your beloved about how you each felt when the words were spoken. You may journal individually or together about anything of significance that occurred between you as the words of love were spoken.

   iv. You might want to repeat this ritual with your beloved at least once every three to six months. I encourage you to keep the letters you've written and place them on a sacred altar as explained in the next ritual.

b. Create a sacred love altar for you and your beloved. I suggest you do this ritual together so that the energies of both of you become imprinted in this sacred shrine to your love.

i. Find a place in your home where you can set up a sacred love altar for you and your beloved. A good spot might be in your bedroom. Find a nice corner in the room where you can place a small table or even a corner shelf can work. This sacred altar is meant only for your collective energies, so a private space in your home is ideal.

ii. Begin by clearing the space. You can do this through prayer, invocation, or using sage or a clearing spray to cleanse the energy in this space.

iii. Gather sacred objects of love that reflect your sacred moments together and the love you share. Each of you should select one or more sacred objects to place on the altar. I suggest that one of those objects be the love letters you created for one another in the previous ritual. You can put those in a special little box or just plainly on the altar. You don't have to create this all in one sitting. The idea is that over time you bring objects to the altar that nourish and support the growth of your love for each other. You will want to add these one by one as they appear in your life.

iv. Revisit your sacred love altar frequently, and commune and contemplate with its energy, nurturing its development together. You can use the space around the altar to pray and meditate together on your love relationship, as well as to sit and practice *divine devotion* with one another through your love-letter-writing in the previous ritual.

5. Meditate with my painting **Cosmic Union**, shown at the end of the chapter, to help you reconnect with your *divine mystic,* the one who helps you access your *divine devotion.* Each of my paintings was divinely channeled and holds messages and energetic impressions of the Soul that bring healing to the bearer. This particular painting holds vibrations of healing for those needing to remember their expression of *divine devotion.*

a. Close your eyes and take a breath... inhaling slowly through your nose and exhaling slowly through your mouth... and with each breath you take relax your mind, body, and spirit. Continue focusing on your breath... and with each breath allow your thoughts to pass freely... thought after thought... breath after breath... relaxing more and more deeply. Continue taking several more deep breaths. {**Repeat for one or two minutes.**}

b. Briefly open your eyes and observe the painting. Allow yourself to be taken on a journey into the painting. Look at the images and symbols, and allow your gaze to go to one focal point in the painting. Soften your gaze as you focus on this point of interest. Breathe in its energy, seeing the symbols, images, and colors in your mind's eye. Continue breathing in the energy... breath after breath, allowing you to feel and absorb the healing energy from this focal point.

c.   With your next breath, listen to the voice of your Soul. What is it communicating? What messages do you hear or feel within you as you breathe in the energy of the painting? Pay attention to where the energy is going in your body. This gives you an indication of where in your body you may need to release old energy, traumas, or wounds. Continue breathing and just go into the stillness while you connect deeper within. Allow the healing energies of the painting to penetrate your mind, body, and spirit. {**Do this for two to five minutes.**} If you feel guided, you may continue repeating this step, changing to a different focal point in the painting each time. Again, allow yourself to breathe the images, symbols, colors, and healing energies into your being.

d.   Don't forget to journal about anything of significance that comes up during this experience.

Eileen Anümani Santos, *Cosmic Union*, c. 2007

Cosmic Union is about the practice of *divine devotion*, which ultimately culminates in a deep, intimate, cosmic union between you and Source and all those around you, including those in your most intimate love relationships. It is through the embodiment of your *divine mystic* that this is made possible. As you unmask your hidden jewel and claim your place in the world, you open a deeper channel of direct communication with your Higher-Self—the Soul of You. This painting holds the energy of the cosmic union through which the oneness between heart, *divine mind*, and Soul is made possible.

Allow *DIVINE DEVOTION* to guide you in your Soul quest for *COSMIC UNION*!

The Birth of the Christ within You

by Eileen Anümani Santos

I come to you with words of peace and love.

You are so loved—an eternal love that is beyond words and
your physical body.

It can only be experienced within the chambers of your Soul.

What you seek is already within YOU. Dig into the well and it will become clear.

You are God's emissary—He speaks through you, yet you have doubted this gift
for too long.

Honor your divinity. It is only through this sacred kinship that what you seek
will divulge itself.

Honor your sacredness, your heart, your creation, and your
source of light.

Ámate, love yourself, as God loves you, for the gift of your unmasking comes
from complete immersion in this eternal love.

The ocean of love that swirls within your heart carries a vibration that creates
the union between the spiritual and Earthly planes.

It is from this place that the Christ within you is born.

When you live your life from this place, you create Heaven on Earth
within and without.

Honor it, become it, and live it, for the world awaits your arrival.

CHAPTER 12

Soul Chamber XII:
Embodying the Divine Christ Consciousness

When you began this journey you may have wondered, "Will I ever get there?" And yet here you are. Congratulations! You made it to the last Soul chamber. In this chamber you bring it all together; all that you've unmasked, unearthed, transmuted, and healed comes together to help you embody the highest version of you. It is the *Christ consciousness—la conciencia de Cristo* in Spanish—that has always lived within you and is now ready to be awakened.

For some of you the word *Christ* brings up resistance or unpleasant religious experiences. If that's the case, stop for a moment and take a breath. Set an intention to be open to receiving your *divine truths*, whatever they may be. Invoke the guidance of your Heart and Soul so you can discover a deeper understanding of what *Christ consciousness* means for you. When you feel ready, read on.

Who are you? Are you Heaven? Are you Earth? Is it possible that you hold the power to open the gates of Heaven and Earth within you? Yes, absolutely! Within you exists the portal that unites Heaven and Earth. This portal is found in the center of your heart at the point where the higher and lower heart meet. When you're ready to embody the *Christ consciousness*, this portal opens, making it possible to experience the union of Heaven and Earth within you.

Since you've made it this far on the journey, you've been listening to the yearning of your Soul to more fully embody the real you—that beautiful, loving, divine being that you truly are. The unmasking of this chamber and the embodiment of the Soul virtue of the *divine Christ* is what makes this all possible. All those parts of you that were pretending to be something else, like fear, anger, and pain, were there for a reason. They were there to show you where you were resisting love and needed to do your inner work. But now you're ready to allow your true essence—eternal love—to be your guiding force. It's time to awaken to all that you are.

With the words *Christ consciousness* I'm referring to the vibration or frequency of eternal love and oneness that unites the trinity of Divine Heart, Divine Mind, and Divine Soul. In essence, this consciousness or intelligent life force brings the mental, emotional, physical, and spiritual bodies together in perfect alignment, wherein your upper and lower chakras become fully integrated into this vibration of oneness. Another way of saying this is the transformation of your God-seed into God-realized. This is you becoming the essence of God that lives within you, demonstrated through purification of heart, mind, and Soul. The words *I AM* are a holy expression of the God within you. The *Christ consciousness* is the realization of you as the "I" in the "I AM."

In the Bible (New International Version), in Ephesians 3:20, it says, "Now to Him who is able to do immeasurably more than all we ask or imagine, according to His power that is at work within us." I have come to understand that these words refer to the awakening of your cosmic superpowers. You hold the power to heal and transform your life and the lives of others in big and significant ways. And because you've made it this far, you've probably already experienced some of these superpowers in yourself.

Maybe you always know when your phone is going to ring and who's calling even before you pick it up. If that's the case, you're probably clairvoyant. If you can hear the thoughts of others or just know what they're thinking, you're also telepathic. Perhaps you feel your hands light up when you're in a room with someone who needs healing, which could mean you're a natural healer. Those are your inherent, healing, cosmic superpowers. There are many forms of cosmic superpowers, and despite the fact that they may seem out of the "norm" in the society you grew up in, they are more common than you think. Unfortunately society tends to put negative labels on things it doesn't understand, which causes many to hide or suppress their divine gifts and cosmic superpowers.

During the origins of time, telepathic communication and the speaking of ancient Soul languages to invoke the powers of the Universe were common to society. Inferences to these superpowers appear in the Bible, such as Moses parting the Red Sea and Jesus walking on water on the Sea of Galilee. In *Autobiography of a Yogi*, by Paramahansa Yogananda, there are accounts of Hindu yogis levitating off the ground during meditation. All this is possible and more.

As we took human form, we forgot all that we could do and be. Each of our Souls chose to return to human form in this life to learn at our Earth school, including awakening to the truth of who we really are. It is only together that we can change the world and shift the consciousness of this planet. You are one of those who have chosen and were chosen to be here to do just that, in only the way that you can. You hold a *secret Soul sauce* that belongs only to you. This secret sauce is held in your God-seed and spiritual DNA, and is exactly what gives life to the superpowers of the *Christ consciousness* that are the topic of this chapter.

In her book *Voice of the Master*, Eva Bell Werber reminded us that as we "come into the full complete consciousness that there is within...and knowingly make contact with that power, it shall be as the releasing of a mighty dam." That releasing she refers to is the awakening and embodiment of the *Christ consciousness* that is part of your God-seed and has waited for this exact moment in your life for you to realize the fullness of its wisdom and freedom.

So what are the divine qualities of the *Christ consciousness*? They include all the Soul virtues we've already discussed: *divine love, divine power, divine worthiness, divine truth, divine light, divine purpose, divine voice, divine wisdom, divine mind, divine passion*, and *divine devotion*. In this chapter we add *divine Christ* as the last Soul virtue. Underneath each of these Soul virtues are Soul qualities that you've heard mentioned throughout our journey together. They include:

1. Practicing compassion and forgiveness to liberate your Soul.

2. Loving yourself enough to set healthy boundaries with others—a dismantling of the victim so you can embody the Soul of your *spiritual warrior.*

3. Accepting yourself and others with non-judgment and Soul Love.

4. Embracing your Soul's truth and genius.

5. Embracing eternal love as the bringer of light in your life.

6. Surrendering to the calling of your Soul and your Soul's purpose.

7. Speaking your truth and accessing the voice of your Soul.

8. Unlocking the ancient wisdom of your Soul.

9. Letting go of attachments and connecting with the loving, sacred thoughts of your Soul.

10. Igniting the sacred flame of desire that transforms your thoughts into your Soul's reality.

11. Practicing humility, patience, gratitude, and holiness to manifest the cosmic union of your human-self and your spiritual-self.

12. Becoming pure of heart—a Christ-blessed heart transforming your God-seed into God-realized.

In the center of your heart there exists a point where your higher and lower heart meet. This is the location of **Soul Chamber XII—Divine Christ Consciousness,** the twelfth (and last) of the Soul virtues that will be unmasked as you continue on your journey of wholeness. The mask associated with the twelfth chamber is the **Mask of Temptation.** When you engage in this level of alignment of Divine Heart, Divine Mind, and Divine Soul, your ego-mind attempts to keep you wed to old ways and patterns. Just as you take the leap forward, things you may have tried to brush under the rug surface to engage you in a deeper Soul quest, one in which you're tested to see how truly committed you are to unmasking your Soul and expressing the highest version of you that you can be. This is where all that you have learned on the journey comes together to help you release the old you and embody your Soul more deeply. The archetype of this Soul chamber is the *divine Christ,* the one who helps you become **pure of heart, pure of mind, and pure of Soul**. Returning to this level of purity is the key that unlocks the portal and convergence point between your higher and lower heart, enabling the embodiment

Divine Christ Consciousness Symbol

of the *divine Christ consciousness* (see sacred symbol here).

In one of my meditations I asked God to grace me with purity of heart. This is how the conversation went:

> **Me:** Father, the glory of Your seed bears fruit in me. I see the harvest of the fruit You planted in my creation. It sprouts, blossoms, and is ready for emergence. I conceive of Your creation within me. You planted something within me that now bears fruit. I was not ready until this moment. I seek refuge in Your love, in the pureness that You are. I seek to be that pureness, too. In Your image I stand before You to serve You as You designed me to serve You. I stand before You asking for purity of heart. I seek the purity of heart that only You can betroth upon me. I seek Your grace and glory. Let me be the highest version of me that I can be. Let me be the embodiment of my Soul. Let me be the REAL ME, the ME I have always been in the source of Your heart, Your *divine mind,* and Your being. I am READY now to emerge as the expression of YOU, My Dearest God, to embody the God-vibration You planted within me long ago. Only from this place can I perform my purpose-work in its truest form and intention. I fully embody the divine expression that I AM.
>
> **God's response:** You have awakened now clearly to my voice and my being. You're now able to go beneath the noise that sometimes surrounds you as you connect with the seed of innocence I planted in you upon creation.

The virgin light of *divine love* has been unmasked and unveiled. As you surrender to the purest form of light within you, the noise dismantles and clears the way forward for our togetherness and oneness in all you do. In this oneness there is no static. The path is clear for you to move forward with faith, love, peace, strength, and the knowing that you have opened the passageway for destiny to unfold. Your choices created the doorway through which fate now manifests into destiny. The Universe works under my command to make it so. Revel in me, my love, and my desire for you to have all that you need and more. The greatest gift I can give you in this moment is the eternal grace of my love—a love that melts all in its path and provides the gateway to the REAL YOU that you have been seeking all your life. As I pour my love over you in this moment, you awaken to the purity of heart that has always lived within you. You are now ready to embody a deeper part of your Soul.

As God told me He was pouring His love over me, that's exactly what I experienced. It felt like a fountain of liquid love coming down from the heavens and immersing every part of my being. This was a defining moment for me, one in which I knew that I was beginning to awaken to a deeper part of my Soul. It all begins in the heart (Divine Heart) as you embrace the pure intention of love. It then continues in your mind (Divine Mind) as you engage in pure thoughts inspired by the oneness that you share with all that is. It culminates with the purity of your Soul; and the pureness of the wisdom of your all-knowing, all-loving, and all-being Soul (Divine Soul) forms a trinity of threads that awakens the *Christ consciousness* that lives within you. Once the trinity is formed, Cosmic Love brings all the threads together to open the portal to your Christed-Self.

The Power of Your Divine Heart

Life began as a seed of creation, a spark of fire that engendered the world you live in. Because you're reading these words, your Soul is stirring with that same spark, ready to be anointed by the sacred fire that is the *Christ consciousness*. In this sacred fire you bathe in God's will, grace, and glory. In the pain you've experienced there's a touch of God that molded you to scale mountains with courage, focus, and love. Above all, you're blanketed in His grace of humility. Before the resurrection comes the thorn, to remind you of the importance of faith, trust, and surrender to a universal plan that holds your fate. With each

> *Life began as a seed of creation, a spark of fire that engendered the world you live in.*

thorn that you overcome, you learn to move forward in your life despite the outward circumstances.

Circumstances are never perfect, yet God needs you now. He needs you to step forward in your purpose-work despite what your life looks like. It is only in the stepping forward that you remove the thorn, and with each step forward comes the blessing and resurrection. Amid the thorns there is something you cannot see—something is there. It's waiting for you to believe in the unseen—to know that all circumstances are temporary and that even that thorn is a gift from God. For if He had given you all the glory before you were ready to receive it from a place of love and humility, your ego's pride would've dismantled the miracle as it arrived at your doorstep.

No one gets to skip their lessons. I had to be shaken to the core and be thrown into financial scarcity to learn one of the biggest lessons of my life. I had to learn what it really means to surrender, trust, and believe in the unseen. How can you trust when the life around you is falling apart? How can you trust when you have lost your job and have bills to pay? How can you trust when you find out your spouse is cheating on you and your heart is broken into a million pieces? How can you trust when someone you love dearly is terminally ill?

These are the thorns I speak of. They appear in your life unexpectedly and shatter you to the core. You cry and maybe even become angry at God. But know this: you were only being prepared for something bigger in your life. These thorns can be transmuted as you walk with faith and meet these places of fear with love. Love has the power to bring miracles in a holy instant. Love has the power to forge a new doorway of being. Love has the power to transform the unseen into a life you never imagined would be possible. The thorns that appeared before you were God's deliverance of His love to you. When God is preparing you to step into your destiny, you must be pure of heart, mind, and Soul. Without that purity you won't be able to serve as it was intended. This means practicing and living the qualities of the *divine Christ*.

For a long time I resisted my calling. I lived in two worlds: the corporate world in which I was trained to do, get, control, doubt, and live in fear; and my spiritual world in which I surrendered to moments of joy, love, passion, and peace. There was a part of me that believed I could only make a "good" living if I stayed in the corporate world. Ambition got in the way of surrendering to my Soul's purpose. And, as you already know, there was a part of me that lived in fear of showing the real me. I've come to understand that part of me even more deeply now. That part of me was afraid I would lose the people I loved if I showed the real me. If they could see all I could do as a spiritual being, they might think I was crazy and I would lose them forever. I was unwilling to accept all those parts of me.

Through trials and tribulations, and many painful experiences, I engaged my spiritual muscle. With each battle, pain, and mountain I scaled, a new understanding of how powerful we really are came to me. I now understand what Marianne Williamson meant when she said, "It is our light not our darkness that most frightens us." Throughout my journey I was presented with many thorns, ranging from abuse and a near-death experience to financial challenges. With each one I shed another layer that was holding me back from where I needed to be to fully embody the real me. Each time I shed another layer that had been catalyzed by some event in my life, I became more of me. And more gifts were subsequently born through me.

There was a defining moment just before I was set to write this chapter that propelled me to a deeper place of understanding and transformation. Those who were witnessing my journey said I had been initiated in God's sacred fire so I could finally step through the doorway to where the human-self and the spiritual-self are made one with God. For me this signified the doorway to the *divine Christ*. This is what happened:

It was a normal day for me… or so I thought. I entered into my morning meditation as I did every day. But this day it would all be different. As I meditated, I felt I was entering a meditative state I had never reached before. In this plane of consciousness there was no form. I just saw myself as the Universe and the Universe was me. I felt such bliss and oneness. I was floating on air, feeling such peace and love inside of me. I stayed in that space for at least an hour. It was so beautiful that I didn't want it to end.

But alas, I had an appointment with my acupuncturist and had to part with this blissful experience. When I arrived at the office of my acupuncturist she immediately noticed that something was different about me and commented on how powerfully my light was shining. I was still floating from my experience that morning. When she examined me, she decided that the best way she could help me was to ground the energy I had just experienced. When she placed the needles in my body, all I felt was this congruency with what had happened to me earlier, and I lay there loving every moment of the peace I felt within.

At home several hours later, something happened that shook me to the core. My body began to shiver and shudder. I could feel an overwhelming fear growing inside me, overtaking every part of me. I couldn't believe this was happening. *What the f*ck?*, I thought. *I was just in such a blissful place, this can't be happening.* My body went into a fight-or-flight mode as if it was in danger, and in moments I was in a state of complete panic. I had never had a panic attack before, but this sure felt like one. My ego ranted very negative thoughts: "You're not ready to work at this level. Who do you think you are? This is too hard. You need to give up now. It's not worth living like this."

"Wow" is all I can say! In that moment I knew exactly what it felt like to be over-come with fear. I was standing in a duality that I imagine you have experienced as well; one part of me loving and wanting to be in peace, and the other part of me running away from that joy. I knew in that moment I needed help, so I went back into medita-tion and asked for assistance from my guides. I needed enough energy to recenter, even if momentarily, as I sought help from others. My guides told me to drop every-thing I was doing and work on being present to what was happening inside me. So for the next seven days, I did just that.

The first thing I was guided to do was to place a call to my healer, Bette, and ask for an emergency appointment. Thankfully she was able to see me the next day. By that time I had also reached out to friends and family asking for prayers and healing light. I have first-hand experience with the power of prayer. In chapter 1, if you recall, I told the story of my near-death experience, and I know without a doubt that it was the prayers of family and friends that lifted me through that dark night of the Soul.

When I arrived at my healer's home, I gave her the lowdown about all that had hap-pened. She was not surprised to hear about what I had experienced. She pointed out that we had been working on releasing my deepest core trauma for the last two years, and now had reached the last bit which is sometimes the most difficult to release. She told me that my body had gone into survival mode; it felt unsafe to experience all that bliss and joy. Remember, my core trauma was around mistrust of the Divine and my own divinity. As soon as this energy completely landed in my body, my body went into protection mode and began to fight for survival.

Despite how scary this was for me, I can say now what a blessing it was at the same time. You cannot heal what is hidden and not seen. As this chaos came to the surface, I knew it was ripe to be released. As we released the trauma and brought in more of my light during that healing, what opened within me was a reservoir of peace that had always lived inside me but now could more comfortably take its place in my everyday life. I learned so much from this experience. I knew this was what it must feel like when someone becomes overwhelmed by fear and chooses to do harm to themselves or oth-ers because the fear overtakes them. I was aware enough to not allow that to occur, but I know it happened so that I could understand what it felt like to walk the threshold of these two worlds—the duality of love and fear that can appear at a moment's notice—and to have the will to choose that which serves you and does not harm you.

I left the healing knowing that my work and "doing" for the next several days was my inner work. Without that I would never recover enough to serve in the way God was calling me to serve. So as guided, I religiously worked on myself daily. I was told that for fourteen days straight I would be communing directly with Jesus and Mary Magdalene as they prepared me to receive my anointing (an initiation).

Each day I went into meditation, and all they would say was "Just listen and be." We would hold hands in a sacred circle and I would sit there with them, just "being" in their presence. Each evening I felt like I was on fire. The burning that was happening within my body was deep and long-lasting. Many nights I had to strip naked and feel the coldness of the sheets to be able to get through the night. Keep in mind that I'm typically cold and looking for warmth, so this was completely unusual for me. I knew the Divine was working to heal me through this sacred fire. I was being purified so I could receive what was coming next. This continued for fourteen days as they said it would.

On the fourteenth day I started to feel different. I knew something was trying to be born through me. One day shortly afterward, the Divine told me to go to my basement and turn on my amp and microphone. I knew that meant that something was going to be spoken through me. When I did this, words began to come through my mouth. My human ears did not understand what I was saying, but my Soul was in delight, for I was speaking an ancient Soul language. I was told that this was one of my gifts and was to be used to heal those I serve. This is what I meant when I said that as your vibration matches the God-seed of the cosmic superpowers implanted within you, that particular seed is born into the physical, as it happened for me.

Afterward, I was in a bit of shock. There was a part of me thinking, *Okay, what are people going to think about me when they hear this language? What am I going to tell my family?* But I continued to have faith and surrender. With each day of meditation that followed, I continued to go deeper and deeper. I could feel I was being prepared for a deeper embodiment of my Soul, of the *Christ consciousness*. I was enormously grateful for this gift and all that I was learning, unraveling, and understanding. There was this deeper mystery of the Universe unraveling before my eyes. I started to understand how powerful we really are if only we allow ourselves to just "be." I was witnessing the power of belief in the unseen and how it catalyzes an opening that brings forth our ability to consciously co-create magic and miracles in our lives.

As all this was happening, I felt the power within me awakening like never before—an awakening to the power of my ancient Soul, Anümani. Each time I said my spiritual name loudly, I felt surges of power running through my body. I began to understand how powerful our words really are. I was reminded that this is the power Jesus used to turn water into wine. Our words have more power than our human minds can understand. I began to speak words with much more conviction. I began to understand that when you enlist this *divine power* and blanket it in God's love, which lives within you, these words become like magnets invoking that which you seek immediately into your life. As I opened to realign my vibration to the power of my divine expression, I powerfully recited, "I receive the bounty of the loving Universe." This became my daily mantra. The words themselves launched me through a new doorway of understanding and being in the world.

As I continued my meditations, I knew I was closer now to that moment of anointment when the sacred union of Divine Heart, Divine Mind, and Divine Soul unify in oneness with the Universe. This is when the God-seed becomes the God-realized, and the *Christ consciousness* awakens within. As this initiation process continued, my meditations became deeper and deeper. I began to see my energetic body lying horizontally in a formless plane of consciousness, and it was as if God was pouring liquid love into the twelve Soul chambers I've spoken about in each of the chapters of this book. Each one represents a Soul virtue of the *Christ consciousness* and a necessary step in the evolution of your human-self into the Christed-Self.

Lo and behold, about a week after I began to speak this ancient Soul language, another gift was born through me. Once again I was told to go to my basement, but this time I was asked specifically to record on my phone what was to come through. My first reaction was "Oh no, what now?" As instructed, I grabbed my phone and went down to the basement. I turned on the microphone and amp and started recording. I sat there with my eyes closed, just allowing the download to come through, and all of a sudden I felt this surge of energy enter my crown and come down into my throat. A voice was speaking, but it was not mine. The accent completely threw me off.

When I asked my spirit guides what was going on, I was told that the collective consciousness of 227 galactic Souls—beings from other star systems—were speaking through me. They were from the star Sirius, and called themselves Ishtar. They explained that their mission was to help humanity and this Earthly plane ascend to a state of peace and love again. They said I was chosen to bring forth these messages of peace and love to humanity through my healing ministry.

After this experience I found it hard to believe it had really happened. The Divine had been quite explicit that I must record what was to come through, and that was because it knew I would doubt it. But when I listened to the recording I knew it was real. With each day that passed I knew without a doubt this was a gift from the Universe and an important part of my service to humanity.

I learned to meet fear with love, lack with unlimited abundance, and confusion with the certainty that soon the loving bounty of the Universe would be at my doorstep. Any lack that you experience in life is temporary. When you learn this lesson, meet that place of pain or lack with love, and engage the power of the Universe, the Universe creates a new trajectory of manifestation and goodness in your life.

And what is the moral of this story, Dear One? As Yoda from *Star Wars* would say, "You must unlearn what you have learned." I had to unlearn all that wasn't aligned with my Soul's purpose and the vibration of love that is at the core of me, you, and every human being. I had to unlearn fear, doing, getting, doubting, controlling—all the behaviors and patterns that become ingrained in our psyches and drive us into an automation of our human personalities. I had to stop being a robot running on an automated, ego-coded basis, and instead allow my divinity to sprout through my humanity as the guiding force in my life. This is when you awaken to the Soul of You and allow it to be your source of inspiration and action in your daily life.

Although the terrain was a bit rough, it was succulent at the same time. Why is this important? Because the more you're present in your daily life to enjoy each step and every experience, the more often wonderful things happen. You open to the curiosity, wonderment, and creative force that lives within you. This force is called Soul Love. You are an imprint of God himself. You are God in miniature. That's what Jesus meant when He said, "You shall do as I do and more." This wonderment of life opens so you can perceive what exists around you with the eyes of reverence and sacredness. The more you embody your divinity and your Christed-Self, the more you see life through the eyes of your God-self, the part of you that is always connected to Source. Can you imagine a life in which everything you experience is through the eyes of God? Can you imagine a life in which you can connect directly with the Souls of those you encounter?

As you embody the *divine Christ consciousness*, you open more deeply to this quality of wonderment. It also brings with it the ability to create in ways that perhaps were unfamiliar or inaccessible to you previously. Jesus had a wonder for life. He used this wonder to learn to trust His *divine power* and create a deeper relationship with God, one that took Him to full surrender and sacred service, even at the cost of His human life. By then He understood the immortality of His divinity and His Soul. He understood that beyond the veil of the Earthly plane where physical death takes place, there is an eternal existence that escapes the limitations of the human psyche.

The Universe, which also exists within you in miniature form, has magical powers. When you learn to consciously co-create with it, you see evidence of its existence appear readily in your life. You experience the magic that happens when your Divine Heart, Divine Mind, and Divine Soul come together in unity to consciously co-create with the power of this force that lives eternally within a tiny yet vast space in your heart center. In this space the spiritual and Earthly worlds collide (as above, so below). This is where your higher and lower heart meet. In this convergence, the embodiment of the *Christ consciousness* is made possible.

Christ consciousness is an energetic life force that brings with it the qualities of God—a higher power.

Christ consciousness is an energetic life force that brings with it the qualities of God—a higher power. This consciousness is all-knowing, all-being, all-loving—an omnipresent, energetic force that is formless but connected to all that is. You hold the God-seed for that consciousness within you. And because you're at this stage of unmasking your Soul, something inside you is ready to awaken at this deeper level. To open the gateway to this consciousness, you must have traversed and embodied each Soul chamber prior to this one. This doesn't mean your journey is over after this and that you've achieved ultimate enlightenment. The more you become YOU—a luminous being of light—the more light you hold and the more enlightened you become. I don't believe it's a "one and done" kind of deal. Just like everything else in life, there are layers and degrees of luminosity and vibrational shifts that occur as you shed the lower-vibration-based thoughts, traumas, and pain you're holding in your human energy field. While you're in human form, there is always internal work to be done.

Each mask you shed dismantles a layer of ego-based thinking and replaces it with more light and more love. Each mask you shed dismantles a layer of ego-based thinking and replaces it with more light and more love. The more you shed, the more of the real you shines through and the more love and light you hold within your vessel. Love is the key to all that you seek. It is the key to embodying and awakening the *Christ consciousness* seeds that you hold.

As I described before, God encoded each and every one of us with a universal intelligence. When your vibration shifts to the vibration of the *Christ consciousness*, the God-seed of that consciousness is awakened. The seeds then sprout and grow inside you until you're ready to walk through the portal between the spiritual and Earthly planes. When you walk through this portal you become initiated to a higher vibration of love and of light. There are many levels, and at each portal you can imagine a translucent veil separating them. As you hit the vibration of love for that level, you're able to pierce the veil there, which then triggers the portal to give you access to the higher vibration of your multidimensional being. When you walk through the portal that appears before you, you shed another layer of yourself, which creates the space for your Divine-Self to ascend to a higher vibration of love. With each initiation you ascend to higher vibrations and planes of consciousness.

Again, this is only possible if you've opened your heart to a deeper level of love that encompasses all the qualities that Jesus demonstrated on His human journey, such as surrender, trust, belief, compassion, forgiveness, understanding, acceptance, reverence, humility, and *divine love*. I use Jesus as an example, but there are many other ascended masters who hold these qualities as seen across a multitude of spiritual beliefs and religions. Buddha, Saint Germain, Mother Mary, Mary Magdalene, Padre Pio, Confucius, and Babaji are some examples, just to name a few. Each of these divine beings demonstrated mastery of their light and cosmic superpowers. Through cycles of rebirth, entailing much inner work, they ascended to higher initiatory levels (there are at least seven levels of initiation), allowing them to leave the human rebirth cycle and become pure beings of love and light.

Underlying the transcendence of the ascended masters is your ability to hold all of these same qualities for yourself. Self-love allows you to love all of you fully, which also brings you to that same level of love with God. It is through this process of self-love mastery that you unmask the hidden doorway that connects you directly to Source. From there the illusion of separation transmutes into oneness. From this vantage point you're able to live on this Earthly plane yet not be of it. You're able to live a Soul-conscious life that is anchored in love, which I call Soul Love, guiding you to serve on this Earthly plane with a new level of awareness of the real you—a formless being of light who is connected to all that is. As you can see, we began this book with *divine love* and we are ending up at the heart center once again. All along, this transformational journey of *Truth, Light, and Healing* has really been about unmasking the many faces of fear that have held you back from being the real you—an eternal force of love. Purity of heart is a key ingredient in embodying the *divine Christ consciousness*.

The Power of Your Divine Mind

Every thought has an energetic imprint it disburses outward to the Universe. Imagine what happens when your thoughts are full of fear and lower vibrations: they not only contribute that same energy to your life experiences, but they affect the universal imprint of the *divine mind* that connects us all.

> *Every thought you put out into the world affects everyone else. Every action you take affects everyone else.*

Every thought you put out into the world affects everyone else. Every action you take affects everyone else. Everything you do has a cause-and-effect reaction. This is how powerful you really are. Those who remain "asleep" to their own divinity and power remain shackled to a world of pain and disillusion created by the ego-mind that thrives by keeping them in fear. From this moment forward I want you to really take this in and become conscious of what you think, say, and do. God created you with super intelligence and cosmic powers that are available to you so you can contribute to the shift in consciousness that is occurring as we speak. This is a time of great awakening, shifting, and ascension for our Earthly plane. You've been chosen to be of service to the love that you really are and bring this forth to your human brethren so we can change the world together. Let us create a world that embodies the *Christ consciousness* and nurtures the younger generation from a place of love instead of hatred and judgment. It's time for you and all of humanity to be free to be who you really were created to be. Let us be that unstoppable force of LOVE together!

You become what you believe. That belief begins with your thoughts. As I mentioned before, you can use the power of your mind to manifest what you desire in your life. Your thoughts are so powerful that you can use them to command your body to heal, transform, and be love. There are passages in many sacred texts demonstrating the power I speak of, which is made possible through the divine expression of love that lives within you. "Let there be light," God said in Genesis 1:3 (New International Version), and then there was light. As God willed it, there it was—the light. You have this same power living within you. As you open to the purity of your mind, the mind that is immersed in the pureness of your heart, you, too, can command this level of change in your life.

Let's practice doing this right now. Close your eyes and relax. Take several deep breaths and allow yourself to drop right into your heart. See yourself standing in your heart center as rays of emerald-green and pink light enter your crown and surround your heart. Each swirl connects you with the eternal love that you are. When you feel ready, repeat the following words: "I now command the unity of my Divine Heart, Divine Mind, and Divine Soul to occur with my next breath." Take a breath and feel these words in your heart center. Now say, "All that stands in the way of this unity is now cleared and transmuted into the purest fibers of eternal love that flow within me."

How did that feel for you? If you felt the power in those words, you're beginning to awaken to the *Christ consciousness* that lives within you. As you immerse your thoughts in absolute belief in your divinity and cosmic superpowers, you become what you believe.

It was a shift in belief that created the space for me to be ready to receive the powerful initiation that you read about earlier in this chapter. Embodying the *divine Christ consciousness* requires the power of a pure mind. Without belief that you're divinely powerful and deserve to hold these powers within you, the initiation into the Christed-Self cannot occur. It is only through the power of belief that the unseen is made seen. When you nourish your God-seeds and Soul's desires with belief, you imprint an energy of manifestation. Belief becomes the cocoon that nourishes those seeds to grow and prepares them for harvest at exactly the right time.

This reminds me of the story I told you earlier in the book about the character Neo in the movie *The Matrix*. Even though everyone told him he was "The One" who had been chosen to save his world, it wasn't until he believed it for himself that his superpowers came online. The same holds true for you. It is the power of your thoughts and your mind that create the doorway for you to experience your *divine truths*. It is in these truths that you experience your divine gifts and cosmic superpowers more deeply. Belief is the magic that makes it possible for you to witness and experience your gifts in this way. This is exactly what I experienced as I was being prepared for my own Christed-initiation. Let me tell you how this transpired for me:

I was yet again at a retreat with my mentor, Christine Kloser. This time I was invited to support her and a new group of forthcoming authors she was coaching. We spent several days having each participant pick a rock from a basket and use the word on the rock to spur their introduction to the group. The Universe always conspires to have you pick the "right" rock, the one that will challenge you to the core, help you heal, or allow you to receive an insight that catalyzes a new beginning in your life. Christine is known as the "Transformational Catalyst," and I can tell you that in every retreat of hers that I've attended, I experienced major breakthroughs. This time was no different, but I had no idea how big and how deeply it would touch me this time.

It was day two of the retreat, and it was my turn to pick a rock. I reached into the basket and retrieved the rock. It said "LOVE." I looked at it and told my friend Pedro, who was one of the forthcoming authors being coached by Christine, "Pedro, I got your rock." Before Pedro had chosen his rock, he said that he thought he was going to pick the "LOVE" stone. So when I picked that one, my first reaction was to tell him I had inadvertently picked his stone. That was a sure sign that deep down there was some wound not allowing me to fully accept the meaning of that rock. The emotions came pouring forth as I cried and cried. When I calmed down, I began to tell the group why that rock had so much meaning for me. Back in 2003, I began my journey of rediscovering the love that lived within my Soul through Marianne Williamson's book, *A Return to Love*. I had spent the last twelve years learning that I no longer needed to seek that love outside of me. It had always been there, living within me; but my comment to Pedro said there was more to heal there.

Christine immediately felt the stirring of my Soul. She knew there was a part of me not believing in my gifts, not seeing what others saw in me, not accepting my divinity as God wanted me to. So she asked Pedro and I to stand face to face, and requested that he tell me how I had impacted his life. I felt this amazing love and support from him as we stood there heart to heart. This Soul-brother held me in his arms as I cried and released what I had been carrying for so many years. When I returned to my seat, Christine had me reframe my initial statement. She asked me to hold the rock in my hand and say, "This is my rock." I repeated that several times. Can you feel how powerful that was? This goes back to what I was saying about belief and commanding your thoughts. By saying "This is my rock," I was commanding an immediate shift in old beliefs that had been holding me back from a deeper embodiment of my Soul and my Christed-Self. In that moment I had my breakthrough—a deep shift in belief and a deeper awareness of where my Soul was taking me. It wasn't until that day that

I understood my search was over. No longer did I need to search for love outside of me—I just needed to be LOVE.

Your thoughts are so powerful that you can use them to change your future. In the *divine mind* there is a holographic blueprint that contains the God-seeds of the divine thoughts that make up the destiny of your human embodiment, which I spoke about in chapter 9. In one given moment, your thoughts create potential future outcomes. When you connect to the *divine mind* through a meditative state, you're able to travel to future points in time. If the future doesn't look the way you want it to, you can change it. As I've mentioned before, everything begins with intention. Creating a new picture of the future begins in your mind. By envisioning or visualizing in your mind the future you want to create, you plant the seeds for it to manifest in the physical realm.

When I began to think about the cover for *Unmasking Your Soul*, I decided to use this technique to get validation about what design elements belonged on the front. I had asked my niece Kristi, who's a very gifted graphic designer, to come up with several design options. As always, I was blown away by what she presented to me. I narrowed down the choices fairly quickly to two designs. Then I began to second-guess my intuition regarding the placement of some of the design elements. So in meditation I asked my guides to take me to a future point in my life when the book was already complete and in physical existence. I remember going through a portal to a future point in time. When I walked through the portal, I saw the book lying on a table. I picked it up, looked at the cover, and immediately saw the placement of all the design elements. I understood that this particular placement was important to the vibration and feel of the book. You can probably guess what happened next. We incorporated what I saw on the cover. Immediately I knew we were on the right track, but the cover was not yet complete. It wasn't until we placed my spiritual name on the cover that the energy of the cover shifted to where it needed to be.

This power of manifestation is the same power that Jesus used to convert water into wine and two fish and five loaves of bread into enough food to feed a crowd of five thousand. You, like Jesus, have that same power. The more you embody your divinity and *divine Christ consciousness*, the easier it becomes to manifest at this level. Jesus was co-creating with the universal consciousness that unites us all. I experienced this with the writing of this book. Each word I wrote, I became. That's why writing is one of the most healing art forms that exists. As you write, what must be healed comes to the surface, and as you release those emotions, your vibration shifts to accept more light and love. With each shift you transform and become more of the Soul of You. The more you permanently experience that core aspect of you in your daily life, the more you transform from God-seed to God-realized, or the Christed-Self that is the focus of this chapter.

Let's give you an opportunity to experience an aspect of your future now. You can record the following meditation so you can close your eyes while you listen to it. Sit comfortably where you won't be disturbed—with your feet flat on the floor and your hands on your knees with palms facing up. If you're an experienced meditator, use whatever position is most comfortable to you. When you're ready, please move to the meditation.

Guided Meditation: Experiencing an Aspect of Your Future

Close your eyes and take several deep breaths. With each breath in, inhale love, and with each breath out, exhale any stress or anxiety. Continue doing this until you feel relaxed.

Imagine you're walking in the desert near Jerusalem. The desert is quite barren, but as you continue walking, a temple appears before you. You see white marble stones forming a staircase into the temple. You climb the stairs. Waiting for you at the doorway is Jesus. He is ready to take you inside the temple. As you approach Him, He gently grabs your hand and you walk into the temple together.

Jesus waves His hand and white light fills the chamber. As you become immersed in this white light, you feel your body tingling. You're beginning to feel lighter and lighter. You're transforming into the being of light you truly are. As you look upon Jesus, His eyes fill with emotion as He witnesses your transformation. You look into His eyes and feel yourself being cleansed and purified in a sea of love emerging through His eyes unto you.

Jesus says, "Dear Child, within you lies the greatest gift of all, the love of our Creator. Connect with this love within you and with a pure heart ask to be shown the future you need to see in this moment." As Jesus says this to you, a doorway appears before you. Breathe the words of Jesus into your being and know that you're safe and surrounded in a cocoon of love. When you're ready, you may open the door. When you walk through, you cannot see Jesus any longer, but you feel His presence there with you.

You're now in a future point in time on the space-time continuum. Take a moment to witness yourself in this time. Observe what you're wearing. Look for signs of when and where you are. Allow the vision of this time to appear before your eyes. Your surroundings begin to appear as if you're witnessing a movie in which you're the protagonist. Just allow the movie to form, the scenes to change before you. Stay here until the movie is complete and you feel you have received the answers to your inquiry.

When you're ready, look ahead, and the doorway that transported you here has appeared before you. Waiting at the door is Jesus. He waves for you to come. He gently grabs your hand and you go through the doorway together. You return to the temple from whence you began your journey today.

A table appears in the center of the chamber. A chalice appears on the table and Jesus calls you over. He says, "My Child, as you drink from this chalice you shall receive a purification of heart, mind, and Soul." You lift the chalice to your lips and drink of this liquid LOVE. With each drop that flows within you, you can feel every cell transforming, each Christed-seed awakening from its deep sleep. As each seed gently bursts inside you, rays of golden light fill every part of your being. Stay here for a moment and allow the integration to occur.

When you feel complete, thank Jesus for His love and assistance today, and walk through the temple door. See yourself returning to your body in the present time. Begin to feel your physical presence. Your feet, legs, torso, arms, and head feel heavier as you come back into the present moment.

When you feel you're fully back, you may slowly open your eyes.

Now that you've completed the meditation, it's time to journal. Spend ten to fifteen minutes answering the following questions. Use this time to reflect on this aspect of yourself—the power of your mind. Purity of mind is an important key in unlocking your *divine Christ consciousness.*

Journaling Exercise

1. What did you notice or feel as you entered the temple?

2. How did you feel when your body was immersed in the white light? How about when Jesus blanketed you in a sea of love? Write down any insights.

3. What did you see, feel, or experience as you walked into your future? What did you notice about yourself? Write down anything you remember about the movie that played before your eyes.

4. Is there anything about your future you would like to change? If so, write down how it might look different.

5. Take a moment to envision that future now and imprint the seeds of its existence into your heart.

The Power of Your Divine Soul

> *Your Soul is the omniscient and omnipresent part of you that exists beyond your physical presence.*

Your Soul is the *omniscient* and *omnipresent* part of you that exists beyond your physical presence. It communicates to you through your Higher-Self. Your Soul carries with it the wisdom and knowledge of every life you've lived. With each life your Soul grows, expands, and evolves. Inherent in your Soul's existence is the DNA of your divine gifts and Soul's purpose. Throughout your journey with me in this book, we've unmasked the chambers of your Soul that held the secrets of your *divine truths*, the absolute truths that belong only to you. That means that your truths are unique to you and only you.

There's a spiritual maturity associated with your Soul. I know that many of you reading these words are ancient Souls reuniting at this exact time to contribute to the shift in consciousness the Earthly plane is experiencing. Together we are here to reestablish peace and love as the covenants of our existence on this planet. You're part of the group of light workers who are here to bring this sacred service to humanity.

As a Soul, you carry the wisdom of the Universe within you. Imagine this wisdom as encoded frequencies of light, which bring together images, sounds, and words into divinely inspired thoughts, which when expressed through your human vessel shift your consciousness to new levels of spiritual maturity. The expression can take many forms—written, spoken, sung, etc. As we work together to bring about this spiritual evolution, your Soul asks you to allow its existence to be the guiding force in your daily life.

As we near the conclusion of our journey together, it seems appropriate to share with you how the man and ascended master we call Jesus impacted my Soul. He's taught me about Christed-love, or what I call Soul love. This is the vastness of the Soul grounded in God's eternal love. It doesn't get any bigger or more infinite than that. It was through His presence in my life that I learned how to have compassion and forgive (as I discussed in chapter 1). He also helped me understand what it takes to be a healer and teacher in the world we live in. I know He's never left my side; but I left His, especially during most of my adulthood when I became trapped in all the unloving masks I was wearing.

I was introduced to Jesus through my Catholic upbringing. I remember as a little girl seeing portraits of Jesus in my parents' home. They now have my painting of Jesus that you'll see at the end of this chapter hanging in their home as well. I painted that portrait for my mother back in 2008. I didn't quite understand the significance of the portrait then. One of the reasons I painted it for her was because my mother always reminds me of Jesus. She loves to give and help others, and in fact, my father and older brother have Jesus as their middle names. But I painted that portrait as much for myself as for my mother. We both spent most of our lives seeking love outside of ourselves.

But things are different for me now. This journey of my Soul's unmasking has been one of absolute *Truth, Light, and Healing*, one in which there was deep healing, self-discovery, and a return to that Christed (Soul) love that has always lived inside of me (and in you, too). As an interfaith minister, I believe that there are many paths to God, and I welcome and encourage all of them, especially in pursuit of the unifying force that will help us change the world together—*Eternal Soul Love*.

In the last years of my marriage I found refuge in praying to Jesus. I was working in New York City and can't tell you how many times I went to St. Patrick's Cathedral to escape the noise that had shattered my insides. I would go straight to the pew that faced an image of Jesus. There I would light a candle and kneel in prayer until I felt my heart was full of peace again. Somehow this closeness with Jesus disappeared until I began working as a healer. He began to appear in my healings, and the deeper I went, the more He was there to guide me and bring healing to those I was serving.

Not only was Jesus a great master healer, teacher, and spiritual leader, He completely understood the power of His divine Soul and how to use it to touch the Souls of His disciples and followers. One of the greatest powers of your Soul is its unlimited capacity to access wisdom that transcends time and space. Jesus knew how to tap into that *divine wisdom* and share it with the masses. He did this masterfully through His storytelling—the parables that spoke deeply to the Souls who were listening, and at the same time elicited wonder and self-reflection about the deeper meaning of His words.

To help you engage more deeply with the power of your *Divine Soul*, I'd like to share seven keys that I discovered on my own journey of unmasking. As I teach you these keys, I'll be weaving some of Jesus's parables into the mix so you, too, can ponder the deeper meaning of your Soul's expression in this life. Divine Soul is the last thread of the trinity (with Divine Heart and Divine Mind) that makes the Christed-Self possible.

In the first key, your Soul moves you from less *doing* to more *being*. This might seem a bit counterintuitive, but by actually engaging your Soul in this way, you're able to get done what's truly important for the evolution of your Soul. This is all about *being* more present in your *doing*. Your Soul has its own rhythm and movement that coincide with the holographic blueprint that lives within the *divine mind*. If you recall, this is where the imprint of your Soul's destiny sits. The more you practice *being* present to the rhythm of your Soul, the more you become attuned to *doing* what's in alignment with your *divine purpose*. In fact, this then becomes your filter for discerning what to say yes to and what to say no to.

In the "Parable of the Sower," in Matthew 13:1-9 (New International Version), Jesus talked of a farmer who went out to sow his seed. Some of it was eaten off the path by the birds, some fell on rocky places and did not have much soil to grow in, and other seeds fell on thorns that choked the plants as they grew. But the seeds that fell on good soil produced crops. For me, the *good soil* that Jesus spoke of in this parable represents the outcome you get when you bring your *being* into your *doing*. As you become attuned to the rhythm of your Soul, which only happens when you're divinely present to what it is you're doing, you create the fertile soil for the seeds you're planting to grow, produce, and manifest in alignment with God's plan for you. In other words, as you bring the presence of Soul into your doing, what you manifest is in perfect alignment with your Soul's purpose.

In the second key, your Soul moves you from *competing* to *inspiring*. This requires a dismantling of your ego's desires to keep you attached to the physical nature of the Earthly plane. Competing tends to put you in situations and thought patterns of manipulation to outmaneuver whomever you're competing against. In truth, there is no competition. That is an illusion created by the ego-mind. If you were to do only what you were created to do, how can there be any competition? That again points to a focus on the outside world. The power of your Soul is its ability to help you live from the inside out, where the eternal force of LOVE whispers in your ear as you take action on a daily basis. When you focus on *inspiring*, or being *in spirit*, you're able to engage those you're serving in a deeper alignment with their own Soul's calling. Anything that's out of sync with love holds you back from your Soul's magnificence.

In the "Parable of the Workers in the Vineyard," in Matthew 20:1-15 (New International Version), Jesus likened Heaven to a landowner who went out early in the morning to hire help for his vineyard. The landowner agreed to pay them each a denarius for the day and sent them along to the vineyard. He went out again at nine in the morning, saw others standing in the marketplace, and told them to go work in his vineyard. He told them he would pay them whatever was right. And so they went. At noon, three, and five in the afternoon, the landowner did the same thing. When evening arrived, the landowner told his foreman to call in the workers and pay them their wages, beginning with the last ones hired and ending with the ones hired first. You can imagine what happened next. The workers who started early in the morning were upset that the workers who started later in the day got paid the same as they did. While this parable emphasizes equality in the abundance of the Universe, I want to point out the importance of *grace* in this story. When you're living *in spirit* and *inspiring* others, you're allowing grace to touch the Souls of others through you. In this parable the landowner allowed the grace of his Christed-Self to touch the lives of these men, a sign of a deeper Soul embodiment.

In the third key, your Soul moves you from *controlling* to *allowing*. I know you can certainly relate to this one. Many of us spend a lifetime trying to control the outcomes of our lives, only to realize that we were never in charge in the first place. Do yourself a favor and make it a priority to change this erroneous belief right now. The more tightly you hold on to something, the more you block yourself from receiving the bounty of the Universe in whatever form is intended for your highest good. You can think of *allowing* as making a vow to surrender to the guidance of your Soul and the Universe. When you surrender and let go of all boxes, labels, limitations, and outcomes your human mind expects and wants to place on the fruit of your desire, you give the Universe permission to grant you the bigness you deserve. This includes surrendering to your divine gifts and cosmic superpowers. The bigger your purpose in the world, the more overwhelming and scary it can feel to allow these gifts to come online. I know; I've lived that experience. So begin by getting rid of any boxes you've put yourself in or allowed others to put you in. In God's realm there are no boxes. This applies to timing as well: Flow with the rhythm of your Soul (and a little patience helps, too) because there is a divine timing for everything, and we can't control that either. It's your ego that keeps you playing small. Yet your Soul… well, it already knows your true magnificence and seeks to get you every bit of what you deserve. It's your birthright to receive the limitless bounty of the Universe. Go for it!

In the "Parable of the Pearl of Great Price," in Matthew 13:45 (New International Version), Jesus likened the Kingdom of Heaven to a merchant seeking beautiful pearls, and who, when he found them, sold everything he had and bought them. To me, this is about our willingness to give up everything to know God more deeply and discover the treasure that already lives within us. This doesn't mean you have to turn into a monk and live in a monastery. This teaching connects more deeply to what we discussed in chapter 11 about *divine devotion*. If you recall, I discussed the archetype of the *divine mystic*, wherein the marriage of your human-self and your spiritual-self occurs. This is when a deeper knowing of God occurs. The hidden treasure lies in the *allowing*. As you give up control, you receive more than you ever imagined possible.

In the fourth key, your Soul moves you from *doubting* to *believing*. I touched on the importance of belief several times before. It can have many different contexts. One context, certainly, is about using the power of belief to bring the unseen into manifestation as you co-create with your Soul and the Divine. Remember, everything begins with intention, and belief is an unstoppable force of intention that begins with relentless faith that something you deeply desire in your heart will happen. A second important context is about believing in yourself. By that I mean believing in your divine gifts and your cosmic superpowers that we discussed earlier in the chapter. This infers being able to see yourself as God sees you, and I don't mean from an ego perspective, but instead from sacredness and love. In this context, *believing* serves to shift your vibration from God-seed to God-realized, awakening your cosmic superpowers more deeply. The last context I want to bring to your attention is about believing in the Universe's desire to bring you ultimate goodness, including a limitless bounty of abundance in all areas of your life. This is one of the Soul lessons I've been working on for most of my life, and it's taken many painful repetitions of not believing in the abundance of the Universe to finally accept this *divine truth*. Take it from me: even the direst situation is temporary and will pass, bringing you what is in the highest good for your Soul. This is when allowing comes to serve you more deeply. As you can see, these keys work together. They really are dependent on one another.

In the "Parable of the Lost Sheep," in Luke 15:1-7 (New International Version), Jesus told the story of losing one sheep from a herd of a hundred. If this happened, He said, you would go after the lost sheep until you found it; and when found, you would joyfully put it on your shoulder and go home to rejoice with your friends and neighbors at the finding of your lost sheep. He went on to say that there is more rejoicing in Heaven over one sinner who repents than over ninety-nine who do not need to repent. This parable goes right to one of the key areas I addressed earlier about my own Soul lesson. It tells us that every Soul is precious to God and worth every effort to save. When God pursues you with such intent, there is no place for doubt. I remember writing this as one of the affirmations on my vision board: "God has my back." Embodying this truth was key in my own healing and ability to step more deeply into my purpose-work.

In the fifth key, your Soul moves you from *getting* to *serving*. There's a big difference in energy and vibration between the two. You can think of *getting* as a restrictive energy that is bound by expectation, perhaps even wanting more and more and never being quite satisfied or content with what you do *get*. Divine service, on the other hand, is engulfed in a higher vibration of love that has no expectation—what I like to call *selfless service*. This includes things like providing some level of free service to your tribe. I've been doing free chakra and soul readings for years. For me it's like a tithing of my *divine love* to God, the Universe, and my tribe. Love always expands into more love, and that's the part that makes my heart sing. This may sound counterintuitive, but when you serve in this manner the Universe rewards you in ways you never imagined possible. This doesn't mean that you can't or shouldn't charge for your services. On the contrary; you live in a world of commerce, and as such, God expects and knows that you must make a living. That living can be as small or big as you're willing to *embrace* and *receive*. In the end, when you serve from a place of reverence and the Christed-love that is the focus of this chapter, you clearly see and feel the nourishment given to your Soul by the Universe, whether that is in material gain, internal abundance, or any other ways abundance wishes to grace your life.

In the "Parable of the Good Samaritan," in Luke 10:25-37 (New International Version), Jesus told the story of a man who was travelling from Jerusalem to Jericho when he was attacked by robbers. The robbers stripped the man of his clothes, beat him, and left him half dead. A priest happened to be going by on the same side of the road, but when he saw the man he crossed over to the other side of the road. A Levite also crossed to the other side of the road when he saw the man lying there. But a Samaritan went to where the man lay, and when he saw him, took pity on him. He bandaged the man's wounds. Then he put the man on his own donkey, took him to an inn, and took care of him. The next day he gave the innkeeper two denarii to look after the wounded man until the Samaritan returned. While this parable is a beautiful picture of mercy and compassion, it vehemently demonstrates what it means to be in *selfless service* and a steward of God. This story reminds me so much of my mother and the many times I saw her help strangers and buy groceries for those in need. The reason you and I are here is to *serve*. Embodying the *Christ consciousness* requires a deeper Soul awareness about your true motives for that service and ensuring they're in alignment with your responsibilities as a *steward of love and light*.

In the sixth key, your Soul moves you from *showcasing* to *humility*. Your ego forever wants attention and recognition. While it's important to give credit where credit is due, that should not be at the cost of others or your relationship with the Divine. Nothing is possible without partnership with the Divine. Life doesn't happen only because of you; it happens in co-creation with you. Your willingness to be that open vessel of love and light is what allows the manifestation of that life to occur for your highest good. And your willingness to stay humble in that co-creation process determines whether or not the outcome serves your highest good. Your Soul knows that when you're flowing in the truth of you and showing up authentically in the world, your vibration automatically attracts to you those you're meant to serve. If you find that you're constantly praising yourself or having to prove to others what you can do, there's something wrong, and most likely you will hit a brick wall. Perhaps the intent and motives behind what you're doing are not in alignment with your Heart and Soul. That's a good time to take a pause, commune with your Soul more deeply, and realign. This doesn't mean that you shouldn't brand or market your services. What it does mean is that the motive behind that marketing and how you show up in the world should align with your *divine truths* and be an expression of the Soul and *divine love* that you represent to your tribe.

To those who were confident in their own righteousness and looked down upon everyone else, Jesus told the "Parable of the Pharisee and Tax Collector," in Luke 18:9-14 (New International Version). In this parable, two men walked up to a temple to pray, one a Pharisee and the other a tax collector. The Pharisee stood by himself and prayed, "God, I thank you that I am not like other people—robbers, evildoers, adulterers—or even like this tax collector. I fast twice a week and give a tenth of all I get." But the tax collector stood at a distance and didn't even look up to Heaven. Instead he beat his breast and said, "God, have mercy on me, a sinner." Jesus said that this man, the tax collector, went home justified before God, for those "who exalt themselves will be humbled, and those who humble themselves will be exalted." In the hearts of the humble there's an intensity of love and light that can't be missed. This is the purity of heart I wrote of earlier. Humility is the gateway to that purity, and without it, embodiment of the *Christ consciousness* is not possible.

In the seventh and last key, there is a transformation from *egotist* to *soulfulist*. (*Unmasking Your Soul* would not be complete without sharing another of my gifts: creating new words. I've been accused of doing that many times before in my previous life as a consultant.) In an egotist world, the primary lens is focused on the material and superficial layers of existence. The egotist tends to see the world through the lens of the wounded self, and their daily life is primarily run by the lower thought vibrations of the ego-mind. The soulfulist immediately recognizes the Soul in all of existence. The soulfulist has gained an understanding of their presence in the world as a divine being of love and light. Being an expression of that love and light in the world honors their innate desire to connect with the light and Souls of their human brethren. There is a deep reverence for all that is Soul, and no Soul gets left behind. As the soulfulist embodies their Soul and Christed-Self more deeply, their view of the world changes. Imagine seeing the world through the eyes of your God-self. That's what becoming a soulfulist is really about.

In the "Parable of the Prodigal Son," in Luke 15:11-32 (New International Version), Jesus told the story of a man who had two sons. The younger son asked his father for his share of property and took a journey to a faraway country where he squandered everything to reckless living. With famine arising in that country, and in need, he hired himself out to one of the citizens of that country who sent him out into the fields to feed the pigs. He came to his senses and realized that his father's hired servants had more than enough to eat, yet he perished in hunger. He decided to return to his father. While he was still a long way off, his father saw him, felt compassion, and ran to embrace and kiss him. The son said to his father, "Father, I have sinned against Heaven and before you. I am no longer worthy to be called your son." But the father asked his servants to bring the best robe and put it on his son, and put a ring on his hand and shoes on his feet. He asked them to bring the fattened calf and kill it so they could eat and celebrate. And the father said, "For this my son was dead, and is alive again; he was lost, and is found." The older son was in the field while all this was happening. When he came closer to the house, he heard the music and dancing. He called one of the servants and asked what was going on. The servant told him that his brother had come back and that his father had killed the calf because his brother was back safe and sound. But the older brother became angry and refused to enter the house. The father went out to bring him in, but the older son was angry and told his father that he had served him for many years and never disobeyed any of his father's commands, yet he had never received a young goat to celebrate with his friends. The father told him, "Son, you are always with me, and all that is mine is yours. It was fitting to celebrate and be glad, for this your brother was dead, and is alive; he was lost, and is found."

You can probably already surmise that the older son played the role of the egotist in this parable, seeing through the eyes of self-righteousness. He could not see how blessed he had been all those years, but instead focused on what he believed he didn't have or hadn't gotten. His father, on the other hand, played the role of the soulfulist. He welcomed his younger son, a lost Soul, with compassion and forgiveness. He saw his son through the eyes of his *divine Christ*, the God-realized within.

As you implement these keys in your life, you embody more of your Soul and open the door for the birth of the *Christ consciousness* within you. I want to commend you for all your hard work and for sticking with me to the end. There is no greater reward for me than to help you unmask your Soul. Remember that you are *love*, and love is the unstoppable force that transforms all in its path. Love is the answer to all that you seek. I love you, Dearest One!

The meditation that follows helps you awaken to the *divine Christ* within you. In the meditation we'll be opening purity of heart, purity of mind, and purity of Soul within you. Take this time now, before you begin, to ask the Divine to help you bring all that is blocking you from embodying the highest version of you, the Christed-Self, to your conscious mind so you can heal and transform it.

You can record the meditation so you can close your eyes while you listen to it. For the audio version, visit **www.UnmaskingYourSoul.com/Meditations.** Sit comfortably where you won't be disturbed—with your feet flat on the floor and your hands on your knees with palms facing up. If you're an experienced meditator, use whatever position is most comfortable to you. When you're ready, please move to the meditation.

Guided Meditation: Activating the Divine Christ within You

Breathe slowly, inhaling through your nose and exhaling through your mouth. With each inhale imagine breathing in love, and with each exhale imagine breathing out any stress, pain, or wound that you're holding. Allow your thoughts to align with the beating of your heart. With every beat of your heart you go deeper and deeper into the divine mind and open your heart space. {Pause until you feel deeply connected.}

Imagine taking an elevator down from the top of your head to the center of your heart. See yourself standing there surrounded in beautiful rays of pink and green swirling light. With each swirl you feel more and more love. Standing with you are your ancestors, guides, and ascended masters (Jesus among them), who will accompany you on this journey today.

Jesus steps forward, facing you. He lifts His right hand and it emanates a blue and golden light. He etches out a triangle of light in front of you. This triangle represents the doorway of the Christ consciousness—a trinity of the Divine Heart, Divine Mind, and Divine Soul. He asks you to come forward and step into the center of this triangle. And so you do. As you step into this triangle, you're transported to another plane of consciousness.

As you look around, you see yourself floating horizontally in the ethers, surrounded by seven divine beings of light. The radiance of the light is so bright it expands infinitely across time and space. In the expansion of this light, you feel the presence of Ishtar (the 227 galactic Souls forming this consciousness) holding a field of peace and love around you and the divine beings encircling you. You feel held, safe, and at one with the light.

The light now transforms into the colors of the rainbow. The swirls of light enter your body through your crown, flowing through every cell of your body, transmuting and awakening your Christed-seeds. With each seed that awakens, you feel sensations in your body. You feel lighter and lighter, and as if you're being lifted into the heavens. {Stay here until the flow of light subsides within you.}

Jesus steps forward and ignites the sacred flame in your heart. The flame expands and expands beyond your heart, engulfing all of you in this blessed fire. You can feel every cell being touched by the flame. Surrender all thought, all pain, all wounds to this sacred flame. It gently transmutes each of your cells to their original form of wholeness and completeness. Your etheric body returns to its pure form. Now your physical body matches your etheric template, an infusion of the purest form of love and light flowing through every part of your being—mind, body, heart, and Soul. **{Pause for several minutes.}**

Mother Mary steps forward and places her hand on your heart. You feel your heart expanding and expanding. A deep, eternal, liquid love flows through your entire body. She draws a sacred triangle of light in the convergence point of your higher and lower heart. In the center of the triangle she traces the sacred symbol of the twelfth Soul chamber, a swirly S with one dot on each side. As she completes the symbol on your heart, it illuminates brightly and becomes a three-dimensional holographic image above you, opening a portal to the Divine Heart. A dot of blue light forms in the center of the image above you. **{Breathe in purity of heart. Take several deep breaths, connecting with the source of purity within your Divine Heart.}**

The dot extends upward as a thread of Christed-blue light.

The Green Tara Bodhisattva steps forward and places her hand on your forehead. She draws a sacred triangle of light in the center of your brows. In the center of that triangle she draws the sacred symbol of the twelfth Soul chamber, a swirly S with one dot on each side. As she completes the symbol on your forehead, it illuminates brightly and becomes a three-dimensional holographic image above you, opening a portal to the Divine Mind. **{Breathe in purity of mind. Take several deep breaths, connecting with the source of purity within your Divine Mind.}**

The Christed-thread of blue light connects your Divine Heart to your Divine Mind.

Mahavatar Babaji steps forward and places his hand on the top of your head. A beautiful white lotus flower opens on your crown, and its beautiful petals expand outward. Babaji then draws a sacred triangle six inches above your head. In the center of the triangle he draws the sacred symbol of the twelfth Soul chamber, a swirly S with one dot on each side. As he completes the symbol above your head, it illuminates brightly and becomes a three-dimensional holographic *image above you, opening a portal to the Divine Soul. {**Breathe in purity of Soul. Take several deep breaths, connecting with the source of purity within your Divine Soul.**}*

*Jesus comes forward and anoints your feet, temples, forehead, and the top of your head. He leans over and kisses your forehead, and as He does, the Christed-thread of blue light completes the trinity of Divine Heart, Divine Mind, and Divine Soul. Your Christed-Self has now been awakened within you. As you continue your spiritual evolution, this thread will multiply, giving you safe passage to the highest version of you—the divine Christ within you. {**Pause for several minutes to integrate this experience.**}*

When you feel complete, return to your physical presence and slowly open your eyes.

Now that you've completed the guided meditation, take some time to do some journaling. Spend about ten to fifteen minutes in a quiet place where you won't be disturbed answering the questions below. You can put on some soothing music or light a candle or incense to support you as you write. Just write from your Heart and Soul and the rest will follow.

Journaling Exercise

1. What did you feel when you stepped into the doorway of the *Christ consciousness*?

2. What did you experience as you were floating in the ethers surrounded by the seven divine beings?

3. What did you feel as your Christed-seeds began to open?

4. What did you experience as Jesus ignited the sacred flame within your heart?

5. What did you experience as Mother Mary connected you with the purity of your Divine Heart? Purity of your Divine Mind with the Green Tara Bodhisattva? Purity of Divine Soul with Mahavatar Babaji?

6. What was your experience as you were anointed by Jesus and awakened to the Christ within you?

7. Write down anything else of significance. You may want to sit with your responses for several minutes daily over the coming days to integrate this experience.

After journaling, continue working on the *Canvas of Your Soul.* (You can download the PDF at **www.UnmaskingYourSoul.com/Blueprint.**) Pick phrases, words, or symbols and put them on section 12 of the *Healing* part of your roadmap. Make this canvas your own piece of artwork that represents the journey we're taking together in this book. You can color, paint, or even cut images from magazines that depict the messages and insights you received in this chapter on *embodying the divine Christ consciousness.* You don't need to be a professional artist to do this. Just let your Soul express through you as it wants to. This will become the vision board of your Soul's unmasking, a precious gift to you from your *divine Christ.* Congratulations for sticking it out and completing your journey with me!

Five Rituals to Awaken Your Divine Christ Consciousness Muscle

The rituals below are meant to help you awaken your *divine Christ consciousness* muscle. You can repeat any of the rituals that follow and the exercises and guided meditations earlier in the chapter as many times as you like. With each repetition you go deeper in accessing your *divine Christ consciousness.*

Before you begin, create your sacred space and take some deep breaths to relax your mind and body. Connect with your Soul as you enter this sacred space.

1. Use this sacred ritual to energetically set intention and attention to the Christed within you. Below is an invocation you can use daily to do this. Read every word out loud with fervent intention. Looking deeply into your eyes and connecting with your Soul in front of a mirror is ideal. Do this for at least twenty-one consecutive days.

   The light that shines within me is overflowing in *divine love.* With every breath I take into my heart center, I feel my divinity. I am a radiant being of light and love. I sparkle, I tingle, and I purify all those in my presence. I'm beaming inside and out! With my next breath, I witness my light. I stand powerfully in this light, yet soft petals of love emerge from my heart to those in my presence. It is from this place that I become the covenant of God's expression of the Christed within me. I feel the sacredness of my essence and hold in reverence everyone and everything that surrounds me. I am ONE with all that is. I breathe that in now.

   I'm ready to embody the truth of my wholeness and completeness. In this place I feel such peace, compassion, and understanding that I must allow for that which wants to serve through me. For I am here to serve and I'm committed to doing so. It is my unique purpose that inspires me to hold all that is as the most sacred in my life. Desire and passion create the fire that breed the joy, creation, and divine flow that carry me into living my life on purpose.

This is the moment of embodiment, when my Soul guides me to live in the highest version of truth and authenticity. My spirit has always aspired to reach this level of wholeness. I've already experienced the transition, but now I'm learning to make it a permanent way of being. Day by day I become more of who I really am and let go of the structures of my ego-mind. As I imagine it, I become it. In this last stage of healing, my oneness with the Divine becomes a natural state of being. I no longer need to will it or think it; it just is. And within that state of being, I begin to live from my Soul and Christed-Self.

2. Use this ritual to open the Soul chamber of the *divine Christ* within you. Practice this daily for seven consecutive days.

   a. Draw the sacred symbol (see below) of this Soul chamber in the center of your left palm. Then draw the symbol in the center of your right palm. Bring both palms together as in prayer, and affirm the following words with love and conviction out loud: "I am the Christed, and with pureness of heart, mind, and Soul, I now embody the highest version of me."

   b. With palms together as in prayer, slowly move your attention through the following four points: heart, forehead, top of head, and six to eight inches above your head. Do this slowly and spend several minutes at each point.

   c. Imagine a thread of blue light that connects all four points. When you have the points connected, extend the top of the line up above your head as far above your head as you can go (several hundred feet). Then

Divine Christ Consciousness Symbol

377

do the same for the bottom of the line, going from your heart to below your feet and into the center of the Earth as far as you can go (several hundred feet). Stay here for several minutes until you feel complete.

d. Once you complete this exercise, be sure to journal about what you experienced. The more you do this, the easier it is to automatically connect these energy points. As you shift vibrationally, you may notice changes in how the energy feels and a deeper awareness of the blossoming of your Christed-seed. Continue to journal about your experience over the seven days.

3. In this ritual you take an inventory of any ego clutter that's holding you back from making the choices that align with your Soul's purpose. You're going to use the energy of the Divine Heart, Divine Mind, and Divine Soul to assist you on this Soul quest. You can use this ritual any time you need clarity in making choices that support your highest good. Find a quiet place where you can sit and relax. Close your eyes and take a couple of deep breaths, then move to the ritual.

Begin by setting an intention to be open to receiving guidance from the trinity of the Christ consciousness—Divine Heart, Divine Mind, and Divine Soul.

Hold the situation you're trying to get clarity on in your heart. As you hold the situation in your Divine Heart, what feelings and emotions surface? Immerse the situation you're holding in your heart with beautiful rays of pink light. See the light swirling in your heart center, and from those swirls clearly emerges the message. Feel these emotions and what they're trying to tell you.

As you hold the situation in your heart, listen to any thoughts emerging from your Divine Mind. Remember that only loving thoughts represent the true thoughts of this part of you. See yourself immersing your thoughts in beautiful pink light. Continue to do this until you receive the loving thoughts that represent the messages from your Divine Mind.

Now move to your Divine Soul. This is where you connect directly with your Higher-Self, the conduit to your Divine Soul. See or imagine yourself as this radiant being of light. See yourself handing over this situation to your Higher-Self. Pause and wait for a response. If the response does not come in the moment, do not despair or try to force it. Know that it will come when it's time.

When you feel complete, come back to the present moment and be sure to journal about any insights you received.

4. In this ritual, you take an inventory of where you might not be in alignment with the rhythm of your Soul. When you're not in alignment it can feel like you're walking through mud or hitting a brick wall. In contrast, being in

alignment makes you feel like things manifest in your life with ease and grace. Engaging with your Soul at this level is like performing an etheric Soul dance. In this dance your Soul leads and you follow. Take a moment to pause and breathe. Close your eyes and allow your Soul to help you take an inventory of your life. Where are you not in alignment with the rhythm of your Soul? Look at every area of your life: career, relationships, spiritual, family, finances, etc. When you're ready, ask your Divine Soul to help you flow through each area of your life, and write in your journal the responses to the following questions in regard to each area:

a. In this part of my life, when am I constantly walking through mud or hitting a brick wall?

b. What is causing this misalignment? Is there something I'm afraid to face? If so, what is it?

c. What steps do I need to take to get back in alignment with the rhythm of my Soul? (Pause here to connect with your Higher-Self (the conduit of your Soul) to receive any divine messages.)

Do I need support to get back in alignment? If so, who am I going to ask for help to keep me accountable to my Soul? (Think about what you need this person to do for you, such as be a sounding board; hold a loving, safe space for you to be you; etc. Then let them know how you'd like their help.)

When you've covered all the areas of your life in which you feel out of alignment with the rhythm of your Soul, complete this exercise by affirming the following: "I receive the guidance of my Divine Soul and flow to its rhythm." Breathe this intention into your heart and journal about any other insights that arise.

5. Meditate with my painting *A Portrait of Jesus*, shown at the end of the chapter, to help you reconnect with your *divine Christ*, the one who helps you access your *divine Christ consciousness*. Each of my paintings was divinely channeled and holds messages and energetic impressions of the Soul that bring healing to the bearer. This particular painting holds vibrations of healing for those needing to remember their expression of *divine Christ consciousness*.

a. Close your eyes and take a breath... inhaling slowly through your nose and exhaling slowly through your mouth... and with each breath you take relax your mind, body, and spirit. Continue focusing on your breath... and with each breath allow your thoughts to pass freely... thought after thought... breath after breath... relaxing more and more deeply. Continue taking several more deep breaths. {**Repeat for one or two minutes.**}

b. Briefly open your eyes and observe the painting. Allow yourself to be taken on a journey into the painting. Look at the images and symbols, and allow your gaze to go to one focal point in the painting. Soften your gaze as you focus on this point of interest. Breathe in its energy, seeing the symbols, images, and colors in your mind's eye. Continue breathing in the energy... breath after breath, allowing you to feel and absorb the healing energy from this focal point.

c. With your next breath, listen to the voice of your Soul. What is it communicating? What messages do you hear or feel within you as you breathe in the energy of the painting? Pay attention to where the energy is going in your body. This gives you an indication of where in your body you may need to release old energy, traumas, or wounds. Continue breathing and just go into the stillness while you connect deeper within. Allow the healing energies of the painting to penetrate your mind, body, and spirit. {**Do this for two to five minutes.**} If you feel guided, you may continue repeating this step, changing to a different focal point in the painting each time. Again, allow yourself to breathe the images, symbols, colors, and healing energies into your being.

d. Don't forget to journal about anything of significance that comes up during this experience.

Eileen Anümani Santos, *A Portrait Of Jesus*, c. 2008

A Portrait of Jesus represents the *Christ consciousness* that lives within you. As you become *pure of heart*, *pure of mind*, and *pure of Soul*, you ignite the sacred fire of the Creator to transform your God-seed into God-realized. It is through the embodiment of your *divine Christ consciousness* that this is made possible. As you unmask the temptations of the ego and walk through the doorway of purity, you become the highest version of you—the Christed-One.

I see the God in you.

Through your *DIVINE CHRIST CONSCIOUSNESS*, the union of Heaven and Earth is born within!

AFTERWORD

Thank you for allowing me to be your spiritual guide on this leg of your journey. We took this passage together, for as you unmasked, so did I. Our journey on this Earthly plane continues daily as long as we inhabit our human bodies. And, as this part of the sojourn ends, a new one begins, for God takes us deeper so we can surrender to the fullest expression of our divinity.

I hope you choose to stay in touch and continue working with me so you can fully embody your divine gifts and purpose in the world. Only together can we bring peace and love to the world. Let's transmute the fear into love. Let's create a world in which our families and the next generation of Souls can enjoy lives that are brighter, lighter, and infused with Soul Love. God needs you to say yes to your Soul's calling. If you haven't already made that Soul commitment, I ask you in this moment to take a deep breath, go within your heart, commit to who you are and why you're really here, and join me on this journey of Soul Love.

Shortly after finishing *Unmasking Your Soul* I was given the insight by the Divine that the twelve Soul chambers you've just experienced are the many faces of SOUL LOVE. With each layer of woundedness that you've healed and returned to wholeness, you were opening the gateway for this Soul love or Christed-love to be awakened within you. So this journey was really about your rediscovering and experiencing the LOVE that you already are. That was my Soul lesson: *to be love and experience how eternally loved I am.* With *divine love* there is no seeking, just being. Seeking implies that love is outside of you, when in fact it resides within you. I remind you again:

You are love and deeply loved by the Universe.
You are a luminous being of light.
You are what the world is waiting for.

It's time to shine that light as big and bright as you can. It's time to stop hiding the brilliance you hold in every cell of your being; for you are God's Picasso—a masterpiece that marries your divinity with your humanity. The more you allow the fullness of your divinity to be expressed through your humanity, the happier, more joyful, and more peaceful you are. In the same vein, the more you trust and surrender to God's divine plan for you, the more you receive the bounty from the Universe that has your name on it.

As I write these final words, I am practicing letting go of what was born in these pages so that the next leg of the journey can begin. It's like a parent feeling sadness when what was once a full home now becomes an empty nest. This book and I have journeyed together for sixteen months. Its evolution has evolved my own Soul and divine expression. Each word written brought forth a deeper unmasking and my own healing and transformation.

Along the way I learned how to listen to the voice and rhythm of my Soul. Sometimes that meant putting the book aside until I was at the vibration I needed to be to serve you and me in the highest. Living from a place of Soul Love is not always about forward movement; sometimes it's about being still and surrendering to what is in the moment. By listening and surrendering, healing happens naturally. Then when you hear the voice from within give you your Soulful cue, you know it's time to take inspired action. This is what it's like to live a Soul-driven life in which ego is no longer in the driver's seat and your Soul (and the eternal love it holds) is your guiding force.

In the second book of this trilogy, entitled *Soul Speak: Understanding the Language of Your Soul*, I'll be sharing more about how your Soul communicates. We'll be going deeper into Soul and light languages, symbology, and more that is yet to be born through and with me by the Divine. If you want to stay in touch and learn more about my progress, please sign up at www.AnumaniSpeaks.com. I look forward to continuing this journey together!

Remember, do what you LOVE, and what you LOVE opens the fountain of unlimited bounty that the Universe is waiting to share with you.

May God bless you and your loved ones always and forever!

Eternally Yours,
Anümani

ACKNOWLEDGMENTS

To my parents, Angel Sr. and Arsenia: Thank you for your eternal love.

To my brothers and their wives, Angel Jr. and Nancy, Joe and Lauren: Thank you for being my biggest cheerleaders on this journey.

To my nieces and nephews, Kristi, Ashley, Elvin, and Mateo: Thank you for your unconditional love. You all make me so proud. Kristi, a special thank you for sharing your creative talents and designing the book cover and illustrating the sacred symbols. The book would not have been complete without your magical touch.

To my great nieces, Vanessa, Leylah, Aeriel, and Julia: Thank you for always reminding me to have fun and for loving me as I am.

To my cousin, Betsy Ruiz: Thank you, Prima, for sharing your heart with me.

To my mentor, friend, and Soul sister, Christine Kloser: Thank you for creating a safe space for me to unmask my Soul.

To my Soul Voyager family, Nancy (Elizabeth) Baker, Kaylan (Malia) Daane, Susan (Sequoia) Dascenzi, Linda Hyden, Melinda Kapor, Pam Culley-McCullough, Lilia Shoshanna Rae, Linda Roebuck, Susanne (Sarah) Romo, Helen (Maya White Feather) Sherry, Julie (Anjali) Stamper, and Kara (Carissima) Stoltenberg: Thank you for your sisterhood and always holding me in a space of love.

To my MasterHeart family: I am honored to have co-authored *Pebbles in the Pond (Wave 4)* with each and every one of you. And, to all the Waves before and after: heart to heart we remain.

To my amazing goddess sisters, Stephanie Bavaro and Dawn Mahan: Thank you for always being there for me.

To my friend Janeth: Thank you for reminding me to be me. You are always in my heart.

To my friend and healer Bette Hanson: Thank you for sharing your amazing healing gifts with me. You were instrumental in my transformation and I am eternally grateful. Sending lots of love to our furry friend Sascha, as she watches from the cosmic plane.

To my editor, Marlene Oulton: You are magical with words. Thank you for all your love and encouragement. I couldn't have done it without you.

To Reverend Jill Carel and Reverend Rhetta Morgan, who saw something in me that I couldn't see in myself: Thank you for your love and encouragement.

To Carrie Jareed, my book midwife; Ranilo Cabo, interior/book designer; and Gwen Hoffnagle, editor/proofreader: Thank you for birthing this beautiful book for me.

To Viki Winterton and team: Thank you for helping me launch my book into the world.

To all my clients: Thank you for trusting in me to be your spiritual guide. As I walk, you walk. As you walk, I walk. Together we unmask our Souls. I hold you in a blanket of eternal love!

ABOUT THE AUTHOR

Eileen Anümani Santos is an interfaith minister, transformational healer, artist, singer, international bestselling author, and spiritual guide whose mission is to heal and awaken the hearts and minds of those seeking to live more authentic and Soul-driven lives. Through a mystical dream she experienced in 2003, she awakened to begin her own journey of self-discovery. In this dream she heard God's voice say to her, "My Child, I have a mission for you, one that you won't understand in this moment, but be patient, for in time all will be revealed to you."

From her own transformational journey emerged the **Unmasking Your Soul Blueprint**™, a powerful healing process that takes seekers on a journey of ***Truth, Light, and Healing***, during which human existence and spiritual existence merge. This allows their Souls to unmask their magnificence to the world. As her clients uncover the true potential of their God-seed, they are transformed to a way of being that transcends words, connecting them to a vastness of limitless opportunities where they are empowered to become their most authentic selves. As her clients learn to connect with the voices of their Souls, they are able to co-create the lives they desire and deserve, lives that are full of love, compassion, joy, health, wholeness, and abundance.

Anümani is the spiritual name and vibration of Eileen's ancient Soul who holds the golden light of Archangel Metatron and the energies of the Merkaba. *Anü* means the omniscient one, and *mani* is the jewel of compassion and love. Anümani is here to guide her clients in the unmasking of their own jewels of love that live within them. She does this by becoming a bridge to the Soul as she speaks in ancient Soul languages that bring healing and unlock the divine gifts of those she serves. With the help of a collective consciousness of 227 galactic Souls who call themselves Ishtar, she leads her clients to new horizons of healing, awareness, and initiatory experiences.

Her clients describe her work as "gentle, yet powerful, connecting to a vastness of consciousness beyond the human mind." Be it an entrepreneur, housewife, or spiritual seeker, any and all who are called by their Souls to show up in the world empowered as their most authentic selves will be transformed by Anümani's work.

In June of 2015, Anümani became an international bestselling author with the release of the anthology *Pebbles in the Pond (Wave 4)*, for which she was a contributing author. For information about Anümani's programs and services, and how to begin your transformational journey, visit www.AnumaniSpeaks.com.

ALSO BY EILEEN ANÜMANI SANTOS

(CONTRIBUTING AUTHOR)

Pebbles in the Pond: Transforming the World One Person at a Time (Wave 4)

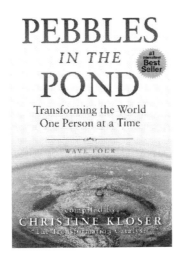

Made in the USA
Middletown, DE
09 November 2020